IN THE HEAT OF THE SUMMER

POLITICS AND CULTURE IN MODERN AMERICA

Series Editors: Margot Canaday, Glenda Gilmore,
Michael Kazin, Stephen Pitti, Thomas J. Sugrue

Volumes in the series narrate and analyze political and social
change in the broadest dimensions from 1865 to the present,
including ideas about the ways people have sought and wielded
power in the public sphere and the language and institutions
of politics at all levels—local, national, and transnational. The
series is motivated by a desire to reverse the fragmentation of
modern U.S. history and to encourage synthetic perspectives on
social movements and the state, on gender, race, and labor, and
on intellectual history and popular culture.

In the Heat
of the Summer

THE NEW YORK RIOTS OF 1964 AND THE WAR ON CRIME

Michael W. Flamm

PENN

UNIVERSITY OF PENNSYLVANIA PRESS

PHILADELPHIA

Published by
University of Pennsylvania Press
Philadelphia, Pennsylvania 19104-4112
www.upenn.edu/pennpress

Printed in the United States of America
on acid-free paper

10 9 8 7 6 5 4 3 2 1

In The Heat Of The Summer
Words and Music by Phil Ochs
Copyright © 1966 BARRICADE MUSIC, INC.
Copyright Renewed
All Rights Controlled and Administered by ALMO MUSIC CORP.
All Rights Reserved Used by Permission
Reprinted by Permission of Hal Leonard Corporation

Cataloging-in-Publication Data is available
from the Library of Congress
ISBN 978-0-8122-4850-0

For Austin and Alexandra

CONTENTS

"Come on, shoot another nigger!"

With tears streaming down her face, the black teenager taunted a helmeted phalanx of New York City policemen. Amid a barrage of books and bottles from two hundred black students, the officers struggled to maintain order outside Robert F. Wagner Junior High School on East 76th Street in Upper Manhattan. The only serious casualty at the scene was the sole black patrolman, who suffered a concussion when hit in the head by a can of soda. He remained on duty for more than an hour before collapsing, and was raced unconscious to Lenox Hill Hospital, where he eventually recovered.[1]

The heated protests spontaneously erupted minutes after Lieutenant Thomas Gilligan, a white off-duty officer in civilian clothes, fired three shots and killed a black student, fifteen-year-old James Powell, on July 16, 1964. The fatal confrontation followed an earlier altercation that Thursday morning between a white superintendent and black teenagers in front of an apartment building across the street from the school. But tensions were already high from a publicized series of violent crimes featuring black assailants and white victims.[2]

At that instant, three thousand miles away in San Francisco, weary aides to Barry Goldwater were putting the finishing touches on his acceptance speech to the Republican Convention. At the Cow Palace the previous night Goldwater had received the greatest prize of his political career—the presidential nomination. Now he would announce to the excited delegates in the arena and the American people watching on television that the conservative moment had arrived and what the nation needed was law and order.

Fourteen hours after Powell bled to death on the sidewalk, Goldwater strode to the podium as the band played "The Battle Hymn of the Republic" and red, white, and blue balloons fell from the rafters. Grim and stern, with black-rimmed glasses that accentuated his political image as an angry prophet of impending doom, he denounced rising crime and "violence in our streets" to roars of approval from the convention. "Security from domestic violence, no less than from foreign aggression, is the most elementary and fundamental purpose of any government," Goldwater intoned, "and a government that cannot fulfill that purpose is one that cannot long command the loyalty of its citizens."[3]

The unexpected conjunction of these two events represented a pivotal juncture in the nation's history, which had previously featured intermittent episodes of public interest in law enforcement and criminal justice. Although the federal government had periodically embarked on crusades against crime or immorality in the past, and plenty of local, state, and national politicians had voiced similar ideas, Goldwater's words combined with impending developments would have an impact in the future that few of his listeners or viewers—not even devoted friends or avid foes—could have anticipated.[4]

On Saturday evening, thousands of Central Harlem residents took to the streets to protest the Powell shooting and other grievances. Most were bystanders, not participants, in the violence that erupted during the next three nights. The unrest then spread to Bedford-Stuyvesant (Bed-Stuy), a section of Brooklyn, for another three nights. In both communities, the rioting and looting were intense, although the vast majority of black residents, regardless of their sympathies or beliefs, never ventured from their homes or apartments.[5]

The Harlem Riot, as most whites called it, was accompanied by hundreds of injuries and arrests as well as at least one death. In both neighborhoods, the business districts were devastated, with white-owned and black-owned stores vandalized and ransacked. Soon the rebellion or uprising, as some blacks described it, spread to other cities such as Rochester, New York, and sent shockwaves across the country.[6] The first "long, hot summer" of the decade had arrived—and with it a new racial dynamic that would drive a wedge between the civil rights movement and many white liberals who had supported it in the early 1960s. The image of the black rioter now joined the symbol of the black criminal, which had deep roots in American history; together, they served as both the real and imagined basis of white anxiety.[7]

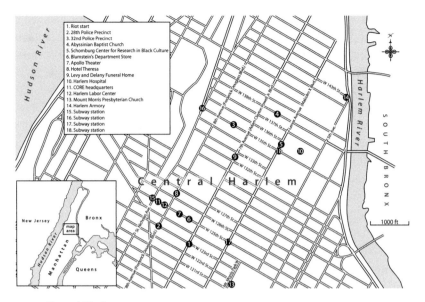

MAP 1. Central Harlem

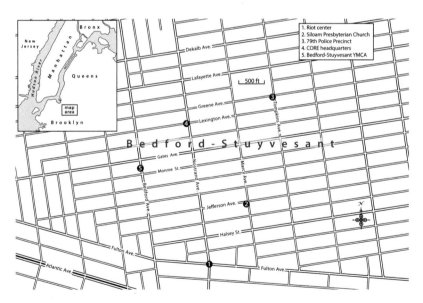

MAP 2. Bedford-Stuyvesant

Goldwater had predicted the outbreak of civil disorder and blamed it on the doctrine of civil disobedience preached and practiced by Dr. Martin Luther King, Jr. and his followers. The Republican nominee also successfully conflated the disparate threats of crime and riots as he borrowed the issue of law and order from Democrats in Dixie, modified it, and propelled "domestic violence" from the margins to the mainstream of presidential politics. For decades southern whites had opposed civil rights in part by claiming that integration would lead to a sharp increase in racial crime and unrest, which conservatives attributed to black immorality. Now growing numbers of northern whites—even those in favor of racial equality—likewise feared that integration would harm public safety.[8]

The conservative appeal to law and order posed a serious threat to the liberal dreams of President Lyndon Johnson, who responded to the political pressure with a dual strategy. As the campaign for the White House reached a climax in the fall of 1964, he promised with extravagant rhetoric that the War on Poverty would combat the social conditions—rising unemployment, failing schools, and poor housing—that plagued urban ghettos and generated racial violence. With broad and bipartisan support from both liberals and conservatives, the president in the spring of 1965 also declared a War on Crime in the optimistic belief that it would raise the level of police professionalism and lessen the incidence or perception of police brutality—another source of black anger and frustration.

Johnson hoped and thought that better policing combined with social programs and a national commitment to civil rights would reduce black crime and unrest, which liberals attributed to white racism. But the War on Crime had limited impact, although it substantially widened the door to federal intervention in local policing. Within three years it had evolved into an anti-riot program in the wake of the unrest that Harlem had foretold—Watts in 1965, Newark and Detroit in 1967, Washington and more than a hundred other cities after the assassination of King in 1968. By then Johnson had decided not to run for another term and the War on Poverty was also in retreat, denounced and defunded by white conservatives who contended that it had encouraged and rewarded black rioters.[9]

After Republican President Richard Nixon moved into the White House, he recast the War on Crime as a War on Drugs, with the addict and dealer now joining the criminal and rioter as public enemies. Building on the political consensus in favor of a larger federal role in law enforcement and appealing to the public demand for law and order, Nixon in the 1970s targeted heroin as a major threat to American society, especially to middle-class suburbs where white youths were portrayed as the innocent victims of the drug trade. As cocaine became a growing menace, Republican President Ronald Reagan escalated the War on Drugs in the 1980s and Democratic President Bill Clinton expanded it even more in the 1990s. During these decades, conservatives and liberals in Congress, white and black, were consistently supportive.[10]

The bipartisan War on Drugs has cost tens of billions of dollars to date. It has also harmed minority families and communities across the nation. In 2014, fifty years after the Harlem Riot, the United States had more prisoners behind bars by a wide margin than any other country in the world—most of them poor young men of color convicted of nonviolent crimes. And it had a rate of incarceration between five and ten times as high as in Western Europe and other democracies. Although on the decline, the rate remained historically high in comparison to incarceration levels in the United States from the mid-1920s to the early 1970s.[11]

In recent years, public attention has also focused on the militarization of policing—a collective legacy of the 1960s riots—and the deaths of unarmed blacks at the hands of armed whites. Sometimes they result from civilian actions—as when Trayvon Martin was shot in Florida by a neighborhood watch volunteer in 2012. Often the killings are a consequence of police actions, justified or not, which have caused sadness and anger in black communities across the nation. And on occasion they have led to renewed outbursts of civil unrest, as in Ferguson, Missouri, in 2014 and Baltimore, Maryland, in 2015.[12]

Today James Powell is forgotten by politicians, policymakers, and even participants in the Black Lives Matter movement. But his death was a catalyst for the Harlem Riot, which holds historical significance because it foreshadowed the disorders of the decade and helped set the stage for the politics of crime and policing, which has affected the lives of millions of minorities for more than half a century.

No one to date has written an in-depth history of the racial unrest in New York City in July 1964.[13] This day-to-day, street-level narrative is intended to recapture that story and, in the process, provide some historical background for our current predicament. It is important to understand how the riots in Harlem and Brooklyn, although not the direct cause of the prison crisis, influenced the political context in which the crime and drug policies of recent decades have unfolded. *In the Heat of the Summer*—the title comes from a song by the folk artist Phil Ochs—shines a spotlight on the extraordinary drama of a single week when peaceful protests and violent unrest intersected, law and order moved to the forefront of presidential politics, the freedom struggle reached a crossroads, and the War on Crime was set in motion.

Why no complete account of this critical moment exists is a mystery. The Harlem Riot typically gets only a couple of paragraphs or pages in the standard versions of urban unrest. Even the *Report of the National Advisory Commission on Civil Disorders* (better known as the Kerner Commission) largely ignored it. Although New York was not the worst riot, it was the first major civil disorder of the 1960s. It also erupted in the media capital of the United States and presaged unrest to come. Yet a comparative silence surrounds the clashes in Central Harlem and Bed-Stuy—an odd oversight given the way the national media have commemorated the racial fires that transformed other cities.[14]

Watts, Detroit, and Washington have all generated important books. Even a smaller city like Rochester—which had a riot the weekend after Harlem—has become the subject of *July '64*, an award-winning documentary film. Perhaps the violent events in New York, which attracted national and international coverage at the time, failed to fit the conventional narrative, which presents 1964 as a year of tragedy and suffering—symbolized by the disappearance and murder of three civil rights workers in the South—that led to triumph and redemption in the form of the Civil Rights Act. Possibly the unrest in Harlem and Brooklyn was simply overshadowed by the far deadlier and more destructive disorders that began in 1965. In the end, it is hard to know exactly why the largest riot of "Freedom Summer" has not received the attention it merits.[15]

To correct this omission and tell the story as accurately as possible, I have supplemented new discoveries from historical archives with personal interviews I conducted with dozens of Harlem residents, police officers, political activists, city officials, and print journalists, black and white. Few of my interviewees had ever spoken for the record of their experiences in July 1964. For many it was difficult, even painful, to reconstruct the past. Yet their memories and observations provided me with insights that I could not have gained elsewhere.

Nevertheless, it is impossible to reconstruct with certainty what happened in Central Harlem and Bed-Stuy more than fifty years ago. Even then the events were hazy; now they are shrouded by time. This account instead concentrates on the human dimension of the urban unrest by incorporating a broad range of personal perspectives—black and white, young and old, Christian and Jewish, angry and fearful as well as radical, liberal, and conservative. On almost every page, it showcases the voices of demonstrators and police, officials and reporters, merchants and looters, community activists and ordinary citizens. In providing these diverse and divergent perspectives, my aim is to present the viewpoints of those who were involved as fully and fairly as possible without making assumptions or passing judgments unless the evidence warrants it.

Some of the figures in this book are readily recognizable, such as Mayor Robert F. Wagner, Jr., Congressman Adam Clayton Powell, Jr. (no relation to James Powell), and Governor Nelson Rockefeller; black leaders like Martin Luther King, Jr., Roy Wilkins, James Farmer, and Malcolm X; black scholars or artists like Kenneth Clark, James Baldwin, Langston Hughes, and Ralph Ellison; and white journalists like Jimmy Breslin of the *Herald Tribune* and Gay Talese of the *New York Times*. Others are undeservedly obscure, such as George Schuyler, a conservative black commentator who served on the grand jury that reviewed the Powell shooting; Earl Caldwell, a black reporter who was launching his career; and Lloyd Sealy, the first black police officer to assume command of the 28th Precinct in Central Harlem and then reach the rank of assistant chief inspector.

The narrative, which moves back and forth from the streets of New York to the corridors of the White House, has two central characters: Lyndon Johnson and Bayard Rustin. It is difficult to imagine two more different people in the summer of 1964: Johnson, the coarse and ambitious Texan politician who was determined to win the presidential election so that he could extend civil rights, build a Great Society, and surpass the historic achievements of his political hero, Franklin Roosevelt; and Rustin, the sophisticated civil rights activist, pacifist, and socialist who after decades of nonviolent struggle against racial segregation was eager to seize the opportunity to advance his dreams of racial equality and economic justice.

Even so, Rustin and Johnson were united by their shared goals and common vision of the Harlem Riot as a major threat to their political ambitions. The racial unrest, they worried, might discredit the cause of civil rights; it might even lead to the election of Barry Goldwater by alienating white liberals and moderates who were sympathetic to the freedom movement but afraid of what the urban protests might portend. And so both the activist and the president worked feverishly, with limited success and unforeseen consequences, to stop the rioting and looting before it could spread.

Night after night, Rustin walked the streets of New York promoting nonviolence and risking his personal safety to pacify the angry youths who had lost patience. Day after day, Johnson worked the phones and levers of power in Washington in an effort to find the right political balance between firmness and compassion, law enforcement and social programs aimed at restoring hope to those who were hurling rocks and debris. Ultimately, the crisis made them allies or partners of a sort and led to greater respect between them—but it also left them vulnerable to criticism from both radicals and conservatives, which prefigured the fate of liberals later in the decade.

A final note of my own: I was born in New York in April 1964. At the time my parents were living on King Street in the West Village. In researching this project, I found a letter in the Municipal Archives that my father, a Brooklyn native, had written to the deputy mayor in charge of police brutality on July 27, three days after the final clashes in Bed-Stuy had subsided. In the letter, which was subsequently forwarded to NYPD Commissioner Michael Murphy, my father contended that the "tension and mistrust" between the police and the public was due in part to a mutual lack of respect or courtesy. A middle-class Jewish American, he observed that uniformed patrolmen, who were typically working-class Irish or Italian Americans, routinely addressed him as "Johnny" or "Mac" (not "Mister") and my mother as "sister" or "girl" (not "Miss").[16]

"Presumably the citizen is supposed to bite his tongue and accept this for the sake of law and order," my father wrote. But he wondered whether officers "insensible to an individual's dignity" were not also "insensible to the individual's rights." If police disrespect was mainly a result of "bad training," as my father hoped, then perhaps better instruction or stricter discipline could make basic courtesy as important to officers as keeping their "shoes shined and uniform pressed," although he conceded that preventing police brutality was a higher priority, especially for minority residents. In response, he received a two-sentence form letter. But today police cars in New York have three words—whether observed more often in the breach or not—emblazoned on the side: Courtesy. Professionalism. Respect.[17]

Discovering my father's letter—which he had long forgotten—was not only an unexpected connection to family history. It was also a priceless reminder that respect for the dignity of all should matter to all. As a wise and generous friend once told me, the most valuable gift a historian can possess is empathy for the people about whom he or she writes. I hope this book meets that standard.

CHAPTER 1

THE GROWING MENACE

Now no one knows how it started
Why the windows were shattered
But deep in the dark, someone set the spark
And then it no longer mattered
    —Phil Ochs, "In the Heat of the Summer"

THURSDAY, JULY 16

The death of James Powell came almost instantaneously according to the autopsy report. The first .38 caliber bullet, perhaps intended as a warning shot, broke a glass panel in the outer door to the apartment building and smashed into the inner door of the vestibule. The second, perhaps intended to disarm Powell, went through the right forearm close to the wrist and then ripped into the chest, slicing the main artery above the heart and lodging in the lungs. It was the fatal wound. The third shot entered the abdomen just above the navel and severed a major vein. But according to the deputy chief medical examiner, Powell probably could have survived that injury if hospitalized promptly.[1]

"There was no evidence on the body of smoke, flame or powder marks," the autopsy report stated, "thus showing that both bullets must have travelled more than a foot and a half before striking [the victim]." There were also no marks in the recently repaired sidewalk. Both findings cast doubt on the claim by some witnesses that Lieutenant Thomas Gilligan had fired the second and third bullets at close range while Powell was lying on the ground. But the forensic evidence would only arrive weeks later—

too late to quell the rumors or quench the outrage felt by many in the black community.[2]

On the final morning of his young life, Powell said goodbye to his mother Annie at 7:30 A.M. and left his home in the Soundview Housing Project, a lower-income apartment complex in the Bronx. At age fifteen he was a relatively small and slight youth, standing five feet six inches tall and weighing 122 pounds. An only child and a ninth-grader at nearby Samuel Gompers Vocational High School, Powell was taking voluntary remedial-reading classes at Wagner Junior High School for the summer term, which had started nine days earlier.[3]

Since the death of his father Harold three years earlier, Powell had begun to get into scrapes with the law, including arrests for armed robbery and breaking a car window. Twice he was also charged with trying to board a subway or bus without paying the fare. None of those arrests had led to convictions. But according to the FBI, Powell ran with a gang and had suffered a knife wound in his right leg that required hospitalization. That might explain why he gave two knives, one with a black handle and one with a red handle, to Cliff Harris and Carl Dudley, two other boys who joined him on the way to the subway on that fateful morning.[4]

Neighbors had a mixed view of Powell. Some believed that he was a good kid and doubted that he would have sought serious trouble. Others contended that he was a troubled youth who "liked to get high on whiskey" and was beginning to develop a wild streak. From interviews with school officials and social workers, the FBI learned that Powell was a chronic truant who had been absent thirty-two days in the spring term, which was why he needed to attend summer school. When he was present, fellow students accused him of bullying them, stealing from them, and starting fights— even in the guidance office.[5]

Powell and his friends were part of a group of about one hundred students who were waiting for classes to begin at 9:30 A.M. Some were standing near the entrance to the school. Others were leaning on cars or sitting on stoops across the street where a superintendent named Patrick Lynch, a stocky thirty-six-year-old Irish immigrant with a strong brogue, was watering the plants, flowers, and trees in front of the apartment buildings at 211 and 215 East 76th Street.[6]

Lynch and his white tenants had little patience for the summer school students, most of whom were black. The Yorkville neighborhood had few minorities, and during the regular term Wagner Junior High School, which had not previously hosted a summer school session, was roughly half white, a quarter African American, and a quarter Puerto Rican. Those students were not a problem according to the superintendent. "They sit on the stoops to eat lunch and I don't pass any remarks," he told a reporter later, in what seemed like a partial confession. "They clean up. They're good kids."[7]

Not so the kids who attended summer school. In Lynch's eyes, they were rude and loud, creating problems for everyone, especially local merchants, and leaving litter everywhere. He repeatedly complained to the school principal, Max Francke, a mild-mannered, white-haired man who was not sympathetic and tended to side with the students. The building superintendent also lodged more than twenty complaints with the police, who were equally unresponsive. "The other day, my wife was on the street when a couple of kids went for each other with bottles," Lynch said later in a tone of sadness and regret. "My wife went upstairs and called the police, but they never came. They always come after something serious. But why couldn't they come before? Then this would never have happened."[8]

What happened on July 16 at 9:20 A.M. in front of 215 East 76th Street was unclear and contested, both then and now. The grand jury, which by law automatically reviewed every fatal police shooting in New York, heard testimony from "all known" witnesses, including those brought to the attention of the district attorney by the Congress of Racial Equality (CORE) and the National Association for the Advancement of Colored People (NAACP). Of the forty-five interviewed, fifteen were teenagers who were friends or acquaintances of Powell. Among them were his buddies Harris and Dudley. But the eyewitnesses offered conflicting testimony about whether Powell was armed or had attacked Gilligan, perhaps because a repair truck parked in front of the building obstructed their views. Whether the officer had issued a warning or identified himself was also contentious.

Despite the controversy surrounding the incident, the basic cause of the deadly confrontation was not in dispute. According to Lynch, he was washing the sidewalk with a hose at 9:15 A.M. when he repeatedly asked a group of students who were standing near the steps to move so that they would not get wet while he watered some flowers on a fire escape above them. They refused and then claimed that the superintendent had sprayed them with water after calling them "dirty niggers" and threatening to "wash the black off you."[9]

Lynch denied the accusation, but Francke backed the teens, asserting that the hosing was done with "malice aforethought." The principal also accused the superintendent of poor judgment and blamed him for the tragedy. True or not, the incident was laden with overtones from the demonstrations in Birmingham a year earlier, when police officers turned fire hoses and water cannons on black children. Now the students began to retaliate by throwing bottles, trash, and metal garbage can lids at Lynch, who quickly darted inside the building. Yet by then it was too late—the confrontation had already attracted the attention of Powell, Harris, and Dudley across the street.[10]

"I am going to cut that [expletive]," said Powell, who asked Dudley for the knife with the red handle. When he pretended not to have it, Powell asked Harris for the knife with the black handle. "What do you want with it?" asked Harris. "Give it to me," said Powell, who added "I'll be back." So Harris gave the knife to Powell, who started to cross the street. A girl pleaded with him and tried to restrain him, but he brushed her aside and, with the knife in his right hand, headed up the steps screaming "hit him, hit him, hit him."[11]

At that moment, Gilligan emerged from the Jadco TV Service Company next door. For the officer, a solid man who stood more than six feet tall and weighed two hundred pounds, the morning was supposed to be quiet and uneventful. The plan was to get a radio fixed at a shop he knew from previous duty in the precinct. A thirty-seven-year-old resident of Stuyvesant Town, a middle-class, virtually all-white apartment project on the East Side, he was off duty and out of uniform, although he had his badge and revolver with him as department regulations required. Like all officers he was obligated to stop crime, arrest offenders, and protect life as well as property at all times.

On this day, Gilligan was assigned to the 14th Inspection Division in Brooklyn, where he was a decorated officer who had joined the force after serving in the Pacific during World War II. In seventeen years on the job, he had received nineteen citations, represented by impressive rows of enameled bars above the gold badge on his dress uniform. He had four citations for disarming suspects without firing his weapon and two for disabling suspects with his revolver (he had never killed anyone until Powell). In 1958, he had fought for his life with a man on a rooftop; despite a broken wrist, Gilligan managed to shoot him as he fled. In 1960, he was able to wound a youth in the right shoulder who was vandalizing cars outside

Stuyvesant Town and had broken two fingers on the officer's gun hand with a fire nozzle.

Gilligan also had numerous citations for saving lives. He had, wrote two reporters, "rescued women and children from a fire, saved an unconscious man by first aid, stopped a man from a suicidal jump, rescued an unconscious man trapped in a basement after an explosion, and used mouth-to-mouth resuscitation to revive a woman who had attempted suicide by swallowing barbiturates." By many accounts, Gilligan was a hero cop. By many others, he was a "Killer Cop" whose face was soon plastered on "Wanted for Murder" posters across Harlem.[12]

The histories of Powell and Gilligan were, of course, immaterial in a court of law. Powell's background had no direct bearing on his actions that day. Gilligan's record was also irrelevant—good officers make bad shootings and vice versa. But in the court of public opinion, which the civil rights movement and press coverage had greatly influenced, the information mattered deeply. As in all controversial police incidents with racial overtones, many whites and blacks fit the "facts" as they understood or perceived them into a simplistic narrative with an innocent or menacing victim and an upright or brutal officer.

When the owner of the appliance store told him that Thursday morning of the trouble with the summer school students, Gilligan had no desire to get involved. But the officer would not have a choice. As the merchant watched through the front window of the shop, the teens begin to hurl objects at Lynch and there was a loud crash as glass shattered. At that point Gilligan ran out of the store, removing from his trouser pockets his badge with his left hand and his revolver with his right hand. He was standing at the bottom of the stoop when Powell turned from the entrance to the building and headed back down the steps to the street.[13]

"Stop, I'm a cop," Gilligan yelled. "Drop it." But Powell kept coming down the stairs. With the knife in his right hand, he tried to strike at Gilligan, who had a split second to make a life-or-death decision. With his heart pounding and adrenalin pumping, he fired a shot. The teen slashed again at the officer, who blocked Powell and pushed him away. The knife, however, sliced Gilligan's arm and when the youth raised it once more, the officer fired again. The bullet struck the teen's wrist and deflected into his chest, but his forward momentum continued. And so Gilligan stepped back and fired a third time into the abdomen of Powell, who collapsed on the sidewalk, face down, his blood pooling underneath him.[14]

Seeing Powell on the ground with his body parallel to the curb, his friend Harris raced across the street. "I ran over to where he was and got down on my knees next to him and said, 'Jimmy, what's the matter?'" he recalled. But there was no response except for a trickle of blood from Powell's mouth as he tried to spit. So Harris turned his attention to the officer, who was looming over them with a gun at his side, and asked him if he could call an ambulance. "No, this black [expletive] is my prisoner," Gilligan replied according to Harris. "You call the ambulance."[15]

From the corner candy store, the teen phoned for help as screams started to come from the crowd of students in front of the school. At the same time, Francke stepped outside, saw the body, and instructed his secretary to call an ambulance. But by the time it arrived Powell was dead. Later, a teacher found the black-handled knife, which Harris subsequently identified, in a gutter between parked cars about eight to ten feet from the body.[16]

That is how most of the adult witnesses interviewed by the grand jury saw the incident, with minor discrepancies such as the precise words Gilligan had used when confronting Powell. Among the adult witnesses, most of whom were white, were a bus driver, a truck driver, a nurse, a priest, two merchants (including the owner of the repair store), five teachers, and eight passersby. But that is not how most of the fifteen black students interviewed perceived the altercation. They maintained that Gilligan had not identified himself as a police officer, had given no warning, and had fired two shots into Powell's back while he lay wounded on the sidewalk. Most of the students also claimed that Powell was unarmed and unthreatening.[17]

"I saw the boy go into the building and he didn't have any knife then," said a teenage girl. "When he came out, he was even laughing and kind of like running and the cop was on the street going into the building and then he shot him." Even if she was wrong about the knife, it was understandable. In Harlem, it was common knowledge that police officers routinely carried throwaway knives because they risked disciplinary or criminal charges if they used deadly force against an unarmed assailant. The standard police jacket, which Gilligan was not wearing at the time, even had a concealed breast pocket—ostensibly for that purpose. Although it seems likely that Powell had a knife, especially since the shooting took place in broad daylight before numerous eyewitnesses, it is easy to see why so many blacks in New York would reach the opposite conclusion.[18]

At the crime scene, more trouble was brewing. As Gilligan was whisked to Roosevelt Hospital to get his arm bandaged (Lynch was also treated there for a possible fracture of his left hand, which was struck by a bottle), the students kept converging despite repeated warnings from police. The arrival of a news photographer caused the confrontation to escalate. "This is worse than Mississippi," yelled female students in reference to the three missing (and presumed dead) civil rights workers from CORE who had disappeared in June during the "Freedom Summer" campaign to register black voters. "It looked bad," said Francke. "I borrowed a bullhorn and tried to calm the youngsters but it was impossible to quiet the crowd."[19]

As the police issued five riot calls, more than one hundred officers arrived in steel helmets. Eventually, the disturbance ended after ninety minutes without more violence or arrests, although three young women were briefly taken into custody and then released. But as the crowd dispersed emotions continued to run high. At the 77th Street entrance to the Lexington Avenue subway station, a group of fifty black students ransacked a newsstand, scattering papers and candy, and threatened a white motorman with a screwdriver. Another group slapped a white woman on the street and hurled a flower pot through the window of a flower store, terrifying the owner. "Are they going to let that cop go free?" challenged a teenage girl.[20]

Francke, the school principal, defended the students in the aftermath. "These children are not hooligans," he said. "They're dedicated to improving themselves and we never had any trouble with them." A deli owner agreed. "This is a racial problem," he observed. "They cry because they feel there's no justice for them. Whether they're right or wrong, we have to change their minds." But other white residents of Yorkville disagreed. "I never thought I'd see the day when I'd be afraid to walk in my own neighborhood in broad daylight," said an older man, "but when I see these kids coming I duck into the nearest doorway." And a retired woman expressed resentment: "They hang around our hallways. When we tell them to leave they act as if we are prejudiced against them. We just don't like having garbage and noisy people in our home."[21]

Within hours of the incident members of CORE's national office and East Side chapter were holding an impromptu press conference at the corner of 77th and Lexington. In front of newspaper reporters and television cameras, they spoke of police brutality and the pressing need for an independent civilian review board not composed of police officials to investigate the shooting. The NAACP also demanded an immediate inquiry by the district attorney. In response, Deputy Chief Inspector Joseph Coyle promised a prompt investigation, but asserted that Gilligan had acted in self-defense.[22]

The man of the hour, however, was silent and out of sight. Had Gilligan made a public statement in the immediate aftermath of the Powell shooting, it is conceivable that some of the rage and anger spreading across Central Harlem might have dissipated. But on the advice of counsel he was already taking a low profile and avoiding the media spotlight. Not so the presidential nominee of the Republican Party, who at that moment was preparing to deliver the biggest speech of his political life at the Cow Palace in San Francisco.

A year before the Powell shooting, Barry Goldwater had anticipated that racial unrest would spread from the South to the North. "I predict," he told an interviewer in July 1963, "that if there is rioting in the streets it'll occur in Chicago, Detroit, New York, or Washington, probably to a greater extent than it will occur in the southern cities."[23] Like most conservatives, he believed that the civil rights movement had contributed to urban black violence. In a letter to a friend, Goldwater wrote that "I am somewhat fearful of what might happen in some of our large northern cities . . . if this type of fire-eating talk continues among the Negro leaders and those whites who would use them only as a means to gain power. . . . I am afraid we're in trouble."[24]

Precisely which black leaders and white liberals Goldwater had in mind is not clear. But like millions of other Americans, he had seen the newspaper photos and watched the television broadcasts from Birmingham, Alabama, where Public Safety Commissioner Eugene "Bull" Connor had jailed Dr. Martin Luther King, Jr. in May and then unleashed police dogs and water cannons on black children marching for freedom and justice. In June, Goldwater had listened to John Kennedy speak to the nation about the pressing need for immediate action on civil rights.

"We are confronted primarily with a moral issue," said the president, only hours after segregationist Governor George Wallace had made his infamous "Stand in the Schoolhouse Door" in a vain attempt to prevent two black students from registering for classes at the University of Alabama. "It is as old as the Scriptures and is as clear as the American Constitution. The heart of the question is whether all Americans are to be afforded equal rights and equal opportunities, whether we are going to treat our fellow Americans as we want to be treated." Kennedy also expressed concern at how prejudice and discrimination against African Americans discredited the image of the United States in the eyes of the world.[25]

Like Goldwater, Kennedy saw a threat to order and security—white liberals and conservatives feared black unrest, although they differed on the causes of it. "The fires of frustration and discord are burning in every city, North and South, where legal remedies are not at hand," the president observed. "Redress is sought in the streets, in demonstrations, parades, and protests which create tensions and threaten violence and threaten lives." To preempt the danger, he asked Congress to enact legislation making public accommodations such as hotels and restaurants, stores and theaters, open to all regardless of race.[26]

The introduction of the civil rights bill placed Goldwater in a challenging but promising political position. Kennedy's action had led more southern whites to reconsider their allegiance to the Democratic Party. But could Goldwater win their votes without becoming known as a racial extremist and losing the support of white moderates elsewhere in the country?

There is no substantiated evidence that the senator was prejudiced in his private life, that he ever made racist remarks or told racist jokes. By the same token, Goldwater was clearly and strongly in favor of gradual and voluntary integration. In his family's department stores, he had welcomed black customers and hired black employees. In his hometown of Phoenix, Goldwater was a founding member of the National Urban League chapter and had played a major role in promoting the integration of schools and restaurants. And in his Air Force Reserve unit he had led the fight against segregation. Although he tolerated the presence, knowingly or not, of racial and religious bigots at campaign events in the South, he never spent a night in a hotel that refused to provide service to blacks.[27]

But in his public life Goldwater had voted against the Civil Rights Act of 1957 and anti–poll tax legislation in 1960 and 1962. Now he opposed the civil rights bill on the stated grounds of property rights and states' rights. With the assistance of ghostwriter L. Brent Bozell, Jr., the brother-in-law of National Review publisher William F. Buckley, he wrote Conscience of a Conservative. In the best seller, which sold more than three million copies, Goldwater objected to forced integration and stated that he was not willing to impose his racial views on "the people of Mississippi or South Carolina. . . . That is their business and not mine. I believe that the problem of race relations, like all social and cultural problems, is best handled by the people directly concerned."[28]

In Goldwater's mind, legislation in general—and laws imposed by Congress in particular—had little chance of changing people's hearts, especially on a matter as personal as race. In Goldwater's heart, he most feared an expansive and intrusive federal government: the United States would become a police state where the executive branch promoted a minority's rights at the expense of the majority's freedoms. That Mississippi, Alabama, and Georgia were already police states for African Americans was seemingly lost on the Arizona senator.

Goldwater instead worried that property owners would no longer have the right to rent or sell to whomever they wanted. Small businesses would no longer have the right to offer or deny service to whomever they wanted. States would no longer have the right to pass or enforce laws that reflected local values or customs, and employers would no longer have the right to hire or fire whomever they wanted. Free association would become subject to governmental regulation. The Founding Fathers' dream of limited government and local control would become a constitutional nightmare.

Across the nation, tens of millions of white Americans agreed with Goldwater. But could he harness their support and use it to capture the Republican nomination in the face of strong opposition from New York Governor Nelson Rockefeller, a prominent supporter of civil rights? Was the "white backlash" against the freedom movement strong enough to sweep him into the White House? By 1963 conservatives were hard at work trying to convince Goldwater to pursue the presidency. But the senator was playing coy and keeping his cards close to his chest. When he met with supporters in January, Goldwater was firm: "Draft, nothin'. I told you I'm not going to run. And I'm telling you now, don't paint me into a corner. It's my political neck and I intend to have something to say about what happens to it."[29]

But in fact he was already considering possibilities and weighing options. In May he received an unexpected political gift when the front-runner Rockefeller, who had divorced his wife the previous December, announced that he was remarrying. His bride was Margaretta "Happy" Murphy, a campaign volunteer and young mother who only a month earlier had divorced her husband. Most shockingly, she had also surrendered custody of their four small children, who ranged in age from eleven years to eighteen months.

The news generated outrage in conservative circles. "A man who has broken up two homes is not the kind we want for high public office," declared Phyllis Schlafly, an Illinois activist whose self-published book about the Goldwater campaign, *A Choice Not an Echo*, became a sudden and surprise best seller. "The party is not so hard up that it can't find somebody who stuck by his own family." Overnight, the polls reversed and Goldwater surged into the lead among Republicans, despite gaffes such as his comment on an ABC-TV news program that the United States could block the flow of weapons from North Vietnam to the Communist guerrillas in South Vietnam by using low-grade atomic weapons to defoliate the dense jungles and expose the supply routes to aerial bombardment.[30]

Although reluctant to declare his candidacy openly, Goldwater was looking forward to running against Kennedy, a political foe and personal friend whom he had come to know and like during their years in the Senate together. But on November 22, 1963, the assassination of the president may also have killed Goldwater's hopes for the White House. Suddenly, he was faced with a race for which he had no zest and in which he had little chance, since his opponent, Lyndon Johnson, could now campaign as the torch bearer for his mourned predecessor.

Goldwater despised Johnson, whom he saw as a "treacherous" opportunist and blatant "hypocrite" who had never "cleaned that crap off his boots." Moreover, conservatives had to endure harsh criticism from the national media, which claimed that right-wing elements in Dallas were responsible for the "climate of extremism" that had somehow contributed to the assassination. Goldwater nevertheless announced his candidacy from his home in Scottsdale, Arizona, in January 1964. "I will not change my beliefs to win votes," he pledged. "I will offer a choice, not an echo."[31] It was a promise he would keep—to his detriment after the nomination.

The campaign got off to a rocky start in New Hampshire in March, when Goldwater lost to former Massachusetts senator and New England favorite son Henry Cabot Lodge, Jr., Nixon's running mate in 1960 and by then the U.S. ambassador to South Vietnam. Of greater significance than the primary defeat was Goldwater's decision to make law and order a centerpiece of his presidential campaign. It was a momentous choice by the candidate, who had guaranteed voters a clear alternative.

The issue of law and order would help Goldwater win the Republican nomination, but in 1964 he could not ride it into the White House because of his reputation as a racist and extremist who might trigger a nuclear war.

Public fear over "crime in the streets" also had not yet reached a critical level. Law and order would nonetheless become a powerful tool for conservative candidates for decades. And it would help make public support for punitive measures by the police and the courts an enduring foundation of the coming crusades against crime and drugs.

Goldwater was not the inventor or originator of law and order. Since Reconstruction in the 1860s and 1870s southern whites had blamed black criminality on the end of slavery and the beginning of integration. By the 1920s, the Great Migration of African Americans had led to similar fears among northern whites. In the 1940s and 1950s, the rise of the modern civil rights movement led conservatives in Congress to warn repeatedly of the great threat racial integration supposedly posed to public safety. In the debate over the Civil Rights Act of 1960, for example, Democratic Senator Strom Thurmond of South Carolina declared that it would lead to a "wave of terror, crime, and juvenile delinquency" in the South as earlier state laws had in the North. Democratic Senator James Eastland of Mississippi likewise asserted that "law enforcement is breaking down because of racial integration" and claimed that the unsafe streets of New York were clear evidence.[32]

But it was Goldwater who introduced law and order to presidential politics in March 1964, when he charged that crime and riots—which conservatives continually if inexactly conflated—ran rampant in America's streets. He refused, however, to place the blame on racial integration, unlike Thurmond, Eastland, and Wallace, who made law and order the focus of his presidential campaign when he entered Democratic primaries later in the spring. Goldwater instead asserted that the fault lay with the widespread practice of nonviolent protest, which in turn had led to disrespect for authority. The Arizona senator also ascribed guilt to white liberals like President Johnson, who in a crass and cynical bid for black votes had condoned and even applauded demonstrators when they violated what they viewed as unjust and immoral laws.

"Many of our citizens—citizens of all races—accept as normal the use of riots, demonstrations, boycotts, violence, pressures, civil disorder, and disobedience as an approach to serious national problems," thundered Goldwater at the University of New Hampshire, where he promised to restore law and order. Passage of civil rights legislation, he predicted, would not lead to lower tensions and less crime—as white and black liberals had asserted for decades—but only to more bloodshed and fewer restraints on individual behavior. Like most conservatives, he saw black criminality as a result of immorality, not prejudice.[33]

Goldwater used law and order to blend concern over the rising number of traditional crimes—robberies and rapes, muggings and murders—with unease about civil rights, civil disobedience, and civil unrest. If the fear factor reached a critical level, conservative politicians, pundits, and propagandists could emphasize that opposition to crime and violence, not support for discrimination and segregation, was the reason for their resistance to the freedom struggle. Of course, liberals could with justification respond that the calls for law and order frequently rested on racial prejudice. Civil disobedience was often the only recourse left to black demonstrators denied basic freedoms and confronted by white officials who exploited the law or white extremists who defied it. But what made law and order such a potentially potent political weapon for conservatives was that they could turn it into a Rorschach test of public anxiety and project different concerns to different people at different moments.

More fundamentally, Goldwater offered a cogent view of a complicated and threatening world by contending that the loss of security and order was merely the most visible symptom and symbol of the failure of liberalism. In his view, the welfare state had squandered the hard-earned taxes of the deserving middle class on wasteful programs for the undeserving poor. These programs had in turn aggravated rather than alleviated social problems by encouraging personal dependence and discouraging personal responsibility. They had also raised false hopes and expectations on the part of the disadvantaged. "Government seeks to be parent, teacher, leader, doctor, and even minister," he argued at a New Hampshire high school. "And its failures are strewn about us in the rubble of rising crime rates, juvenile delinquency, [political] scandal."[34]

It was a powerful, if premature, indictment of the War on Poverty that Johnson hoped to launch and Goldwater wanted to forestall. But for the moment law and order enabled the Arizona senator to focus on what he and other conservatives claimed were the negative consequences of civil rights without directly opposing what had become a moral imperative to most liberals and many moderates. In the primary campaign, the issue might also help him broaden his appeal in southern and western suburbs. And by enhancing Goldwater's popularity with working-class and lower middle-class whites, especially ethnic Catholics in northern cities, law and order might facilitate a successful challenge in the general election, if he could first claim the Republican nomination.

In April the campaign continued to stumble, but in May it gained momentum and delegates, including 271 of 278 from southern states. At a rally in Madison Square Garden before eighteen thousand enthusiastic supporters, Goldwater said he supported the right to vote but not the effort to legislate integration, calling it a "problem of the heart and of the mind." He added that "until we have an Administration that will cool the fires and the tempers of violence, we simply cannot solve the rest of the problem in a lasting sense." The comment met with scorn from Roy Wilkins, executive secretary of the NAACP. He warned that the patience of blacks was wearing thin as the civil rights bill remained stalled in Congress. "If [our] pleas continue to be met with sophistry and antebellum oratory there will certainly be violence in the streets and elsewhere," he predicted. "There is nothing left. There is no place to turn."[35]

At a Memorial Day rally in Riverside, part of Goldwater's all-out effort to defeat Rockefeller and win the critical California primary, he again rejected the liberal claim that passage of the civil rights bill would reduce black crime and promote racial harmony. "Some wobbly thinkers think that laws will stop you from hating, laws will make you generous," he said with disdain. "But when I read about street crimes, about hatred covered with blood, I ask what's happening to the land of the free." Three days later, he attracted 51 percent of the vote and clinched the Republican nomination. Southern California had provided the vital votes. In morally traditional Orange County, Goldwater swamped Rockefeller, whose new wife had given birth the weekend before the election, by an almost two-to-one margin. Now it was on to the convention—but first the senator had to return to Washington, where the debate over the civil rights bill had reached a climax.[36]

Back in February the House of Representatives had overwhelmingly approved the measure. But in the Senate a core group of southern Democrats had blocked it. After a seventy-five-day filibuster, the longest in history, the Senate took a cloture vote on June 10. Supporters of the bill needed sixty-seven votes to halt debate; in the end, they received seventy-one, including the "aye" of Democratic Senator Clair Engle of California, who was in a wheelchair and had to point to his eye because he could not speak due to a brain tumor.[37]

On June 18, Goldwater was one of twenty-seven senators—only six of whom were Republicans—to vote against the Civil Rights Act, which Johnson signed into law on July 2. The racial question was "fundamentally a matter of the heart," Goldwater declared on the floor of the Senate. "The problems of discrimination cannot be cured by laws alone." He added that "if my vote is misconstrued, let it be, and let me suffer its consequences. . . . This is where I stand."[38]

As anticipated, Goldwater's vote attracted harsh criticism from liberals. But he received strong praise from conservatives like Ezra Taft Benson, former secretary of agriculture in the Eisenhower administration and later president of the Church of Jesus Christ of Latter-day Saints. Like Goldwater he agreed that the bill would lead to more violence, but he blamed communists—not liberals. "The plans made some years ago for the use of the Negroes in stirring up strife and contention, if not civil war, is being carried out effectively," warned Benson.[39]

At the Republican Convention in San Francisco, most of the delegates shared Goldwater's opposition to civil rights and support for law and order. On July 14, the second night, Dwight Eisenhower arrived and, in a last-minute departure from his prepared text, warned of the danger posed by crime. "Let us not be guilty," he said, "of maudlin sympathy for the criminal who, roaming the streets with switchblade knife and illegal firearms seeking a helpless prey, suddenly becomes upon apprehension a poor, underprivileged person who counts upon the compassion of our society and the laxness or weaknesses of too many courts to forgive his offense." As the journalist Theodore White observed, the former president was "lifting to national discourse a matter of intimate concern to the delegates, creating there before them an issue which touched all fears, North and South. The convention howled."[40]

Two nights later, on July 16, Goldwater again brought the convention to a fever pitch. In no mood to offer conciliatory words to the moderates who had called him an extremist and sought to block his nomination even after he had secured a majority of the delegates, he made it clear that conservatives were now in charge. "Those who do not care for our cause, we don't expect to enter our ranks in any case," he declared. And then he offered the aphorism for which he is best remembered. "I would remind you that extremism in the defense of liberty is no vice," he stated. "And let me remind you also that moderation in the pursuit of justice is no virtue."

FIGURE 1. Senator Barry Goldwater addresses the Republican Convention on July 16 and accepts the presidential nomination. © Bettmann/CORBIS.

A reporter in the auditorium was stunned: "My God, he's going to run as Barry Goldwater."[41]

But while journalists and historians subsequently focused on that phrase and moment, the part of the speech that ignited and united the delegates was the nominee's invocation of law and order. Demanding in loaded language with racial overtones that public security "not become the license of the mob and of the jungle," Goldwater blamed the Democrats for allowing crime to flourish as the more than thirteen hundred delegates, only fifteen of whom were black (none of them from the South), roared their approval.[42]

"The growing menace in our country tonight, to personal safety, to life, to limb and property, in homes, in churches, on the playgrounds and places of business, particularly in our great cities, is the mounting concern—or should be—of every thoughtful citizen in the United States," he growled as the crowd hooted and hollered. "History shows us, demonstrates that nothing, nothing prepares the way for tyranny more than the failure of public officials to keep the streets from bullies and marauders."[43]

In the final draft of his nomination speech, Goldwater had scrawled in the margins even stronger and more personal language, which he opted not to deliver. "Our wives dare not leave their homes after dark," he wrote. "Lawlessness grows. Contempt for law and order is more the order than the exception."[44] Later he would use these lines when he gave his first post-convention speech in Prescott, Arizona, in September.

But for now Goldwater retired to his headquarters at the Mark Hopkins Hotel, where he answered questions from reporters and stressed his determination to make law and order a centerpiece of his fall campaign. "I think law, and the abuse of law and order in this country, the total disregard for it, the mounting crime rate is going to be another issue" he said, "at least I'm going to make it one because I think the responsibility for this has to start someplace and it should start at the Federal level with the Federal courts enforcing the laws."[45]

Goldwater then cited a New York case in which a woman who had defended herself with a knife against a rapist was facing possible criminal charges while her assailant would probably go free. "That kind of business has to stop in this country," he said, "and as the President, I'm going to do all I can to see that women can go out in the streets of this country without being scared stiff." In fact, the rates of murder and rape in Phoenix were substantially higher than in New York, as Democrats would hasten to note in coming days.[46]

For the moment, however, the top Democrat was silent, almost certainly by design. During a light day of staged domesticity, Johnson in the morning visited the Tidal Basin, where he and Lady Bird viewed the Darlington Oak Tree, which she hoped to plant on the South Lawn of the White House. In the afternoon, the two took a carefully orchestrated stroll from the White House to Decatur House and then through Lafayette Park. In the evening, the First Lady appeared while the president was reading a newspaper. "What time are you going to eat dinner?" he asked. "The minute you are ready," she replied. "What are your plans for later?" Johnson said he had some mail to sign and would join her in thirty to forty minutes.[47]

But first the president had one more call to make—to former Senator Ernest "Mac" McFarland, chairman of the Arizona delegation to the Democratic Convention. His surprising loss to Goldwater in 1952 had lifted the conservative Republican to national prominence—but had also opened the door for Johnson, who at forty-six became the youngest Majority Leader in

American history when the Democrats regained control of the Senate after the 1954 elections. Now the two old colleagues shared reminiscences as they prepared to watch Goldwater accept the GOP nomination in a few hours.

"Gosh, this fellow you sent up here has caused us a lot of problems," said the president. "Well, I know what you're talking about," chuckled McFarland, who had failed to unseat Goldwater in 1958 despite winning races for governor in 1954 and 1956. "He caused me some." Then the two men got down to business: Would the president like him to make a statement to the press about Goldwater, given their history? McFarland thought it was a bad idea, but said "if you want me to make one I will and I'll say whatever you want me to say." Johnson demurred since he had already informed reporters that he would make no comment at this time: "I just told 'em I was going on sawing my wood and doing my work."[48]

But the president was clearly annoyed by Goldwater's charges. "He'll call me a faker and he called me a phony and a lot of ugly names, but I didn't have anything to say about him," Johnson maintained. "And so I noticed he backed up this morning and said he didn't want to engage in any personalities." McFarland was sympathetic—and skeptical. "Well, last night he said there might be a few brickbats," he noted. Johnson, however, remained adamant: "I'm just going to let him go and we're going to give him lots of rope."[49]

After dinner with the First Lady the president retired for the evening. Presumably, he watched Goldwater's speech, which began at 11:20 EST on Thursday night, but no aides were present to record his immediate reaction. On Friday morning, as organized protests began in New York, Johnson traveled to his ranch outside Austin for the weekend. From there he phoned special assistant Bill Moyers, who at his request read back to him Goldwater's already-notorious claim that extremism in the defense of liberty was no vice. "Well, extremism to destroy liberty is," responded the president. Offering a window into how he viewed the speech, he informed Moyers that he wanted to issue "a balanced statement, not a vicious, violent Goldwater one."[50]

Back in the White House, Goldwater's address and comments to the press about crime and race set off alarm bells. In private, aides worried about an anti–civil rights reaction by whites. "I am disturbed about the continued demonstrations and what I see on radio and TV," wrote an official. "I am convinced that a great deal of the Negro leadership simply does not understand the political facts of life, and think that they are advancing their cause by uttering threats in the newspapers and on TV. They are not sophisticated enough to understand the theory of the backlash unless they are told about it by someone whom they believe." Another staffer urged Johnson to initiate a dialogue with Wilkins, CORE leader James Farmer, and other civil rights leaders as soon as possible, which the president would do the week after Harlem exploded.[51]

But for now Johnson expressed optimism in public. On July 18, the Saturday after the Republican Convention, the president stated at a news conference on his Texas ranch that the United States did not possess, need, or want a national police force, which would contradict Goldwater's belief in limited government. "If we are going to give the federal government the responsibility for all law enforcement, in the cities and towns, even here in the hill country," Johnson said, "I would think that the people would believe that it would do more than anything else to concentrate power in Washington."[52]

The response was carefully crafted and fully indicative of the confidence the president felt as the polls showed him with a large lead. But at that moment he had no inkling of the storm brewing in Central Harlem.

CHAPTER 2

THE GREAT MECCA

Drunk with the memory of the ghetto
Drunk with the lure of the looting
And the memory of the uniforms shoving with their sticks
Asking, "Are you looking for trouble?"
  —Phil Ochs, "In the Heat of the Summer"

1873–1963

In the summer of 1933, Bayard Rustin made his first visit to Harlem. A tall and handsome young man with a restless mind, athletic build, and musical talent, he was born in Pennsylvania in 1912, the son of unmarried parents he never really knew. He was raised mostly by his grandmother, who was educated in integrated Quaker schools and influenced by Quaker ideas. But she could not shelter him from the realities of the world. One of Rustin's earliest brushes with discrimination came when, as a member of the West Chester High School football team, he was denied service in a restaurant in the nearby town of Media and decided to stage his own sit-in, three decades before the famous Nashville protests of 1960. "I sat there quite a long time," he noted later, "and was eventually thrown out bodily. From that point on, I had the conviction that I would not accept segregation."[1]

After his first year at Wilberforce University in western Ohio, Rustin came to New York to see his aunt, a teacher who lived in Harlem. By then the Great Depression was in full force—only months earlier newly elected Franklin Roosevelt had taken the oath of office and assured the nation that "the only thing we have to fear is fear itself." But pure excitement was the twenty-one-year-old Rustin's initial reaction when he arrived in Harlem. "A totally thrilling experience," he recalled. "I'll never forget my first walk on 125th Street. . . . I had such a feeling of exhilaration."[2]

New arrivals often had a similar response because 125th Street was the main artery of Central Harlem, the historic and symbolic heart of black America. Stretching roughly from 110th Street (the northern border of Central Park) to 145th Street, Fifth Avenue to Morningside Park and St. Nicholas Park, the neighborhood was overwhelmingly African American. By contrast, East Harlem and Spanish Harlem were more mixed, with large numbers of Italian Americans, Jewish Americans, and Puerto Ricans.

"Harlem is indeed the great Mecca for the sight-seer, the pleasure-seeker, the curious, the adventurous, the enterprising, the ambitious, and the talented of the whole Negro world," James Weldon Johnson, the noted author, poet, lawyer, diplomat, and first black executive secretary of the NAACP, wrote in the 1920s. "It is a city within a city, the greatest Negro city in the world." But the energy of Harlem could not disguise the fact that it was also a ghetto, with all of the underlying social and economic problems that typically added fuel to the fires of outrage. Periodically, the community exploded, most notably in 1935 during the Great Depression and in 1943 during World War II, even as the same conditions persisted into the 1950s and 1960s. To appreciate what happened in 1964 it is important to understand the history of Harlem.[3]

After the Civil War, New York City underwent an urban revolution. New neighborhoods were needed as the population surpassed a million, and in 1873 Harlem was annexed. By 1881 the elevated railroad had reached 129th Street and a building boom soon followed, with row upon row of elegant brownstones and exclusive apartments constructed on broad and leafy streets in the next two decades. It was, predicted a magazine in 1893, inevitable that "the center of fashion, wealth, culture and intelligence must, in the near future, be found in the ancient and honorable village of Harlem."[4]

The real estate speculators assumed that if they built it, wealthy whites would come to Harlem in search of fresh air and living space as well as an escape from the noise and congestion of the city. But not if they had to share the area with blacks, who were not welcome. So commercial banks were pressured not to offer mortgages to African Americans. Property owners were forced to sign restrictive covenants stating that they would rent or sell only to Caucasians. And neighborhood associations were formed to defend the color barrier. "We are approaching a crisis," declared the founder of the Harlem Property Owners Improvement Corporation in 1913. "It is the question of whether the white man will rule Harlem or the Negro."[5]

But by then it was too late. A wave of speculation in Harlem had swamped the housing market, causing it to collapse in 1905 amid a sea of unsold and unrented buildings. Meanwhile, black migrants from the South and immigrants from the Caribbean were flooding into other parts of the city, causing apartment shortages and rising rents. Tensions also festered between longtime residents and new arrivals, both the native- and foreign-born, which caused lasting divisions within the black community. At the same time, urban renewal and commercial expansion, such as the construction of the original and ornate Pennsylvania Station, were destroying affordable housing and dislocating black residents in Hell's Kitchen on the West Side and in Midtown Manhattan.

Into the breach stepped entrepreneurs such as Philip Payton, founder of the Afro-Am Realty Company, which began to lease Harlem properties from white owners and then rent them to black tenants. Payton was a graduate of Livingston College in North Carolina who had moved to New York in 1899 to make his fortune. After working as a handyman, a barber (his father's trade), and a janitor in a real estate office, he saw his chance and seized it. Another opportunist was Solomon Riley, a barrel-chested Barbados native with a Caucasian wife who followed the same strategy as Payton. "I decided to turn the sword's edge the other way" was how he put it.[6]

The Interborough Rapid Transit (IRT) line along Lenox Avenue, completed in 1904, opened the floodgates to black families eager to enjoy the good life and spacious apartments in Harlem. Their ranks grew as the economic stimulus of World War I created job opportunities in northern factories and reinforced the Great Migration of African Americans from the rural South. In the decade after 1918, almost a hundred thousand blacks moved to Central Harlem, which by 1930 was home to almost two hundred thousand African Americans, more than 65 percent of New York's black population and 12 percent of the city population.[7]

By the Jazz Age Central Harlem had become the place where African Americans could enjoy the "fundamental rights of American citizenship" according to Johnson, whose mother hailed from the Bahamas. "In return, the Negro loves New York and is proud of it, and contributes in his way to its greatness." During the 1920s and 1930s, greatness was everywhere as the Harlem Renaissance attracted the most gifted and talented blacks from across the United States and the West Indies.[8]

Entertainers like Bill "Bojangles" Robinson, Florence Mills, Bert Williams, Bessie Smith, Duke Ellington, Fletcher Henderson, and Fats Waller graced the stages of the Apollo Theater, the Cotton Club, Small's Paradise, and the Savoy Ballroom. Writers and poets like Langston Hughes, Claude McKay, Jean Toomer, Countee Cullen, and Zora Neale Hurston dazzled the literary world. And scholars like E. Franklin Frazier, a Howard University sociologist, and Alain Locke, the first African American Rhodes Scholar and author of *The New Negro*, produced important studies of black society.[9]

At the same time, institutions both sacred (such as the Abyssinian Baptist Church, which soon had the largest Protestant congregation in the country) and secular (such as the Schomburg Center for Research in Black Culture) enriched life in Harlem. It was also the center of African American political thought and hosted *The Crisis*, a magazine published by the NAACP and edited by W. E. B. Du Bois and Jessie Faucet; *Opportunity*, a journal published by the National Urban League and edited by Charles S. Johnson; and the *Messenger*, a monthly originally sponsored by the Socialist Party and edited by A. Philip Randolph and Chandler Owen.

But the glamour and sophistication of the Harlem Renaissance could not hide the fact that the community was not monolithic. On the contrary, it was diverse, with deep divisions between the "respectable" churchgoers and the "rebellious" street people, the middle class and the lower class, the native-born and the foreign-born, the light-skinned and the dark-skinned. In the 1920s, most blacks also could not escape the strains of everyday life in Harlem, where it was a constant struggle to make ends meet amid low incomes and high rents (whites continued to own the vast majority of properties and businesses). With crowding and congestion at extreme levels, death by violence and disease was rampant. Mothers in Harlem died in childbirth at twice the rate of mothers in other parts of the city; the infant mortality rate for blacks was almost twice as high as for whites. Rickets, a bone disorder caused by malnutrition, was common.[10]

No wonder that when the Great Depression arrived it "didn't have the impact on the Negroes that it had on whites," observed George S. Schuyler, a novelist, journalist, and skeptic of the Harlem Renaissance, because "Negroes had been in the Depression all the time." He was essentially right, but by the early 1930s a bad situation had grown even worse. Across New York the homicide rate fell—but not in Central Harlem, where it rose significantly. Malnutrition among children was three times the rate of the rest of the city. And disease remained at epidemic levels—the rate of tuberculosis among blacks was four times the rate among whites, although mortality rates on the whole declined due to better health care and free medical clinics.[11]

Led by Mayor Fiorello H. La Guardia, a liberal Republican with strong ties to the black community, New York offered relatively generous relief assistance. Federal aid also came from the New Deal of President Franklin D. Roosevelt, a liberal Democrat and former governor of New York who actively sought black votes. But although African Americans in Central Harlem enjoyed real benefits that prevented mass hunger and deprivation, in general they received less than their fair share of public welfare, often as a result of racism and discrimination. In response, private institutions like Abyssinian Baptist, headed by the influential minister Adam Clayton Powell, Sr. and his son Adam, the assistant pastor, tried to meet the growing need with soup kitchens, clothing drives, and homeless shelters.

Under the dynamic leadership of Powell Sr., who was named pastor in 1908, Abyssinian Baptist had a congregation of ten thousand and was the most prominent church in Harlem. Powell Jr. was an only son, the adored and pampered child of mixed-race parents. With straight hair and fair skin, he could pass as white, which he briefly chose to do while a student at Colgate University. After college he returned to Harlem in 1930, earned a master's degree in religious education from Columbia University, and entered the ministry at his father's side. Handsome and charismatic, he became a popular civil rights leader during the Great Depression, and in 1938 succeeded his father as pastor. Three years later, he was the first black elected to the city council; in 1944, he joined Congress as the first black representative from New York State.[12]

The root of the problem, Powell Jr. believed, was a lack of jobs. Last hired and first fired, blacks suffered from an unemployment rate at least several times that of whites. In Central Harlem, whites owned three-quarters of the businesses including Blumstein's, the largest department store on 125th Street. And only one-quarter of those businesses would hire blacks, even for entry-level positions. Frustrated, a broad and uneasy coalition of moderate, radical, religious, and nationalist organizations launched a "Don't Buy Where You Can't Work" campaign, which persuaded

Blumstein's to agree to hire fifteen black female clerks, all of them light-skinned and attractive.[13]

But the department store reneged on promises to hire more black employees, other businesses followed suit, and in 1935 the campaign collapsed amid charges of corruption and anti-Semitism (a majority of white store owners in Harlem were Jewish). "I remember meeting no Negro in the years of my growing up, in my family or out of it," recalled James Baldwin, the celebrated writer and Harlem native, "who would really ever trust a Jew and few who did not, indeed, exhibit for them the blackest contempt."[14] In the bitter climate of dashed expectations and mutual distrust, the stage was set for an explosion whose causes and aftermath were similar to the 1964 riot.

On the cool afternoon of March 19, 1935, Lino Rivera walked into the Kress Five and Ten store on West 125th Street across from the Apollo Theater. Unemployed and broke, the sixteen-year-old Puerto Rican had spent the day looking for work in Brooklyn and catching a movie. As he strolled through the store around 3 P.M., he noticed a ten-cent penknife on a counter. "I wanted it and so I took it," he later admitted. Two employees (both white) saw him and grabbed him, but Rivera bit one of them in the hand, drawing blood. They managed to restrain him and summon a police officer, who took the youth to the basement for questioning.[15]

As a group of onlookers formed, a black woman screamed that they were going to beat or kill Rivera. After she was arrested and charged with disorderly conduct, the arrival of an ambulance—to treat the employee—added to the rumors flying through the crowd. Then the driver of a hearse stopped at the scene and another woman shouted, "There's the hearse come to take the boy's body out of the store." In fact, Rivera was already on his way home—uninjured, he had left Kress through a rear exit after the manager had chosen not to file charges against him. The manager also tried to inform the bystanders, but many had dispersed and so word of the supposed brutality spread like wildfire throughout Central Harlem.[16]

With counters overturned and merchandise scattered in the aisles, the police began to clear the Kress store and ordered it closed at 5:30 P.M. But as people returned from work and heard the rumors, a fresh crowd gathered. Between 6 and 7 P.M. two groups of young communists, black and white, arrived with newly painted placards and printed pamphlets alleging that Rivera was near death and that the police had broken the arms of the

woman who was arrested (neither charge was true). The radicals also organized a picket line and made inflammatory speeches at street meetings.
Suddenly, bottles or rocks shattered the large plate glass windows and hundreds of looters swarmed into the five-and-dime, grabbing whatever items
they could reach. Thousands of others quickly joined the fray, smashing
windows and robbing stores along 125th Street from Fifth to Eighth Avenue.[17] The Harlem Riot of 1935 had begun.

The rioters were not solely the "riffraff" or hoodlums as many blacks
and whites later claimed—they were a mix of the poor, the provoked, and
the prominent. "One of the most unusual was a Harlem playgirl and relative of one of the most conservative of Harlem's ministers," wrote Claude
McKay, the gifted author and poet from Jamaica. "Under her coat she was
carrying a bag full of bricks and was taxied from place to place hurling
them through the plate glass."[18]

Sixteen years earlier, during the race riots that marked the "Red Summer" of 1919, McKay had composed "If We Must Die," an anthem for the
"New Negro" movement. "Like men we'll face the murderous, cowardly
pack," the poem declared, "pressed to the wall, dying, but fighting back!"
Now McKay belittled the 1935 riot as little more than a "party." Few whites
were affected, he observed, and then "not nearly to the extent they might
be during the celebration of a Joe Louis victory."[19] But as always, blacks
who lived and worked in Harlem would pay for the party and suffer the
hangover.

After a desperate search, the police located Rivera and brought him
back to the Kress store at 2 A.M. to demonstrate that he was unharmed. But
they failed to make effective use of radio stations or sound trucks and by
then the looting had spread south to 120th Street and north to 138th Street
as owners rushed to post signs indicating that the business employed African Americans or was black-owned. In his classic novel *Invisible Man*,
Ralph Ellison described the scene: "The crowd was working in and out of
the stores like ants around spilled sugar. . . . I saw a little hard man come
out of the crowd carrying several boxes. He wore three hats upon his head,
and several pairs of suspenders flopped about his shoulders, and now as he
came toward us I saw that he wore a pair of gleaming new rubber hip boots.
His pockets bulged and over his shoulder he carried a cloth sack that swung
heavily behind him."[20]

More than five hundred officers raced to Harlem and flooded the area.
In the streets, squads of mounted and foot patrolmen waded into the

crowds, which had grown to around three thousand, using their night sticks and gun butts on rioters. On the rooftops, police combed tenement buildings in an effort to arrest snipers and halt the fusillade of "Irish confetti" (bricks, bottles, and bats) that rained down on their fellow officers below. Emergency units and prisoner wagons occupied strategic positions throughout Central Harlem while radio cars cruised the blocks and tried to coordinate operations. The next morning order was restored, but not before one male was dead (two more would die later) and more than a hundred (including seven officers) were wounded. Another 125 were arrested (mostly black youths charged with disorderly conduct or inciting to riot), and more than two hundred stores were vandalized if not looted.[21]

The overwhelming majority of police were white, which aggravated the confrontation. Before the riot began, several black residents politely asked officers in the Kress store about the condition of Rivera. It was, they were gruffly informed, "none of their business." An older woman made another plea: "Can't you tell us what happened?" She was warned to move on "if you know what's good for you." Once the looting was under way, witnesses asserted that one of the victims, a high school student coming home from a movie with his brother, was shot and mortally wounded by a white policeman who never fired a warning shot or told the black youth to halt when he ran from the officer as part of a crowd outside an auto supply store.[22] More black police, testified the ranking African American officer in the NYPD at the first public hearing of the mayor's commission to investigate the riot, could have made a difference because they were better suited to handle trouble in Harlem.[23]

In the debate over who caused the explosion, Mayor La Guardia and city officials immediately cast blame on the communists, who in their view had sought to exploit the racial unrest for political gain. "We have evidence," charged Manhattan District Attorney William Dodge, "that two hours after the boy stole that knife the Reds had placed inflammatory leaflets on the streets." He announced that he would convene a grand jury "to let the Communists know that they cannot come into this country and upset our laws."[24]

Black conservatives were careful to finger white radicals and agitators. "The peace of Harlem was disrupted by people from other places last night," stated Fred R. Moore, editor of the *New York Age* (an African American newspaper) and a former alderman. "These people were dissatisfied with the place they came from and they are dissatisfied with American ways.

They were determined to incite irresponsible people to revolt against law and order. . . . We are a peace-loving people who never subscribe to so-called 'red' notions." An elderly waiter called white communists the "prime instigators," and a window washer concurred.[25]

Black radicals in turn initially pointed to the white police, whose "brutality and provocation against the Negro people" had triggered the "race riots" according to James Ford, executive secretary of the Harlem section of the Communist Party.[26] But most African Americans—including the communists in time—placed primary responsibility on the economic pressures in Central Harlem.

"Continued exploitation of the Negro is at the bottom of all the trouble, exploitation as regards wages, jobs, and working conditions," contended the younger Powell. A porter stated that the "rioting was due to economics" and a barber agreed. "The Communists are only responsible for setting off the fuse; the situation already existed," he told a reporter for the *Amsterdam News*. In "Declaration of 1776," educator Nannie Burroughs outlined a broad and deep history of oppression and discrimination. "The causes of the Harlem Riot are not far to seek," she asserted. "Day after day, year after year, decade after decade, black people have been robbed of their inalienable rights. . . . That 'long train of abuses' is a magazine of powder. An unknown boy was simply the match."[27]

After the initial hysteria had subsided, La Guardia had second thoughts about the communist plot, alleged or otherwise, and convened a commission with E. Franklin Frazier as researcher to explore the underlying causes of the Harlem Riot of 1935. Chaired by Dr. Charles H. Roberts, a black dentist and city alderman, the commission held twenty-five hearings and interviewed 160 witnesses; ultimately, it concluded—as would the FBI report after the 1964 riot—that the "outburst was spontaneous and unpremeditated" with "no evidence of any program or leadership of the rioters." At first looters targeted white stores, but soon "property itself became the object of their fury."[28]

The report was highly critical of the NYPD in general and how it reacted on March 19 in particular. "The police practice aggressions and brutalities upon the Harlem citizens not only because they are Negroes but because they are poor and therefore defenseless," the commission stated. "But these attacks upon the security of the homes and the persons of the citizens are doing more than anything else to create a disrespect for authority and to bring about mass resistance to the injustices suffered by the community."[29]

The bulk of the 135-page report, however, focused on the social and economic ills of Harlem. Like the War on Poverty and Great Society programs of the 1960s, it touched on the pressing need for vastly improved public health, education, and housing. The report focused on widespread discrimination in employment and relief, public and private, at both the city and federal levels. And it offered a sweeping set of recommendations —so sweeping, in fact, that when finished a year later, La Guardia opted not to release the report, perhaps because it highlighted problems he could not solve and raised expectations he could not meet. Or perhaps the findings simply were, in the words of the *Amsterdam News*, which published the full document in July 1936, "too hot, too caustic, too critical, too unfavorable" to his administration.[30]

The report nevertheless inspired La Guardia to take a more direct interest in the community. "He was not prepared to place Harlem at the center of his agenda," wrote his biographer, "but he did place it far higher on his list of priorities." That summer, on his way to a concert, he heard the police broadcast news about a murder in the area and raced uptown to assume personal control and defuse the tense situation. And over the next four years he acted upon many, though by no means all, of the commission's recommendations. He appointed the city's first black magistrate, named African Americans to many other municipal posts, integrated the staffs of the city hospitals, built two new public schools, constructed the Harlem River Houses, and added a Women's Pavilion to Harlem Hospital. For La Guardia, who would serve as mayor from 1934 to 1945, it was a start, albeit overdue and incomplete.[31]

Two years after the Harlem Riot of 1935, Bayard Rustin moved to New York, where he first lived with his aunt and then found an apartment of his own on St. Nicholas Avenue. The exact reason for his departure from Pennsylvania remains murky. It is possible that he had little choice: Rustin by then had accepted that he was gay and had begun to act upon his sexual desires. The West Chester police may even have caught him having sex in a public park with a prominent young white man and made it clear to him that he had no future in the small town. But it is also likely that he was attracted by the political and cultural opportunities presented by Harlem— not to mention the personal anonymity and social freedom it offered.[32]

Once Rustin arrived in the fall of 1937, he quickly embraced New York, where he would spend the rest of his life. With his polished tenor voice, he became a member of the Carolinians, a singing group that performed regularly at the Café Society Downtown, a popular club in Greenwich Village. He also joined the Young Communist League (YCL), which was dedicated to the struggle for racial equality and the defense of the Scottsboro Boys, nine black Alabama teenagers falsely accused of rape. In 1941, after Nazi Germany invaded Soviet Russia and Moscow insisted that the struggle against racism take a back seat to the fight against fascism, Rustin left the YCL. But he was not bitter because his experience as a Communist had given him—a man who never earned a college degree—a crash course in planning and organizing. "It taught me a great deal," he readily admitted later, "and I presume that if I had to do it over again, I'd do the same thing."[33]

Even when Rustin was an active Communist, he continued to sing in church choirs and attend Quaker meetings. So it was not surprising that in 1941, with war on the horizon, he joined the Fellowship of Reconciliation (FOR), a Christian pacifist organization led by the socialist A. J. Muste. Like Rustin, Muste was a former Communist, and for a time he served as a sort of father figure to his gifted protégé. He also enabled Rustin to join the crusade of the man who would become his great mentor and patron: A. Philip Randolph, the head of the most important black union in the country, the Brotherhood of Sleeping Car Porters, and the inspiration behind the 1941 March on Washington protest and movement.

As the United States mobilized for war under President Roosevelt, who had won an unprecedented third term in 1940, an economic boom began and the Great Depression at last came to end. Hopes rose in New York, where the black population had grown by another 150,000 since 1930. But prices and rents in Harlem remained high, while discrimination and segregation in training programs and war plants remained common—90 percent refused to hire African Americans, who represented less than half a percent of the workforce.[34] In 1941, Roosevelt issued Executive Order 8802, which had the strong support of La Guardia and banned racial discrimination in defense industries. The action came in response to Randolph's threat of a mass demonstration in Washington, and it led to the creation of the Fair Employment Practices Commission, which had some effect. Eventually, African Americans received real benefits from war mobilization as jobs arrived and paychecks grew. But as with the New Deal, blacks again failed to receive their fair share of government programs and contracts.

Frustration and resentment mounted. In 1941, at the age of thirty-three, Adam Clayton Powell, Jr. was elected to the city council and became a

harsh critic of La Guardia, who had failed to implement many of the recommendations in the 1935 report. "The Mayor is one of the most pathetic
figures on the current American scene," Powell wrote in 1942. "Now that
his political future is finished, we are no longer potential votes for him. We
are therefore ignored."[35]

A year later, a race riot erupted in Detroit, where tensions between
southern whites and blacks who had migrated north in search of jobs had
reached a crisis level. On June 20, a hot Saturday evening, crowds clashed
in Belle Isle as rumors swept the city that blacks had raped and murdered
a white woman while whites had murdered a black woman and her child,
then dumped the bodies in the Detroit River. Over the next three days,
thirty-four people were killed, twenty-five of whom were black (seventeen
were shot by white officers). Hundreds were injured. Only the arrival of the
U.S. Army, ordered to Detroit by President Roosevelt, restored a fragile and
bitter peace. The nation watched in shock and horror.

In New York, the fear was that Harlem was next. On June 24, Powell
demanded that La Guardia meet with him and said at a city council meeting
that if a riot erupted in New York "the blood of innocent people . . . would
rest upon the hands" of the mayor and police commissioner.[36] La Guardia
refused, perhaps understandably, to meet with Powell, but conferred with
other black leaders. In July he made plans in case of violence to close bars,
divert traffic, place guards at stores that sold weapons, and protect passengers using public transit. The mayor also had the police commissioner
emphasize that officers should demonstrate restraint by using tear gas and
deadly force only as a last resort against physical harm.[37]

At the same time, La Guardia prodded the NYPD to promise to hire
more blacks—of the roughly 19,000 officers on the force, only 140 were
African American, with 130 stationed in Central Harlem or Bedford-
Stuyvesant. Another twenty cadets (the largest group to date) were in the
Police Academy. Among them was Robert Mangum, who in 1943 helped
found the Guardians, an association of black officers, because the Patrolmen's Benevolent Association (PBA) refused to accept them. At first the
Guardians had to meet secretly at the Harlem YMCA because of opposition
from supervisors. Not until 1949—with the support of Powell, who in 1944
had joined the U.S. House of Representatives—would the Guardians
receive a charter of recognition from the city.[38] It would take far longer for
them to gain respect from their fellow white officers.

La Guardia's efforts in the summer of 1943 were in vain, although they may have limited the bloodshed to come. On August 1, a hot Sunday evening, everyone in Harlem was outdoors, trying to beat the heat in the absence of air conditioning. At 7 P.M. Marjorie Polite registered at the Hotel Braddock on West 126th Street, which was under surveillance for prostitution. Unhappy with her room, she demanded a refund and then got into an argument with the elevator operator, who refused to return a dollar tip that she had allegedly given him. Patrolman James Collins, who was on duty inside the hotel, first tried to calm Polite and then ordered her to leave. When she refused and began to curse at him, he arrested her for disorderly conduct.[39]

In the hotel lobby was a Connecticut woman, Florine Roberts, who was meeting her son Robert Bandy, an Army private on leave from the 703rd Military Police Battalion in Jersey City. Together, they demanded that Collins release Polite. He refused. What happened next was a matter of dispute. According to Collins, he was attacked for no reason by Roberts and Bandy, who seized his nightstick and began to strike the officer in the head, forcing Collins to use his revolver when the soldier fled and refused to halt. According to Bandy, he objected and intervened only when Collins shoved Polite; the officer then threw his nightstick at Bandy, who caught it and was shot in the shoulder when he was slow to return it.[40]

Fortunately, the injuries of both men were not serious. Unfortunately, word quickly spread that a white officer had killed a black soldier attempting to protect his mother. The police tried to correct the false rumors, but by 8 P.M. a crowd estimated at three thousand was gathered outside the 28th Precinct, threatening to take revenge against the officer responsible for the alleged atrocity. At 9 P.M. La Guardia rushed to the station house, which was already surrounded by army infantry and military police, and conferred with the police and fire commissioners. With almost manic energy, La Guardia began to give orders and speak to the crowd, urging people to go home. He also took a tour of the riot area, accompanied by local black leaders. Meanwhile, efforts were made to recruit volunteers from the community and bring in reinforcements by keeping all patrolmen on duty when their shifts ended at midnight. Soon Central Harlem was flooded with five thousand police officers and contingency plans went into effect.[41]

But it was to no avail. At 10:30 P.M. the sound of breaking glass rang through the streets. Claude Brown, author of the memoir *Manchild in the*

Promised Land, was six at the time and thought Harlem was under attack from German or Japanese bombers. He asked his father, a sharecropper from South Carolina, where the sirens were. "This ain't no air raid—just a whole lotta niggers gone fool," he replied. But the noise kept Brown scared and awake in his bed for hours.[42]

Soon looters were rampaging the streets from 110th to 145th, Lenox to Eighth Avenue, filling the air with screams and laughter, although there was a deep undercurrent of anger. "Do not attempt to fuck with me," a young man told the *Amsterdam News*. Author Ralph Ellison again found himself in the middle of a riot when he exited the 137th Street subway station after dinner with friends. In the *New York Post*, he wrote that he sensed shame in some looters like "the woman with her arms loaded who passed me muttering 'Forgive me, Jesus. Have mercy, Lord.'" Still others seemed filled with self-disgust when "faced with an embarrassment of riches and took only useless objects."[43]

By Monday morning Harlem was calm even if 125th Street, the epicenter of the riot, was littered with shattered windows and scattered debris from ransacked businesses. "It would have been better to have left the plate glass as it had been and the goods lying in the stores," commented novelist James Baldwin, who was in New York to attend the funeral of his estranged father and celebrate his nineteenth birthday. "It would have been better, but it also would have been intolerable, for Harlem had needed something to smash. To smash something is the ghetto's chronic need. Most of the time it is the members of the ghetto who smash each other, and themselves. But as long as the ghetto walls are standing there will always come a moment when these outlets do not work." For his part, Ellison saw the riot as "the poorer element's way of blowing off steam."[44]

At 9:50 A.M. La Guardia, exhausted, went on the air for the third time. "Shame has come to our city and sorrow to the large number of our fellow citizens, decent, law-abiding citizens, who live in the Harlem section," he said. "The situation is under control. I want to make it clear that this was not a race riot, for the thoughtless hoodlums had no one to fight with and gave vent to their activity by breaking windows [and] looting many of these stores belonging to the people who live in Harlem." He also had praise for the police, who were "most efficient and exercised a great deal of restraint." And he informed the people of Harlem that he expected "full and complete cooperation" while pledging that he would maintain law and order in the city.[45]

To ensure he would keep his promise, La Guardia had fifteen hundred volunteers, most of whom were African Americans, and six thousand police (civilian and military) patrol the riot zone. In reserve and on standby at several armories were eight thousand New York state guardsmen, including a black regiment. They were not needed, for the rioters were also exhausted. Over the next week life slowly returned to normal as the mayor lifted the liquor and traffic bans and city workers began a cleanup campaign. But the toll was costly. At least six persons, all black, were dead. Almost seven hundred were injured and nearly six hundred were arrested (most of whom were young adult males from a broad range of backgrounds), with property damage as high as $5 million.[46]

In the aftermath, the *Amsterdam News* echoed La Guardia when it declared that "we take our stand on the side of law and order, firmly asserting that those persons who violate the law ought to be arrested and punished." Yet many officers routinely employed excessive force and expressed contemptuous attitudes. "Policemen can be efficient without being brutal!" it editorialized. Officers who were "efficient and understanding" would find the community supportive and sympathetic. But "Harlem will not be bullied, brow-beaten, or bull-dozed," warned the newspaper.[47]

Langston Hughes also offered an ode to the woman whose arrest had led to the riot. In "The Ballad of Margie Polite," he celebrated her refusal to accept her fate as a victim or go gently into the night. "If Margie Polite had of been white, she might not've cussed out the cop that night," wrote Hughes. "In the lobby of the Braddock Hotel, she might not've felt the urge to raise hell." But she was black and she had resisted arrest. In the process, she had become more than a footnote to history. "Margie warn't nobody important before," the poem continued. "But she ain't just *nobody* now no more."[48]

From a comparative perspective, the Harlem riots of 1935 and 1943 had similar roots and outcomes. In the words of Robert M. Fogelson, a noted urban historian, both were "spontaneous, unorganized, and precipitated by police actions." Both featured looting aimed at property rather than people (unlike in Detroit). And both were, according to Fogelson, "so completely confined to the ghetto that life was normal for whites and blacks elsewhere in the city." Even if the riots were a form of political protest, the prompt actions of black leaders and city officials effectively contained the violence and damage. "Nevertheless," wrote Fogelson, who praised the "virtuoso performance" of La Guardia, "these efforts (and the riots themselves) indicated the inability of the moderate black leaders to channel rank-and-file

discontent into legitimate channels and when necessary to restrain the rioters." Thus the clashes of 1935 and 1943 were, in a sense, the "direct precur-
sors" to the Harlem Riot of 1964.[49]

But for now what was more critical was how little had changed in the
aftermath of the upheaval of 1943. More than three hundred thousand
African Americans continued to face "obscene living conditions" as they
crowded into substandard housing intended for seventy-five thousand.
Harlem was still, asserted an article in *Collier's*, "very inflammable, dynami-
cally race conscious, emotionally on the hair trigger, doggedly resentful of
its Jim Crow estate."[50] It remained ready to explode—all it would take was
another spark.

Bayard Rustin was not in Harlem when it erupted in August 1943. At
the time, he was on the road, tirelessly moving from city to city organizing
and recruiting for Muste and Randolph. He was also working as a trainer
for the newly formed Congress of Racial Equality (CORE), which fellow
FOR field secretary James Farmer had launched in an effort to promote
racial justice through nonviolent resistance. Then in November Rustin
received his draft notice and was arrested when he refused to report for
civilian public service. He spent the next two years in federal prison, where
he protested against segregated dining facilities, studied the ideas of Gandhi, and endured hunger strikes. He also faced homosexual misconduct
charges, which delayed his release until 1946.[51]

The following year, Rustin and CORE executive secretary George
Houser organized the Journey of Reconciliation, the first Freedom Ride to
protest segregation in interstate travel. As a participant, Rustin was sen-
tenced to a chain gang in North Carolina. But the arrest that shattered his
life came in 1953, when he was taken into custody in Pasadena, California,
and charged with lewd vagrancy for performing oral sex on two white men
in the backseat of a car. It was not his first arrest for illegal sex, but it
brought his homosexuality to public notice. After pleading guilty to a single
charge of "sex perversion" (the official term for consensual sodomy at the
time), he was fired from his position as director of race relations with FOR
after twelve years of dedicated service.[52]

Feeling abandoned and adrift, Rustin struggled to make himself again
acceptable and respectable in the eyes of the friends and allies he had once
had. For the rest of his career, his sexual orientation would shadow him
even more than his communist background. In 1953, he joined the War

Resisters League (over the objections of Muste) and soon became executive director; four years later, Rustin was instrumental in persuading King to form the Southern Christian Leadership Conference. But in 1960 Congressman Powell (a board member and social conservative) forced Rustin to resign by threatening to expose his sexual orientation on the floor of Congress and feed false allegations to the press that he and King were lovers.[53]

While Rustin fought to restore his reputation, demographic change swept across many neighborhoods in New York in the 1950s, generating racial tension and conflict. Segregation, especially in housing and education, remained a serious problem. Economic factors—especially deindustrialization, automation, and discrimination—affected the workplace and job market, which in turn contributed to the depressed social conditions experienced by a large majority of African Americans in Central Harlem. And youth crime, often connected to the drug trade, was a growing concern of many residents.

The black migration to the North from the South, where the mechanization of cotton farming led to an exodus of millions of sharecroppers from rural areas, continued unabated after World War II. By 1950 more than one million African Americans lived in New York—a 30 percent increase since 1948. During the 1950s, almost half a million more blacks arrived, only to discover that the federal government and local banks preserved residential segregation by "redlining" neighborhoods and restricting loans. Meanwhile, more than a million whites departed for the suburbs of New Jersey, Long Island, and Westchester County, where blacks were usually not welcome. Even more whites might have left if not for the Lyons Law, which required city residency for municipal employees. But in 1960 the state legislature added a loophole for police officers, which enabled many of them to relocate and reinforced the sense in Harlem and Bed-Stuy that the NYPD was an outside force of occupation and oppression.[54]

The inflow of blacks and the outflow of whites changed the complexion of neighborhoods and boroughs. It also increased the pressure on housing as conditions worsened, especially in Harlem, where almost half of the buildings predated 1900. In an unpublished article on the first mental health institution in the area, the Lafargue Psychiatric Clinic, Ellison provided an almost hallucinogenic description of the plight of the community. "Harlem is a ruin," he wrote, "[and] many of its ordinary aspects (its crimes, its casual violence, its crumbling buildings with littered area-ways, ill-smelling halls and vermin-invaded rooms) are indistinguishable from the distorted images that appear in dreams, and which, like muggers haunting a lonely hall, quiver in the waking mind with hidden and threatening significance."[55]

Dr. Kenneth Clark offered a similar assessment in *Dark Ghetto*, his classic study of Harlem. "The most concrete fact of the ghetto is its physical ugliness—the dirt, the filth, the neglect," he wrote. "The parks are seedy with lack of care. The streets are crowded with the people and refuse. In all of Harlem there is no museum, no art gallery, no art school, no sustained 'little theater' group; despite the stereotype of the Negro as artist, there are only five libraries—but hundreds of bars, hundreds of churches, and scores of fortune tellers. Everywhere there are signs of fantasy, decay, abandonment, and defeat." Like Ellison, Clark saw a psychological dimension to the physical deterioration. "The only constant characteristic is a sense of inadequacy," Clark observed of Harlem. "People seem to have given up in the little things that are so often the symbol of the larger things."[56]

Here Clark's analysis was not entirely fair or correct. Plenty of residents had not given up—on the contrary, they often engaged in political activism and mobilized against racial discrimination and segregation where they lived, worked, and went to school. In the 1930s, blacks in Harlem had participated in "Don't Buy Where You Can't Work" demonstrations. In the 1940s, they had enthusiastically supported the successful campaigns of Powell for Congress and Benjamin Davis, a Harvard Law School graduate and staunch member of the Communist Party, for city council. They also picketed against Stuyvesant Town, a middle-class apartment complex that refused to rent to blacks despite the fact that the developer, Met Life, had received tax exemptions from the city. In the 1950s, a group of African American mothers who became known as the "Little Rock Nine of Harlem" pulled their children from three junior high schools as a protest against segregation.[57]

As overcrowding intensified, resentment over segregation deepened. In Harlem, where the number of residents had doubled since 1940, the number of apartments had not increased despite the construction of the Riverton Houses, a large middle-income housing development created by Met Life in response to the protests over Stuyvesant Town. White store owners, observed Jesse B. Semple (the Harlem character created by Langston Hughes), "take my money over the counter, then go on downtown to Stuyvesant Town where I can't live, or out to them pretty suburbs, and leave me in Harlem holding the bag." By 1952 blacks had finally won, after an unrelenting fight by a coalition of political and religious organizations, the right to live in the apartment complex—but only after it was fully occupied. Eight years later, when Lieutenant Gilligan was a resident, only a tiny handful of his neighbors were black.[58]

During the 1950s, the population of Harlem fell by 10 percent, mainly because poor blacks were moving to other ghettos like Bed-Stuy in Brooklyn. But a few middle-class black professionals were also starting to take advantage of the opportunity to relocate to the suburbs, among them Clark, who moved his family to Westchester in 1950 because it had better public schools than Harlem. "My children have only one life," Clark said. "I can't risk that." It was, nevertheless, a difficult decision for the distinguished psychologist who with his wife produced the famous "doll study," which documented the harmful effects of school segregation and influenced the landmark Supreme Court decision in *Brown v. Board of Education* in 1954. "More than forty years of my life had been lived in Harlem," Clark wrote. "I started school in the Harlem public schools. I first learned about people, about love, about cruelty, about sacrifice, about cowardice, about courage, about bombast in Harlem."[59]

The departure of middle-class professionals like Clark coincided with the loss of decent-paying jobs for working-class residents. During the 1950s, deindustrialization came to New York as factories began to relocate to the South. Automation also invaded the service sector, leading to fewer opportunities for those with poor English or dark skin, little experience or limited skills. The first Latino borough president and member of Congress, Herman Badillo, arrived in New York from Puerto Rico with his mother in 1941. In the early 1950s, he was able to attend City College and law school by working as a pin boy in a bowling alley and as an elevator operator in an apartment building—both jobs threatened or eliminated by technology.[60]

Coincidentally, when Harlem erupted in 1964, both Mayor Robert Wagner and Congressman Powell were in Europe to attend a conference in Geneva on the impact of automation on cities. Meanwhile, blacks remained largely excluded from the skilled trades because labor unions and apprenticeship programs refused to accept them. Together, deindustrialization and discrimination ravaged Harlem. In 1962, Clark received a large grant from the President's Committee on Juvenile Delinquency, which believed that black teens posed a significant threat to urban peace. The grant funded the Harlem Youth Opportunities Unlimited (HARYOU) project, which employed two hundred "associates" to conduct interviews and gather information about the community. Their research, which would become the statistical basis of *Dark Ghetto*, showed that most black families maintained a "marginal subsistence," with a median income of $3,995 compared to $6,100 for white families.[61]

Compounding the inequity was the fact that blacks often paid more in rent than whites even though almost half the housing in Central Harlem was substandard compared to 15 percent in the city as a whole. Residential segregation led to higher rates of population density and left residents with fewer options about where to live. "Cruel in the extreme," wrote Clark, "is the landlord who, like the store owner who charges Negroes more for shoddy merchandise, exploits the powerlessness of the poor."[62]

The perception of exploitation by white merchants—especially Jewish businessmen—was real and widespread. But whether it was accurate is more difficult to determine given that store owners of all races and religions had to operate in a "high-cost, high-crime, high-risk environment," with narrow profit margins and limited returns on investment. Beyond debate, however, was the reality that African Americans owned or managed only 4 percent of Harlem businesses. By comparison, southern cities like Atlanta often had substantially greater numbers of black-owned businesses because of commercial segregation.[63]

Other measures of social distress were more obvious and less open to dispute by 1964. For example, the mortality rate for blacks as a whole remained 60 percent higher than for whites—73 percent for infants. Even the streets were, literally, less safe—in Central Harlem, a child was 61 percent more likely to get killed by a car than in other neighborhoods. And for black adults the unemployment rate was twice as high as for the rest of the city. Among young men eighteen to twenty-four, it was five times as high for blacks as for whites.[64]

The problem was likely to worsen, predicted Clark, as the number of teens rose and the number of jobs available to them fell. "The restless brooding young men without jobs who cluster in the bars in the winter and on stoops and corners in the summer are the stuff out of which riots are made," he wrote. "The solution to riots is not better police protection (or even the claims of police brutality) or pleas from civil rights leaders for law and order. The solution lies in finding jobs for the unemployed and in raising the social and economic status of the entire community. Otherwise the 'long hot summers' will come every year."[65]

"Brooding young men" on street corners were not new to Harlem. But in the two decades after World War II, the disappearance of jobs and, to a lesser extent, the departure of individuals like Clark weakened the social fabric of Harlem and contributed to the rise in social disorder. According to the NYPD, arrests of teenagers rose 60 percent between 1952 and 1957, with African Americans disproportionately implicated, although the statistics are open to interpretation and challenge.[66] The figures nonetheless concerned the NAACP, which feared that conservatives might use them as proof of black criminality and evidence against racial integration. Executive secretary Roy Wilkins stated in 1959 that reducing youth crime was vital because "many of our enemies are using incidents of juvenile delinquency to buttress their fight against us and against desegregation of the schools."[67]

Drugs—especially heroin—were a major cause of youth crime. In the 1950s, heroin claimed the lives of author Claude Brown's brother and many of his friends. By the 1960s, "there were a lot more drugs than we ever saw in our life, a lot more burglaries, and a lot more assaults," recalled Detective Sonny Grosso, a native of Harlem who also served there. "And that's all tied to the addicts trying to get more money to pay for their drugs." Dope pushing and gang banging—although the term was not yet invented—were rampant. According to a Harlem supervisor with the Youth Board, many leaders and members were heroin users, which led to internal conflict and gang disintegration as well as more crime and turf wars.[68]

At least half of New York's thirty thousand addicts lived in Central Harlem, where narcotics arrests were more than ten times higher than in the rest of the city by 1964. "Property crimes skyrocketed to pay for habits, and then violent crimes followed, not only in the competition between dealers, but also in the disciplinary and debt-collecting functions of the gangs," wrote a police historian. "Heroin created thousands of rich killers and millions of derelicts, whores, and thieves. In short, it created crime as we know it."[69]

Dealing drugs was not, however, the only visible and profitable criminal activity in Harlem. Gambling was also widespread because "people were always looking for a way out," recalled Detective Barney Cohen, who also served in Bed-Stuy. "The numbers game remains a community pastime; streetwalking still flourishes on 125th Street; and marijuana is easy to get," Michael Harrington wrote in *The Other America*, his famous 1962 exposé of urban and rural poverty. "These things are not, of course, 'natural' to the Negro. They are by-products of a ghetto which has little money, much unemployment, and a life to be lived in the streets. Because of them, and because the white man is so ready to believe crime in the Negro, fear is basic to the ghetto."[70]

Disillusionment and disenchantment were also pervasive according to a black journalist who testified before the state legislature in June 1963. "The mood of the Negro, particularly in New York City, is very, very bitter," said Louis Lomax, who co-produced the documentary *The Hate That Hate Produced* about Elijah Muhammad and the Nation of Islam. "He is losing faith. The Negro on the streets of Harlem is tired of platitudes from white liberals." Adding to the impatience and frustration was a sense of invisibility and inadequacy, because while Harlem simmered and suffered in the shadows, the national media spotlight shone brightly on the civil rights struggle in the South.[71]

In the North, African Americans now felt mounting pressure to become more active and visible in the freedom struggle. "Southern Negroes have shown bravery and should shame the Northern Negro," said the entertainer Sammy Davis, Jr. "They seem to have more spunk and backbone," said a machinist in Harlem. The protests in Alabama were the turning point—the televised images had a searing impact, especially on urban teenagers. "For the black people of this nation," wrote Rustin after a visit, "Birmingham became the moment of truth." The civil rights movement, he believed, had reached a new stage. "The Negro masses are no longer prepared to wait for anybody," he added. "They are going to move. Nothing can stop them."[72]

With the civil rights bill facing an uncertain future in Congress, Rustin in July brought his idea for a march on Washington to the "Big Six" movement leaders—King, Randolph, Wilkins, Farmer, Whitney Young of the Urban League, and John Lewis of the Student Nonviolent Coordinating Committee (SNCC). At a meeting in New York at the Roosevelt Hotel, Rustin called for a mass, nonviolent demonstration, which would require extensive planning and organization. But Wilkins immediately and strongly objected to him serving as director. "He's got too many scars," the NAACP leader said, citing Rustin's flirtation with communism in the late 1930s, his prison term during World War II, and his arrest in Pasadena in 1953. "This march is of such importance that we must not put a person of his liabilities as the head."[73]

Farmer, however, defended him, and after Randolph cleverly volunteered to serve as director (with Rustin as his assistant), Wilkins reluctantly

FIGURE 2. Bayard Rustin briefs reporters at the March on Washington in August 1963. Photo by Warren K. Leffler. Library of Congress, Prints and Photographs Division, U.S. News & World Report Magazine Collection (LC-U9-10332 frame 11).

agreed on the condition that Rustin remain in the background and avoid the limelight, which proved impossible. With less than two months to prepare, Rustin instantly set to work, hiring a staff, inventing policies, raising funds, and maintaining unity among the many organizations sponsoring the demonstration. It was the most intense period of his lengthy career, but he achieved a remarkable feat, earning forever after the title of "Mr. March" from his mentor, Randolph.

An estimated quarter million people of all races and religions gathered in the nation's capital in August to demand jobs, freedom, and passage of the civil rights bill. Behind the scenes, it was a tense time as debates erupted between the White House and civil rights leaders over the length of the demonstration, the tone of the speeches, the role of whites, even the dress of the participants. But in the end, after King had made his iconic "I Have a Dream" speech, most Americans saw the March on Washington as a great triumph of the human spirit and a historic occasion when racial reconciliation at last seemed like a realistic possibility. The demonstration, Rustin believed, had also prevented violent unrest in northern cities by channeling hostile energy.[74]

A month later, the optimism generated by the March on Washington was shattered by the explosion of a bomb at the 16th Street Baptist Church in Birmingham, where four little black girls waiting for the start of Sunday school were tragically murdered. For the slender and soft-spoken Clark, a liberal integrationist, it was a fateful moment. "The present battle for racial justice in America is in its showdown stage," he wrote in *Ebony*. "Negroes and committed whites will either remove the last barriers to racial equality in America within the next year or two, or will witness a frightening and revolting form of racial oppression and moral stagnation." No middle ground existed.[75]

But on his public television program *The Negro and the Promise of American Life*, Clark managed to strike a cautiously positive note after a series of conversations with Baldwin, King, and Malcolm X, with whom he was friendly even though they disagreed on most issues. "We have come to the point where there are only two ways that America can avoid continued racial explosions: one would be total oppression; the other total equality," Clark concluded. "There is no compromise. I believe—I hope—that we are on the threshold of a truly democratic America." In the coming year, the violence and unrest in New York would sorely test, if not dash, his faith in the future.[76]

CHAPTER 3

THE GATHERING STORM

Down the street they were rumbling
All the tempers were ragin'
Oh, where, oh, where are the white silver tongues
Who forgot to listen to the warnings?
—Phil Ochs, "In the Heat of the Summer"

FRIDAY, JULY 17

The morning after James Powell's death at the hands of Thomas Gilligan, fifty officers arrived at Wagner Junior High School, site of the confrontation. The patrolmen were armed with nightsticks, not standard equipment for a daytime assignment. Consultations immediately began between the NYPD, school principal Max Francke, and Madison S. Jones, executive director of the City Commission on Civil Rights, who had offered his services to Francke in the wake of the shooting and protests on Thursday. After the police received assurances that only students would participate in the demonstration planned by CORE for later that morning, the nightsticks were returned to the 19th Precinct on East 67th Street. The officers, however, remained in place, hoping for the best but prepared for the worst.[1]

By 8 A.M. around seventy-five demonstrators had arrived, many with their school textbooks. Led by Chris Sprowal, the tall and slender chairman of Downtown CORE, they chanted "Police Brutality Must Go" and "Freedom Now." They waved placards that proclaimed "Save Us from Our Protectors" and "Stop Killer Cops." And they sang civil rights freedom songs

FIGURE 3. Police observe as demonstrators on East 67th Street protest the killing of James Powell. Photo by Marion S. Trikosko. Library of Congress, Prints and Photographs Division, U.S. News & World Report Magazine Collection (LC-U9-12259 frame 1).

such as "We Shall Overcome." The protests were peaceful and organized in contrast to Thursday's demonstrations. "We all know there are agitators around who profess violence," said Sprowal. "We saw who they were and we weeded them out." The pickets also were integrated. Most of the demonstrators were black, but several were white or Puerto Rican—one sign read "Demandamos El Fin De Brutalidad Policia."[2]

At noon the ranks of the demonstrators swelled with the addition of a hundred or so summer school students who had finished their morning classes. "People around here just want you to get into trouble," warned Sprowal through a bullhorn as they prepared to march to the 19th Precinct. "Act like the young ladies and gentlemen that you are. Don't act like they expect you to act. Hold your heads up." Because the station house was on the same block as a firehouse, the Russian Mission to the United Nations, and the Kennedy Child Study Center, only a token group of twenty-five demonstrators was permitted to picket in front. The remainder paraded a block away next to the Lexington School for the Deaf, whose students came outside to observe and discuss the protest in sign language. An hour later, the demonstration ended and Sprowal urged the students to return daily until the date of the funeral was set.[3]

As the students began to disperse, three members of the Organization of Afro-American Unity arrived. Followers of Malcolm X, who had formed the group after he split with Elijah Muhammad and the Nation of Islam, they counseled the teens not "to let people push you around." But their leader was not in New York at the time—he was in Cairo attending a meeting of the Organization of African Unity. In his capacity as an observer, Malcolm X issued a statement that linked the struggles in America and Africa. "Our problem is your problem," he informed the delegates. "It is not a Negro problem, nor an American problem. This is a world problem, a problem for humanity. It is not a problem of civil rights, it is a problem of human rights."[4]

Segregation and discrimination in the United States, Malcolm X added, were worse than apartheid in South Africa because white Americans hypocritically preached integration and equality. "Out of frustration and hopelessness our young people have reached the point of no return," he wrote. "We no longer endorse patience and turning the other cheek. We assert the right of self-defense by whatever means necessary, and reserve the right of maximum retaliation against our racist oppressors, no matter what the odds against us are."[5]

The implied threat triggered an immediate reaction from Police Commissioner Michael J. Murphy. "Nobody will be allowed to turn New York City into a battleground," he declared. Local activists like Malcolm X, he contended, had a "lust for power" and "other sinister motives."[6] Many blacks in Central Harlem would nevertheless heed the message in the coming days, although without the leadership and direction Malcolm X might have provided. His absence contributed to a vacuum that others would try, without success, to fill.

The Progressive Labor Party (PLP) also had representatives at the protest on East 67th Street that day. Formed by dissident members of the Communist Party in 1961, the group believed that both the Soviet Union and American leaders had betrayed the revolution by advocating reformist positions such as "peaceful coexistence" with the noncommunist world. The PLP was dedicated to an immediate grassroots class struggle based on the Chinese Communist model of resistance. The most prominent black member was William Epton, chairman of the Harlem branch, who was later convicted of conspiring to riot and criminal anarchy in the aftermath of the violence that would erupt on Saturday night. But on Friday morning he too was not present. Instead, a teenager from Monroe, North Carolina, was representing the PLP and distributing leaflets. In his hometown, the youth said, "If the cops shoot a Negro, we arm ourselves and get that cop worse than he got us." Such talk alarmed the CORE officials, who urged the students to remain peaceful and orderly.[7]

But as the demonstrators started to head home, a white passerby saw the "Stop Killer Cops" placard and yelled, "He [Powell] deserved killing." The students made a rush for the man, but the police got to him first, hustled him behind their barricade, and told him to keep his mouth shut and leave. When asked by reporters to give his name the man refused to answer, but offered two rhetorical questions: "What the hell business do they have carrying knives? What was the cop supposed to do, stand there and get stuck?" Other white New Yorkers were likely having a similar reaction to the Thursday shooting because of a rash of crimes in the streets and on the subways.[8]

On Friday afternoon, two white men were assaulted and robbed in the Bronx by roving bands of black teens who were not part of the CORE demonstration. On a southbound train, an elderly actor named Julian Zalewski was attacked by a gang of youths, who threw him to the floor and took his wallet and watch. "I got my Polish up and began to fight," he said. "I yelled in my best theatrical voice, so loudly that the whole gang took off." But not before he was punched and kicked. Elsewhere, a white pharmacist from Yonkers was accosted on a downtown express by two dozen black teenagers, six of whom punched and kicked him while their friends watched. None of the fifteen other adult passengers in the car came to his assistance, which the victim found disappointing though understandable. He would, he admitted, have done the same. Neither incident was unusual—according to the Transit Authority, subway crime had increased 30 percent in the past year.[9]

In early 1964, the subways were not the only unsafe place in New York, where police neglect, corruption, and brutality as well as disrespect had caused tensions between black residents and white officers for decades. According to the NYPD, every category of violent crime experienced a double-digit surge between June 1963 and June 1964. Rapes and robberies soared by 28 and 26 percent, respectively. Assaults rose by 18 percent and murders—usually a statistic beyond dispute because of the presence of a body—increased by 17 percent. Not since 1953 had the crime rate swelled so dramatically across the board. It was not surprising, then, that fear and anxiety over violence in the streets had reached a crescendo by mid-July, especially since New York historically experienced more homicides in the summer, when temperatures climbed and tempers flared, than in any other season.[10]

Many liberals, black and white, refused to accept the statistics at face value. Some contended that they were the product of new data systems or the public's growing willingness to report certain crimes, such as rape or burglary (for insurance purposes). Others argued that the police had a vested interest in either minimizing crime (to demonstrate effectiveness) or exaggerating it (to justify more funding). Even the FBI at times expressed doubts about the NYPD's numbers. Selective enforcement (lax or strict) of certain laws could also affect the statistics, as could the biased actions of prosecutors, judges, and juries. Black leaders such as Congressman Powell regularly asserted that the disproportionately high arrest rate of African Americans was proof of police racism.

Beyond dispute were the racial tensions created by police neglect of minority neighborhoods, which was a long-standing issue. In the aftermath of the Harlem Riot of 1943, the *Amsterdam News* had insisted that the NYPD had a duty and an obligation to provide black residents with the same degree of protection as white citizens elsewhere in the city. "While unalterably opposed to police brutality, we are equally strong and all-out for police efficiency," it editorialized. "[W]e cannot agree that the interest of Harlem or New York—its welfare, its health, its morals, its safety—is being served by allowing a criminal element, however small, to overrun any special community."[11]

Twenty years later, however, many white officers remained leery of inciting trouble in black communities. David Durk was an unusual recruit, an Amherst graduate from the Upper West Side whose father had a medical practice on Park Avenue. After a year at Columbia Law School, he decided to join the NYPD in fall 1963 and was assigned to the 28th Precinct in Central Harlem. At roll call a veteran sergeant offered clear instructions to the rookie patrolman: "Don't lose sight of your partner, don't go down any block alone, don't go into any buildings, and no arrests unless you're personally assaulted." In other words, be careful, avoid trouble, and leave the residents to fend for themselves.[12]

Not surprisingly, a survey conducted on the eve of the riot in 1964 revealed that although 51 percent of African Americans in New York credited the police with doing a "pretty good job," 39 percent disagreed and an equal number named "crime and criminals" as the "biggest problem" facing the city. The fear cut across gender, class, and generational lines in the black community. "There's just too many junkies and drunks around here," said a teenage woman who lived in a rundown apartment on West 146th Street and had a scar on her arm from a slashing by a wino. "It's hard for decent people to live right. I feel like I'm smothering."[13]

Ten blocks north, in a cool and spacious apartment, a middle-aged city official offered his view from a comfortable sofa. "You don't know how much it tears me up to say this," he admitted, "but the most hellish problem Negroes up here have to worry about, next to bad schools and bad housing, is personal safety from muggers and thugs. I don't let my wife go out, even to the grocery store, at night unless she is escorted or takes a cab." In Queens, a subway motorman argued that blacks could not depend on the police. "The only solution to all this mugging and stealing is to organize block associations or civilian patrols," he said, bemoaning police indifference. "It's time we did something to protect our own."[14]

Police corruption was another source of hostility between many residents of Harlem and the officers who patrolled it. A housewife interviewed in 1964 was blunt: "The real criminal in Harlem is the cops. They permit dope, numbers, whores, gangsters to operate here, and all the time they get money under the table—and I ain't talkin' about $2 neither." A college-educated Brooklyn resident was equally direct: "A ghetto police force is a force in league with all of the underworld, a bribed force. If this is not so, why is it that anyone can buy narcotics, alcohol, women or homosexuals freely on Harlem's streets—even on Sunday?"[15] Other socially conservative African Americans held similar views.

Congressman Powell spoke for these residents when he gave a series of speeches on police corruption in 1960 on the floor of the U.S. House, where he had immunity from charges of libel or slander. In his remarks, he offered what a historian has described as a "phone directory of the Harlem underworld" and a detailed description of the regular police protection pad. With names and dates, facts and figures, the congressman outlined how the bribes were distributed in the NYPD chain of command. Noting that all 212 captains and 59 of 60 inspectors were white, Powell charged that organized crime and police graft were "pauperizing Harlem" by siphoning funds from poor blacks to white mobsters and officers.[16]

Few paid attention, with the important exception of the *New York Post*, which assigned a team of investigative reporters led by Ted Poston, who had moved from Kentucky to Harlem in the 1920s and become the first black journalist at a major white newspaper. He confirmed the substance of Powell's allegations. But then the congressman appeared on local television, where he had no immunity, and named a black woman, Esther James, as a courier of money from gamblers to the police. She decided to sue him for libel. When Powell arrogantly chose not to attend his own trial, the jury reacted negatively and found him guilty. In 1963, the court imposed $211,500 in damages. He in turn refused to pay, which led to a self-imposed exile from Harlem for five years. Powell could visit only on Sundays because, by state law, no one could serve civil contempt warrants on that day. As a result, he was unable to play a major role in restoring peace in 1964, even after he returned to Washington from his latest European excursion.[17]

The full extent of police corruption became public knowledge in 1970, when the Knapp Commission held hearings and heard testimony from dozens of witnesses, many of whom vividly described decades of bribes and payoffs in Harlem. Inspector Paul Delise, a decorated twenty-seven-year veteran with six kids and retirement on the horizon, told how, as a mounted cop in Harlem in the 1950s, he had arrested a drug dealer outside a pool room on 116th Street. The dealer offered him a wad of cash. When a squad car arrived, he reported the bribe. The officers suggested he take it. "You son of a bitch. How can you suggest something like that?" replied Delise heatedly. "We're all doing it," the officer responded. "We kick these guys in the ass, we take their works from them, we put 'em on a subway train, and whatever they have in their pockets is what we take."[18]

Other policemen offered similar accounts. Jim O'Neil recalled how in 1964 he and his partner always gave the duty officer a half share of the "hat"—a tradition where "illegal gamblers, wanting to show their gratitude, would walk up to a detective and stuff a twenty in his shirt pocket and say, 'Why don't you take this and buy yourself a hat?'" It was, according to O'Neil, "more of a thank you than a bribe."[19] But according to Robert Leuci, who joined the force in 1961 and also appeared before the Knapp Commission, a captain told him that Harlem alone contained forty numbers operations that paid $100 a day, 365 days a year, to remain open. "The money was major, the backbone and heart of corruption in New York City," testified Leuci, who became a pariah in the department and was the subject of the film *Prince of the City* starring Treat Williams and directed by Sidney Lumet. "The pad went all the way up, right through police headquarters into the mayor's office."[20]

The verdict of the Knapp Commission was blunt: "We find corruption to be widespread." The "nut" (the monthly share per officer) ranged from $400 in Midtown to $1,500 in Harlem, which was known as the "Gold Coast" because it offered so many opportunities for bribes and payoffs. The "meat-eaters" were those who actively sought them; the "grass-eaters" were those who passively accepted what came to them. "You can't work numbers in Harlem unless you pay," testified a runner. "You go to jail on a frame if you don't pay." Police corruption weakened "public faith in the law and police," concluded the commission. "Youngsters raised in New York ghettos, where gambling abounds, regard the law as a joke when all their lives they have seen police officers coming and going from gambling establishments and taking payments from gamblers."[21]

No joke to many blacks was the ever-present possibility of police brutality, a constant source of conflict in Harlem, where black citizens often viewed white officers with hatred and suspicion. James Baldwin perhaps put it best. "It was absolutely clear that the police would whip you and take you in as long as they could get away with it," he wrote in *The Fire Next Time*. "They had the judges, the juries, the shotguns, the law—in a word, power. But it was a criminal power, to be feared but not respected, and to be outwitted in any way whatever."[22] Sometimes the police would not even bother with an arrest. According to the NAACP, which took an active role in investigating police brutality, forty-six unarmed blacks were shot and killed by officers in New York between 1947 and 1952—only two unarmed whites met similar fates.[23]

Two incidents in particular generated outrage. The first came in 1950, when two white officers shot and killed a black Korean War veteran discharged from the Army twelve hours earlier. John Derrick was in uniform and missing $3,000 in discharge pay when his body was identified on 119th Street at Eighth Avenue. "John never even had a gun," a witness told a crowd of three thousand at a rally the next day. "He was murdered." The *Amsterdam News* pledged that "while there is an ounce of ink in our presses, we will pursue this case until justice is done." But Republican Mayor Vincent Impellitteri refused to express remorse, offer condolences, or take action until Congressman Powell demanded that the commissioner transfer the officers out of Harlem within twenty-four hours. "We don't call them that," said Powell angrily, "but we do have lynchings right here in the North. If a lynch mob can be investigated in Georgia, the murder of a Negro by two police officers in New York should be investigated." It was, but both local and federal grand juries failed to indict.[24]

The second incident came in 1951, when white officers beat William Delany unconscious outside his home. A polio victim with severe disabilities, Delany was the nephew of Justice Hubert Delany, a political powerbroker who had served officially as the tax commissioner in the La Guardia administration and unofficially as the mayor's liaison to the black community. The justice was enraged by the attack on his relative. The "police in Harlem consider that they have the God-given right . . . to keep the peace with the nightstick and blackjack whenever a Negro attempts to question their right to restrict the individual's freedom of movement," he said. "Police brutality has been the mode in Harlem for years. The nurses and staff at Harlem Hospital see the bloody results daily. No policeman in Harlem has been convicted for police brutality or murder in over thirty years of many unnecessary killings, and hundreds of cases of brutality."[25] And none were in the Delany case.

Police brutality was a major cause of racial tension in Central Harlem. But it is difficult to determine how widespread or prevalent it was. On the eve of the riot in 1964, the *New York Times* had conducted a survey of blacks from all walks of life and all over the city. More agreed that there was no police brutality (20 percent) than "a lot" (12 percent). More than half of those surveyed believed that it was not common or routine; 85 percent had never witnessed a single act of police brutality, compared to only 9 percent who said they had. For most African Americans the main problems were jobs and housing, followed by crime and education.[26]

At times some black police may have used excessive force on the job. Jim O'Neil joined the NYPD in June 1963. One night, his first alone on post, he was stationed at the corner of 129th Street and Lenox Avenue when he heard a commotion from a nearby bar. Before he could take action, three large black officers in uniform—"at least a thousand pounds of cop on the hoof"—had exited a 1959 Chevy and entered the establishment. O'Neil watched as one of the policemen moved behind the man who was screaming at the bartender, "balled his hand into an enormous fist, and brought it down on top of the guy's head in a pile driver-like motion." With the man on the floor unconscious, the officer walked out and said to O'Neil, "If you want him, kid, take him, he's your collar." But O'Neil was afraid to take credit for what seemed like police brutality. He told his sergeant, who laughed at him. "You were just introduced to the King Cole

Trio," he said. "There isn't a person in Harlem who doesn't know them. They're famous up here and probably do more to keep the peace than all the other cops in the precinct combined."[27]

For Baldwin, however, white officers were primarily responsible for police brutality. "[T]he only way to police a ghetto is to be oppressive," he wrote of them. "Their very presence is an insult, and it would be, even if they spent their entire day feeding gumdrops to children. They represent the force of the white world, and that world's criminal profit and ease, to keep the black man corralled up here, in his place." In Harlem, the white policeman was simply hated. "There is no way for him not to know it: there are few things under heaven more unnerving than the silent, accumulating contempt and hatred of a people," continued Baldwin. "He moves through Harlem, therefore, like an occupying soldier in a bitterly hostile country; which is precisely what, and where he is, and is the reason he walks in twos and threes."[28]

But Police Commissioner Stephen Kennedy refused to station more black officers in Harlem, ironically because of liberal pressure. "It seems to me this would be turning back the clock and you would be segregated in the department," he said in a decision applauded by major civil rights organizations, now opposed to what they saw as the ghettoization of black patrolmen. Kennedy added that "an integrationist believes that a policeman is a policeman, regardless of color." Whether he truly believed in the wisdom of dispersing the department's relatively few black officers—African Americans were 16 percent of the city's population but only 5 percent of the police force in 1964—is impossible to know. But not until after the unrest in Harlem was a black captain—Lloyd Sealy—placed in command of the 28th Precinct.[29]

Sensing trouble, Commissioner Kennedy created a special unit to handle urban unrest in 1959. The Tactical Patrol Force (TPF) was an elite squad of physically imposing young men (all under thirty years old and most over six feet tall) with special training in the martial arts and unit tactics. It attracted officers with a taste for adventure and the rough side of urban policing. For O'Neil, the son of a city fireman, the path to the TPF was circuitous. After leaving high school and serving in the Navy, he worked in retail management for five years before a friend asked him to take the Police Department's entrance exam with him. They made a bet to see who would get the higher score.[30]

O'Neil won the bet—and his reward was a spot in the academy, where a veteran sergeant informed the cadets that they had to become proficient in the use of their weapons. "Just remember once you pull the trigger only the hand of God can take that bullet back," he warned. Then he offered what O'Neil described as "unofficial department policy": "Never shoot to wound, always shoot to kill." Before graduation in 1963, O'Neil applied for an assignment to the TPF. At his interview, he met the commanding officer, Inspector Michael J. Codd, who was tall and fit "with a full head of neatly combed gray hair and blue eyes that cut the air like sharpened steel." Codd was courteous but curt, and O'Neil assumed that he had not made the cut. But then he got the word and was ecstatic. "I was going to be part of an elite, ass-kicking, crime-fighting, gut-busting squad," he recalled in his memoir *A Cop's Tale*, "and I couldn't wait to get started."[31]

Robert Leuci joined the TPF in 1962 after calling every day for weeks in search of an opening, despite the fact that he was only five feet nine inches tall. What excited him was the work and that most of the men in the unit were "ex-marines and paratroopers, all with an appetite for the things that active street cops enjoyed, the jobs that most other cops avoided as a matter of course." He was from a poor family in Bensonhurst, an Italian section of Brooklyn, and his brother had died of a drug overdose, which was probably why narcotics graft continued to trouble Leuci long after many other police officers ceased to see it as "dirty money." His father was a union organizer who read four newspapers a day and was a staunch liberal (it was only during the Red Scare of the 1950s that he had stopped reading the *Daily Worker* and dropped his membership in the Socialist Party). At first he opposed his son's choice of career, but during the social change and racial turmoil of the 1960s he came to support it. "Just be a good cop, don't be a schmuck, treat working people fairly," he counseled.[32]

Leuci tried his best to follow the advice, but it was difficult. On his first night with the TPF, he recalled assembling on a street corner and receiving the hostility of the neighborhood. "We thought we were there to help," he wrote in his memoir *All the Centurions*, "but they saw it as an invasion of their neighborhood. Back then I didn't understand the rage I saw in their faces, the contempt." Aggressive policing was the only kind practiced in the TPF, and in the ghetto that created anger and antagonism. "They didn't like us, simple as that," he remembered. "They felt we were intruding in their lives. And we were. TPF didn't only patrol the streets—we went into the alleyways, the basements, onto the rooftops, through the tenement hallways."[33] But for Leuci the job provided an adrenaline rush like no other, even if the price was alienation from the community.

By 1964 the corrosive combination of police neglect, corruption, and brutality had led many blacks in Central Harlem to question and challenge, directly or indirectly, the authority and legitimacy of the NYPD. But of perhaps equal or even greater importance, although less publicized, were the daily discourtesies inflicted upon many residents by white officers. It was the "small indignities"—the constant rudeness and casual racism—that most offended Percy Sutton, a prominent lawyer and future borough president. He wondered why the Police Academy could not devote more time to training cadets in basic civility. Police harassment of black residents was, admitted then-Lieutenant Anthony Bouza, who visited 125th Street regularly, "a form of Chinese water torture" that led to a flood of resentment and anger.[34]

At the same time, the growing violence and disorder in New York posed a classic case of cognitive dissonance for many whites. Intellectually, they knew that most blacks were not muggers; emotionally, they could not ignore the sense that most muggers seemed black. Adding to the racial tension and providing human faces to the grim statistics were a dramatic series of high-profile events and a disturbing number of sensational black-on-white crimes in the first six months of the year.

Even before the Harlem Riot, Bayard Rustin was a well-known figure in New York. In mid-January, on the heels of the March on Washington, he received an urgent call from Milton Galamison, a Brooklyn minister. He wanted to know whether Rustin was willing to dedicate his organizing talents to a citywide boycott designed to protest the rampant segregation and glaring inequities in the school system. More than 40 percent of the students were minorities; fewer than 3 percent of the teachers were black. A decade after the *Brown* decision, spending on white students was seven times higher than on nonwhite students. Despite reservations about the mercurial Galamison and the shaky coalition of parents and activists behind the boycott, Rustin agreed. But he had only two weeks to work his magic. No matter—with extraordinary energy and unrelenting attention to detail he largely succeeded.[35]

At Siloam Presbyterian Church in Brooklyn, Rustin established a "war room" staffed around the clock with volunteers. At age fifty-three, he still had the energy of a much younger man, routinely putting in eighteen-hour days and at times sleeping at the church in pajamas, a bathrobe, and slippers rather than returning to his Manhattan apartment on 28th Street and

Eighth Avenue. "Do not think," he told others in reference to the white in his hair, "that just because there is snow on the roof there is no fire in the furnace." To keep the fire stoked, he subsisted on cold coffee and cheese sandwiches while making endless lists and taking copious notes on yellow legal pads. The holes in his shoes were a testament to his dedication and a reflection of his pay—around $71 a week for a labor of love and principle.[36]

On a cold and blustery Monday in early February arguably the largest civil rights demonstration in history took place. More than 450,000 mostly African American students (45 percent of total enrollment) boycotted classes in an effort to promote school integration. An estimated hundred thousand students attended almost five hundred freedom schools staffed by supporters of the protest. The president of the Board of Education was dismissive, but Rustin was publicly elated by the turnout (more than three times the normal absentee figure) and predicted that "we are on the threshold of a new political movement." In a prescient moment, he also cautioned that the "winds of change are about to sweep over our city" and that those "who stand aloof from the frustrations and deprivations of the ghetto" could expect more unrest in the near future.[37]

The next day an exhausted Rustin canceled a speaking engagement at Syracuse University and agreed to meet with peace activists from Eastern Europe at the Soviet consulate. When he arrived he was greeted by photographers and reporters from the *Journal-American* and the *Daily News*, both conservative tabloids. "Boycott Chief Soviets' Guest" blared the headline on Wednesday in the *Daily News*, which blasted Rustin for "consorting with the Soviets." The presence of the press was not coincidental. The FBI, which back in November had tapped Rustin's phone and planted a bug in his apartment (with Attorney General Robert Kennedy's approval), had alerted the newspapers to discredit Rustin and the movement.[38]

In public, Rustin stood his ground, calling the controversy a "red smear." But the damage was done and he knew it. In private, he told a friend that visiting the Soviet consulate was "a mistake." The incident again made him persona non grata, at least officially, to moderate black leaders like Roy Wilkins and King, who now distanced themselves from him. After his long and arduous return from exile and isolation, Rustin was once more back on the outside.[39]

As the publicity surrounding Rustin subsided in March, white fears of racial violence resurfaced with news of the brutal murder and rape of Catherine "Kitty" Genovese, a twenty-eight-year-old Italian American bar manager. She lived in the Kew Gardens section of Queens in an apartment that she shared with her lesbian partner Mary Ann Zielonko. On the ground floor was the Interlude Coffee House, where folksinger Phil Ochs, who later wrote a song about the murder called "Outside of a Small Circle of Friends," performed from time to time between bigger gigs. As Genovese was returning home from work in the early morning, she was attacked by Winston Moseley, a twenty-nine-year-old African American who later confessed to killing two other women and committing at least thirty burglaries. Genovese saw Moseley approach as she walked from her car to the building. She tried to run, but he caught her and knifed her in the back twice. "Oh my God, he stabbed me!" she screamed. "Help me!"[40]

A few of her neighbors heard her, but it was a cold night and, with the windows closed, they were not sure what she had said. When one man shouted, "Leave that girl alone!" Moseley fled and Genovese staggered toward the building, seriously injured. She was alive, but not visible to the residents and unable to enter because of a locked doorway. Ten minutes later, Moseley returned and found Genovese, who was still conscious. Despite her efforts at self-defense, he stabbed her several more times, stole $49, and raped her while she lay dying. Media accounts subsequently claimed, dramatically but inaccurately, that thirty-eight of her neighbors had heard her cries for help and failed to respond, which spurred psychological research into the "bystander effect" and led to an overhaul of the NYPD's telephone reporting system.[41]

Ten days after the murder of Genovese, the police commissioner met Abe Rosenthal, metro editor of the New York Times, for lunch at Emil's, a popular restaurant close to City Hall. Murphy, a large man with grim blue eyes, took his usual position (back to the wall) and ordered his usual meal (shrimp curry with rice). Three years into his tenure, he still resembled, in Rosenthal's description, "a tough Irish cop because he is a tough Irish cop." But unlike many of his fellow officers, Murphy was not born into the job. A native of Queens, he spent six years after high school with the Equitable Life Insurance Company. The work was monotonous, however, so he responded to an ad to become a state trooper. From the start he loved it. "One day I was solving a homicide," he said, "and the next day I was on a motorcycle chasing speeders."[42]

But after Murphy was married he joined the NYPD in 1940 so that he would not have to worry about a transfer out of the city. After five years he made sergeant—the fastest rise in the history of the department. At age thirty-two he was the youngest sergeant on the force; within nine years he was promoted to deputy inspector and put in charge of the Police Academy, where he instituted the equivalent of a college curriculum. A dedicated student, Murphy earned three degrees while working full-time. "He had a great legal mind," said the dean of Brooklyn Law School, where Murphy graduated summa cum laude and first in his class in 1945. "You rarely get a student with the combination of alertness, pleasant personality, curiosity, and the power of analysis that this man had."[43]

After the Academy Award–winning film *On the Waterfront* depicted brutal racketeering among dock workers, Murphy took a leave from the NYPD in 1955 to become executive director of the New York–New Jersey Waterfront Commission. Four years later, he returned to the department as chief inspector. In 1961, he became police commissioner, succeeding Stephen Kennedy. By then he was above all an administrator, but he remained an officer at heart. "Police work is the most fascinating in the world," he said. "I don't know of any other occupation that can approach it for variety and challenge."[44]

On the day Murphy dined with Rosenthal at Emil's, the challenge that most worried the commissioner was not the Genovese killing. "In the spring of 1964," the *Times* editor wrote in *Thirty-Eight Witnesses*, his account of the case, "what was usually on the mind of the Police Commissioner of New York was the haunting fear that someday blood would flow in the streets because of the tensions of the civil rights movement." Murphy was supportive of activists—to a degree. "If New York had a whole system of laws I considered unjust, I'd probably be out there breaking them," he said. "But we don't have those kind of laws here." Nevertheless, he defended the actions of protesters—within limits. "I think they have a right to demonstrate," the commissioner said, "and I'm prepared to protect and assist them so they can have their say with a minimum of interference to other men and women in the community."[45]

Later in March, art imitated life—with a surprising and deadly twist—when a one-act play by LeRoi Jones (who had not yet changed his name to Amiri Baraka) premiered at the Cherry Lane Theater. *Dutchman* was a short but brutal play about Lula, a thirty-year-old white temptress in a tight dress, and Clay, a twenty-year-old black professional in a three-piece suit. They meet on the subway, where Lula first tries to seduce Clay. Then she challenges his authenticity and manhood as the dialogue crackles with insults and innuendo. Finally, Lula provokes Clay into slapping her twice and threatening to cut off her breasts.[46]

"Shit, you don't have any sense, Lula, nor feelings either," Clay explodes. "I could murder you now. Such a tiny ugly throat. I could squeeze it flat, and, watch you turn blue, on a humble. For dull kicks. And all these weak-faced ofays squatting around here, staring over their papers at me. Murder them too. Even if they expected it. That man there . . . as skinny and middle-classed as I am, I could rip that paper out of his hand and just as easily rip out his throat." Clay finishes and prepares to leave the train. But Lula grabs a knife and stabs him twice. She and the other passengers quickly remove his body from the car. And when another young black professional enters and takes a seat behind her, she turns and gives him a long, slow stare.[47]

Dutchman was an immediate sensation and turned the twenty-one-year-old Jones into an instant celebrity. A year later, radicalized by the assassination of Malcolm X, he divorced his Jewish wife, moved from Greenwich Village to Harlem, changed his name to Amiri Baraka (or "blessed prince"), and became a founder of the Black Arts Movement. Baraka was later elected to the American Academy of Arts and Letters and named the poet laureate of New Jersey. But *Dutchman* was his first success, perhaps because it truly captured the tensions of 1964. "If this is the way the Negroes really feel about the white world around them, there's more rancor buried in the breasts of colored conformists than anyone can imagine," wrote the *New York Times* reviewer after opening night. "If this is the way even one Negro feels, there is ample cause for guilt as well as alarm, and for a hastening of change."[48]

By the spring even moderates like Kenneth Clark were losing patience. The city's failure to implement a comprehensive plan for school integration and Congress's refusal to pass the civil rights bill rankled. "I must confess that I now see white American liberalism primarily in terms of the adjective 'white,'" he wrote in *Commentary*. "And I think [that] one of the important things Negro Americans will have to learn is how they can deal with a curious and insidious adversary—much more insidious than the out-and-out bigot." Increasingly, Clark saw liberalism as an ideology of words rather than deeds, which "attempts to impose guilt upon the Negro when he has to face the hypocrisy of the liberal."[49] The fragile alliance of whites and blacks in the freedom struggle was fraying as disappointments multiplied and strains deepened.

More tensions flared in early April. With the World's Fair set to open in several weeks, the Brooklyn and Bronx chapters of the Congress on Racial Equality (CORE) announced that they would conduct a massive stall-in unless the city immediately addressed the problems of police brutality, substandard housing, and failing schools. On the roads, bridges, and tunnels leading to Queens, black motorists would deliberately run out of fuel, pretend to have car trouble, or simply abandon their vehicles to block traffic. "Our objective is to have our own civil rights exhibit at the World's Fair," declared Oliver Leeds of Brooklyn CORE. "We do not see why white people should enjoy themselves when Negroes are suffering." The plan generated an instant and negative response from James Farmer, executive director of CORE, who called it a "hare-brained idea" and suspended Leeds's chapter. Similar reaction from city officials, daily newspapers, ordinary citizens, and liberal officials in Washington was equal parts outrage at the possible disruption and fear that the protest might damage public support for civil rights.[50]

Most mainstream civil rights leaders agreed with Farmer that the stall-in was a tactical mistake. King and others found it difficult, however, to condemn the activists for proposing nonviolent civil disobedience. "Which is worse, a 'Stall-In' at the World's Fair or a 'Stall-In' in the U.S. Senate?" King asked in reference to the filibuster against the civil rights bill. "The former merely ties up the traffic of a single city. But the latter seeks to tie up the traffic of history, and endanger the psychological lives of twenty million people."[51]

Aware that he was losing control of CORE, Farmer stated that he would lead a protest at the exhibit halls of southern states that supported segregation. Meanwhile, Mayor Robert Wagner, who called the stall-in a "gun to the heart of the city," announced that he would have more than a thousand police officers on the road and in the air, supported by three command centers and dozens of tow trucks, to act if needed. In the end, they were not—only a dozen motorists were arrested. But significant protests unfolded at subway stations and the opening ceremony, where Lyndon Johnson gave one of his first public speeches since becoming president. Farmer was taken into custody with supporters after blocking the doorway to the New York City Pavilion.[52]

Back in Harlem, crime continued to create anxiety. On April 11, a young white social worker named Eileen Johnston, who had only recently moved to New York from Chicago, went to Count Basie's Night Club with a black co-worker. A few steps from the front door, two black youths confronted them. "This one's mine," said one of the assailants as he jammed a knife into Johnston's back. Six days later, seventy-five teens overturned a fruit stand on Lenox Avenue near 128th Street and began to throw apples, oranges, and melons at each other. When four patrolmen arrived on the scene, they were greeted with a barrage of fruit and rocks. After twenty-five more officers responded to calls for assistance with pistols drawn and nightsticks swinging, the melee ended with five arrests and charges of police brutality at the station house where the suspects were taken. On April 29, a black teen stabbed to death a middle-aged Hungarian immigrant whose husband was critically injured when he tried to come to her aid in the used clothing store they operated.[53]

The crimes generated headlines in the mainstream media because they crossed racial boundaries. But in reality most acts of violence were either white-on-white or black-on-black, with African Americans disproportionately represented as both victim and perpetrator. That, however, was not news. "If a reporter phoned in what he believed was an interesting robbery or homicide in which the victim happened to be black, the editor invariably muttered, 'Forget it,'" recalled Arthur Gelb, deputy metro editor of the New York Times. "Reporters, of course, knew better than even to suggest stories about crimes involving blacks against blacks. That was copy more suited for the Harlem-based weekly, the Amsterdam News."[54]

Violent crimes that featured white victims and black assailants attracted national attention—even on the floor of the U.S. Senate, where the debate over the civil rights bill was under way. In mid-April, Democratic Senator Olin Johnston of South Carolina, an opponent of the measure, repeated the common conservative claim that the black freedom struggle encouraged lawlessness. Southern states, Johnston asserted in defense of segregation, "do not have the high rates of crime and juvenile delinquency of those states which are hotbeds of agitators against so many American institutions." Another foe of the bill, Democratic Senator Richard Russell of Georgia, later raised the grim specter of Kitty Genovese during a verbal confrontation with liberal Republican Jacob Javits of New York, a staunch advocate of civil rights. "I say that couldn't happen in the South, demean it as you may," Russell heatedly charged.[55]

Individually, the crimes caused concern among whites. Collectively, they generated panic when a recently hired black reporter for the New York

Times, Junius Griffin, reported in May that a new Harlem gang known as the "Blood Brothers" had formed with the "avowed intention of attacking white people" without provocation as part of an initiation ritual. "Why shouldn't I hate all white people?" a member told the reporter. According to Griffin, the gang numbered between two and four hundred, although exact figures were hard to find. Allegedly, it was responsible for the murder of Johnston as well as the melee at the fruit stand and other crimes. Based on information supposedly provided to the reporter by a researcher for Harlem Youth Opportunities Unlimited (HARYOU), who had conducted taped interviews with many of the members, they were trained in martial arts and taught how to construct homemade weapons.[56]

A leader interviewed by Griffin said that "the main reason the gang started was to protect ourselves in a group against police brutality. If they're going to hit one of us, and we're by ourselves, then there's no protection." The "Blood Brothers," he claimed, received financial support from numbers runners and drug dealers in Harlem. The NAACP and CORE wanted to help and had staged the school demonstrations. "But who wants an education," he asked, "when you are going to have your brains knocked out or see your brothers or cousins shot by policemen?"[57]

Griffin was only the fourth black reporter on the *New York Times*, which like every major daily in the city had few African American writers on staff, a practice that would start to change during the summer of 1964. George Streator, a Fisk graduate, was hired in 1945 but fired four years later when it was found that he had fabricated quotes. Layhmond Robinson, Jr. was a Syracuse graduate and U.S. Navy photographer in World War II who joined the paper in 1950 after he earned his degree from the Columbia School of Journalism. Theodore "Ted" Jones was raised in Harlem and worked for the *Amsterdam News* while attending City College. After graduation, he joined the *New York Times* as a copyboy, and in 1960 was promoted to reporter. He was "the paper's authority on Harlem," recalled Gelb in his memoir. "But there weren't many stories about Harlem that the *Times*—or, for that matter, any other white newspaper—deemed newsworthy."[58] Griffin was hired to rectify the situation.

Like Robinson, Griffin got his start in journalism in the military after growing up in a coal town and attending the two-room Stonega School for the Colored in Virginia. "I was in the Marines. I wanted to be another Ernie Pyle," he recalled. "I struck a bargain: I agreed to reenlist; after a year, I'd get a transfer to Tokyo and be assigned to *Stars and Stripes*." In

Korea, he became one of only two black correspondents working for the military paper. In 1962, Griffin was discharged and headed to New York, where he joined the Associated Press and was nominated for a Pulitzer Prize as one of eight reporters who wrote the series "The Deepening Crisis" on the civil rights movement. Two years later, he joined the *New York Times* when Rosenthal decided that he "wanted me in Harlem; Abe thought I could bring more depth to the black coverage."[59]

Whether Griffin added more depth remains a matter of controversy within journalism circles—Ted Poston of the *New York Post* later contended that police had peddled the story for weeks before Griffin jumped at it, in part because "Negro scare stories" were a time-honored tradition at the metropolitan newspapers. Five days after his front-page article on the "Blood Brothers" appeared, the NAACP challenged his account. In a statement, it demanded that the state attorney general "put an end to the slanderous lies being propagated concerning the Harlem Community by daily press exaggerations of the so-called blood brothers." Executive Secretary Roy Wilkins added that "from my own information, reports on [the gang] are without foundation." And the Reverend Dr. Donald Harrington of the Community Church of New York was equally scathing. "I believe that this is an irresponsible story patched up out of fear and malice and a few instances of violence," he said. "Not only will it be used to justify police violence in Harlem, but it has already further alienated the great racial communities."[60]

Although the NYPD affirmed the gang's existence, other newspapers were quick to criticize the Griffin article. It was, wrote Gay Talese, a *New York Times* reporter in 1964, "an opportunity they never miss when they think *The Times* has overstepped its traditional caution." Even some veteran reporters on the paper wondered, however, when other journalists were unable to make contact with any gang members. In the newsroom, some began to describe the "Blood Brothers" story as "Rosenthal's Bay of Pigs," a reference to John Kennedy's disastrous decision to approve an invasion of Cuba by armed exiles in April 1961.[61] Like the former president, both Gelb and Rosenthal were relatively inexperienced—they had assumed their editorial positions only in the fall of 1963. More important, both were unfamiliar with what was happening in Harlem.

Rosenthal, the son of a house painter from the Bronx, was familiar with poverty. But his specialty was foreign reporting—he had won a Pulitzer Prize in 1960 for his coverage of Eastern Europe. Gelb was equally unprepared. "We did not know how to cover the wants and dreams of black people," he admitted. "Harlem—it was like a foreign country." When he and Rosenthal questioned Griffin, the reporter always claimed that the gang had dispersed after the attention and notoriety it had received. Twenty years later, when Gelb again spoke to Griffin, who by then was working for Motown Records in Los Angeles, he still "insisted that every fact in his stories had been the truth. Even though at times I had harbored some doubts, overall I found Griffin's sincerity convincing." Gelb also pointed out in an interview that no one has ever proven that Griffin fabricated the article. But fifty years later, Talese had no doubts. "That story was a fake," he declared.[62]

The "Blood Brothers" article had a lasting and insidious impact. "The press, the radio and television had been building a kind of horrified lynch mob in the rest of the city against Harlem," wrote a radical white journalist in a book about the "Fruit Stand" incident in April 1964. "The phrase about the long hot summer coming on was taken as a direct threat against whites. Every act of casual rowdyism involving black people was reported as an atrocity story. The Negroes were beginning to be described as completely out of control, tearing up subways, molesting and raping white women. White neighborhood vigilantes organized into roving patrols stopped and questioned every black man straying out of his home block. New York sounded to the rest of the country like some frontier town helpless before the uncontrollable violence stalking its streets."[63]

Regardless of whether the "Blood Brothers" were fictitious, the fear that crime was causing in New York was all too real. In May, the Hasidic community in Brooklyn formed a civilian patrol quickly dubbed the Maccabees after the fierce Jewish tribe whose resistance to the Greek occupation of Judea is celebrated every Hanukkah. On the Sabbath, the patrol was augmented by Christian volunteers, both black and white. The decision to create the Maccabees came after a gang of fifty black teenagers attacked a group of Hasidic children and a rabbi's wife was the victim of an attempted rape. The hope was that, if nothing else, the patrol might prevent another Genovese tragedy. "Yet no sooner do you rush reinforcements to Crown Heights than the terror leaps out in another part of the city or moves along underground," commented *National Review*, a conservative magazine, "and the knife may be at anyone's throat."[64]

Tensions between the Police Department and many liberal New Yorkers had also risen to dangerous levels. In mid-May, Councilman Theodore Weiss introduced a bill with the support of CORE and the NAACP to create

FIGURE 4. The Maccabees, a Jewish anticrime organization, patrol the streets of Brooklyn. Photo by Marion S. Trikosko. Library of Congress, Prints & Photographs Division, U.S. News & World Report Magazine Collection (LC-U9-12191 frame 24).

a new civilian review board composed of individuals without ties to the NYPD. The existing review board, created in 1955, consisted of three deputy police commissioners. As a result, observed Arnold Fein, chairman of the New York Committee of Democratic Voters, it lacked credibility. "In much of the public mind," he wrote to Mayor Wagner, "such a board is engaged in the business of self-investigation and self-justification." This perception was especially dangerous given the unrest and distrust in the city. "In the current period of racial tension, picketing, and demonstrations," Fein added, "it is almost inevitable that there will be misunderstandings and clashes involving police, with recurrent charges of police brutality." Even if most charges were false, which he believed was the case, a truly independent review board was needed to "clear the air, increase respect for legitimate police operations, restrain the lawless cop, and restrain those who make unfounded charges."[65]

Although the proposed review board would have limited authority—it could only make recommendations to the mayor and police commissioner —it met with fierce and immediate resistance from Commissioner Murphy.

"In my opinion," he stated at a city council public hearing, "this entire push for a citizens' board is a tragedy of errors compounded by half-truths, innuendos, myths, and misconceptions." The allegations of police brutality were "maliciously inspired," he charged, and came from "self-aggrandizing, self-appointed leaders" whose "blind assertions" are "aimed at destroying respect for law and order and are, in effect, calculated mass libel of the police."[66]

The Patrolmen's Benevolent Association, which represented the twenty-six thousand officers of the NYPD, was equally critical. In a letter to Mayor Wagner in May, President John Cassese called the new board a "deliberate slap in the face" to his rank and file, who were overwhelmingly committed to the fair and impartial enforcement of the law despite a few isolated and inevitable abuses of power. Moreover, the police already worked under careful and constant scrutiny from the existing board, the general public, and Commissioner Murphy, who "is tougher and more stringent than any group of civilians would dream of being." Above all, the police labored in a city filled with watchful, if not hostile, eyes.[67]

"Nowhere is there greater awareness of, sensitivity to, and sympathy with, the cause of civil rights and civil liberties," Cassese contended. "Nowhere are the courts more vigilant, the news media more pervasive and aggressive." He also offered two predictions or warnings. The first was that civilian appointees to the new review board would no doubt be "members of pressure groups that cannot be impartial," such as CORE. The second was that an independent board would "deal a devastating blow to police morale and lead policemen to ignore sensitive situations rather than take the chance of getting into trouble with a civilian board with a special axe to grind."[68] Civilian oversight would cause the police to handcuff themselves and a city on the brink of chaos would become even more dangerous.

In June, Commissioner Murphy attempted to reassure the public. "All of us together can turn the threat of a long, hot summer into a cool, calm, constructive period of progress," he said at the seventh annual pre-summer conference of the Police Department and the Youth Board. Among the gangs discussed were the Tiny Tims, the Buccaneers, the Imperial Lords, and the Medallion Lords, with an estimated total of seven to eight hundred members. No new information about the supposed "Blood Brothers" was made available, although the NYPD continued to claim the gang existed. Murphy made no mention of subway crime, including the nine incidents reported since May 29 alone, but emphasized that he did not believe that "this city will explode into bloodshed in the coming months."[69]

At a press conference, Whitney Young, Jr. also tried to calm the racial fear by providing some perspective and balance. The executive director of the Urban League emphasized that he had always deplored violence "whether inflicted by Negro youth in urban settings like Harlem or by those who dynamite Negro churches in Alabama." But he observed that "crime of all sorts—murder, rape, robbery, burglary and assault—has been no stranger to Harlem. Its citizens have been victimized for years with amazing indifference on the part of the general public, which turned its eyes and thoughts elsewhere. The only new dimension to the current violence is that the frustrations of the ghetto are spilling out beyond its boundaries and directly affecting the public at large."[70]

Young recited the facts for all to hear—if they were willing to listen. The crime rate in Harlem was significantly greater than in the rest of the city. The murder rate alone was six times higher. In the overwhelming majority of cases, which the white media almost always chose not to report, it was black-on-black, with African Americans both the victims and perpetrators. It was time, Young added, to eliminate racial identification in crime stories. Reporters should not assign false motives or promote racial bias. "Crime does not carry a racial label," he asserted. "There has always been crime and rioting, particularly among the poor of all races and nations, and especially wherever full citizenship, liberty, and opportunity were denied."[71] It was a brave but ultimately futile effort to soothe the jangled nerves of white residents.

The subways in particular seemed to provide daily tales of terror even as Mayor Wagner ordered an extra shift for all city and transit police, who were also told to wear their uniforms to and from work as an added deterrent. On one train, reported *Newsweek* in mid-June, a group of four black teens threatened to cut off the head of a motorman; on another, a group of five black youths demanded $10 from a white teen and then stabbed him in the shoulder when he refused to pay. "They're animals, vicious animals," said a middle-aged white woman. "And they talk about civil rights." But Rustin objected strongly to what he saw as a false equivalence. "When such acts of hooliganism are carried out by whites," he noted, "it is then called 'juvenile delinquency' and not 'Irish delinquency' or 'Italian delinquency.'"[72]

In Washington, President Lyndon Johnson and Attorney General Robert Kennedy met to discuss the summer's likely hot spots. On the top of the agenda were New York and Mississippi, where CORE volunteers James Chaney, Andrew Goodman, and Michael Schwerner, part of the "Freedom

Summer" voter registration campaign, disappeared in June after police officers and Klan members had beaten, tortured, and murdered them. "It is clear," warned special assistant Richard Goodwin, "that the one domestic issue which could cause real trouble for the party this year is civil rights. . . . The chance of violence is high." Rising expectations and temperatures might lead to a "series of explosions" in the South and the North that could have "serious political repercussions" and might require federal action. "We might well treat this as if we were waging a war," he advised.[73]

In New York, two new anticrime measures went into effect in July. The "No-Knock" law enabled officers who had obtained warrants to search private residences without first notifying the occupants. The "Stop-and-Frisk" law allowed the police to question individuals and gather evidence on the basis of "reasonable suspicion." Governor Nelson Rockefeller, a liberal Republican who later championed harsh antidrug measures in the early 1970s, had signed both laws four months earlier despite protests from the *New York Post* and *Amsterdam News*, which contended that they would give a "green light" to the most "bigoted or sadistic" officers. The NAACP also argued that "aggressive preventive patrol"—a common practice in urban policing by the early 1960s—would lead to greater harassment of racial minorities.[74]

Aggressive policing certainly led to greater tensions in Central Harlem, where the battle to control the street corners escalated. A member of the "Blood Brothers" declared that the gang planned to protest the new laws by staging a "hit" on either a patrolman in the 32nd Precinct or an officer with the elite TPF, which had flooded the area in pairs since the wave of high-profile crimes in April. Even if the threat was a bluff or bravado, it put the police on edge and made them apprehensive.[75]

As the school year ended, the panic among whites was growing and spreading. On July 16, two weeks after President Johnson signed the Civil Rights Act and the same day that Thomas Gilligan shot and killed James Powell, *National Review* reminded readers that over Memorial Day weekend, twenty black teens had vandalized an entire subway car, punching, kicking, and knifing the terrified passengers. It was not simply another incident of urban mayhem. "What is happening," asserted the conservative magazine, "or is about to happen—let us face it—is race war."[76]

Forty-eight hours later, the riot began. "Harlem's history is made on Saturday night," observed author Claude Brown, "because for some reason or another, Negroes just don't mind dying on Saturday night."[77]

CHAPTER 4

THE FIRE THIS TIME

> In the heat of the summer
> When the pavements were burning
> The soul of a city was ravaged in the night
> After the city sun was sinkin'
> —Phil Ochs, "In the Heat of the Summer"

SATURDAY, JULY 18

The minister was rueful and shaken. "This has got out of hand," admitted the Reverend Nelson C. Dukes of the Fountain Spring Baptist Church shortly after 10 P.M. on Saturday night. "If I knew this was going to happen, I would not have said anything." He then disappeared from the 28th Precinct, located on 123rd Street between Seventh and Eighth Avenues, but it was too late. The fire this time had arrived and it would burn for three nights in Harlem.[1]

At a rally earlier that Saturday evening at the corner of 125th Street and Seventh Avenue, Dukes had told the assembled crowd that the time for talk about the senseless murder of James Powell was over. "Let's go to the station," he shouted from the sidewalk, and approximately 150 persons followed him as he marched two blocks to the precinct house. By 9 P.M. the crowd, which had grown to 250, was chanting "murder, murder" and singing "[Police Commissioner Michael] Murphy is a bastard, he must be removed" (to the tune of "We Shall Not Be Moved") in front of the station house. As police reinforcements and barricades arrived, the confrontation escalated and expanded until by midnight a large portion of Central Harlem was engulfed in rioting and looting.[2]

By dawn on Sunday morning the official figures were one dead, thirty-one injured (including twelve officers), and thirty arrested (the low number was because every arrest meant another officer had to leave the line when none could be spared). Among those taken into custody was *Life* photographer Frank Dandridge, who faced charges when he refused to stop taking photos of an officer arresting a woman. More than thirty businesses were vandalized. Hospital records subsequently showed that at least a hundred persons had sought medical treatment for serious injuries caused by gun shots, building tiles, nightsticks, and other objects. By law the police had to report all injuries to medical personnel, but many residents probably chose to treat their own wounds, which meant the actual figures were in all likelihood even higher.[3]

As the sun rose, the streets resembled a battle zone and the sidewalk leading to the emergency entrance at Harlem Hospital was splattered with blood. "Murphy's Gestapo," muttered a subdued man in a dark suit as the sidewalks began to fill with churchgoers. "It looks like a war out there," said a young woman with a baby in her arms as she entered the Hotel Theresa.[4] For many it was.

Saturday began quietly. It was also hot—scorching hot. By noon the temperature was ninety-two degrees in Central Park, a relatively cool green space. In the concrete jungle of Upper Manhattan, it was undoubtedly warmer. And in the crumbling tenements and brownstones of Central Harlem, where air conditioning was a rare luxury, the temperature might have reached a hundred degrees or more. To escape the heat, people naturally congregated on the street corners, fire escapes, rooftops, and building stoops. For the police and the residents of Harlem, it was going to be a hot night in every sense of the word.

At the same time, many important leaders, black and white, were away from the city, state, and country—Mayor Robert Wagner and Congressman Adam Clayton Powell, Jr. were in Europe preparing to attend a conference in Geneva on the impact of automation on cities, Malcolm X was in Cairo observing the African Unity Conference, and NAACP executive director Roy Wilkins was in Wyoming vacationing with Governor Rockefeller at his family's ranch. Their absence would prove a major problem in coming days, as self-proclaimed leaders with few followers would seek to fill the void in Harlem.[5]

At 2 P.M. two events took place in two parts of the city, reflecting partially the racial divide and conflicting views of recent events. At the Levy and Delany Funeral Home in Central Harlem, more than three hundred visitors filed the past the open casket of James Powell and paid their respects to his mother, Annie Powell, who became distraught at the sight of her son. "They killed my baby. They murdered my baby," she cried as she was led to her car. "That's all it was. Murder." The crowd seemed tense, sullen, and emotionally on edge. The police had barricades and were on hand in force if needed, which they were not.[6] Instead, they stood on the sidelines, silently watching and waiting.

In Yorkville on the Upper East Side, the site of the shooting on Thursday and the protest on Friday, officers were also present as a tiny band of white extremists gathered to blame civil rights activists for the rising tide of urban disorder. A small group of white spectators was scornful of both the white extremists and the CORE demonstrators. "The fact that the boy was killed is a terrible thing," said a woman. "But [the protesters] aren't helping things by going around the streets like wild animals." A middle-aged man in the publishing trade contended that "many people are exploiting the Negro problem" and that the civil rights movement was attracting "the support of other minority groups, the lunatic fringe, the bearded and the unwashed." A cab driver who had witnessed the demonstration on Friday called it counterproductive. "Instead of giving the civil rights laws an opportunity to be applied," he asserted, "there are crackpots advocating violence."[7]

The rest of the afternoon was uneventful. But three CORE chapters—Downtown, East River, and South Jamaica—had scheduled a rally for the early evening on the corner of 125th Street and Seventh Avenue. The original focus was the lack of progress in the search for the missing civil rights workers in Mississippi. After Thursday's shooting of James Powell, however, the theme was changed to police brutality. A few minutes before 7 P.M. a young woman from the Bronx chapter of CORE climbed onto a shaky blue chair next to a small American flag. "I'm mad. I'm so damn mad tonight. I'm not much older than that boy and I'm scared of every cop out here," said seventeen-year-old Judith Howell, a high school student dressed in a button-down shirt, skirt, and loafers without socks.[8]

Under the watchful eyes of a dozen officers, the crowd of a hundred or so, neither rowdy nor violent, began to stir amid the steaming heat. "That's the way to go, little girl," yelled someone in support. "James Powell was shot because he was black," Howell continued. "We got a civil rights bill and along with the bill we got Barry Goldwater and a dead black boy." Slowly, the mood of the listeners shifted as anger, frustration, and impatience—with Harlem life, white policemen, black leaders, the presidential election, the scorching heat, the slow pace of racial progress—started to reach the boiling point.[9]

The next few speakers encountered a less sympathetic audience. "White people dictate your policy," shouted one man in reference to CORE's integrated membership. "It is time to let 'the man' know that if he does something to us, we are going to do something back," responded a frustrated Chris Sprowal, chairman of Downtown CORE and organizer of Friday's protest. "If you say 'You kick me once, I'm going to kick you twice,' we might get some respect." Conceding that CORE was committed to nonviolence, he countered that "when a cop shoots at me, I will shoot back."[10]

The crowd replied with cries of approval: "That's right, brother" and "blood for blood." But Sprowal's final appeal for peaceful protest was greeted with hoots of derision—a sign that some younger blacks in New York were losing patience with nonviolent civil disobedience. "Let's go down to that precinct and take it apart brick by brick," yelled Howell. After Sprowal spoke a member of South Jamaica CORE charged that "45 percent of the cops in New York are neurotic murderers."[11]

By now the crowd was excited and had grown to several hundred. Yet no real news appeared imminent, and so most of the reporters headed home or to a bar with ice. Among the few who remained was Paul L. Montgomery of the *New York Times*. A twenty-seven-year-old assistant religion editor, he became captivated by the action and opted to stay. As a result, he found himself on the front lines of a big story.[12]

After the CORE rally ended, Dukes spoke for twenty minutes, followed by Edward Mills Davis and James Lawson of the United African Nationalist Movement. Then the minister led the march to the 28th Precinct, where the protest resumed and became confrontational. Outside, a handful of officers donned helmets and linked arms to keep the crowd at bay while others raced to get their gear and offer assistance. As patrolmen rushed to the rooftops to halt the light rain of bottles and bricks, Montgomery asked the precinct captain how many officers he had. "Enough," the captain replied. The actual number was only twenty. Inside, an ad hoc grievance committee consisting of a CORE member, two Black Nationalists, and Dukes met with Deputy Chief Inspector Thomas Pendergast. They demanded that the commissioner immediately suspend Gilligan and personally come to Harlem to make the announcement; Pendergast responded that the incident was under investigation and offered the committee a bull-horn to address the crowd in the street.[13]

At this point, the protest was a tense but predictable drama for Harlem. "This is their version of city hall," Deputy Chief Inspector Casimir Krus-zewski, commander of the 28th Precinct, observed later. "If they're going to demonstrate against the government, they have to do it here." Typically, the activists would offer some words, the followers would vent, the crowd would disperse, and everyone would call it a night. But July 18 was not a typical Saturday, especially for two Bronx teenagers who were at the head-quarters of Harlem CORE, a second-floor walk-up on West 125th Street, when they learned about the protest and decided to witness it for themselves.[14]

Quentin Hill and Wayne Moreland were friends who lived in the Throgs Neck housing project. Like Powell, they were fifteen, which made his death resonate strongly with them. On weekends they both worked at Orchard Beach, where on hot days they earned good money by selling ice cream and soft drinks. After work Hill and Moreland usually liked to take the subway into Harlem to see the sights and shop. But on that night they decided to join CORE because the Powell shooting had convinced them that the free-dom struggle in the South needed to become more assertive in the North.[15]

When the teenagers arrived at the 28th Precinct, the crowd was shouting at the officers, who "silently snickered and grinned" according to More-land. At 9:20 P.M. a truck loaded with barricades arrived, and as darkness fell Pendergast raised a bullhorn. "This has become a disorderly gathering," he announced. "I am instructing the police to clear the street." But then both Hill and Moreland heard—"as vividly as if it happened yesterday"— the chief inspector state, "Okay, boys, you've had your say. Now why don't you go home?" As he spoke, cries of "we're not boys" erupted and someone hurled a rock. "That's it," said Pendergast as the officers and demonstrators clashed. "Lock them up." The police immediately arrested sixteen people and dragged them roughly into the station house. Then a bottle struck Patrolman Michael Doris in the head and knocked him to the pavement with a concussion—the first officer injured.[16]

Angered, the police charged. Now the crowd broke and the teenagers ran. Moreland heard the "dull thud" of nightsticks hitting bone and flesh; Hill saw a Molotov cocktail (a glass bottle filled with flammable liquid and capped with a cloth fuse) float through the air and explode into flames. Amid the chaos and the sound of gunfire both were able to evade capture and duck into the Chock Full O'Nuts on 125th Street, where they dived to the floor along with the employees and other customers. At one point, Hill tried to raise his head to see what was happening. "Stay down," ordered an older man. "I was scared," recollected Moreland. "I recall thinking, just let me get out of here." But Hill had a different reaction. "When you're fifteen you're not afraid of much," he remembered, "and things were unfolding so rapidly that I'm not sure we had time to be afraid."[17]

After the disorder abated, the teenagers went home to the Bronx. But the protest was a formative moment. For Moreland, who later became a professor of literature at Queens College, it was a radicalizing experience. "Whatever illusions I had about the political process or the inherent righteousness of justice" disappeared that night, he recalled. For Hill the rebellion confirmed his sense of the world. In "Time Poem," which was published as part of the Black Arts Movement, he wrote, "go to the precinct / say hello to the sergeant / put your spear between his eyes and pull the trigger." Hill later changed his name to Basir Mchawi and became an activist, editor, photographer, and educator in the public schools. He also taught at Queens College with his lifelong friend.[18]

While Hill and Moreland were able to avoid arrest, another protester was less fortunate. "I didn't do it—you've got the wrong man," the youth yelled as he was hauled into custody. "They're beating him—they're beating him," chanted some bystanders. The false rumor quickly spread to 125th Street, where Mills and Lawson heard it. They rushed to the 28th Precinct, where they demanded to see the prisoner. The lieutenant on duty brought him from his cell and the protester denied the allegation. "They may have been a little rough when they arrested me," he said, "but they haven't bothered me in here." Out there the correction made little difference as misinformation continued to circulate.[19]

By 10 P.M. Deputy Chief Inspector Harry Taylor, in charge of the entire Manhattan North area, had assumed command and reinforcements had started to arrive from other precincts. Many of them were off-duty detectives and patrolmen with police badges pinned to their civilian clothes. With the additional manpower and tactical support provided by two squads of TPF officers bused from Midtown, the police managed to clear 123rd Street in front of the station house and establish barricades at both ends of the block. On Eighth Avenue the crowd drifted away, but on Seventh Avenue it swelled as the curious came to contemplate the commotion. Soon the intersection contained an estimated thousand demonstrators.[20]

A convertible driven by a white couple became trapped in the intersection at 124th Street and Seventh Avenue. The crowd smashed the headlights and pounded the sides of the car. The blond woman inside was badly hurt. "I asked her if she was all right," recalled TPF officer Robert Leuci. "Her voice was weak and trembling. I remember the way she turned away, wiping her eyes and her face with her forearm. Her hair was a bloody mess and it hung across her face. I had never seen such wide-eyed fear on the face of anyone, nothing like the fear on that woman's face." The officer tried to clear the intersection and keep traffic moving, but it was almost impossible. "Bottles and bricks were exploding everywhere," recollected Leuci. "Some cops were hit, some went down, some of us shot above the car into the night."[21]

Other motorists were more fortunate. Peter Drew, a German Jew who had come to the United States after Kristallnacht in 1938, was driving from Queens to a Van Cliburn concert at Lewisohn Stadium with a friend's daughter around 7:30 P.M. At 124th Street and Lenox Avenue, the graduate student encountered a large crowd shouting, "Get Gilligan!" He made it safely to the open-air amphitheater, where he could hear siren after siren during the concert. After it ended, he wisely decided not to try to drive back through Harlem. Instead, he took the West Side Highway and then headed home. "That could have been us," he thought later as he looked at newspaper photos of overturned cars.[22]

"Why don't you go home?" pleaded a tired and sweaty policeman with a bullhorn on 125th Street. "We are home—this is our home, baby," replied a voice from the crowd. It was a powerful reminder of who the occupied and the occupiers were in the minds of many Harlem residents. Then, without warning, the TPF officers went on the offensive. Shouting "Charge!" and swinging clubs, they jumped over the barricades and launched into the intersection. "The idea is to make a lot of noise—run right at them; that usually breaks a crowd," a sergeant explained later.[23]

If that was the intent, it worked—but the large crowd now broke into small clusters of twenty or thirty against which tear gas and smoke grenades were less effective. The groups then scattered. Most went north to 125th Street, chased by the police. From there some turned left and headed west to Eighth Avenue; others turned right and headed east to Lenox Avenue. Any hope of restoring order evaporated as violence and vandalism spread in every direction, although mostly uptown to 135th Street.

Montgomery, who was trailing the police, stopped outside the Hotel Theresa for a moment to survey the broken glass and strewn garbage. As he stood on the corner of 125th Street and Seventh Avenue at 10:30 P.M., he saw a youth hurl a Molotov cocktail at a police car; he missed the target, but a sheet of flames spread across the street. When Patrolman Frank Strazza exited the car he stepped into the burning gasoline, badly injuring his leg. His four fellow officers drew their weapons and fired repeatedly into the air. The gunshots sounded like firecrackers to Montgomery, who could see the flashes. "It was a sound," he wrote with considerable under-statement, "that was to become familiar the rest of the night."[24]

Looting was widespread despite the precautions taken by many owners, who shuttered their businesses as soon as evening fell. Using crowbars, the crowds removed the folding metal gates from the doors and windows; in some instances, drivers may have used heavy chains attached to tow hooks to rip the gates from their frames and drag them into the street, where they resembled twisted pieces of sculpture. The shelves of grocery stores were cleared. An insurance agency, a men's clothing store, and many other busi-nesses were ransacked. A black reporter with the *Amsterdam News* saw a ten-year-old looter struggle with a cache of clothes as large as he was. Per-haps most frightening of all, every rifle in two pawnshops on 135th Street was stolen, although it was later determined that officers had removed them as a precaution. But the police remained anxious about the weaponry some groups might possess.[25]

The most immediate and worrisome problem for the police was the roof-tops. In the spring, Inspector Taylor had ordered his officers to check them and remove any potential missiles or weapons, but it was a futile task. The bricks and mortar in many tenements were crumbling; anyone could easily pry them loose and hurl them at a target five or six floors below. To add to the threat, between each building lay a parapet covered with tiles, which were also effective weapons when thrown with accuracy. And then there were the bottles left by those who, in the summer months, regularly sought relief from their sweltering apartments by relaxing on the cooler rooftops.

To protect themselves from the aerial bombardment, officers fired their pistols at the roof line in hopes of forcing their assailants to retreat. Tear gas and nightsticks were useless. Mounted policemen on horseback were vulnerable. Fire hoses were rejected, perhaps because of their use in Bir-mingham in 1963, perhaps because the International Association of Fire-fighters was in principle opposed to having its members engage in crowd control. Ironically, German shepherds like those unleashed by "Bull" Con-nor were seen on the streets of Harlem—but they belonged to residents who wanted protection from the disorder.[26] James Farmer nonetheless made the comparison the next day. "I saw New York's night of Birmingham horror," the CORE executive director declared.[27]

Soon the night air of Central Harlem was filled with the acrid smell of gun smoke, as hundreds of officers discharged thousands of shots. Precisely who gave the order to fire weapons and when is not known. What appears to have happened is that commanders in the field gradually and informally authorized the use of unrestricted gunfire as a suppressing tactic. Hours later the commissioner personally and officially gave his stamp of approval when he arrived at the 28th Precinct. By then Central Harlem seemed like a war zone, with screams from people and cracks from bullets as they ricocheted off brick walls and cement sidewalks.[28]

Robert Leuci and his partner, a TPF rookie named Ronnie Heffernan, were clearing debris from a rooftop on 124th Street near Lenox Avenue when the shots proliferated. "For the first moment or two I thought the sound was firecrackers; it couldn't be gunshots, there were so many," Leuci recalled. "'Firecrackers?' I said. Ronnie shook his head. And then for maybe five seconds, we stood there looking at each other. Popping noises, not deafening but not soft either. There had been days of demonstrations and threats, and now on a sweltering Saturday night, the meltdown had come." The two men separated, but the noise kept growing. "A continuous roar rose from the crowds, an ocean of sound that just kept coming," Leuci remembered. "There were wailing sirens, flashing red lights that reflected off the windshields of cars and storefront glass . . . 125th Street was a battleground, with cops and looters in hand-to-hand combat."[29]

In the city room of the *Herald Tribune*, a phone call from a black man caused a white reporter to ask what the background noises were. "That Goldwater stuff has started," the caller said after asking how he could get in touch with Governor Rockefeller, who was still at his Wyoming ranch with NAACP leader Roy Wilkins. "They're shooting at people up here in Harlem," the caller added with a touch of panic. "The police are chasing the people here at Eighth Avenue and 125th Street and shooting at them." The reporter asked if there were any deaths. "No, they're shooting in the air," the man said. "The crowd runs when they shoot, then, when they stop, the crowd comes back again."[30] It would become a familiar dance in the coming hours.

The rioters smashed the windows of police cars and alternated between taunting and mocking the officers. Some shouted "killer cops must go" (even at patrolmen trying to help a hit-and-run victim); others screamed "Murphy's rats." Their numbers swelled as passengers exiting from the subway station and patrons spilling from the Apollo Theater joined the crowd as either spectators or participants. Rumors added to the volatile mix. "They walk all over me in Greenville, South Carolina," said a drunken woman. "They might as well run over me here." She then lay down in the middle of Seventh Avenue. "Did you see that?" a man said to his companion. "They shot that woman down in cold blood."[31] The story no doubt spread quickly.

Between 11 P.M. and 1 A.M. the city tried to contain the unrest by cordoning off Central Harlem from the rest of New York. With false fire alarms ringing constantly, the Fire Department brought in fire engines to block major thoroughfares and remain close at hand. The Transit Authority stationed additional officers at all Harlem subway stations and diverted buses from regular routes. The Police Department placed barricades on many streets and kept all officers in Harlem on duty even after their shifts ended. The extra manpower was desperately needed—police radios crackled with urgent 10-13 calls (code for assistance requested). At one point, twenty patrol cars had to run an obstacle course of broken glass and assorted debris to Lenox Avenue and 125th Street, where officers were trapped in the intersection, surrounded by hundreds of rioters on all four corners and showered by bricks and bottles.[32]

Heavily outnumbered in Central Harlem, the NYPD called in hundreds of officers from other boroughs. The total number of police on the front lines on Saturday night was reported at five hundred, but it was probably much higher—as a matter of policy, the department never released specific figures. A journalist later suggested to Murphy that he could easily deploy that many officers to any point in the city within an hour. "We can do a lot better than that," he snapped. Although the commissioner resisted a full-scale mobilization because he feared that the violence might spread and wanted to have a reserve ready if necessary, he ordered every on-duty TPF member from Manhattan and Brooklyn to Harlem.[33]

Among those who reported were Davy Katz and his partner Jim O'Neil, who had expected trouble since the Powell shooting. He had seen the posters with Gilligan's picture and the words "WANTED FOR MURDER" plastered across Harlem. "I still have one of the posters," wrote O'Neil, "and to this day I have no idea how they got his picture."[34]

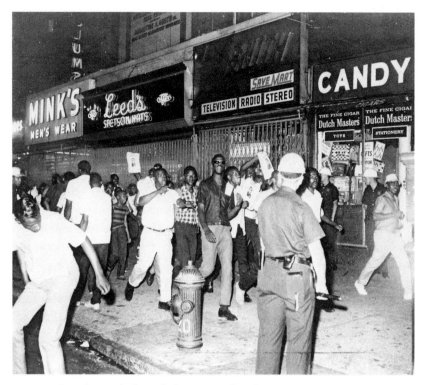

FIGURE 5. Crowds march through the streets of Harlem carrying pictures
and flyers of Lt. Gilligan. Photo by Dick De Marsico. Library of Congress, Prints
and Photographs Division, New York World-Telegram & Sun Collection
(LC-USZ62-136895).

The signal to mobilize came at 8 P.M. Katz and O'Neil ran three blocks
to the station house in Lower Manhattan, where a sergeant with a mega-
phone briefed them on the situation on Eighth Avenue between 115th and
135th Streets. "The precinct cops are not trained in riot suppression so the
department pulled them out of there," he said. "You're going to take their
place and meet the monster head on. . . . When you get there [125th Street]
form up around Inspector Codd, he'll tell you what to do. Good luck men,
it's rough out there."[35]

The forty-two officers who composed the 1st, 7th, and 12th Squads (to
which Katz and O'Neil belonged) grabbed their white air raid warden's
steel helmets, whose design dated from World War I. It was their sole piece

of protective riot gear. "Unlike today's well-dressed riot cop," noted O'Neil, "we had no bulletproof vests, full helmets with shatterproof face plates, handheld shields, or high-laced combat boots." As they rode in patrol cars with lights flashing and sirens wailing, their "faces showed no emotion, mouths spoke no words, and blank eyes stared straight ahead." For O'Neil, it was a moment for reflection: "I was wondering if tonight was going to be the first time I would fire my service revolver in the line of duty."[36]

When the 12th Squad arrived at 125th Street, the officers could hear shots and see fires in the darkness. "My inexperience shielded me from what I was about to encounter," remembered O'Neil. Standing with his back to Eighth Avenue was Lieutenant Codd, who gave the men simple but explicit orders: "You're here to suppress looting, discourage and suppress rioting or unlawful demonstrations. Now go get them." As the squad began to patrol, it encountered Molotov cocktails and sporadic gunfire in O'Neil's recollection. The officers returned fire. One man kept hurling bricks at them from the roof of a four-story tenement.[37]

"Would somebody shoot that fuck's head off?" asked a frustrated sergeant. "Hey Sarge, I'll get him," said James "Jimmy" Dexter, an expert marksman with wavy hair and a baby face who stood six feet seven inches tall. He waited, aimed, and fired when the man came back into his sights. "Shit, I think I got him, I think I got him," yelled Dexter. According to O'Neil, he, Dexter, and Katz followed the sergeant to the roof, where they found the man "with a bullet right between his eyes; we all cheered."[38]

Then Inspector Codd arrived. After determining who had fired the fatal shot, he congratulated Dexter. "Assign an officer to stay with Jimmy, and tell him to bring some sandwiches and beers for the both of them. Here's ten dollars—my treat." Next he turned to Katz and O'Neil: "Gentlemen, let's get back to the streets."[39]

The victim was Jay Jenkins, a forty-one-year-old ex-convict with ten arrests for crimes ranging from receiving stolen goods to carrying concealed weapons. He was, officially, the only person killed in six nights of unrest, but O'Neil and others were skeptical. "The rash of floaters pulled out of the waters surrounding Manhattan, in the weeks following the end of the riots, was obviously a very large coincidence," he commented without further explanation.[40]

It was a common perception in Harlem that night that the police had no intention of making arrests or taking prisoners unless absolutely unavoidable. "They want to kill all of us," an elderly woman said. "They want to shoot all the black people." The NYPD would never have acted so aggressively in a white neighborhood, said an elderly man. "They wouldn't do all this gunslinging and clubbing on 42nd Street."[41]

O'Neil and Katz rejoined their unit and began to look for looters. "We'd enter any store that had broken windows, and if we found anyone inside we would beat them to the ground with our axe handles, then move on to the next store without making any arrests," O'Neil recalled. "No need to, when you're dispensing well-deserved instant justice." He never shot any looters, but he saw an officer wound a black woman who had stolen several pairs of shoes.[42]

Then O'Neil and Katz spotted six men running from a mattress store. With a motorcycle cop they gave chase, but the looters ran into an alley and slammed a heavy door in their face. "Suck dick assholes if you want to come and get us," they shouted. "Suck on these," retorted the motorcycle cop, who fired six rounds through the door. "We moved on without a thought as to who was dead or alive on the other side of the door," wrote O'Neil.[43]

Whether it was "instant justice"—as O'Neil believed—or excessive force is a matter of perspective. Allegations of brutality were numerous that night and the next day. "A man was standing and crying, 'They shot me!'" said a young woman angrily. "A cop walked over to him and split his head open. Yes, just like that!" A middle-aged man was equally agitated. "They gonna kill everybody before it's over," he said. "Whitey don't care who he kills up here." A twenty-four-year-old entertainer with the Peace Corps, who had just returned from a European tour, said that he was clubbed, handcuffed, and arrested when he exited a subway station.[44]

A twenty-three-year-old black woman declared that a white officer shot her in the leg while she was trying to hail a taxi. "I remember screaming at him, 'You shot me! You shot me!'" she stated. "He looked at me and said, 'Well, lay down and die then.'" The woman was shocked. "I really don't know how I should feel," she remarked afterward. "But I do know that cop shot me intentionally. I think he was hating all of us when he did it."[45]

White officers rejected the claim that they had employed excessive force. "They'd scream brutality for anything," said a detective. "Don't believe it," said another policeman. "We asked them to move back. They didn't. They became abusive. We had to get a little tough." A black Transit Authority officer had words of praise for his fellow officers of both races. "I can see why they call 'em New York's finest," he said. "They're scared to death, but if you think they're gonna let any bums out here tonight take over this city, you can forget it."[46]

Some Harlem residents were particularly critical of black officers, who often faced cries of "Uncle Tom" or worse. "If you were my husband, I'd beat you to death," hissed a woman. "Some of the Negro cops," said a student, "I suppose got to prove to the white cops they're not biased. So they overdo it."[47]

But a black policeman disputed the idea that honest and upright citizens were mistreated. "The type of element you encounter in a street riot is the exact same element you deal with outside of a gin mill or a pool hall on a Saturday night," he said. "A small, but active and loud hoodlum element just out deliberately seeking any opportunity to go looting or stealing." An older African American with salt and pepper hair seconded his opinion: "I'll be damned if these guys are demonstrating for civil rights or anything else. They're just stealing and they've been waiting for this chance all summer."[48]

At 1 A.M. Farmer received a frantic phone call at his apartment in Lower Manhattan (like many civil rights leaders, he did not live in Harlem). "Jim, you'd better get your ass up here fast!" begged a co-worker from CORE headquarters on 125th Street. "Harlem is blowing like a volcano! Bottles and bricks are flying everywhere, and the cops are shooting like cowboys." Farmer rushed there by subway after a vigorous debate at the national office on Park Row. "Dammit, I cannot not go," he told staffers after they expressed concern about his physical safety. "It's a war," he was informed when he arrived. "The cops are like occupation troops. They've gone crazy, shooting in windows and beating up women and little children."[49]

From a window Farmer could see a confrontation brewing on the street between a group of youths and a cluster of officers: "The two armies—one white, one black; one with lethal weapons, the other with bottles and bricks—stood staring at each other." Farmer sent a volunteer to mingle with the teens and discover their intentions. When he returned he told Farmer that they planned to raid the office because about a third of the two-dozen volunteers present were white. Farmer quickly devised a plan to evacuate the four white women (against their wishes) through a rear exit with black escorts. The white men would remain while he would speak to the crowd to draw their attention.[50]

"Listen, you guys, I want to talk to you," said Farmer in his deep baritone voice. "I want to make a speech." The response was not positive. "Don't tell us about no nonviolence," said a young man. "We don' wanna hear *that* shit." Undeterred, Farmer began to speak about the promising achievements of the freedom struggle. "Now, I'm bringing that movement north so we can deal with the problems of the northern ghettos," he told the crowd, "the rat-infested firetrap housing; the garbage piling up because no sanitation trucks come by; the unemployment, when there are jobs for whites but not for blacks; and the police brutality."[51]

The youths were listening. Farmer added that at a Friday meeting with the deputy mayor, Paul Screvane, he had demanded that the NYPD assign more African American officers to Harlem. "We know that black cops can be brutal too," he conceded, "but we know that the black cop is not going to beat up our mothers and sisters and little brothers, because it could be *his* mother and sister and little brother." Now they were applauding—and the CORE leader even managed to get some laughter when he observed that he had met with the deputy mayor because Mayor Wagner was in Mallorca, not Manhattan. "I think he'd better stop in Africa and do some campaigning," Farmer said. "He might learn something there."[52]

"What can we do to help?" came a voice from the darkness. "Get off the streets and go home," boomed Farmer. The idea met with immediate disapproval. "No, we'll go home when those storm troopers go home," said a chorus of voices. "They stay, we stay! They go, we go!" So Farmer organized a demonstration in an effort to channel their rage and frustration until they were tired and ready to go home. For a few blocks they marched two abreast, clapping and chanting in an orderly fashion. But on Amsterdam Avenue they encountered officers firing their revolvers as quickly as possible (it sounded to Farmer like they had machine guns).[53]

Four youths rushed to form a human shield around Farmer. "It was a futile but heroic gesture," he recalled. "Some were muggers, I'm sure, and maybe even rapists and possibly killers, and certainly there were haters; but the spark of humanity, scarcely born, had not yet died in them." Convinced there was nothing more that he could do ("It was a Pied Piper effort that failed"), Farmer returned to CORE headquarters, where a white volunteer tried to offer medical attention to a black youth. "What's that whitey doing here?" he screamed. "Get 'im out of here! Kill 'im. Don't let 'im touch me!"[54]

At that moment, King's glorious vision of a peaceful community rooted in interracial harmony seemed like an impossible dream. "Tortured by that hate and the hate that spawned it," reflected Farmer, "I went to the window and gazed out into the blackness."[55]

In the darkness, Jim O'Neil and Davey Katz were running out of bullets. "Jim, how many rounds you got left?" asked Katz around 2 A.M. "I got one left and how about you?" asked O'Neil. "Three. Here, take one and save it for yourself," said Katz. "I don't think they're taking any prisoners." They were not the only officers in Harlem who were down to their final rounds. But then O'Neil and Katz saw a patrol car without flashers rolling down 125th Street with two officers. When the car reached them the policeman on the passenger side leaned out his window and said, "Hang in there, an ammo truck from the Rodmans Neck Range is five minutes behind us."[56] And so it was—right on schedule.

In desperation, the department had loaded boxes of thirty-eight-caliber bullets from the police pistol range in the Bronx into a silver van. The vehicle, as if part of a climactic scene from a classic western, now drove slowly down the street, the rear doors tied back to keep them open. As policemen emerged from the cover of shadows, a uniformed officer flanked by two men with Thompson submachine guns handed out boxes of ammunition. Both Katz and O'Neil took four boxes with fifty rounds each. "When we got back to the relative safety of our doorway," he recalled, "we reloaded our service revolvers, filled up our bandoleers and our dump pouches, and went back to war."[57]

The "war" continued to rage at 3 A.M. Sunday morning despite the show of force and firepower by the NYPD. The sounds of sirens and gunfire were constant. Confusion was commonplace and the chain of command broke down. "I remember during the Harlem riots in 1964," said one patrolman later, "I saw guys down there shooting up at the rooftops trying to pin down people throwing bricks. . . . And a lieutenant came along and said, 'Put that gun away. You have no authority to fire!' The cop told him, 'If you are afraid of getting hurt with gunfire around here, then get the hell out of here. I'm a cop sent up here to do a job and I am going to do a job.'"[58]

The use of gunfire as a suppressing tactic was unprecedented for the NYPD. In both 1935 and 1943 the department had ordered officers not to draw their weapons unless either they or civilians were in clear and immediate danger. The response in 1964 was also a departure from standard procedure, which dictated first a show of force, then an order to disperse, followed by the use of nightsticks, tear gas, and—as a last resort only—

FIGURE 6. Police fire into the night in an effort to suppress the barrage of bottles and bricks. Photo by Warren K. Leffler. Library of Congress, Prints and Photographs Division, U.S. News & World Report Magazine Collection (LC-U9-12287 frame 2).

firearms. And after the riot the NYPD again banned warning shots—officers now faced possible charges if they disobeyed. Five years later, the department also established the Firearms Discharge Review Board, which required officers to account for every use of their weapon.[59]

Luckily or miraculously, only one rioter was officially killed, perhaps because of pure luck, perhaps because of "superhuman restraint by cops with guns in their hands" according to a police captain. Apparently, the bullets fired above the rioters or at the rooftops fell harmlessly to the ground once their muzzle velocity was spent. The resort to firearms was nevertheless a risk of enormous, potentially tragic, proportions. Had the crowds become more assertive, officers would have had to retreat or aim their weapons at people in the street—and the death toll might have been far greater.[60]

The warning shots were a "tactical error" according to a black educator. Now the people of Harlem, who had protested when unarmed, were no longer intimidated. "They have no fear of the policemen's guns and the sound of firearms, and it's only logical that they will come out with their own weapons," he said days later. "Then we will see how brave these cops are, the cops that have been volunteering to go into Harlem and Brooklyn. No man in his right mind volunteers for the front line, when he knows that his enemy has the same weapons that he has." It was a frightening prediction, which fortunately never came to pass.[61]

"We felt this means of control would be more effective and less harmful than the alternatives available to us, and we have been proven right," said Deputy Commissioner Walter Arm, bluntly and unapologetically, about the use of gunfire. "If our men had been firing recklessly, the people hit by bullets would certainly far outnumber the injured policemen." But he refused to explain why the department had not made more use of smoke grenades or tear gas. "I'm simply not going to discuss any details of our tactics or planning," he stated.[62]

Arm's analysis failed to convince Harlem's elected leaders. "Not in the history of New York City has such a technique of open gunplay been practiced by the police," read their statement. "It is a miracle that such an act did not produce more homicide and incitement to a real riot and wholesale deaths." Only a minority neighborhood, it continued, would have received such treatment from officers, who would not have dared to display such "wanton firing" in a white community.[63]

The hail of gunfire—more than six thousand rounds were fired—may have inflicted only a single fatality, but it resulted in plenty of casualties. A young woman who said that she was searching for her mother around 4 A.M. was shot in the right knee near 127th Street. "I thought they were just shooting blanks until I got hit in the leg," she reported, "and then the cops just left me and I had to take a taxi to the hospital." A bartender on his way home from work said he was shot in the back by officers chasing a crowd. "They were beating up everyone, and there was nothing but smoke and gunshots for blocks around," he said. "I wasn't throwing anything or doing anything; they just shot me." But black journalist Les Carson of the *World Telegram and Sun*, who said that he was "too dumb to be afraid," recalled that "I never saw anybody shoot at anybody" in Harlem.[64]

Bloodied heads were, however, a common sight, usually caused by nightsticks swung with abandon. One man stated that he was beaten after he sidestepped a barricade "just to see what was going on." Another said that he was clubbed after throwing a brick at a policeman who had called him a "nigger." But not only residents were at risk. So too were the reporters who now rushed to Harlem to cover the breaking story.[65]

Francis X. Clines of the *New York Times*, a twenty-six-year-old white journalist from Queens who worked the police beat, arrived by subway at 125th Street to reinforce Montgomery. As he left the station with his notebook and press card, "there was this roar, this din." Then a black youth clobbered Clines from behind with a plank of wood and kicked him as he fell to the ground. It was "the end of innocence," he later recalled. But an older black woman chased the teen away and helped Clines, the first journalist injured in Harlem, to a police car. "The whole night was a shock to me," remembered Clines, who had naively assumed that as a reporter he was immune from the wrath of the crowd. "It was a great education. It was a lesson in everything you need to know in my business."[66]

For the rest of the evening, Clines rode with two veteran white officers, who became "alarmed and frightened" when bricks from a parapet struck their parked car. As he stared out the window, Clines watched the men draw their weapons. "Are we shooting at them?" one asked the other as they aimed at the rooftop. "Then they started shooting," recalled Clines, "and it elevated and escalated before my eyes." Although the firing in his view was not indiscriminate, he recognized that it was "more dangerous than getting hit over the head" and could easily "be lethal or fatal for civilians." The next day, the newspaper offered a hard hat imprinted with the company logo to Clines. But he refused to pose with it for *Times Talk*, the in-house publication, or wear the helmet on the street for fear that it would make him a target.[67]

On the east side of Lenox Avenue, Montgomery was standing next to a squad car when it suddenly moved to the west side, leaving him alone and exposed. A large black man immediately grabbed and shoved him several times against a metal grating that covered a shattered window. Montgomery saw broken glass next to his face and a broken bottle in someone's hands. A track star in high school, he made the instantaneous decision to run and made it to the police barricade at Seventh Avenue.[68]

Often the line between spectator and participant blurred or shifted. In the early hours of Sunday morning, a middle-aged black man in sport coat, Bermuda shorts, and madras tie approached Montgomery and Clines, who had press badges pinned to their jacket lapels. "These are not the real people of Harlem," he said solemnly. "These are not the people who make Harlem great. Tell your readers that there is a good element in Harlem, that most of the people in Harlem are respectable and law-abiding." The reporters carefully jotted down the man's words. A few minutes later, they saw a group charge at the police screaming "Kill the mother---- whiteys!" It was led by the man who had just spoken to them. "Some of the good people just got caught up in it, I guess," said Montgomery.[69]

Later he and Clines made light of what had happened to them and described their strategy for covering the riot in *Times Talk*. "In essence it was simple—run with the mobs when they attacked the police, then run away from them when it looked like they wanted to attack you," they wrote. "The advantage was that we definitely did not feel left out. Just about everyone we saw wanted to have a talk. 'Hey, whitey, we gonna get you' was the second most popular conversational opening. I cannot repeat the most popular because the Style Book Committee has not yet determined whether it should be hyphenated." While the committee deliberated, the newspaper supplied other reporters with bright blue hard hats from Con Edison, the electric company. "It was hated almost as much as the police in New York," recalled Fred Powledge, a white southerner who spray painted his helmet black and never wore it, although he kept it as a souvenir. "Any reporter who was fool enough to walk into a riot wearing one of those" deserved what he got.[70]

At 4 A.M. replacements arrived for Katz and O'Neil, who headed home for some rest, but the rioting and looting had not abated. At the corner of 123rd Street and Seventh Avenue, Montgomery observed a lone white youth, sobbing and bloody, cross the police barricade and head into the 28th Precinct. Through "numb lips" and with "glazed eyes" he explained that he was a sailor from California who had simply exited at the wrong time from the wrong subway station, where a group of blacks had attacked him. "They beat me and took my watch and I yelled," he said in a soft monotone.[71]

Thirty minutes later, Commissioner Murphy arrived at the station house. He had received an early morning call at his summer home on Long Island and rushed straight to the 28th Precinct. Immediately, he went to the second floor detectives' room, where he met with Bishop Alvin Childs, honorary mayor of Harlem, Madison S. Jones, executive director of the City Commission on Human Rights, Farmer, Lawson, and others. Murphy expressed his deep concern and agreed to draft a statement to be read in Harlem churches in a few hours. It was the commissioner's fifty-first birthday.[72]

At 5 A.M. the crowds started to grow larger and louder on Lenox Avenue. By then Lez Edmond, a young photographer and interviewer, had arrived by car from his apartment in Queens. A part-time student who worked in the electronics industry and had a press pass from the United Nations, Edmond was an activist who knew most of the leaders and organizations, although he was not a member of any of them. "All of a sudden the shooting started right in front of the car," he recalled. "In fact, policemen were leaning on the car . . . and emptying their guns so fast that they were throwing live bullets away on the ground."[73]

Edmond had no time for fear. But twice he and a friend had to crawl under the car for safety. Then he decided to explore Harlem by foot. When he saw a Black Nationalist approach Inspector Pendergast, he raced to record the conversation. "You can't do any worse than you're doing now," said the man. "Let the people of the community, the businessmen, try to straighten this out. Give us a chance." Pendergast replied that there was nothing he could do, he was simply following orders. "You try that," he said. "I wish you luck."[74]

At the corner of 126th Street and Lenox Avenue, a man and a woman had no patience for luck—they cursed any and all white faces in sight, whether they belonged to police officers or bus drivers. "I served in the Army for 20 years and protected you white---- and look what I came back to!" he said. "Let's burn down the precincts and get all these bastards out of here," she said. The exhausted patrolmen paid them no heed—they were too tired. They had also seen and heard far worse by that time.[75]

Eventually, fresh officers under the command of Captain Lloyd Sealy, one of the highest-ranking African Americans in the NYPD, eased the tension by walking slowly, speaking softly, and keeping their nightsticks sheathed. "As long as you have all these policemen, and the majority is white, you're going to have this problem," said a bystander. "I understand," replied Sealy, "but this is a problem someone else is going to have to solve."[76]

At 7 A.M. Murphy gave a brief press conference at the precinct house and released his statement. He reminded the residents of Harlem that both the Civilian Complaint Review Board and the district attorney were investigating the Powell shooting. "Let us be fair and not make a judgment until all the facts are in and all the witnesses are heard," he pleaded. Then he urged the black community to disavow violence and disown those who "have used this unfortunate incident as an excuse for looting and for vicious, unprovoked attacks against police." He added that their "crimes have been met by swift and necessary police action." Finally, the commissioner offered his assessment of why the riot had occurred: "In our estimation this is a crime problem and not a social problem."[77]

By 9 A.M. a tenuous peace seemed to have returned to Harlem. The crowds had dispersed, the churches were filling, and the streets were at last calm. It was evident, however, that many residents—even those unlikely to have participated in the riot—were not convinced of Murphy's sincerity. Deputy Commissioner Arm, who had distributed the commissioner's statement to local churches, expressed shock at the hostility he encountered. "I never met such hatred," he said. "And these were the respectable church-going people. I couldn't understand it."[78] His reaction was common among many whites.

Among many blacks, Murphy's analysis of the riot rang false. In the view of Kenneth Clark, it was not simply a "crime problem" or a community reaction to police brutality. It was, instead, the product of pathologies fed by the "disease of racism." Harlem residents, he contended in the *Herald Tribune*, "do not have the political or economic power to obtain even the most minimally adequate public services in housing, sanitation, health, police protection, and education." Poor schools, high unemployment, broken homes, drug use, and juvenile delinquency—these were the root causes of the civil unrest on Saturday night and Sunday morning. "Harlem is a community dominated by chronic frustration, stagnation, despair, and a pervading sense of powerlessness and hopelessness," Clark wrote. "The real danger of Harlem is not in the infrequent explosions of random lawlessness. The frightening horror of Harlem is the chronic day-to-day quiet violence to the human spirit which exists and is accepted as normal."[79]

Given the daily degradation Clark described, it was not surprising that many blacks—perhaps most—questioned the good faith of white people. At Harlem Hospital a cluster of bystanders watched the police bring the injured to the emergency room. "Butchers! Rotten butcher bastards!" they yelled. "You proud of yourself, white man?" The group celebrated when a stretcher bearing a white man went past. "He's white, he's white," someone cheered. "That's good! They got one!"[80]

The spectators temporarily dispersed after a barrel-chested black patrolman waved his club and confronted them. "I don't take —— from anyone—white, black, blue, or green," he shouted. "I've been on the job fourteen years. You're not going to tell me what to do. Now get the hell out of here." But most of the onlookers soon returned.[81]

On 125th Street, meanwhile, an older black veteran offered his view of events. "I fought the Japs in World War II who were my friends," said the stocky man with vehemence. "But I didn't know it then. This time we're fighting our enemy." The man then jabbed his finger at a white man and shouted, "You're no good. You never have been and you never will be."[82] On this Sunday in Central Harlem, peaceful reflection and quiet contemplation were hard to find outside the houses of worship.

CHAPTER 5

THIS MOST MARVELOUS CITY

Barricades sadly were risin'
Bricks were heavily flyin'
And the loudspeaker drowned like a whisperin' sound
When compared to the angered emotions
—Phil Ochs, "In the Heat of the Summer"

SUNDAY, JULY 19

By 8 P.M. on Sunday evening more than one thousand people lined both sides of Seventh Avenue outside the Levy and Delany Funeral Home at 132nd Street. Inside around one hundred mourners listened to the Reverend Theodore Kerrison of St. Augustine Baptist Church deliver an understated eulogy for James Powell. "Death has to come to us all sooner or later," he observed. He then began to recite the Twenty-third Psalm. "Though I walk through the valley of the shadow of death, I will fear no evil," the reverend intoned as the crash of broken bottles and the crackle of gunshots pierced the air.[1]

Sobbing, Annie Powell was led from the funeral parlor to a waiting automobile. As she departed, a sound truck arrived in front and Bayard Rustin, the influential behind-the-scenes organizer of the March on Washington in August 1963 and the New York school boycott in February 1964, climbed aboard and began to address the agitated crowd.[2]

"I urge you to go home," Rustin said. "We know there has been an injustice done. The thing we need to do most is respect this woman, whose son was shot." From the street came cries of "Uncle Tom. Uncle Tom." Rustin, a pacifist who possessed an absolute commitment to nonviolence, was calm and steadfast. "I'm prepared to be a Tom if it's the only way I can save women and children from being shot down in the street," he replied, "and if you're not willing to do the same, you're fools."[3]

A cascade of boos descended upon Rustin, who in tears soon abandoned the sound truck to seek medical attention for a youth whose clothes were splattered in blood. The man who had orchestrated a peaceful demonstration of a quarter million at the Lincoln Memorial less than a year earlier could not convince a few hundred Harlem residents to follow his direction now. The dramatic moment was a symbolic showdown between two versions of the freedom struggle, two visions of social protest. It was also a clear sign of the changing times and different generations within the civil rights movement as it faced the complex and entrenched challenge of northern racism and segregation.[4]

"We want Malcolm X," chanted the crowd in the face of the police. "We want Malcolm X." But he was at the Organization of African Unity conference. "There are probably more armed Negroes in Harlem than in any other spot on earth," commented Malcolm X from Cairo. "If the people who are armed get involved in this, you can bet they'll really have something on their hands."[5]

Back in April, in front of a white audience in New York, Malcolm X had predicted that "1964 will be America's hottest year; her hottest year yet; a year of much racial violence and much racial bloodshed." Unlike in the past, both blacks and whites would suffer. "So far only the Negroes have shed blood," he warned. "White blood has to be shed before the white man will consider the conflict a bloody one."[6]

Malcolm X would probably not have encouraged the uprising—he loved Harlem too much to want to see it devastated—but his rhetoric certainly caused tempers to rise. At the same time, it is doubtful that Malcolm X could have halted the riot or would even have tried, as some suggested, although he considered it self-destructive and suicidal. "Black people didn't start the riot and they don't have any obligation to stop it," he told his friend and attorney, Percy Sutton, the next day. "It's bad destroying our own community because someday we should own it. But I don't advise you go get on the tops of any [sound] trucks. I wouldn't if I were there. Angry people don't know who their friends are. And if I were there, I'd be doing the same thing."[7]

Such comments angered CORE executive director James Farmer, who like Rustin was a proponent of integration and nonviolent civil disobedience. "[Malcolm X] was lucky that he was not there at the time," Farmer reflected later. "Had he been in the country then, he would have had the awful dilemma of putting up or shutting up. He'd have been talking violence and guys [would've] said, 'OK, here we are now, tell us what to do. Join us.' He'd just have to keep quiet, or he would be telling them to 'shit or get off the pot.'"[8] The CORE leader was understandably annoyed, if not bitter, because he had already tried in vain to stop the riot on Saturday night and faced a similar dilemma on Sunday afternoon.

Now the unrest and violence were resuming as darkness fell. To disperse the crowds pouring from behind the barricades, three busloads of TPF officers charged with nightsticks held high. Nearby, police intercepted more than a hundred black youths who were headed for the funeral home. Many were carrying pieces of lumber scavenged from construction sites, but they scattered after a brief confrontation with a black sergeant. Soon the streets of Central Harlem were again filled with the sight of bricks and bottles, police batons, and Molotov cocktails. "Die, you dirty white bastards," screamed a black woman at white officers after a near miss from the fourteenth floor. "I hope you all get killed." Gunshots reverberated as the police once more tried to suppress the aerial barrage by firing at the tenement rooftops.[9]

The riot had resumed. "At the sound of the shots, Seventh Avenue began to look like a town under siege," wrote a reporter who was told to seek shelter in a church doorway. "People raced in every direction, scurried into hallways, shouted, screamed. Police crouched against buildings and spread-eagled themselves on the mall grass." By Monday morning the official toll was another twenty-seven policemen and ninety-three civilians injured, although area hospitals reported treating more than two hundred. Thankfully, there were no more fatalities, at least according to the NYPD, but another 108 individuals were arrested while forty-five more stores were damaged or looted.[10] If the fires of rage and fury were subsiding, it was difficult to tell.

Earlier, on Sunday afternoon, merchants had taken stock of the toll inflicted in property damage and lost merchandise. Of the twenty-three businesses looted or ransacked on Saturday night, sixteen were on Lenox Avenue—and the block between 126th and 127th was perhaps the hardest hit, with only one of four small markets left untouched. "We just kept all the lights on and stayed open all night," explained a clerk. "Looters won't come in when you're open."[11]

But as Sam Zaben, the owner of Paul's Supermarket, which had closed at 9 P.M., waded through aisles littered with canned foods, broken eggs, and meat packages, he tried to assess the costs. The looters also took $300 in cash from the cash registers that he usually left open because they cost $3,000 apiece and he did not want them destroyed. "I don't think they were trying to do anything to me," Zaben mused. "This thing just got hot and we got caught in the switches. I've been in Harlem 27 years and I've never had a cross word with my customers."[12]

Possibly Zaben was naive and had little sense of how his customers viewed him. More likely, the looters chose his store for other reasons, such as ease of access, and were not his regular customers, since only a tiny fraction of Harlem residents had directly participated in the riot. Normally, he spent Sundays (his only time away from work) at his home in Rego Park, Queens, but he came right to the market when his brother called in the morning. "Someone, either me or my son, will have to stay here tonight," Zaben said. "With the window open they can just walk right in if there is more trouble."[13]

As merchants swept the broken glass from the sidewalks, the owner of the B&B Grocery on the other side of the same block noted that the looters had largely ignored his food items. But they had, he calculated, taken two hundred cartons of cigarettes, fifty to seventy-five cases of beer, and $2,000 in cash.[14] Now he would most likely have to absorb some of the loss, pay higher insurance premiums, and pass on much of the costs to his customers, most of whom had probably chosen not to join the looting. In the end, they would have to pay even higher prices, assuming that the businesses elected to reopen, which was not always the case. Often it was not clear who the true victims of the looting were.

But at City Hall the acting mayor was clear about what he believed was at stake in Harlem. "This most marvelous city in the world could be a shambles almost overnight without law and order," said City Council President Paul Screvane in a prepared statement. "It is the basis of survival, and nowhere more so than in New York City. Those with even the least stake in our society have a stake in law and order."[15]

Screvane stressed that he was in close contact with Commissioner Murphy and Mayor Wagner, who remained in Spain. "The nation and the world are watching us to see whether we have both the flexibility and the firmness to deal with our internal problems," Screvane declared. "Let no one deliberately strike a hole in the dike of peace and order which protects us all."[16] The hopeful sentiment was widely shared by most whites and blacks, although many in Harlem were dubious.

Among them was Farmer, who remained deeply disturbed by what he had experienced on Harlem's streets Saturday night. At 2:45 P.M. he made an appearance on the WABC-TV program *Page One*, which was broadcast live. On the air Farmer, who seemed physically exhausted and emotionally distraught, made a series of inflammatory statements, which were out of character for him and perhaps a reflection of the pressures he faced within CORE. He demanded that the NYPD arrest Lieutenant Gilligan and charge him with murder because CORE had evidence "which we consider conclusive" that Powell had no knife when he was shot. He said that he had personally witnessed police officers "shooting into windows, into tenement houses, and into the Theresa Hotel." And Farmer claimed that they had also attacked innocent people after screaming "Let's get those niggers."[17]

Farmer added that "I saw a woman who walked up to the police and asked them for their assistance in getting a taxicab so that she might go home. This woman was shot in the groin and is now in Harlem Hospital." And he offered a graphic description of the racial unrest in New York and compared it to what he had experienced elsewhere: "I walked through the streets for four hours and saw the most nauseating demonstration of police malfeasance. It was an orgy of blood, violence, and sadism on the part of the police . . . I say with much sadness that I have not seen anything like this before, not even in Alabama or Mississippi."[18]

Reaction to Farmer's comments from police officials was swift and furious. At a special news conference, Deputy Commissioner Walter Arm assailed them as "in complete contradiction to the facts" and "dangerous and not a bit helpful." The woman in question, he asserted, was treated and released by Harlem Hospital after she had suffered a superficial wound when she was struck in the left thigh by a bullet that had ricocheted off the pavement. The department's top community relations specialist and a former reporter who had covered the 1935 Harlem Riot for the *Herald Tribune*, Arm vigorously defended the conduct of the police and denied reports that officers had used automatic weapons or rifles.[19]

The deputy commissioner also emphasized that Commissioner Murphy had remained on duty almost continuously since 4:30 A.M. except for a breakfast break and a church visit with his family. Arm further pledged that "force will be met with force" and held the "criminal element" responsible for the disorders. "The thousands of decent Negro law-abiding citizens in

FIGURE 7. James Farmer speaks to reporters outside the Hotel Theresa. Photo by Stanley Wolfson. Library of Congress, Prints and Photographs Division, New York World-Telegram & Sun Collection (LC-97519454).

Harlem are not to be blamed for the looting and the acts of violence," he said, adding that the damage in 1935 was far worse. "Could you imagine what would have happened to the poor, honest people of Harlem if the cops hadn't been around?" asked another police official.[20]

Less than thirty minutes after Arm spoke, Farmer convened an informal and impromptu press conference in front of the 28th Precinct. He said that if the police failed to stop brutalizing the people of Harlem, he would ask Governor Rockefeller, who remained on vacation in Wyoming, to deploy the National Guard. Farmer was not the only person imploring Albany to intervene.[21]

Whites in Upper Manhattan were also flooding the governor's office with desperate letters. In a typical appeal, a woman reported to Rockefeller that a large sign reading "Kill All Whites" marked the entrance to her subway station at 125th Street and Broadway. "Murderous assaults now take place even in daytime under protection of large gangs in the face of a more and more frightened citizenry," she wrote, along with a request that the governor take action since she could not go to work without fear of robbery or assault. The form letter that she received in response said that Rockefeller was closely monitoring developments, but that "primary responsibility for maintaining law and order in the situation rests with New York City authorities."[22]

Political leaders outside the city would repeatedly take that position in the days to come. At a briefing for reporters in Austin, Texas, on Sunday afternoon, White House Press Secretary George Reedy said that Lyndon Johnson was relaxing at his ranch, staying informed but not contemplating any federal action or intervention at the moment. "The President has made it clear that any time local authorities need help in keeping law and order we stand ready to help," said Reedy, offering the first indication of the intense interest recent events in New York would soon draw from the White House.[23]

But at his press conference Farmer demanded immediate assistance from Albany or Washington as the price for his efforts to calm Harlem. "I cannot make an appeal to the Negro community until I have something concrete to tell them," he stated. "At this point, I have not received any assurances from the police officers that this brutality will end."[24] Farmer's actions and statements drew national attention—but they also generated serious dissension within CORE, which was increasingly riven by disputes.

As the unrest in Harlem continued, white supporters of the freedom struggle questioned the leadership offered by the executive director. In the days and weeks after Farmer's comments appeared in print and on the air, letters poured into CORE headquarters expressing disappointment and anger with him. "How does it feel to be responsible for setting back the civil rights movement about 10 years?" asked a Pennsylvania man. "As an active supporter of Martin Luther King and his sit-ins, peaceful picketing, and orderly demonstrations *with purpose*, I can only view the past nights in New York as mass violence and unbridled savagery."[25]

The civil rights movement, wrote a CORE supporter from New Jersey, was "good and noble . . . in the eyes of men of good will and God." Surely police brutality was a major factor in Saturday's violence. "But why do you fail to admit in a frank and honest way that a segment of the Negro community did act in an uncivilized manner which can do nothing to help the cause of civil rights?" he asked. "Plundering liquor stores and pawn shops do not share in the noble aspect of storming the Bastille or Fort Ticonderoga." A Wisconsin member was equally blunt. "When a Negro is denied the ballot, and you defend him, I am with you," he wrote. "But when a Negro knifes a policeman, and you defend him, I wonder if you are not losing perspective." Nagging at the CORE letter writer was the conservative contention that rising crime and disorder were the result of black activism. "If this makes me one of the phony parlor liberals, so be it," he concluded. "I think we must draw the line when the demand for equal rights becomes a demand for special license to act irresponsibly."[26]

The Harlem Riot left Farmer at a personal and professional crossroads. Born in Texas in 1920, he was the grandson of a slave and the son of a demanding, self-made man who was reputedly the first African American to earn a doctorate in the state (he could read, write, and speak French and German as well as Hebrew, Greek, Aramaic, and Latin). Farmer himself was also gifted—by first grade he could read, write, and count. By age fourteen he had won a series of debate tournaments and earned a full scholarship to Wiley College, where he captained the debate team (the film *The Great Debaters* details his extraordinary success) and planned to become a doctor.[27]

But when Farmer learned that he could not stand the sight of blood, he enrolled in 1938 at Howard University's School of Religion, where he discovered Gandhi's ideas on nonviolent civil disobedience. A large man with precise diction and a commanding voice, he seemed like a natural for the pulpit. But again he veered from the chosen path, this time because southern Methodists accepted and enforced racial segregation. "I didn't see how I could honestly preach the Gospel of Christ in a church that practiced discrimination," he recalled.[28]

During World War II, Farmer became a conscientious objector and staff member of the Fellowship of Reconciliation (FOR), a pacifist organization. In 1942, he and a white friend were denied service when they tried to buy coffee and doughnuts at Jack Spratt's Coffee Shop on the South Side of Chicago. For Farmer, who had encountered segregation as a small child in Texas and a college student at Wiley, where he had to sit in the "buzzard's roost" at the local movie theater, it was the final straw. He and others organized a successful sit-in at Jack Spratt's and formed the Committee on Racial Equality, which later became the Congress of Racial Equality (CORE).[29]

A year later, Farmer moved east because "I thought that anyone who would cut wide, new swaths in the forest of American bigotry must hone his axe on the pavements of New York." Soon CORE had more than seventy chapters, and by the early 1960s it was the most integrated civil rights organization with more than eighty thousand white and black members. It was CORE that the students in Greensboro turned to after the first sit-ins in 1960; it was CORE that organized the Freedom Rides in 1961; and it was CORE that supplied the three student martyrs—Schwerner, Chaney, and Goodman—to the Mississippi "Freedom Summer" campaign in 1964.[30]

A tireless advocate of racial integration and interracial cooperation, Farmer became the executive director of CORE in 1961, shortly before the Freedom Rides, which he joined for the final leg from Montgomery to Jackson, where he spent forty days in jail for disturbing the peace. Two years later, he was almost killed when Louisiana state troopers armed with cattle prods, shotguns, and tear gas conducted door-to-door raids in the small town of Plaquemine, where he was organizing demonstrations. He escaped by "playing dead" in the back of a hearse that smuggled him out of town. Eventually he was again arrested and was behind bars when the March on Washington took place in August 1963. But Floyd McKissick, a fellow CORE member, read his speech for him. "We will not stop," Farmer wrote, "until the dogs stop biting us in the South and the rats stop biting us in the North."[31]

Within six months, however, CORE was in crisis—as were other civil rights organizations like the Student Nonviolent Coordinating Committee (SNCC)—as radicals and liberals clashed over the principles of nonviolence and integration as well as the question of what role, if any, whites should play in the movement. Other cleavages in CORE included the importance of community organization versus partisan politics and the authority of the national office versus the autonomy of local chapters like those in the Bronx and Brooklyn, which often failed or refused to clear or coordinate their actions with Farmer no matter how ill conceived. The chairman of Bronx CORE, for example, attempted with two other members to make a citizen's arrest of Mayor Wagner at City Hall; as a result, he spent five days in Bellevue Hospital undergoing mental observation. Brooklyn CORE launched the stall-in at the World's Fair despite Farmer's firm opposition.[32]

As executive director, Farmer found himself under fire from all directions. "Somebody has to walk the dangerous road," he told a reporter. "Somebody has to keep in contact with both the white middle classes and the Negro masses, knowing all too well that neither will be satisfied. . . . Neither understands the other's dilemma." As he later recalled, "I lived in two worlds." But by the spring of 1964 the CORE leader was trapped in the middle, struggling to walk a tightrope between different audiences who questioned his authority and credibility. "Farmer was not like King—he was not prepared to cross that mountain," recalled Fred Powledge. "He was a normal human being who didn't want to get killed." Perhaps that also helps explain the balancing act Farmer sought to strike between discouraging violence and encouraging resistance during the unrest in Harlem.[33]

On Sunday afternoon Farmer was not invited to address or attend the rally at Mount Morris Presbyterian Church on 122nd Street. But he could not ignore the blunt question scrawled in hand-drawn letters on the home-made flyer: "Is Harlem Mississippi?" Underneath the question was a series of statements: "THE POLICE MUST NOT BE PERMITTED TO TAKE THE LAW INTO THEIR OWN HANDS! Your Son, Daughter, Sister, Brother May be Next! HARLEM IS NOW AN ARMED CAMP!" The poster demanded the immediate resignation of Police Commissioner Michael Murphy and the indictment for murder of Lieutenant Thomas Gilligan. It also called for a true civilian review board and the removal of all "armed forces" from Harlem. And on behalf of the Community Council on Housing and the NAACP it invited everyone to come "ALL OUT FOR MASS RALLY."[34]

The rally was planned by Jesse Gray, a former member of the American Labor Party and a longtime community activist who was an advocate of tenants' rights and an organizer of rent strikes, including a successful pro-test in the winter and spring. A native of Louisiana, the youngest of ten children, he had a genuine gift for political theater and a healthy appetite for media attention. To protest public subsidies for the World's Fair in Queens, Gray had promoted the "World's Worst Fair" in Harlem in May. The sidewalk show featured grim photos of dilapidated housing and a per-sonal appearance by former heavyweight champion Joe Louis. "We don't need a World's Fair—We need a Fair World" was the theme of the event.[35]

Gray appeared at the Sunday rally at 4 P.M. with a swollen face, an eye patch, and a bandaged cheek—the result, he said, of a police beating on Saturday night. Before a crowd of four hundred, half of whom were Black Nationalists, he lambasted the NYPD, which he characterized as "99 percent white," fundamentally corrupt, and "deeply rooted with hatred and rac-ism." Gray alleged that "there is money in murder in Harlem" and charged that "graft is a concession for loyalty to the police from white merchants and other persons in the power structure." To a burst of applause he added that "we have one of the most corrupt, rotten police departments in this country. Murphy is nothing but a crumb-snatcher and a stooge for Mayor Wagner. Last night the police looked better than German Storm Troopers." The crowd roared with approval as Gray moved to a rhetorical climax.[36]

"We're about to witness in New York City what we have heard about in Mississippi," Gray declared. "Somebody has said the only thing that will solve the situation in Mississippi is guerrilla warfare. I'm beginning to wonder what will solve the problem here." From the excited audience came the desired cry: "Guerrilla warfare!" A week later, Gray would claim in a courtroom that he meant Mississippi only, not New York. But in the heat of the moment, he called for "a hundred skilled black revolutionaries who are ready to die." If each platoon captain recruited a hundred loyal followers, Gray declared, revolution was inevitable. "This city can be changed by 50,000 well-organized Negroes," he claimed as a young woman handed out blue cards for new volunteers. "They can determine what will happen in New York City."[37]

Gray added that if Powell had not died in Harlem, he would have died in Vietnam—a prescient comment given that the Gulf of Tonkin Incident, which President Johnson would use as a pretext to widen the conflict in Southeast Asia, would take place in two weeks. "We've got to decide whether they (young black men) die in Vietnam or the U.S.," he stated. "I'd rather it be in the U.S." Gray then called for a demonstration at the United Nations on Monday to see if it would intervene to halt "police terror" in the United States.[38]

"Let's bomb them," screamed a female voice. "Let's get bombs and destroy them." By now the crowd's bloodlust was fully aroused. "Before the day is over, we'll separate the boys from the men and the girls from the women," said Isaiah Robinson, leader of the Harlem Parents Committee, who argued that Patrick Henry was not charged with inciting a riot when he demanded liberty or death. "Stand up like men and die for democracy," he urged.[39]

The leader of Harlem CORE, Marshall England, followed Gray to the podium. With tears in his eyes and his voice cracking, he called for peaceful protest. "The Negro people must vote and organize," he said. As he left the stage he was showered with boos. "We are black men, not Negroes," shouted a man.[40]

Next came Edward Mills "Porkchop" Davis, a fifty-three-year-old street speaker and Black Nationalist, who calmed the audience by stressing the need for unity. "You are not going to solve the problem by an emotional outburst or by undirected violence," he said. Black veterans, he added, should share their knowledge of guerrilla warfare with the people. "If we must die," he ended in words that echoed Claude McKay in 1919, "let us die scientifically." Once again, the crowd responded with fervor and vehemence.[41]

As Farmer warily approached the podium, he was greeted with jeers and cries of "whites are not wanted." But he was a powerful orator and soon had the crowd with him. "I saw the white cops united against the black man," he said with passion as he called for the immediate arrest of Lieutenant Gilligan. "I saw the blood pouring off the heads of men and women. [James Powell] was my son and your son and every black mother's and father's son who died before that policeman's bullets."[42]

People jumped to their feet and shouted, "Let's go. What are we waiting for?" But Farmer stopped them with a raised hand. "If you go out of here, one running one way, one running another, it will be a slaughter," he said. "I am not ready to die. I want no Negro to die." Frustrated, the crowd grew restive. But Farmer regained their support when he repeated his televised claim that he had seen an officer deliberately draw his weapon and shoot a woman in the groin after she had asked him to help her hail a taxi.[43]

Percy Sutton, the Democratic candidate for State Assembly, was among the next group of speakers. A native of San Antonio, he was beaten at age thirteen for distributing NAACP flyers. During World War II, he served with the Tuskegee Airmen and became the first black to enter Army Air Corps Intelligence. He experienced firsthand the Harlem Riot of 1943 when he visited to court his future wife. "I had no sense of the depth of the revolution," he recalled. A year later, he was arrested for dining with a white colonel on board a train. After the war, he moved to New York and earned a degree from Brooklyn Law School. On Saturday night he was with a troop of Boy Scouts in New Jersey. On Sunday afternoon he delivered a plea for peace in a cool but strong voice.[44]

The final speaker was Bayard Rustin, who was booed loudly but stared the crowd into silence. "There is nobody in this room who cares more than I do that a young boy was shot down like an animal," he said in a calm, firm tone. "There is nobody that has gone to jail more often than I have." But violence was the wrong way to achieve peace and progress. "I want no human being to die or be brutalized," he said. To add to these "monstrous deeds is to make an animal of me as the police were animals."[45]

A wave of boos drove Rustin from the altar and as he stepped down a group of Black Nationalists approached him in a threatening manner. But CORE supporters formed a protective shield around him and escorted him from the church. As seventy-five members went to headquarters to prepare white armbands with CORE written in blue letters, Rustin briefed them on what he expected them to do. "I want volunteers to man a command post at 125th Street and Eighth Avenue tonight where we can deploy young men to help disperse teenagers and give protection to women and children who are on the street."[46]

For Rustin the rally was a sobering moment, a bitter clash that he had seen coming. In June, he had decided he would no longer debate Malcolm X in public, not when "the ballot or the bullet" was his constant refrain. "For just so long as he advocates rifle clubs and a mau-mau type movement, is anti-Semitic and anti-civil libertarian, he falls outside the civil rights movement as far as I am concerned," Rustin wrote in response to an invitation. "There is too much to be done on the grassroots level . . . for us to waste time with demagoguery, no matter how appealing it might be." In July, two days before the Powell shooting, he remarked to a friend that "Negroes have been put in a desperate situation and yet everyone—myself included—must urge them to behave not with desperation but politically and rationally."[47]

At the age of fifty-two Rustin remained a striking figure with piercing eyes, chiseled cheekbones, and a dense mass of salt-and-pepper hair. After decades of activism, he was widely respected as a political philosopher, movement tactician, and skilled organizer who was a master of detail and planning. Now, however, he was in a difficult if not impossible situation and he knew it. But he also believed that social progress could come only from social justice achieved through nonviolent protest.

After the rally, Rustin was incredulous. "He literally called on people directly and indirectly to use violence," he wrote of Gray to a friend. "Nobody in his right mind would have called for that kind of demonstration at the height of this conflict." When Rustin tried to lead a peaceful march with Farmer on Sunday night, he found himself "spat upon and insulted" by angry youths who "revolted in the only way left to them." Most were between the ages of eighteen and twenty-five, "the unemployed, the forgotten, the poorest of the poor—without hope and with no faith in

a society which has doomed them to utter despair," Rustin contended as
he journeyed to local playgrounds to tell some basketball players that a
local union had found jobs for them.[48]

Rustin was himself close to despair after walking the streets from dawn
to dusk for four consecutive nights. "I am frankly, terribly depressed," he
privately admitted to Whitney Young of the Urban League after Rustin's
largely futile effort to aid the injured, stop the violence, and protect the
innocent. But he continued to believe that he could change the course of
history. And Rustin publicly stressed that the Harlem Riot had only
strengthened his faith in nonviolence, even after he witnessed a white police
officer whom Rustin knew "beat a woman to the ground mercilessly" and
then attack him when he protested.[49]

The brutality by both races seemed to confirm the worst views of
human nature and deeply distressed Rustin, who also saw a black church-
woman rob a white taxi driver after her sons had "beaten him almost to
unconsciousness." He chose, however, to accentuate the positive rather
than the negative, to focus on the CORE members who had come to his
aid at the Gray rally rather than the Black Nationalists who had physically
threatened him. More than ever, Rustin maintained, he was committed to
peaceful protest because he had observed firsthand how "violence dehu-
manizes all who are caught-up in its whirlpool."[50]

Not everyone was trapped in the vortex of violence. While Jessie Gray
was advocating guerrilla warfare at Mount Morris Presbyterian Church,
another gathering that represented another side of Central Harlem was taking place at Union Baptist Church, which James Powell had attended with
his mother. Before one hundred mostly elderly women, Powell's aunt spoke
with tears streaming down her cheeks. Dressed in black for mourning, she
spoke of the pain her sister was experiencing. "I asked the kids if my
nephew had a knife and they said no," Marsh said. "He had a garbage pail
cover and was trying to protect himself. I don't know what it's going to do
to my sister. She's sick, and I don't know what it's going to do to her. . . .
Oh, Lord! What am I going to do?"[51] As murmurs of sympathy swept the
church, her question lingered in the air: What were most people in Central
Harlem going to do?

For journalists, black and white, the questions were different. Who was
going to report what happened and how would they do it? After the rally on
Sunday afternoon, three white *New York Times* journalists—photographers
Eddie Hausner and John Orris, joined by reporter Joseph Lelyveld—met at

FIGURE 8. James Powell's aunt breaks down in tears outside Union Baptist Church in Harlem. Photo by Marion S. Trikosko. Library of Congress, Prints and Photographs Division, U.S. News & World Report Magazine Collection (LC-U9-12259 frame 4).

the Hotel Theresa. Everything seemed calm, so they decided to walk up Seventh Avenue, which proved a mistake. Within a block an angry group of black teens had attacked them. Lelyveld broke free, but Hausner had his elbow bloodied and, despite shielding his body, took "a few solid kicks." Orris had the worst of it—he almost had his right eye dislodged from the socket before four black Housing Authority officers came to the rescue and managed to move him into a basement, where they called Harlem Hospital.[52]

For Lelyveld the experience was rife with ironies. On July 10, his father Arthur, a Cleveland rabbi, was hospitalized in Mississippi after white segregationists attacked and beat him with their fists and a lead pipe—and then received only suspended sentences. The elder Lelyveld was a volunteer with the "Freedom Summer" campaign and would later speak at the funerals in New York for Michael Schwerner and Andrew Goodman, who had disappeared on June 21 and whose bodies were found on August 4. Now the younger Lelyveld found himself under threat from a different side of the freedom struggle—on Lenox Avenue he ducked into a postal van seconds before a dozen bottles crashed into the sidewalk where he had stood.[53]

Even black reporters were not immune to the hostility of the crowds. Lester Carson, a reporter for the *World-Telegram and Sun*, heard the cries of "Uncle Tom" and opted not to display his press badge. Edward Cumberbatch of the *Post* at first kept his press badge in plain sight so that the police would know who he was. But then he made the same choice as Carson "so the rioters wouldn't know who I was." In print Cumberbatch was candid about his fear of stray bullets: "When hell broke I was scared. . . . And I didn't have a helmet."[54]

In the hours after the memorial service for James Powell on Sunday night, Central Harlem once more grew dark and dangerous, although the rioting and looting were more sporadic than on Saturday night. The parade of projectiles—bricks and rocks—again made helmets a necessity for officers, who resumed firing their revolvers in an attempt to clear the roof lines of tenement houses. And the barrage of bottles—whiskey, soda, and milk—continued.

But in general the community was quieter, in part because fewer residents were in the streets, whether to watch the action or participate in it. In part, too, it was because the NYPD was ready for the disorder. On Saturday night, the department was caught by surprise and hesitated to overreact. "It was the problem of trying to get the men in and also wondering where it would break out next—South Jamaica, the South Bronx, or Bedford-Stuyvesant," explained Commissioner Murphy. On Sunday night, the NYPD placed the entire twenty-five-thousand-man force—responsible for staffing eighty precincts and patrolling forty thousand city blocks—on twelve-hour shifts until further notice. Then it got the men in, flooding Central Harlem in advance with several hundred additional officers and providing better command and control once they were there.[55]

The Police Department also deployed helicopters from the Aviation Bureau to act as spotters for suspicious activities and persons on the roofs of Harlem's tenements. And it used motorcycle officers to block off the fifty-seven blocks of Central Harlem between 116th and 135th Streets,

Eighth and Lenox Avenues. The commissioner remained opposed, however, to the use of mounted police because he was convinced that horses were too vulnerable to projectiles from above.[56]

Meanwhile, the Transit Authority placed additional officers on Harlem trains and directed motormen not to stop at 125th Street, although regular service was restored at midnight. By then, however, almost all of the bars and restaurants in the area had voluntarily closed in an effort to calm the neighborhood and shrink the crowds, which had some effect. By 1:30 A.M. on Monday morning Harlem was largely peaceful and, according to an NYPD report, "improving very rapidly" despite isolated "groups of hoodlums . . . still roaming the streets." It was a considerable improvement over twenty-four hours earlier. But four more black men in their teens and twenties were in the hospital after policemen had shot them.[57]

The toll might have gone much higher if not for Rustin, who personally disposed of three cases of dynamite—enough to destroy a city block—after two young black men agreed to give it to him instead of using it. The amazing saga began at 10 P.M., when a stranger approached Rustin at the corner of 125th Street and Lenox Avenue and pointed out the men. Rustin went to them, promised them anonymity, and asked if they in fact had explosives. They took him to their basement apartment and showed him the dynamite. He told them that violence was not the solution and urged them to get rid of it. "You call yourself a leader," they said. "Let's do something."[58]

So Rustin led them to the 28th Precinct even though he was unsure what to do until he ran into Civil Court Judge James L. Watson, a former state senator and respected black official. Without mentioning the explosives, Rustin told him that it was urgent that he speak with Screvane. Persuaded, Watson placed a call to the acting mayor, who called the station house. Rustin informed him of the plot and of his plan to dispose of the dynamite (in case the police caught him with it). He even put one of the two young men on the line with Screvane, who promised to meet with Harlem leaders.[59]

Without informing Watson or the police, Rustin phoned a friend on Long Island for instructions on how to render the dynamite harmless. Then he borrowed a car and purchased some oil at a gasoline station. Next he returned with the two young men to their apartment, where they poured oil on the dynamite and placed it on newspapers in the floor of the car. Finally, Rustin drove to an undisclosed river at 2:30 A.M. and dumped the dangerous explosives into the murky waters. The lack of verifiable details made the story seem implausible. But when contacted by a reporter Watson said that a week after the incident Rustin had told him what he had done and the judge had spoken with Screvane, who confirmed the incredible account.[60]

Despite Rustin's efforts, the weekend's events left many youths in Harlem angry and resentful. Among them was a seventeen-year-old basketball sensation named Lew Alcindor (better known today as Kareem Abdul-Jabbar), already a two-time All-American at Power Memorial Academy. The son of a transit officer, he was born in Harlem in 1947 and lived on West 111th Street just north of Central Park, where he played as a baby. Three years later, he and his family moved to a city-owned, middle-class apartment in the Dyckman Street housing project in the Inwood section of Upper Manhattan. But in July 1964 Alcindor was part of a Harlem Youth Opportunities Unlimited (HARYOU) journalism workshop, whose office was in the basement of the 135th Street YMCA. Down the block was the Schomburg Center for Research in Black Culture, where he discovered Harlem's rich and exciting past.[61]

The present was more troubling for Alcindor, although Harlem remained a refuge for a sensitive and angry black student who felt isolated and out of place at a white parochial school. Part of his resentment flowed from the bombing of the 16th Street Baptist Church in Birmingham in September 1963. The death of the four little girls awaiting Sunday school hit him hard. "My faith was exploded like church rubble," he wrote in his memoir *Giant Steps*. "I would gladly have killed whoever killed those girls by myself."[62]

But Alcindor was also frustrated by the sense of exploitation he felt as he strolled the streets and browsed the shops of Harlem during the spring of 1964. "Who was gouging the neighborhood on groceries, clothing, and rent?" he asked. Then he answered his own question: "White people. Who controlled the jobs that these guys playing craps on the stoop couldn't get? And who was making money selling them wine? Landlords, storeowners, pawnbrokers—white people."[63]

On Saturday Alcindor went to the beach. "It was sticky, and the heat that I had picked up on the sand combined with the subway musk to bake me like a traveling calzone," he recalled. On his way home he stopped at 125th Street to buy records and look at shoes. "I poked my head out of the subway entrance and was faced with a firefight," he wrote. "There was smoke in the sky, fire around the corner. . . . Harlem was rioting, [which] scared the shit out of me."[64]

For a moment, Alcindor watched from the subway steps and then he ran. "I didn't stop until I was at 137th St. and Broadway," he remembered. "Anger wasn't new to me, nor was power, but I was burning without release. No amount of running would give those people control of that street—I knew that—and that made me angry. The fact that I understood, felt the impulse to put a brick through Woolworth's front window, didn't make me any less aware that it would not do any good. I knew cops shot kids, I knew the cops were white and more often than not the kids weren't."[65]

On Sunday Alcindor examined his feelings more closely. Even though the Powell killing was a tragedy, it was the "excuses, denials, explanations" of the police that cut the deepest. "It was not the death—that happened all the time, everybody had a friend who'd died—but the lie that was intolerable," he reflected. "It made all of Harlem face the fact that they didn't even have the strength to exact an acceptable apology. What else was there to do but go wild?" Yet those who wanted to avenge the shooting or repudiate the lie had little chance now. "The police were better prepared, given twenty-four hours warning, and injected with an element of pride—these niggers were trying to run their city, to abuse their regulations, to usurp their turf," he noted. "The fight was more than a simple order now, it became a personal challenge to each individual cop."[66]

After the riot, Alcindor and the other students in the journalism workshop produced a special issue, with an editorial blaming the police and articles that featured interviews with eyewitnesses. But he could not cleanse his heart of hate. He was often sullen and suspicious in the presence of whites, especially strangers, and he could not easily hide from the limelight (sportswriters had dubbed the high school junior, standing six feet ten inches, the "tower from Power"). A week later, Alcindor returned to Harlem and found that "the anger was still in the streets, but the nights were less fiery." City Hall had made promises and the black community had accepted them—for now. "It was hard to stare a dead end in the face; most people wanted to step back," he observed. "It was if the whole of Harlem was heaving after a fight."[67]

As Alcindor struggled to make sense of what had happened, he had plenty of company. At the *Herald Tribune*, a white columnist from Jamaica,

Queens, was also trying to sort his emotions and put into words what he had witnessed in Harlem on Sunday. "Here was the answer to all the talk and all the speeches and all the ignorance and all the history of this deep, vicious thing of black man and white man which they put down under the nice name of civil rights," wrote thirty-four-year-old Jimmy Breslin in a front-page column. And it had taken place in his hometown, not in a locale known for racism and segregation. "This was New York City you were in last night. It wasn't Mississippi or Alabama or any place else where these things are supposed to happen," he commented. "This is how far down we came in New York City last night. Civilization was gone. It was gone in a rash of guns and flying bottles, and kids screaming, 'We want Malcolm X. We want Malcolm X.'"[68]

Breslin saw police brutality and racial discrimination as serious and legitimate problems. He also had little sympathy for Republican nominee Barry Goldwater, who might profit politically from the riot because his "followers want to see this business of loving niggers come to a decent halt before it gets too far and something is done." But for Breslin the real issues in Harlem were the shortage of responsible black leadership and the surplus of angry young people who had run amok without proper supervision. "They were 14 or 15 or 18 or 21 and there were some adults with them," he wrote, "but age didn't matter because all of them were trying to hit a cop in the face with a bottle and, if they killed a cop, they would have cheered."[69]

Although the youths were not reflective of the community as a whole, they "wanted everything they got" in Breslin's words and "represented the part of Harlem that couldn't wait for trouble with white police." Or, for that matter, white people in general—the columnist had his own encounter with a vengeful teenager when his car was blocked on a side street in Harlem. Even though a firefighter with an axe was only a few feet away, the black youth told Breslin that he wanted to stick a knife "in your fat, white belly."[70]

NAACP leader Roy Wilkins shared Breslin's concern about Harlem's youth and the potential impact of their actions on the presidential campaign. "I don't care how angry the Negroes are," Wilkins argued from his comfortable vantage point at the Rockefeller family ranch in Wyoming. "For the sake of the city and its people and getting to a solution to see that this kind of thing doesn't happen again, we've all got to keep our heads. We can't leave it to the bottle-droppers and rock-throwers."[71]

As the most traumatic weekend in recent New York history came to a close, Wilkins knew that he and other moderate leaders, black and white, would have to take immediate and effective action in the coming days or risk potentially devastating political consequences for the White House and the freedom struggle.

CHAPTER 6

HEAT AND DIRT, ANGER AND FURY

> On and on come the angry
> No longer following reason
> And all the stores were the target now
> Where just the other day they were buyin'
> —Phil Ochs, "In the Heat of the Summer"

MONDAY, JULY 20

The question seemed to catch Arizona Senator Barry Goldwater by surprise. At an impromptu press conference held at Chicago's O'Hare International Airport during a refueling stop on the way from Phoenix to Washington, reporter Edward Folliard of the *Washington Post* asked if the Republican candidate was willing to make a joint appeal with President Lyndon Johnson to reduce racial discord on the campaign trail and in America's cities. In his informal style Goldwater, who had earlier stated that he had "no pat answer" for the strife in Harlem, called it "a very good idea" and said that he would "welcome the chance" to meet with the president so that nothing "we or our associates might say in words should add to the feeling of tension that exists today."[1]

It was Monday morning, and after two nights of racial unrest the political fallout from the Harlem Riot had now moved far beyond New York. The pressing issue now was whether the Johnson administration could contain it.

In public, the White House responded positively to the Goldwater offer. Press Secretary George Reedy quickly said that Johnson was also open to the idea. "Certainly as a man who has asked for observance of the civil rights law and has signed the law and who is implementing the law, the President would not do anything to incite or inflame tensions," he stated. Twice he declared that Johnson would give Goldwater's proposal for a summit meeting "serious consideration." But Reedy cautiously added that he could not give a direct answer as to whether the president would meet one-on-one with his challenger until the White House had received a formal invitation from the senator's campaign.[2]

The hesitation was because the political stakes were so high. At the moment, Johnson was far ahead in the polls and seemingly had little to gain from a face-to-face summit with Goldwater, who might use it to improve his stature and shed his image as an extremist. But declining the meeting might cause large numbers of white Democrats to switch parties or, more likely, not vote at all. The bottom line: the administration had to handle the sensitive offer with extreme care.

"We wouldn't carry a state in the South if the vote was tomorrow," Johnson anxiously informed Reedy by telephone on Monday evening. He added that he wanted the press secretary to "assure everybody that we're not going to do anything to incite anybody," but work hard to "give the impression that [Goldwater] is, without saying so."[3] It was a delicate situation and the president knew it. Both he and his aides were also deeply skeptical and suspicious of the senator's motivations and intent.

In private, the White House was divided over the proper response to Goldwater's invitation. Ignore it, advised Bill Moyers, Richard Goodwin, and Jack Valenti, because if the meeting failed to produce an agreement Goldwater could claim that "Johnson failed to agree because he knows he has to have the Negro vote." A summit between the two candidates would also make the senator appear more statesmanlike. Above all, a private meeting would create the impression that real matters of political principle were not at stake, cautioned the aides, and suggest that we doubt "whether he will really take a racist tack in the campaign even though we know perfectly well that is the heart of his hopes for the Presidency. He can win on the race issue, yet we will be giving him camouflage for just the kind of campaign he intends to run."[4]

But another staffer focused on the political risks of declining the senator's offer. "I hate to think of the backlash from a 'No,'" wrote Horace Busby, who contended that the Republicans "would be screaming that the Kennedy-Johnson people will talk to Communists . . . but won't talk to Goldwater about keeping peace in the streets." On that issue, Busby feared, the president and the party were vulnerable. "You, not Goldwater, are tagged as the candidate hoping to benefit from racial exploitation," he warned. "The GOP thus is able to plead 'clean hands' and to ascribe every CORE picket ruckus to the Democratic Party."[5] The White House was trapped between two undesirable options.

At the same time, Johnson was under intense pressure from conservatives in Congress and the South to intervene in Harlem with force if necessary. The mayor of Notasulga, Alabama, for example, urged him to send troops "to protect the lives and property of the white minority in the area" and to reassure his white constituents, who were "greatly alarmed at the apparent breakdown of law and order" in New York. He added pointedly that the president had placed several thousand soldiers in his city back in February, when the mayor had defied a federal court order by physically trying to prevent six black students from integrating a local high school.[6]

Johnson was acutely sensitive to the supposed double standard regarding federal intervention in the South and the North. "Everybody thinks . . . that if we denounce the killings in Mississippi . . . we ought to denounce it in Harlem too," he told Reedy. "And we haven't done a damn thing about it."[7] Accordingly, the president agreed to a private meeting with Goldwater on the date (Friday, July 24) and in the place (the White House) of his choosing. The challenge in the meantime was to end the racial unrest in New York, which would not prove simple or easy.

On Monday morning, Annie Powell arrived at the Levy and Delaney Funeral Home, the site of clashes between the police and protesters the night before. "My baby, my baby, oh my God, I want to see my baby," she cried as two men escorted her into the building at 9 A.M. A quiet crowd of a hundred or so watched as a police helicopter hovered in the sky above, scanning the rooftops of Seventh Avenue for potential trouble. After a few minutes Powell left the funeral home and climbed into a limousine.[8]

The crowd remained silent until six men carrying the gray coffin of James Powell emerged. As a white photographer moved into position to take a picture, a black teenager shouted at and shoved him. An older man and woman pulled her back as the police started to approach. "For shame, for shame," said a woman. "You devils! You devils!" bellowed a man who shook his fist at the officers. But the solemnity of the scene acted as a restraint and there was no violence.[9]

An hour later, on a bright and sunny day, James Powell was buried on a grassy hill at Ferncliff Cemetery in Hartsdale, New York. The coffin was placed in the same grave as his father, Harold, who had died in 1961. The brief service was led by the Reverend Theodore Kerrison of St. Augustine Baptist Church, who had presided at the memorial on Sunday evening. But his words failed to console Annie Powell, who remained bereft despite the support of family and friends. "Harold, Harold, look how they've sent you my baby," she wept as fifteen fellow mourners and seven police officers from Westchester County (three of them African American) bore witness to her pain and sorrow.[10]

As James Powell was laid to rest, merchants in Harlem continued to assess the damage to their businesses from the weekend. With forty-five stores looted or vandalized, the impact was extensive and expensive. On Eighth Avenue at 131st Street, the A&P supermarket was heavily damaged—to replace the plate glass window in the front would alone cost more than $15,000. "This is what a Molotov cocktail did," said the manager, pointing to a charred portion of the linoleum floor. "We wouldn't have a store here today if the police had not been alert and extinguished the flames with grapefruit juice taken from the shelves." It was, the manager added, "the best use we've discovered for grapefruit juice since I've been in the business." He also insisted, perhaps naively, that those responsible for the vandalism were "winos and junkies"—not his regular customers who lived in the St. Nicholas Housing Project across the street. "I've been manager here for seventeen months," he said in a refrain heard often in coming days, "and this is the first trouble we've had."[11]

The trouble seemed to center on corner bars, pawn shops, clothing stores, dry cleaners, and supermarkets—which over a decade would largely disappear from Harlem. On Lenox Avenue at 130th Street another A&P was vandalized, as was the Spotless Store, a dry-cleaning business. "The only thing I regret is that they broke into the cleaners and took the clothes," said a young man who was watching black handymen repair doors, windows, and interiors. "They are just harming our people who live in this neighborhood when they do that. I don't care about the bar. It's owned by 'whitey' anyway." Many residents in Central Harlem shared his view, but almost all of the white-owned businesses targeted by looters employed at least a few African Americans, including some in supervisory or managerial positions, who now faced an uncertain future.[12]

Most of the white merchants had acquired their businesses thirty or forty years before, when Harlem was more diverse and less contentious. Now they were ready to sell but could not because few whites wanted to buy and most blacks lacked sufficient cash or could not qualify for bank loans. "I tell you what they ought to do," said a store owner who was so eager to relocate that he was willing to take a loss on his property. "They ought to take all that Federal money coming in to Harlem and buy all the small stores. Then give them to Harlem. Let them hold all the demonstrations they want." Fear of more crime and disorder was also widespread among the merchants. "If they bust Gilligan [the officer who shot Powell] no cop up here is worth 10 cents," said another owner who declined, like all of those interviewed, to give his name out of concern for retaliation.[13]

The tensions were growing. A Jewish merchant described how a Black Nationalist had visited his store and pointed to the black teen who worked for him. "White man, see that girl there?" he had asked. "In five years she will own the store and you will be sweeping." The owner was unfazed. "So I told him they wouldn't have to wait five years, that I have always done the sweeping here and I will still do it," he recounted. "I told him as a Jewish man that we have had troubles, too, but that you people want to start at the top, and we are willing to start at the bottom."[14]

The brief and pointed exchange, with the phrase "you people" lingering in the steamy air, reflected a long history of conflict and misunderstanding between blacks and Jews in Harlem. It was also indicative of the deeper problems that would remain even after the current violence had subsided.

While the cleanup continued in Harlem, Paul Screvane (the acting mayor) and Michael Murphy (the police commissioner) were conducting all-day meetings at City Hall with various groups of civil rights leaders and activists, including Percy Sutton, James Farmer, Madison Jones, and Cleveland Robinson of the City Commission on Human Rights, the Reverend Eugene Callender of the NAACP, and Joseph Overton of the National Negro American Labor Council. Screvane was optimistic that open dialogue would lead to constructive results. "I believe, the way Mayor Wagner believes, that as long as people can sit down and discuss the problems, something can be worked out," he said on Sunday night. "It is to be expected that irresponsible elements would take advantage of the situation to stir up race hatred among our citizens, just as lawless elements under cover of the turmoil . . . looted and robbed innocent citizens and merchants." But he was "confident that cooler heads will prevail" and stated that he had kept in close touch with the mayor, who remained on vacation in Spain and still planned to attend the conference in Geneva.[15]

After Monday afternoon was relatively calm and peaceful, a hopeful Screvane stated that "all those with whom we met today spoke with one voice in regretting the spilling of blood and the infliction of injury upon police and civilians alike in an outbreak which is projected to the world as reflecting shame and discredit on New York City and the United States." It was an open acknowledgment that the unrest in Harlem had become front-page news across the nation and around the world. A Swedish journalist claimed that he saw police officers "shooting to kill, not to scare" and a British reporter wrote that "now there is just heat and dirt, anger and fury in Harlem." Photos of the riot appeared on the front pages of newspapers in Paris, London, and other European cities.[16]

The civil unrest had major implications in the Cold War propaganda battle for the hearts and minds of Africans, Asians, and Latinos. In Moscow, the headline in *Izvestia*, the Soviet organ, read "Harlem Drenched in Blood." The article described the community as resembling a "newly occupied enemy city" and linked the racial violence to Goldwater's extremism. A political cartoon in the *Daily News* depicted Soviet leader Nikita Khrushchev dancing with a newspaper whose headline read "New Riots in Harlem." The caption was "Happy Days!" But not for the White House, which feared lasting damage to the nation's image, or City Hall, which feared major harm to the tourist trade.[17]

The only beneficiaries of the unrest in Harlem, according to Screvane, were "racists and demagogues." Expressing faith in the Police Department and vowing to maintain law and order, he announced a five-point program intended to bring a halt to the violence. Two concerned community relations. First, City Hall pledged to expand "channels of communication" between minority groups and municipal government by expanding existing opportunities for community input and feedback at various social service agencies already located in black neighborhoods. Second, the police commissioner, who had reportedly received several telephone death threats, agreed to establish and head a "community affairs committee" that would meet regularly with Harlem activists. Neither recommendation was particularly controversial—but neither seemed likely to accomplish a great deal or satisfy a great many.[18]

Two other points in the Screvane program dealt directly with the Police Department, which promised to withdraw many of the white officers deployed to Harlem on Saturday and Sunday. "The stationing of so many policemen in Harlem inflames the people," said the Reverend Joseph H. May of Mount Carmel Baptist Church. "This is not Commissioner Murphy's fortress." The NYPD also pledged to hire more black patrolmen (about seventeen hundred of the twenty-six-thousand-man force were African American) and reassign more of them to the 28th and 32nd Precincts in Central Harlem.[19]

Murphy remained committed, however, to the ideal—or illusion—of the Police Department as an integrated institution. He was adamant that the assignments would be temporary and that race would not be the determining factor. "We don't make assignments by race," he snapped. "They'll be serving a special purpose up there, just as if we were to assign Spanish-speaking police to do a special job."[20] For black officers, the unrest in Harlem certainly posed a special challenge.

Many patrolmen, especially veterans who had joined the force in the 1940s and 1950s, had a strong sense of professional duty. "We're cops first," said an older officer. "We're proud of it and we'll do our jobs as cops come what may." Blue not black—that was often how critics described them and they saw themselves. But the reality was more complicated for younger officers who had joined the NYPD in the 1960s. In their eyes, they had dual identities that merged and shifted depending on the moment. "I become a different person," said a twenty-four-year-old officer who added that he might have become an electrician if a union had accepted him. "I become—or try to become—impartial. I demand respect for the uniform I'm wearing, and yet when I take it off, I know I feel different than when I have it on. I feel more Negro."[21]

Black officers often chose to join the Police Department out of a desire to serve the community. But overnight it had seemed to turn on them. In front of the Levy & Delany Funeral Home on Sunday night, Captain Lloyd Sealy and Lieutenant Robert Johnson had received special attention from the jeering crowds. "Look at those Uncle Toms," said a young man leaning against a wooden barricade. "Whitey can always get some of us to do his dirty work," replied an older man in disgust. Both policemen—close friends who had joined the NYPD in the 1940s—could hear the remarks aimed at them, but they kept their cool during their second straight night of extended duty under the most difficult of circumstances. On Monday night, they would face more of the same.[22]

A sense of pride also motivated many black officers. But the turmoil and taunts in the streets took a toll on their self-esteem. "I took this job because I didn't want to be ashamed of myself," said a twenty-six-year-old patrolman named Frank (no officers wanted to give their full names or speak on the record) who had served for three years at the precinct house on West 123rd Street. "Before, being a police officer was something nice. Now the people out there want to make you feel ashamed. They make you feel like a bum."[23]

A handsome, muscular man with a short mustache and cropped hair, Frank winced when asked how it felt to pull his revolver on a large crowd of young blacks. "It's a damn thing. A stinking thing," he said. "You know the frustration and how all of it is built up. And you know what happens when Malcolm X and the other rabble rousers start to heckle them up. But somebody said a cop's got a tough skin or he ain't a cop." Yet Frank also contended that his special knowledge and understanding of Central Harlem gave him a deeper empathy for black residents, which in turn made him better able to patrol the area. "I lived in Harlem," he said. "I know the community. I know things you just can't learn in schools."[24]

Another officer stressed the enormous value of shared experience. When he was with black friends in Harlem he never let the white officers who sometimes hassled them "know I'm a cop too. I'm just a Negro in the street then, and I know how it feels." A fellow patrolman put it in different terms. "We're needed in Harlem," he said. "We can talk to the people, our people. They don't fear us in the same way they fear the white boys—and their fear is a real fear whether or not there's a valid reason for it." Of course, there was a reason for it—the possibility or perception of police brutality, which often caused Harlem residents to view a white officer with trepidation and hear what a black officer described as "this little edge to the white cop's voice when he says, 'Break it up.'"[25]

At times the mere presence of a black face in a blue uniform calmed tensions. "We don't infuriate each other," observed another patrolman. "There's a natural line of communication that can span the gulf between the uniform and the sport shirt." It was not always the case, however, according to a third officer. "It is a little difficult when I arrest some of these kids in the neighborhood," he admitted, "because I see a lot of me in them. And sometimes, when I'm with a few white cops making an arrest, I catch some of these Negro kids looking at me, they keep looking and seem to say, 'Help me get out of this,' or sometimes they get mad and whisper, 'Hey nigger cop, don't you know you're only enforcing the white man's rule?'"[26]

Despite their differences, all of the black officers wanted to see Central Harlem patrolled by more African Americans. The veterans were anxious to return to the practices of the 1940s and 1950s, when a platoon of sixty to seventy policemen on a tour of duty might contain twenty to thirty black officers. In principle, they maintained, it was a good idea to desegregate every precinct, but not in practice. "I don't think any of us as cops or citizens opposes integration," said a patrolman to George Barner of the *Amsterdam News*. "Our feeling . . . is simply that in terms of the situation in Harlem and New York, it would have been more useful, more meaningful and safer to have kept a substantial body of Negro officers in Harlem than to accomplish what is at best a token integration." He and others also objected to the politicization of the issue. "Now, suddenly, there's a howl that we should be brought back," he noted. "We sometimes feel as though we are being used as pawns at the willy-nilly whim of somebody calling himself a leader."[27]

Barner, a Harlem native and Korean War veteran who was thirty-three at the time, recalled decades later the black officers that he had known. Under difficult if not impossible circumstances they had done their personal and professional best to serve the residents, most of whom viewed the policemen with favor even after the riot. "They were intelligent, mature, dedicated officers who were race men in the best sense of the word," he said. "They were prepared to bring the weight of their common sense, their experience, and their understanding of their sworn duty" to protect and defend "the citizens of Harlem who were not engaging in criminal acts."[28]

As Screvane tried to fulfill his sworn duty in July 1964, the most important and contentious element of his five-point program was the city's assurance that it would undertake a comprehensive study of the current system of handling citizen complaints of police brutality. Since 1954 the civilian complaint review board, which consisted of three deputy police commissioners, had handled under two hundred cases a year on average and found 90 percent of them unsubstantiated. Now the possibility of a true civilian review board not under the control or influence of the Police Department was on the table for discussion and already on the legislative roll of the City Council in the form of the Weiss bill.[29]

Throughout the day, bipartisan support for such a measure, which backers believed might have prevented or limited the looting and rioting, appeared from various groups and quarters. In Washington, Republican Senator Jacob Javits issued a statement in favor of a new review board with at minimum a majority of civilians as members; in Manhattan, the New York County Democratic executive committee (better known as Tammany Hall) also voted unanimously to ask Mayor Wagner to establish an independent board by executive order. The Police Community Relations Board of East Harlem and the Social Action Committee of Grace Congregational Church both urged the City Council to convene a special meeting to enact the Weiss bill, which gained the endorsement of radical organizations like the Workers Defense League as well.[30]

The groundswell of support from liberal-left groups was reflected in the pages of the New York Times, which approved of the appointment of one or two civilians to the existing board as an intermediate measure that might improve relations between the Police Department and the black community. But it opposed the immediate suspension of Lieutenant Gilligan, asserting that he was "entitled to the same presumption of innocence as any other citizen." Above all, the newspaper stated that "it is as unjust to blame all policemen for the possible misdeeds of a few as it is to blame all Negroes or all whites for the crimes of some of their number."[31]

The New York Post also stated that "indiscriminate cop-hating is a sickness." It conceded that civilian oversight would not "accomplish overnight miracles," but argued that an independent review board was an essential and overdue first step. "Too many citizens—and newspapers—have contended too long that such a civilian body would impose undue curbs on the police in the war against hoodlumism," the editorial asserted. "Now the nightstick brigade has received its ugly answer. Unbridled force is no solution to the problems of our city; a sense of oppression and injustice can turn even peaceful citizens into hell-raisers, create a playground for demagogues of many varieties, and subject the most innocent policemen to harassment by angry protesters."[32]

Leading the "nightstick brigade" was the conservative Daily News, a staunch opponent of any changes to the existing board. Under the headline "Kibitzer Council" it declared that the acting mayor should "draw the line" at a new review board. "This notion is backed by 'liberals,' bleeding hearts, and the Communist publication calling itself The Worker," the newspaper proclaimed. "These specimens hope to load such a board with looters, Communists, and other troublemakers." They in turn would seek to handcuff the NYPD as it sought to prevent more unrest and disorder. Next to the editorial was a cartoon with hands labeled "Proposed Civilian Council" about to grab hands labeled "NY

Police" as they attempted to corral still another set of hands labeled "Crime." The title read: "Would-Be Interloper."[33]

The most impassioned voice in favor of a civilian oversight was the *Amsterdam News*, which had a circulation of almost sixty thousand readers. In a front-page editorial it asked, "Does anybody believe that a panel of top white police officers is going to find Lt. Thomas Gilligan guilty of homicide or manslaughter or any other serious offense in the death of this 15-year-old Negro whom he shot and killed? Nobody in Harlem does." The newspaper denounced "the irresponsible people who elected to take the law into their own hands." But it expressed understanding of their actions: "At the seat of this trouble is the strong public feeling that no matter what a policeman does to a Harlemite, no matter how brutal [sic] a policeman may treat a citizen of Harlem . . . any charge against that policeman will be whitewashed by a board of review on which there sits no one else but policemen." The *Amsterdam News* demanded the immediate suspension of Gilligan and the creation of a board composed of upstanding citizens who will "judge the rights of a man on the receiving end of a nightstick by the same yardstick it judges the policeman who wields it."[34]

The fervent plea was echoed by Farmer, who shortly after meeting with Screvane issued his own four-point agenda. In addition to demanding a higher percentage of black officers in Central Harlem, the CORE leader called for the immediate suspension and arrest of Lieutenant Gilligan, who he claimed was undergoing treatment at a Veterans' Administration mental institution (in fact, although the officer received a $77 per month pension from the military for a service-related disability, he was at home on sick leave with a hand injury as a result of his altercation with Powell); the immediate creation of an independent review board; and the immediate return of Mayor Wagner to New York.[35]

In response to further rioting, the acting mayor agreed to expedite the investigation of the officer and send his case to the grand jury the next day. But that was not enough for Farmer, who called Screvane's program and concession "too little too late." They were, he added, "welcome but inadequate in this moment of crisis." At a press conference later, a tired and sweaty Farmer was asked whether the actions he advocated against Gilligan might lead to widespread retirements from the police force. "If there are mass resignations," he quipped, "there should be a massive recruitment drive."[36]

Other black activists felt the Screvane program failed to address the underlying causes of the racial unrest. Cleveland Robinson of the City Commission on Human Rights emphasized that the problems of Harlem were "not just the question of police brutality but the whole social structure—housing, education, lack of jobs." The prevalence of street crime and police corruption added fuel to the flames. "Part of the reason why in Harlem there is such disdain for law and order is the high crime rate and the number of unsolved crimes—numbers, prostitution, dope peddling— going on under the noses of the police," he asserted. "There is a feeling that Harlem is a lucrative field for police who are paid off and who do not pay attention to crime." Robinson concluded that it was "not the time for street rallies and open demonstrations" because so many of the lawless were leaderless and beyond the control of individuals or organizations.[37]

From his vantage point in Los Angeles, labor leader A. Philip Randolph, a Harlem resident for fifty years, agreed with Robinson that it was necessary to curtail more protests, primarily because of the political impact they might have on the presidential campaign. "Violence and bloodshed is not the remedy," he asserted. "It will destroy our community and set back the Negro cause. It only plays into the hands of our enemies." In particular, it could make Goldwater president, "which would be the greatest disaster to befall Negroes since slavery." Because the Civil Rights Act was now the law of the land, Randolph argued, "let us declare a moratorium on demonstrations and peacefully test it and work for its enforcement."[38] The proposal came as a result of conversations with Bayard Rustin, who had relayed to his patron, mentor, and friend just how volatile the situation in Harlem was.

Both leaders were also concerned about the implications of Alabama Governor George Wallace's withdrawal from the presidential election on Sunday. With the avowed segregationist and independent candidate no longer in the race, his followers were now free to back the Republican nominee. "We do not know whether Senator Goldwater wants the support of anti-Negro extremists," commented the *New York Times*, "though many of the things he has and has not said recently suggest that he does want their votes."[39] In any event, he was likely to benefit from Wallace's decision not to run, which made the declaration of a moratorium even more pressing. Consequently, Randolph advised Rustin to approach NAACP leader Roy Wilkins, who was surprised by the idea but delighted to endorse it.

Together, Wilkins and Rustin sent a telegram to the rest of the "Big Six" in the freedom struggle—King of the Southern Christian Leadership Conference, John Lewis of the Student Nonviolent Coordinating Committee, Whitney Young of the Urban League, Farmer, and Randolph. It warned that the "Civil Rights Act of 1964 could well be diminished or nullified and a decade of increasingly violent and futile disorder ushered in if we do not play our hand coolly and intelligently."[40] The time had come to halt all mass demonstrations that might strengthen white opposition to civil rights, to change tactics until after the November election.

The other leaders quickly agreed to meet in New York to discuss the urgent matter in person the following week, five days after the private conference between Goldwater and Johnson already set for July 24 in the White House. Pressure was mounting from all directions. For now, the basic task remained—to restore peace to the streets of Harlem as soon as possible.

On Monday afternoon, normalcy seemed to return as children played and stores reopened. "Nobody feels ashamed of what has happened," said an African American who owned a small business in Central Harlem. "Everybody feels it's just a hoodlum element." It was a common view in the black communities of New York. Many were critical of white policemen in general and Lieutenant Gilligan in particular. But they also had little patience with the protests and disorder of the weekend.[41]

"You can't accomplish anything with violence," said a Bronx construction worker. "What good are these demonstrations doing the people in Harlem?" asked a Manhattan housekeeper. "Stores are broken into and that just means that the Negro girls who work there can't go to work." And a Queens postman blamed "hoodlums and drug addicts" for the looting and vandalism. "This trouble is being instigated by people who stand around on corners and talk and talk, loaf around and do nothing—just look for trouble," he said. "It certainly is not helping our cause."[42]

But the sudden appearance of blue leaflets were an indication of the tensions and divisions that existed. The flyers were signed by Jesse Gray's rent-strike organization and the Harlem Defense Council, a new group that shared office space with the Progressive Labor Party (PLP). Headed by William Epton, a self-proclaimed Maoist revolutionary, the PLP was a radical offshoot of the Communist Party and had sent a representative to the Friday CORE rally at Powell's summer school. The leaflets emphasized the importance of "defending each and every block" of Harlem against "the enemy" and urged residents to come to the United Nations to protest "terrorism and genocide committed against Black Americans."

At 6 P.M. Gray told a crowd of several hundred at the rally that "there will be more demonstrations and riots whether we like it or not"—a clear signal that not all accepted the proposed moratorium. He also called for a large protest next Saturday at the 32nd Precinct on West 135th Street—an ominous reminder of last Saturday's mass rally at the 28th Precinct.[43] More trouble was brewing in the streets.

On Monday evening, firefighters had to extinguish two small blazes. The first was in the balcony of the RKO Alhambra, a movie theater between 126th and 127th Streets. The second fire was in the three-story brick building across the street that housed the National Memorial African Book Store. It was owned by Harlem legend Lewis H. Michaux, a Black Nationalist who originally sold books from a wagon and strongly objected to the term "Negro," which he considered a word for slaves. "Negro is a thing," he often said. "Use it. Abuse it. Accuse it. Refuse it." Firefighters were able to douse both blazes without serious damage to the theater or the store's collection of more than two hundred thousand books, paintings, and photos on black history, civil rights, and African nationalism.[44]

As night fell, the crowds swelled with curious onlookers, many of whom were drawn by the air of excitement and anticipation. The police used fire trucks to block traffic on 125th Street between Amsterdam and Fifth Avenues as well as Lenox and Seventh Avenues between 116th and 135th Streets, which left pedestrians free to roam at will. CORE officials with black armbands and medical supplies tried to bring order to the chaos. But by 9 P.M. angry and gleeful youths, many carrying posters with the caption "Wanted for Murder" below the photo of Gilligan, roved Central Harlem.[45]

In groups ranging from a few dozen to a few hundred, the teenagers smashed windows, set fires, and screamed epithets at officers who strained to show restraint. The youths demanded justice and hurled debris at the police, who scattered them with nightsticks or warning shots fired into the air. "Where the hell are those kids' parents?" asked a black sergeant in disgust. "They must have some kind of parents. Don't they care what they do?"[46]

At 9:35 P.M. Screvane placed an international call to Spain to provide Wagner with a status update. After a brief report on the latest disturbances, which made it clear that Harlem remained at a flashpoint, the mayor asked for advice. "You have been closer to the situation than I have," he said.

"What is your judgment?" The acting mayor was blunt: "I suggest you come back." Wagner readily agreed. "I should be there to take care of it," he replied. After the call ended he canceled his trip to Geneva and made plans to fly to New York on Tuesday afternoon. It was none too soon. "He should have been back many hours ago," the *Post* editorialized. "Surely this is no time for him to be abroad. His continued absence is an abdication."[47]

By 10 P.M. hundreds of officers were on duty across Harlem and hundreds of people had gathered on 125th Street between Eighth and St. Nicholas Avenues. The block contained the Harlem Labor Center and CORE headquarters. As the crowd grew more hostile, white reporters and photographers found themselves the targets of bottles tossed from alleys and BBs fired from a building across the street. A drunk man shouted, "You want war? We'll give you war." He was ignored, but as the pandemonium rose a sound truck arrived.[48]

"Attention, Mr. Overton requests your presence in 312," the voice intoned over and over again. It was effective—more than three hundred listeners left the sidewalk in front of the CORE office and drifted into the Harlem Labor Center at 312 125th Street. There they heard Overton, who was born in North Carolina but had moved to Harlem and worked on the "Don't Buy Where You Can't Work" campaign of the 1930s, urge them to take their demands to City Hall. "All you're doing here is tearing up your own stores, your own property," he pleaded.[49]

Back at CORE headquarters the mood was tense. Unsure of what was about to happen, Farmer decided to tell white members who were phoning the office to stay out of Harlem so that CORE's effectiveness in the black community was not compromised. He also decided to confine those whites who were already present—four volunteers and Gay Talese of the *New York Times*—in a back room for what he claimed was their own protection. The reporter was skeptical and angry. "At the behest of this prophet of doom" who was "playing on fear," Talese later recalled, he could not do what he saw as his job, which was to float through the streets in search of minor characters for sidebars and features. "Don't you think this is a little ridiculous?" a white woman asked. "Look, the situation is mad down there," replied a black worker as shots and sirens sounded in the distance.[50]

When the crowd of mostly teenagers returned from the Harlem Labor Center at 10:45 P.M., Farmer emerged from CORE headquarters. He told them that Wagner was headed back to New York and that Gilligan's case would go before a grand jury the next day. "They should kill him," the

FIGURE 9. Captain Lloyd Sealy confers with another officer. Lloyd George Sealy Papers, Special Collections, Lloyd Sealy Library, John Jay College of Criminal Justice/ CUNY.

youths yelled. Farmer insisted that it was time to go home. "We're not going home," the crowd replied. "We are home." At that point, the CORE director decided to organize a march to keep the youths occupied until they were ready to go home. Linking arms with Overton and Rustin, he started a chant of "we want justice" and led the teens toward St. Nicholas Avenue.[51]

"Farmer's going to move them away from here," said Captain Sealy to a white superior. "We'd better let them go." It was a calm and cool assessment, delivered in the quiet and reassuring manner for which he was known. "In the middle of it all," observed Jimmy Breslin of the *Herald Tribune*, "Lloyd Sealy, tall and dignified, walked the way that a man walks when the game calls for a man." The captain routinely inspired that kind of respect from both whites and blacks of all ages.[52]

Born in 1917 in Manhattan and raised in Brooklyn, Lloyd George Sealy was the son of immigrants from Barbados, who named him for Britain's prime minister during World War I. In high school he was one of only twelve African Americans in his class, but he was elected chief justice of the arbitration court and president of the student council. After graduation he worked for several years as a railroad clerk and federal employee in the General Accounting Office in Washington. Then he returned to New York and joined the Police Department in 1942. While walking a beat full-time in Bedford-Stuyvesant, he managed to earn a sociology degree from Brooklyn College in 1946. A year later, he became a sergeant. But it was not until 1959 that he made lieutenant, seven years after he had received a law degree. In 1963, he became only the third black captain in NYPD history and the first black officer to attend the FBI Academy in Quantico, Virginia.[53]

A slender, handsome man who relaxed by reading, swimming, and listening to jazz or classical music, Sealy assumed command of the 28th Precinct in mid-August after Murphy made the decision to promote him ahead of several other candidates. It was a popular choice in Central Harlem, where he was the first African American to hold the position and only the second in NYPD history to lead a precinct house. The Amsterdam News applauded the appointment, even though it came only in response to the riot. "I believe that a policeman is a policeman regardless of color," said Sealy, "but at this time Negroes may respond better to a Negro policeman than to a white officer." He added, however, that poverty was no excuse for breaking the law and harming the community: "I have lived in poor neighborhoods. I have been without, but that did not make me take the road to crime."[54]

Sealy soon became a fixture in the Harlem neighborhood by walking the streets in full uniform at all hours and speaking to everyone he could. His philosophy was simple: "I try to explain to the Negro groups the role of the policeman and why he's here. [And I] try to show the police that this is a community of decent people with the same values and same standards as any other community." He also promoted better relations between the police and residents by insisting that officers follow proper procedures. Under Sealy's watch, Central Harlem was relatively quiet for the next two summers despite racial unrest in other cities such as the Watts section of Los Angeles.[55]

But on this night gangs of teenagers, some allegedly equipped with walkie-talkies so they could coordinate looting activities and pinpoint police positions, continued to roam the streets and clash with officers. Near the CORE office on 125th Street Sealy had to intervene with a rare display of temper, perhaps from frustration or exhaustion after three straight nights on riot duty. "The cops grabbed this youth and began beating him as if there were no tomorrow," recounted Overton, who witnessed the incident. "Well, Sealy comes running up and I've never seen him so mad. And he yells, 'Damn it, if you're going to arrest the man, arrest him. Don't stand there and beat him.' Well, the crowd had been moving in at that point, and if he hadn't made that move, I don't know what might have happened."[56] The phrase the captain used—arrest them, don't beat them—would become his mantra as he rose through the ranks.

Despite Sealy's presence, chaos remained commonplace. The march led by Farmer encountered a blue-helmeted riot squad at 128th Street. "It was wall-to-wall police," recalled Bronx teenager Wayne Moreland, who had returned to CORE headquarters and found the mood in Harlem more "mischievous" than on Saturday night. He even saw someone lean out a bus window and snatch a hat from an officer's head. The demonstrators scattered when the police fired a series of shots into the air in response to what they claimed was a deluge of debris, although Farmer had not heard a single bottle shatter. "What's the matter, can't you see what we're trying to do?" the CORE leader asked in frustration.[57]

Suddenly, Rustin arrived with an urgent message for Deputy Chief Inspector Pierce Glynn. "There's a group leaving for Times Square that must be stopped," he said, exhausted after another long night in Harlem's streets. "You must stop them." Rustin was not sure what the group's intentions were, but Glynn went to a patrol car and radioed instructions to the Transit Authority, which halted the trains and dispersed the youths before they headed to Midtown.[58]

At midnight a young man from South Carolina who had arrived in New York two weeks earlier hurled a Molotov cocktail through the plate glass of a drugstore on 124th Street at Eighth Avenue. While the flames roared, the crowd cheered the arsonist as the police led him away in handcuffs. Then it booed the firefighters as they battled the blaze despite extreme fatigue. And the bystanders watched as a well-dressed black man complained that officers had struck him in the head with a nightstick.[59]

"I was trying to put out a fire in front of my own damn building," protested Joseph Monroe, a resident of Harlem for fifty years and a business owner since 1937. "The kids set those damn barrels on fire . . . [and] the cops hit me on the head for trying to stop the fire." But the police beating bothered him less than the unequal treatment he had received. "The cops protect all the white man's business in Harlem," charged Monroe. "You see the white business with big iron rails all in front of them and white policemen standing outside, but a black man gets no protection at all." And without insurance—it was too costly—he could not compete. Monroe nevertheless promised to do all he could to save Harlem and offered to speak to the kids, which seemed unlikely to make a difference.[60]

The mayhem had abated by 1 A.M. But less than an hour later heavy gunfire exploded and patrol cars with lights flashing and sirens screaming raced north on Eighth Avenue. Their destination was Sam's West Side Bar, located next to the A&P at 131st Street that grapefruit juice had saved the night before. A gang had thrown a trash can through a window and threatened the two officers standing guard inside, who had then requested assistance. According to a sergeant, when additional police arrived they saw two perpetrators run into the bar and lock the door. Then a fusillade of bottles and bricks poured from the roof so the officers had to enter and clear the building. The bartender, his bloody head bandaged by a CORE volunteer, claimed that he had bolted the entry earlier "so we wouldn't get involved, but [the police] broke through the door and came in hitting and shooting and wrecking the place."[61]

Outside the bar an enraged crowd of several hundred teenagers began to throw bricks and bottles at the police. A Molotov cocktail narrowly missed a patrol car. Rustin arrived on the scene and tried to help the injured to a hospital, but hecklers silenced him. "We don't want no liberal niggers here," they shouted. As the accusations and denials of police brutality flew back and forth, officers made six arrests and medics treated three injured black patrons. All of them had nonserious head wounds, but they bled dramatically under the glare of television cameras. "I just got off work," ranted a short man in a porkpie hat with blood trickling down the sides of his face. "I just had one drink and I was sitting there and I got this."[62]

The role of the media in covering the unrest soon came under close scrutiny. Theodore White, author of *The Making of the President 1964* and a print journalist by training, was especially critical of television reporters who broadcast unsubstantiated allegations on the air while the violence raged. "Television, with its insatiable appetite for live drama, found in the riots gorgeous spectacle," he wrote. "Protected by the police from mobs, cameramen could thus catch the police at work in the ugly business of grappling with rioters, subduing them by clubs if necessary." According to White, the media also ignored the voices of decency and goodwill; instead, television provided a platform to the most extreme and irresponsible, who made statements and charges "as inflammatory and provocative as any ever

FIGURE 10. Bayard Rustin offers assistance to a bloodied man. Photo by David
McAdams. Courtesy of Bayard Rustin Estate.

heard in so delicate a situation." As a result, he contended, police were
denied the vital support of public opinion when it was most needed.[63]

Other critics wondered why television coverage of the actual rioting was
so limited. In fact, some local news editors privately admitted that they had
withheld dramatic and disturbing film footage of looting and vandalism as

well as officers flailing away with their nightsticks until competitors forced their hand. This practice of self-censorship drew criticism from an unexpected source—the Police Department, which described full and live coverage as healthy and helpful. According to deputy commissioner Walter Arm, "it's the best answer we have to the cries of police brutality. The camera, after all, cannot distort or lie; the worst that can happen is that the film is edited. But what you see on the home screen is the actual occurrence."[64]

In Central Harlem on late Monday and early Tuesday, at least twenty more were arrested and seventeen more were injured, including three officers. No one was killed or wounded by bullets, but the night was not over. Just as an uneasy peace seemed to have settled over the neighborhood, police radios crackled with a fresh 10-41 call. It was an appeal for reinforcements. This time, however, it was coming from Bed-Stuy in Brooklyn, where a rally organized by a local CORE chapter had spiraled out of control.[65] Suddenly, the police faced a new front in a widening conflict.

After midnight a membership meeting ended and about three dozen CORE volunteers, half of whom were white, marched down Nostrand Avenue to Fulton Street. On the way they gained followers as men and women leaving bars decided to join them. At the intersection they continued to parade around the four-block area in an effort to gather enough participants to block traffic. When they returned at 1 A.M. they began a demonstration in which speaker after speaker exhorted the crowd to take action. As the listeners grew more agitated, the number of policemen guarding the intersection rose from six to twenty, which further incited the crowd. Cries of "Uncle Tom" greeted the black officers while the white officers endured taunts of "killer cops" and sexual epithets. The captain in charge, Irving Levitan, kept his men in check despite the provocations. "Let's get the Jews before this is over," shouted a demonstrator who may have had Levitan in mind.[66]

With at least a thousand angry people milling in the street, the CORE leaders sensed that the protest was getting out of hand and asked Levitan to remove his men. It was a request he could not consider—in his mind retreat was tantamount to surrender, which would only lead to more trouble in the future. At 1:30 A.M. the crowd launched the first projectiles just as police reinforcements arrived from across the borough. Emboldened, the sixty officers raised their nightsticks and charged. The battle of Brooklyn was under way, with both the guilty and innocent among the casualties. By the time the initial skirmish had concluded, around 7 A.M., scores of windows were broken and stores were looted. An unmarked police car was a charred piece of metal, one person was treated for injuries (officially), and three were arrested.[67]

The epidemic of violence had now spread, with no end or cure in sight. A new day had dawned, but it seemed unlikely to bring order or peace.

CHAPTER 7

TAKE THE "A" TRAIN

"For shame, for shame," wrote the papers
"Why the hurry to your hunger?
Now the rubble's resting on your broken streets
So you see what your rage has unraveled"
　　—Phil Ochs, "In the Heat of the Summer"

TUESDAY, JULY 21

"Deke, you and the FBI have got to stop these riots," implored Lyndon Johnson to his Bureau liaison, Cartha "Deke" DeLoach, assistant to the director. "One of my political analysts tells me that every time one occurs, it costs me 90,000 votes."[1]

By Tuesday morning the president was deeply worried about the political ramifications of the racial unrest in New York, especially if communists or radicals were somehow involved. The night before, he and aides had spent hours drafting and honing a statement, knowing that the words and tone were delicate. It had to stress that the protection of law and order was as important as the promotion of civil rights, whether in the South or the North. It also had to emphasize that public safety was primarily the responsibility of local and state officials, but that the federal government stood ready to provide all necessary assistance, including social programs to correct the root causes of the riot or rebellion.

Johnson was, however, unwilling to take any chances—the statement had to cause no complications. And so before he released it he made a round of calls on Tuesday afternoon to Attorney General Robert Kennedy,

FBI Director J. Edgar Hoover, and City Council President Paul Screvane, the acting mayor.

The first call went to Kennedy at 12:25 P.M. The attorney general reported that Police Commissioner Michael Murphy believed that the Progressive Labor Party (PLP) was behind the disorder. According to an informant, PLP members had distributed pamphlets on how to make Molotov cocktails. Kennedy wanted permission from the president to send the FBI to New York to investigate. "I think I ought to wait until I talk to the mayor [Wagner]," replied Johnson, who added that he wanted to respond as he had to crises in Mississippi and Georgia. "Just so people at least don't think we just jump on the South," he stated, again revealing his fear that conservative critics would claim that he had a double standard when it came to enforcing law and order. "Murphy runs a good department," the attorney general reassured him, "and you know I think that Screvane, Wagner, [will] do whatever has to be, or can be, done."[2]

The president read the proposed statement to Kennedy, who approved of it. "It's a question of the timing for it," said the attorney general. Johnson replied that he wanted to release the statement after he had first shared it with Screvane so that he would not "think that we're trying to put them on the spot."[3] At that moment, the acting mayor was on another line so Johnson immediately switched to it.

"We're getting wires and calls and Congress denouncing us and saying it's damned easy to run into Mississippi and jump on Georgia," the president complained to Screvane, "but when New York happens, we don't open our mouths." Johnson promised to have Hoover contact Murphy. The president then dictated the prepared statement to Screvane, who listened without comment and gave his approval. "Okay, pardner," replied Johnson, who quickly ended the brief conversation and called Hoover, his close friend and longtime neighbor in northwest Washington.[4]

The president needed the FBI in New York. "Do you want me . . . to go up there personally?" Hoover asked. As soon as possible, said Johnson, who also inquired about death threats against King in Mississippi. On Sunday the FBI director had flown to Jackson to open a new field office and announce that he was sending 153 agents to probe white extremism, especially Klan terrorism. Hoover then asked if he should also meet with the mayor. Again, the president answered in the affirmative and offered the use of one of his airplanes. "But get up there," he stressed, "and just tell them that we're not taking over any law enforcement . . . but that we do have to watch these federal violations, and you do have a role to investigate."[5]

Johnson also added a warning. "I'd be careful not to do anything that would inflame the people or the Negroes," he cautioned, "but you handled it perfectly in Mississippi and I think you just say that we're not . . . interested in any race or creed or color, we're interested in all Americans, and that we're going to see there is no violence or lawlessness."[6]

Minutes later, Kennedy phoned to voice his concern about the plan to send Hoover to New York. The call was predictable. It was no secret to Johnson or most of Washington that the attorney general and the FBI director viewed each other with contempt. Kennedy, who was thirty years younger, considered Hoover a relic from the past, a fervent racist whose unyielding opposition to King and the civil rights movement raised questions about his loyalty and utility to the administration. In Hoover's eyes, King was a sanctimonious hypocrite (because of his extramarital affairs) and a "notorious liar." He was also the most dangerous man in America because he was the witting or unwitting tool of communist agents or sympathizers who wanted to manipulate or exploit the freedom struggle to sow racial discord in the United States and weaken public support for law enforcement.[7]

At the same time, Hoover saw Kennedy as an undeserving and callow figure who had ridden his older brother's coattails to power. The attorney general's studied informality—his habit of putting his stocking feet on the desk and wearing shirtsleeves in the office—offended the strait-laced Hoover, who always had his close-cropped and clean-shaven agents attired in suits and ties with starched white dress shirts. Kennedy's well-publicized vigor—he had promoted and completed a fifty-mile hike—also threatened the older man, who was increasingly sensitive about his weight and fitness. In the Justice Department, Kennedy's cult of personality challenged Hoover's control of his agents. When John Kennedy was in the White House, the FBI director had barely tolerated the attorney general, his nominal superior. Now Lyndon Johnson, a political ally who shared his antipathy for Robert Kennedy, sat in the Oval Office. Legend has it that when the attorney general tried to use the direct line to Hoover's telephone shortly after the assassination, the FBI director pointedly refused to answer it and then had the buzzer Kennedy used to summon him restored to his secretary's desk, "where it belongs."[8]

Now the attorney general told the president that giving Hoover a direct and public role was a mistake. The local authorities in New York, unlike in

Mississippi, could and would do their jobs without federal oversight. Kennedy also insisted that if the FBI director personally intervened in Harlem, he would face intense political and media pressure to do the same when similar crises inevitably erupted in other cities like Chicago or Los Angeles (where Watts in fact exploded in 1965). "I see your point of not having him go everywhere," said Johnson, "but if he's working with them . . . I think it might put some of these Communist organizations on notice that we're not going to let this stuff go unattended." It was a hint of how seriously the president viewed the question of whether radicals had organized or incited the riot.[9]

Johnson added that he had not initiated the plan to send the FBI director to New York. "Well, can I just tell you, between ourselves," replied Kennedy, "[Hoover] said to me, 'I think it's a bad idea, but I do it,' so he's giving me a little bit of a different story." The president reiterated what he had said. "Well, now you want the FBI involved, don't you?" he asked. "Yeah, I want them involved, but . . ." the attorney general responded, hesitantly. "But you don't want him involved," concluded Johnson. Kennedy returned to his position that local responsibility was paramount and that the federal government should not take charge of "getting Harlem cleaned up." The president hedged. "I have no deep feeling one way or another," he said, indicating that he was content to wait and see what Wagner thought when he returned later in the afternoon. "I didn't want to veto [Hoover's idea] and I didn't suggest it."[10]

Johnson naturally placed his next call to Hoover. "[Kennedy] thought it would be very unwise for me to go," related the FBI director. "I said I of course was merely complying with the orders of the President." He hastily added that "if you think it's desirable, I need not go, but I could get in touch with Mayor Wagner by telephone." Johnson concurred and also urged Hoover to call Murphy and Rockefeller. According to the FBI director, the governor believed that both radical agitators who wanted revolution and conservative extremists who backed Goldwater were behind the violence and unrest in Harlem.[11]

"We're getting floods of wires and telegrams," said the president, who read the FBI director a sample: "I'm a working girl. Please send the militia to New York. I'm afraid to leave my house. . . . I fear the Negro revolution will reach Queens. Situation is alarming. . . . Please send troops immediately to Harlem." Tell the local authorities, he stressed to Hoover, that "we've got to investigate the possible federal violations" and see if you can "put a quietus on that Malcolm X and all that stuff." Then Johnson offered his personal assessment: "I think the Communists are in charge of it."[12]

Several hours later, the president announced that the FBI would send a team of agents to New York, but that Hoover would remain in Washington to coordinate and oversee the investigation. Johnson also released his statement on Harlem, which was scrupulously balanced and carefully calculated to appeal to liberals, moderates, and conservatives. First, he emphasized that "in the preservation of law and order there can be no compromise— just as there can be no compromise in securing equal and exact justice for all Americans." Second, Johnson stressed that in combating unacceptable violence and lawlessness "New York officials shall have all of the help that we can give them. And this includes help in correcting the evil social conditions that breed despair and disorder."[13]

Finally, the president declared that region was irrelevant: "American citizens have a right to protection of life and limb—whether driving along a highway in Georgia; a road in Mississippi; or a street in New York City."[14] The statement was a masterpiece of evenhandedness and a testament to the sensitivity of the situation. The search for political cover and consensus— no matter how fleeting and fragile—was fully under way as the Harlem crisis drew national attention.

By Tuesday editorial writers from across the United States were expressing their opinions of the civil disorders in New York, which many saw as a boon for Republicans. "The rioters of Harlem who attacked police and looted stores wrote a postscript to Barry Goldwater's acceptance speech beyond the fondest dreams of those who oppose civil rights," wrote the *Kansas City Star* in words that reinforced what Johnson already knew. "Extremist Negro agitators for civil rights can create an atmosphere that helps touch off the stoning of policemen. In so doing they play into the hands of the most dedicated opponents of civil rights."[15]

But other newspapers stressed the need to address the root causes of the racial violence. "The tinder that flared in Harlem is present in Negro ghettos in every major city," wrote the *Milwaukee Journal*. "There must be a redoubled effort to give Negroes a stake in the maintenance of law and order," advocated the *Washington Post*.[16]

Most newspapers, however, stressed the importance of restoring peace first, then redressing grievances. "Anarchy and chaos await those seeking to put the law into the hands of mobs," asserted the *Cleveland Plain Dealer*. In the South, a common theme was the need for fair and balanced regional treatment. The *Raleigh News and Observer* declared that "violence in Manhattan must arouse as much or more indignation as violence in Mississippi." And the *Clarion-Ledger* of Jackson, Mississippi, offered, with a touch of bemusement, some "unsolicited advice" to northern officials faced with racial disturbances: "Don't negotiate with people who want to hold a pistol to your temple. Decline all demands which are couched in terms of a threat. Refuse to discuss peaceful settlements while offenders make war on law and order."[17]

In New York, the *Daily News* warned of violent offenders inspired or incited by radical extremists. "Harlem is a natural stamping ground for Communists," it editorialized, noting the activities of Jesse Gray and the PLP as well as the presence of walkie-talkies on Monday night (although Bayard Rustin later asserted that they were part of an effort to keep the peace). "Let's have these gentry dug out from their assorted rocks and exposed to full and glaring publicity." The sentiments echoed those expressed by Manhattan District Attorney William Dodge in the aftermath of the 1935 riot.[18]

Now the fear of radicals was reflected in the comments of officials like Johnson, Hoover, and Screvane, who in the final hours of his brief mayoralty offered his personal thoughts on who was and was not responsible for the violence and vandalism at an impromptu press briefing recorded by radio station WINS in a City Hall corridor. "Question: Is there evidence that the Communist Party has been fostering the—some of the—civil strife here in New York? Answer: Well, I don't think there's any question about it." Screvane added that "I assume to sponsor these rallies, they must have funds. I haven't been able to pin down where the money is coming from." Radicals, he insisted, were partially responsible, not the "rank-and-file persons living in the Harlem community. They're as frightened as people who live outside the community."[19]

Other groups Screvane held culpable were professional criminals who sought to exploit the opportunity to steal and "young kids who have nothing better to do and get great fun out of throwing a bottle or a stone at policemen or anyone else." The comments about the Communist Party generated headlines—he would later claim that his remarks were misinterpreted—but as the acting mayor spoke, the actual mayor was on his way across the Atlantic on an Iberia Airlines jet from Madrid.[20]

For Mayor Robert Wagner, the Harlem Riot represented the greatest challenge of his lengthy and mostly successful political career. It also came at a critical moment, when he hoped at last to achieve his ultimate ambition and move from City Hall to the U.S. Senate, where his father had served almost four terms from 1926 to 1949. The elder Wagner, who had emigrated from Germany at age nine, was a towering figure in the Democratic Party. During the New Deal, he was instrumental in the passage of the Social Security Act, the Public Housing Act of 1937, and the National Labor Relations Act (often known simply as the Wagner Act). He also took charge of raising his son after his wife died when Robert was nine. The powerful senator regularly took the future mayor to the Metropolitan Opera and let him observe poker games with notable politicians like Governor Al Smith. Together, father and son resided in Yorkville, a German-American neighborhood on the Upper East Side, where the junior high school named after the senator was located and where Powell was shot.[21]

The younger Wagner entered the family business after World War II, when he served as an intelligence officer in the Air Corps (he lost hearing in his left ear after a returning bomber jettisoned its payload too close to the base). In 1953, he was elected mayor with the support of the Tammany Hall Democratic machine. Three years later, he suffered his biggest political disappointment when he lost a Senate race to Jacob Javits, the Republican nominee, who rode the Dwight Eisenhower reelection wave to victory. Never again would Wagner have a chance to reclaim the seat from which his father had resigned in 1949 due to illness. In 1957, he was reelected mayor by almost a million votes—the largest margin in the city's history. Four years later, Wagner broke with Tammany Hall, sided with the self-styled reformers, and won a third term by attracting strong support from Jewish voters and union members, as well as African Americans and Puerto Ricans who had migrated to New York in large numbers in the 1950s.[22]

In City Hall, Wagner cultivated a deliberate decision-making style inherited from his father, whose philosophy was "when in doubt, don't." A chain-smoker with a colorless public image, the low-key mayor brought the World's Fair to Flushing Meadows and Shakespeare productions to Central Park—he strongly backed theatrical impresario Joseph Papp in the face of charges that he was a communist. And Wagner passed the nation's first antidiscrimination law against landlords. But he also promoted slum clearance and built massive public housing complexes, which disrupted urban neighborhoods, reinforced residential segregation, and exacerbated suburban flight.[23]

By all accounts, Wagner was honest—neither he nor his administration was ever hit by a major corruption scandal during his twelve years in office. But by 1964 the city's problems were mounting and his energy was waning—typical problems for third-term New York mayors. Personal tragedy had struck as well. After more than two decades of marriage, his beloved wife Susan died of lung cancer at Gracie Mansion with her husband and their two sons at her side. The ten-day trip to Europe was in part an effort to escape the pain and loneliness caused by her death in March.[24]

The racial unrest offered a test of his political leadership and an opportunity to receive national attention. Ultimately, Wagner would win accolades from many constituents—though certainly not all—for his handling of the crisis. A confidential survey commissioned in August revealed that he had regained his favorable job rating—back in January it was negative—and that he was the clear front-runner in the 1965 mayoral race. The major factor, according to the survey, was his decisive handling of the Harlem crisis, which countered his public image as a passive leader. It was good news for Wagner, but the true reward he sought—another chance at the U.S. Senate—would again elude him.[25]

At 4:04 P.M. Wagner's plane landed at the newly named John Kennedy International Airport. Although tired—the mayor had awakened at 2 A.M. to catch the flight—he greeted his youngest son at the foot of the ramp and was whisked through the immigration and immunization checkpoints. He then met behind closed doors with Screvane, Murphy, and Deputy Mayor Edward Cavanagh, Jr. for fifty minutes. At a press briefing, the mayor refused to classify the racial disorders as the "worst crisis" of his ten years in office until he had more time to gather the facts and study the situation. But Wagner expressed his firm belief that the National Guard and U.S. Army were not needed. And he issued a strong vote of confidence in the police chief. "I have complete faith in Commissioner Murphy," he told reporters.[26]

Next Wagner avoided City Hall, where protesters were waiting, and went to Gracie Mansion. For more than two hours he huddled with aides on the back porch, where the scenic view of the East River provided a calming background to the intense discussions. At 9 P.M. he announced that he would give a televised address the following night, and at 10 P.M. he ate a late dinner with his son at a Chinese restaurant around the corner.

He then returned to the official residence and retired to his bedroom at 1 A.M., still in the same light-gray suit he had worn when he left Spain twenty-three hours earlier.[27]

As the mayor conferred and dined, disturbances were breaking out elsewhere. At City Hall, Isaiah Robinson of the Harlem Parents Committee and four others were arrested and charged with trespassing and disorderly conduct after they refused to leave the building at 5 P.M. Robinson, who at the afternoon rally organized by Jesse Gray Sunday had urged listeners to "Stand up like men and die for democracy," now accused the Tactical Patrol Force (TPF) of carrying out "a sadistic bloodletting orgy" in Harlem.[28]

In Brooklyn, the local CORE chapter had decided not to hold another protest at the corner of Fulton and Nostrand. "It is [our] feeling that rallies and demonstrations, no matter how peaceful in Bedford-Stuyvesant, could get out of hand," said CORE chairman Oliver Leeds, who had decades of experience dating back to the "Don't Buy Where You Can't Work" campaign in 1930s Harlem. "Elements we could not control could seize the lead and do something we do not want." An Army veteran and former communist, Leeds had correctly read the mood on the street and so the decision was made to organize protests in Manhattan.[29]

Accordingly, Brooklyn CORE transported pickets by car—since the Transit Authority had closed the City Hall subway station—to various locations, including Governor Rockefeller's private residence on Fifth Avenue and police headquarters on Centre Street, where demonstrators clashed with counterdemonstrators. "Go home, you nigger-loving bastards. Go home," shouted two hundred or so Italian teenagers, who also yelled "Goldwater for President!" The CORE volunteers responded with chants and signs reading "Gilligan Must Go" and "Murphy Must Go."[30]

Eventually, the police dispersed the white youths, who regrouped and returned with rotten eggs, which they hurled at the protesters. "They should turn this thing over to the Mafia," said an adult bystander. "They would clean this up." An egg struck Deputy Commissioner Walter Arm in the leg, but he and other officers were able to keep the counterdemonstrators at bay while they escorted the CORE picketers to the Spring Street subway station at 11 P.M.[31]

By that time Wagner was taking an unannounced tour of Central Harlem in an unmarked police car driven by a plainclothes detective. With him was Commissioner Murphy. Together, they rode from 110th to 135th on Lenox, Seventh, and Eighth Avenues, stopping from time to time to speak with residents, some of whom recognized the mayor and wanted to shake hands. According to Wagner and Murphy, there was no violence and no hostility—not even for the police commissioner, who usually attracted the demonstrators' ire. In his televised address the next night, the mayor said, "I saw the boarded up windows, I saw the crowds, the itinerant gangs, residents clustered on their stoops and looking fearfully out of their windows." He also reported that he witnessed the "debris of battle," but that many streets were undamaged and most were quiet—at least on Tuesday night.[32]

Wagner was right. After three nights of rioting and looting, Harlem was spent. James Farmer sensed it—after three days without rest the CORE leader went home to sleep, leaving instructions not to call him unless "hell breaks out again." Only sporadic and scattered incidents of violence took place. On 125th Street a group of youths were listening to music outside a record shop next to CORE headquarters. At 9:30 P.M. they grabbed a stack of Gilligan "Wanted for Murder" posters and headed south on Eighth Avenue to 124th Street, where they scattered with whoops of delight when the police fired shots. On Lenox Avenue, small gangs of teenage looters, occasionally with an adult or two present, targeted Spotless Cleaners at 116th and 118th Streets. At 122nd Street, a large cluster formed a human chain to remove clothes from a third dry cleaner until they were chased away by around one hundred officers.[33]

At the Harlem Armory on Fifth Avenue at 142nd Street, a small group of white soldiers who had reverse integrated the legendary 369th Regiment, the "Hellfighters" of World War I fame, managed to rejoin their unit. A company officer told them to gather in the Bronx and put on their uniforms. Then he instructed them to choose a single car, notify him of the make and model, and put a white flag on the antenna for safe passage. "Scared for our well-being and scared of disobeying an order," recalled one of the soldiers, they followed instructions and had no trouble. "Apparently, order can occur within chaos," he observed, "when a revered community institution communicates" with those in charge for the moment.[34]

Back on 125th Street a white reporter spotted Bayard Rustin and asked him if he thought the communists were in charge or somehow involved. "I can smell organization in Harlem," he said, "and this has not been organized." The thirsty reporter ducked into a bar for a beer around 11 P.M. and struck up a conversation about the looting with the black bartender, a middle-aged working man.[35]

"That shit, it ain't doing anybody any good," the bartender said. "These riots make a paradise for dope addicts and thieves. Our kids break the windows and the junkies grab everything inside. They gotta steal to feed their habit, and this makes it easy for them." Launching into a diatribe that seemed to transcend racial differences and reflect the generation gap, he continued, "If the parents would take charge of the kids, they couldn't get mixed up in this. The kids are out of school now and they got nothing to do but spend the whole day gathering bottles, making Molotov cocktails and bombs and all those little playthings, just waiting for the night."[36]

But the bartender also expressed an understanding of why the teenagers rebelled. "They got all these influences working on them," he said. "They got the civil rights groups, they got the nationalist groups, they got the churches and they got the newspapers. The civil rights groups feed them . . . well, they feed them shit! The nationalists feed them shit; the churches feed them shit. And those newspapers. . . ." He looked directly at the reporter: "I'm pretty well off. I got a job. I live all right, I'm happy. But I pick up the paper and start reading it, and all of a sudden I find myself saying, 'those dirty rotten bastards! They can't do that to us!' No wonder these kids get mixed up in that shit."[37]

As if on cue, about an hour later officers encountered a teenager on 114th Street and Eighth Avenue distributing mimeographed sheets titled "Harlem Freedom Fighters" (Bulletin No. 1 July 1964) with directions on "How to make a Molotov cocktail." By now the directions were probably unnecessary for anyone who had any interest:

INSTRUCTIONS: ANY EMPTY BOTTLE

FILL WITH GASOLINE

USE RAG AS WICK

LIGHT RAG

TOSS AND SEE THEM RUN!

The police made the decision to confiscate the leaflets and let the teenager go.[38]

But in a doorway on 125th Street, Lez Edmond found a twelve-year-old boy lying on the ground with a bloody head. "I was walking down the street when the cop come over to me and said, 'Get out of here,'" he recounted. "As I turned to go he hit me and then they began to beat me up. The reason I was beat up is because I didn't run." Edmond next saw a black man in a bloody white shirt run down the street. His wife, who was bleeding in the face, pleaded with him to stop. "Let's go home," she said. "I don't want any trouble." But her husband angrily confronted a police captain, who claimed he could not help. "Don't tell me a damn thing—just line up all these white faces and let me show you the one that hit my wife," replied the man.[39]

It was now after 1 A.M. and a cool breeze wafted through the evening air. Despite what Edmond had witnessed, the crisis in Harlem finally seemed to have calmed a bit. But in Brooklyn the violence on Tuesday night and Wednesday morning would reach heights not seen since Saturday. Once again regular and TPF officers would unleash their full arsenal in an effort to halt mass rioting and looting. And once again cries of police brutality would echo on the streets and in the newspapers.

It was hardly surprising that the violence and unrest had spread to Bedford-Stuyvesant (Bed-Stuy). Although overshadowed by Harlem historically, socially, and culturally, it was by many measures the largest and poorest black community in New York by 1964. In the late nineteenth century, Bed-Stuy consisted of about one hundred square blocks in north central Brooklyn. By the mid-twentieth century, it was "defined racially more often than geographically," according to the New York Times, and extended informally to Flushing Avenue in the north, Washington Avenue in the west, Broadway in the east, and Eastern Parkway in the south. As Bed-Stuy's black population grew and spread, it encroached upon formerly white neighborhoods in Brownsville, Crown Heights, and East New York, whose residents often fled to the suburbs of Long Island and New Jersey. In Brownsville, for example, the Jewish community shrank from almost 175,000 in the early 1940s to fewer than 5,000 by the late 1960s.[40]

Like Harlem, Bed-Stuy in the late nineteenth century was almost entirely rural and white. But again like Harlem, the combination of public transportation and land speculation transformed the area. The extension in 1888 of the elevated train to Myrtle Avenue made it possible to travel easily between Manhattan and Brooklyn. Developers soon raced to construct row after row of beautiful brownstones, priced to sell to upper-middle-class white families. The fashionable section became known as "Stuyvesant Heights," and as affluent whites purchased homes their black servants established their own community in Bedford. Other black laborers, masons, waiters, coachmen, and barbers arrived and settled across Brooklyn, many of them lured by houses seen as superior to the slums of Harlem. During the next four decades, property values soared and the black population rose as the Great Migration brought southern families to New York in droves.[41]

Property values in Stuyvesant Heights collapsed, however, during the Great Depression. Real estate agents and speculators capitalized on the economic and racial fears of whites by blockbusting. They bought low from desperate whites and sold high to eager blacks, who repaid the exorbitant mortgages by taking advantage of the lack of zoning regulations and subdividing the large brownstones into small apartments and rooming houses. Life in Brooklyn had its advantages—backyards and green space were more abundant than in Manhattan. But it was a cultural backwater compared to cosmopolitan Harlem, as the NAACP's Roy Wilkins haughtily highlighted when he termed the CORE stall-in at the World's Fair as "strictly Brooklynese." Fortunately, the glamour, sophistication, and excitement of Harlem were only a matter of taking the "A" train after it was finished in 1936. Immortalized in song by composer Billy Strayhorn and bandleader Duke Ellington in 1939, it took only thirty minutes or so to ride from Brooklyn to Harlem.[42]

During the 1940s, African Americans from the rural South continued to flock to Bed-Stuy, drawn by affordable housing and decent jobs in war plants. The community had other charms. Many streets boasted active block associations dedicated to improving properties. Churches catered to growing families, many of them stable and middle-class. The low-rise brownstones, which were usually only three or four stories, helped create a less stressful, more relaxed environment than in high-rise Manhattan. Although no Harlem, Bed-Stuy even had its own homegrown celebrities, such as the singer and actress Lena Horne, who was born in 1917.

As the black population of Bed-Stuy doubled, "For Sale" signs sprouted on white properties, encouraged by bank officers, mortgage companies, and blockbusters, who sent postcards with the message "We have a buyer for your house" to nervous residents. After World War II the federal government also offered subsidized loans to white veterans who wished to move to the segregated suburbs. "One family just walked out," recalled a white resident. "They left everything behind. In their haste, they didn't even bother to lock the doors behind them." In their wake came blacks who overpaid and assumed debts that soon overwhelmed them. By 1960 Bed-Stuy had surpassed Central Harlem in population and was 83 percent African American or Puerto Rican as white Brooklynites departed in droves.[43]

Young and poor, the new arrivals contributed disproportionately as both perpetrators and victims to a probable increase in the crime rate. A black minister in adjacent Brownsville requested more African American police officers because most of the violence and vandalism involved black gangs, although the victims were of all races. Brooklyn Judge Samuel Leibowitz, a staunch defender of the Scottsboro Boys (nine black teenagers grossly mistreated by the Alabama judicial system), even proposed that the federal government restrict Latino immigration from Puerto Rico and black migration from the rural South. But other liberals, like Borough President Abe Stark and Democratic Congressman Emanuel Celler, strongly opposed the idea, which nonetheless highlighted the growing fear of white residents.[44]

Decrepit and segregated housing aggravated the crime wave. A 1948 survey by Con Ed showed that Bed-Stuy had the oldest buildings in New York. More than 90 percent of them predated 1919 and were in horrible condition. A 1952 fire that claimed the lives of seven Puerto Rican women and children living in an illegal basement tenement led Stark to decry the "appalling living conditions" and declare that many of the private buildings were "unfit for human habitation." But by then most were owned by white landlords who had little concern for their tenants. In an effort to improve living conditions, New York constructed massive high-rise projects like Fort Greene and the Marcy Houses, where more than forty-five thousand residents of central Brooklyn soon lived. By the early 1960s, however, public housing too was frequently overcrowded and in bad condition.[45]

Economic inequity was another factor. In Bed-Stuy, the average family income of around $3,000 in 1964 was well below the city average and the federal government's minimum standard "for health and well-being." Brooklyn factories had traditionally employed large numbers of unskilled and undereducated workers in their packing, shipping, and mailing operations. But machines now threatened those jobs, which accounted for 70 percent of black employment in the borough. Meanwhile, the male unemployment rate was already 17 percent—more than three times the city average. "Automation will precipitate the crisis that is inevitable," said the Reverend Milton Galamison, pastor of Siloam Presbyterian Church for fifteen years.[46]

The son of a Philadelphia postal clerk and holder of a master's degree from Princeton Theological Seminary, Galamison was a powerful voice on behalf of his community, which he vigorously defended against critics who blamed the residents and failed to see what discrimination, automation, and segregation had wrought. "This is not a community of slum-dwellers," he contended. "It is more so a haven for corrupt, absentee landlords and real estate speculators. This is not a community of shiftless husbands. It is a world of wounded men historically deprived of the right to equal employment. This is not a vast neighborhood of negligent mothers. It is a congregation of homemakers without homes and toilers without rest."[47]

In Brooklyn, as in Harlem, many men, women, and children refused to accept passively their unequal treatment and conditions. They demanded better hospitals and integrated schools. They agitated for more playgrounds and swimming pools open to all. They protested against neighborhood segregation, which dictated where even prominent blacks like baseball star Jackie Robinson and the distinguished historian John Hope Franklin could and could not live. They organized boycotts of companies that discriminated against minorities in hiring, such as the Ebinger Baking Company, a Flatbush institution. And they successfully mobilized to elect black officeholders at the local and state, though not federal, level.[48]

In Congress, the black residents of Bed-Stuy lacked political representation because of racial gerrymandering. Unlike Central Harlem, the core area was subdivided into three congressional districts, all of them represented by whites, which meant that Bed-Stuy lacked a single voice in Washington like Congressman Powell who could speak for the community as a whole. Evidence of the powerlessness came in early July, when Kenneth Clark's Harlem Youth Opportunities Unlimited (HARYOU) project was promised a $117 million grant. Three weeks later, the Brooklyn equivalent, Youth in Action, received a token grant of $223,000 almost as an afterthought, even though Bed-Stuy contained an at-risk population of black juveniles at least as large. Unimpressed, the *Amsterdam News* caustically noted that the paltry funds would go not to those in need but to the "high salaries of the directors, analysts, and what-not of the research project."[49]

Now it was Tuesday, and after three days of hearing about Harlem, the teenagers of Brooklyn would have their turn. The youth would take action, but not in the way the federal government or City Hall hoped or wanted.

On Tuesday morning, as desk officers correlated the damage reports from Monday night, Captain Edward Jenkins was worried. As the commanding officer of the 79th Precinct, located in the heart of Bed-Stuy, he sensed that the disorder was only a preview of what was to come. CORE had scheduled a demonstration (not yet moved to Manhattan) for 8:30 P.M., and Jenkins knew the police would need the cooperation of the community to handle the disturbances likely to follow. And so he began to comb the precinct files for black activists to contact. Once he had a list of thirty-five names, he started to make calls and extend invitations to an afternoon meeting at the Bedford YMCA. Even though he had a framed photo of himself with King hanging on his office wall, he understood that no one would view the station house as neutral ground.[50]

Despite the choice of venue, the meeting went poorly. From the start it was clear that neither side could deliver what the other needed or wanted. Jenkins lacked the authority to meet any of the demonstrators' demands. His boss, the commissioner, had already voiced his strong opposition to civilian review and refused even to consider suspending Gilligan pending the outcome of the grand jury hearing. The "leaders" who attended the meeting had few "followers" in the sense that they lacked the street credibility to influence those most likely to riot that night. And Jenkins could not give them any leverage, especially when it came to the pressing issue of police brutality. "The police are heavy-handed here," said Assemblyman Thomas Jones, who represented one of Bed-Stuy's two districts in the state legislature. "You feel like a fool telling people not to protest in the face of this kind of treatment."[51]

Pastor Sandy Ray of the Cornerstone Baptist Church, the chairman of the meeting, shared the sentiments expressed by Jones. Like the assemblyman, the minister felt powerless and was unwilling to exert what little influence he may have had. "The feeling was there was nothing we could do with the people on the street," he said. "We told the captain that politicians had tried to talk to them, and that preachers had tried to talk to them. And they would say things like, 'Shut up, you have milk for your babies, we don't.' And like, 'Did whitey send you out here to talk at us, Uncle Tom?' It's pretty difficult to tell people to go home if you don't have any suggestions that will aid their grievances."[52] The sense of hopelessness was pervasive and growing.

The meeting ended with a vague resolution that offended no one but satisfied no one. "Violence and disorders do not occur in a vacuum," it stated. "In dealing with riots and disorder, we are dealing with symptoms rather than causes. Therefore the basic evils from which the community suffers must be corrected, because the people can no longer be restrained." And then everyone went home—except for Jenkins, who had to prepare for the night ahead. Meanwhile, Inspector Walter Clerke, deputy commander of Brooklyn's Patrol Borough North, was making tactical plans with his deputy, Dominic Hallinan. They decided to dispatch Hallinan with thirty officers to the corner of Nostrand and Fulton, the likely epicenter of any disorder, with twenty others held in reserve. It was also agreed that the officers would have the authority to fire warning shots if necessary.[53] As always, the motto was hope for the best but prepare for the worst, which on Tuesday in Bed-Stuy would surpass expectations.

By twilight hundreds of people had gathered at Nostrand and Fulton. CORE was nowhere in sight. The few signs that it had posted about the change in location ("Demonstrate tonight at City Hall") quickly disappeared. The crowd milled around the intersection, waiting for a protest to start or something to happen. Into the vacuum stepped an anonymous Black Nationalist speaker with a podium and a "Buy Black" sign. In the past, he and others had spoken several times a week on the northeast corner. But "they never attracted any crowds at all," according to a black patrolman. "They had two to four people looking on, they'd think they had something. And nobody ever listened to what they had to say."[54]

Now the speaker had an audience of five hundred or more, which clapped and cheered as he declared that "no white man has ever done anything for us." On the four corners watching him was Hallinan's detachment, white and black, clad in caps (not helmets) with nightsticks in hand. Darting through the crowd were young girls and boys with "Gilligan Wanted for Murder" posters printed by the Harlem Defense Council earlier in the afternoon. After fifteen minutes a small detail of helmeted officers arrived, ready for trouble, which visibly raised the tension level. Sensing it, the speaker began to moderate his comments. "I would like you to remain calm," he urged his listeners, who laughed at the change in tone. "You are under the impression that by emotionalism you will impress the world, but you will not impress anybody."[55]

Suddenly around 9:30 P.M. there was the sound of broken glass. The front window of a drug store on the northeast corner of Nostrand and Fulton had shattered. Without waiting to see what the police would do, the crowd scattered. In an instant, the intersection was eerily empty. But the officers took no action—the speaker was not inciting his listeners and the store display seemed to contain little of value. In a few minutes, the crowd reassembled, larger than ever, and the man on the podium resumed. Then a young women grabbed something from the store window and ran east on Fulton.[56]

FIGURE 11. Black youths observe the action in Bedford-Stuyvesant. Photo by Warren K. Leffler. Library of Congress, Prints and Photographs Division, U.S. News & World Report Magazine Collection (LC-U9-12287 frame 1).

At that moment, from a block away at Arlington Place, came the sound of what Clerke would later describe as fireworks. But what officers, bystanders, and reporters on the scene heard was gunfire. Patrolmen were shooting at a rooftop in the mistaken belief that someone had thrown a bottle from it. In fact, the beams of light were from two officers trying to signal their companions. "No! No!" cried the speaker as everyone began to race toward the gunshots. "That's what the man wants you to do. He wants you to riot so he can shoot you down!" His words went unheeded as the crowd stampeded in a flash.[57]

During the next ten hours, Bed-Stuy would experience what a police sergeant characterized as "pure, undiluted hell." According to a police chaplain, the rioting and looting were "much more serious" than on previous nights in Harlem. "Let's get the Jews first," chanted some in the crowd. On this night in Brooklyn, more than five hundred store windows were

FIGURE 12. Police officers at the 79th Precinct make an inventory of items recovered from looters. Photo by John Bottega. Library of Congress, Prints and Photographs Division, New York World-Telegram & Sun Collection.

smashed (many in small businesses owned or operated by Jewish merchants), fifty persons were arrested, two looters were shot (neither fatally), and one officer was injured. "In the first three hours, before the fireworks, we had only three broken windows," reported Clerke. "But afterward, everything went." He was not exaggerating. By morning the 79th Precinct resembled a furniture warehouse, with piles of phonograph records, television sets, tables, chairs, and lamps retrieved from looters by police. Losses to businesses were estimated at $350,000. "This is a black store," read the cardboard sign in a grocery store that was ransacked.[58]

On Herkimer Street, just south of Fulton, lived Ophelia Bryant, an older woman with an unobstructed view of the looting. "While the cops were down at Nostrand and Fulton, people would go up on Bedford and Herkimer," she recalled. "They started stealing, taking things like chairs and linens. I was standing outside my house looking till they came up the street.

A lot of people came by with TV sets and they came up the street. And then more came by with more TV sets, and radios, beautiful chairs, red velvet things, and whisky by the quart. They were selling whisky for $3 a quart, good Scotch. I think everybody on Herkimer Street was drunk." For a time it was quiet as the looters moved north to DeKalb Avenue, but then they returned to Fulton Street. "A crowd was coming up the street then, running, the cops behind them," Bryant continued. "We didn't know who the cops were going to shoot, and we ran in the house, then after they passed, we came out again. It must have happened that way half a dozen times."[59]

A reporter with an inside view of the rioting was the *Herald Tribune*'s Fred Shapiro, who in search of the gunshots followed the crowd as it flowed west on Fulton and found himself in the middle of a group of looters. All around him well-dressed men and women shopped selectively for items of interest. One older man in an expensive blue suit delicately stuck his arm through a broken window and carefully selected two suitcases—one for himself and one for a friend. Later that evening Shapiro responded with derision when CORE leader Oliver Leeds, who by then had returned from Manhattan, criticized the police and said the looting was "Negroes taking revenge for years of being squeezed, penny by penny, by greedy shopkeepers."[60]

For now, Shapiro had more immediate concerns. While he was observing the looters, a group of eight or nine teenagers was observing him. "Let's get whitey," they chanted in unison. Realizing that he was in trouble and that, unlike Paul Montgomery of the *New York Times*, he could not outrun his pursuers, he began to angle toward a lighted movie theater marquee near Bedford Avenue. There a crowd had gathered, perhaps in anticipation of the triple feature: *Cop Hater*, *The Hanging Tree*, and *When Hell Breaks Loose*. The youths trailed him, switching to "let's kill whitey." As he neared the theater, a young man peeled away from the crowd in front and approached Shapiro, who had no idea what to expect.[61]

"Let him alone," the youth yelled at the teenagers chasing the reporter. They took off at the sound of his voice and, simultaneously, glass breaking. As Shapiro walked west from Bedford in search of police, a black motorist offered him a ride. "Let me drive your ass out of here before you get yourself killed," he said, spotting the press badge on Shapiro's suit.[62] The best and worst of humanity, it seemed, was on display that night—not to mention the many variations in between.

Unlike in Harlem, the police in Brooklyn had opted not to halt traffic, which continued to flow in both directions on Fulton and elsewhere. The reason, Clerke explained, was "to keep [the crowds] from making a ball in the middle of the street, to keep them from gathering into a surge which would have washed us right off the street." From the vandalized doorway of a dress store Shapiro could see his logic, which rested on the fact that the hundreds of police on duty were heavily outnumbered by the thousands of people on the prowl. As a crowd from Nostrand Avenue streamed past him, he watched the officers wave the people through with cries of "Go on, you bastards, run" and "yippee-yi-yo-ki-yay, get along little dogies" (among the more printable remarks). Others were not repeatable.[63]

At 10:25 p.m. the 79th Precinct issued the first call for reinforcements, followed minutes later by a second 10-41. "There doesn't seem to be any particular gripe at the police," said one officer, "they're just on a looting spree." But the spree continued as gangs of looters and small clusters of excited onlookers rampaged through the streets, turning Bed-Stuy into what the *Herald Tribune* called a "raging battleground." One official reported that he was "having a hell of a time keeping my men all over the area. Whenever we get them corralled in one place, they spurt out at another." By 11 p.m. the police had made two more requests for additional manpower.[64] Among the units racing to respond was the TPF's 12th Squad, which included Jim O'Neil and Davy Katz.

The two men were on duty in Central Harlem, where it was relatively quiet. Then word about Brooklyn arrived and they sprinted to Third Avenue, where they boarded a large green school bus filled with other officers. At the head of the bus was a small elderly man dressed completely in black. It was Monsignor Joseph Dunne, who offered a general absolution for all present: "All your sins are forgiven in the name of the Father, of the Son, and of the Holy Ghost. May God be with you." Katz quickly asked, "What about me, Monsignor? I'm Jewish." Dunne was nonplussed. "Son, tonight you're Catholic," he replied as the bus raced down East River Drive at seventy miles per hour with two police cruisers as escorts.[65]

On the way, Captain James Quenton briefed the men. "The riots are much worse in Brooklyn and that's where we're headed," he said. "Tonight you'll get a chance to put into practice what you learned about riot control. We're being sent in to break the back of the riot. I can tell you we're looking at an estimated four thousand rioters. Keep your heads, remember your training, and you'll make it through the night." The bus was silent. Then someone began to bang the floor of the bus with his axe handle. Others joined him and it became rhythmic. Next someone started to chant "Kill" on every beat until the entire bus was repeating it. "Kill . . . Kill . . . Kill . . . again and again, over and over, louder and louder, like a deadly mantra," recalled O'Neil.[66]

The bus stopped at Fulton and Nostrand, one block from the main riot at Bedford Avenue. "Remember," said Quenton, "keep your heads and keep your guns holstered. Good luck men." The officers exited the bus and, despite orders, immediately began to fire in response to a hail of debris, rocks, and bottles. "Every cop was slapping leather and firing off rounds into the surrounding buildings," remembered O'Neil. "My revolver was empty before I even made it to the cover of a doorway." He looked for his partner, started to reload, and saw the captain doing the same. So much for orders. But according to O'Neil the gunshots were effective—the three hundred or so rounds the three TPF squads (forty men in all) had fired within ninety seconds had calmed the area, at least for the moment.[67]

The use of gunfire was not limited to the TPF. Other officers had also exercised their discretion to fire warning shots above the heads of threatening crowds (rooftops were less of a threat in low-rise Brooklyn). "This was deliberate firing in the air," asserted Commissioner Murphy later, somewhat defensively and inaccurately. "These men were kneeling, being careful. Nobody was running down the street going boom, boom, boom. What these shots prevented was hand-to-hand combat; in hand-to-hand you will have a lot of deaths and injuries." But since most officers bought their own ammunition and rarely carried more than two dozen rounds, they were soon down to their final bullets. Once again, as on Saturday in Harlem, the Police Department had to rush ammunition to the center of the action. This time it was Nostrand Avenue, which was first cleared of looters and then of photographers who wanted to take pictures of officers frantically crowding around the resupply car laden with six thousand additional rounds.[68]

With Fulton and Nostrand under control, Captain Quenton ordered the TPF to Fulton and Bedford, the heart of the riot, where thousands of looters had congregated in a single block of one-story buildings. "It was wall-to-wall chaos, with looting everywhere," recalled O'Neil, who saw a short man in suit, tie, and helmet approach. He was Phil Walsh, the three-star chief of detectives. "All right, TPF, get over here, you're working for me now," he ordered. Facing the riot, he clasped his hands together above his head in the shape of a pyramid, the signal for the squads to form an inverted "V" flying wedge formation. "Let's get those sons of bitches," commanded Walsh and the men obeyed, waving their axe handles and chanting "Kill" as they marched down Fulton Street. "We were one unit, with one purpose," said O'Neil. "And that purpose was to break the back of the riot as quickly as possible."[69] Ten minutes later, it was mission accomplished, although sporadic looting continued for hours.

By 1:30 A.M. the scene had cooled to the point where the police could begin to remove officers from the streets. But two more black men were in the hospital with gunshot wounds. Harry Britton, thirty-six, was shot in the stomach as officers were clearing a grocery store of looters. The police contended that Britton had hurled a can of vegetables at a patrolman, hitting him in the chest; an eyewitness claimed that Britton was shot when officers fired into the crowd. Willie McDowell, twenty-three, was also shot in the stomach when he tried to take advantage of the police concentration on Fulton Street and rob a shoe store on Eastern Parkway, south of Atlantic Avenue. When Patrolman James Barrentine spotted him and ordered him to surrender, McDowell leaped at him and the officer fired. He remained with the victim until an ambulance arrived despite the ominous presence of a large group of angry onlookers.[70]

In the aftermath, eyewitnesses testified that the vast majority of the participants were onlookers and bystanders, while the police attributed most of the vandalism and looting to gangs and hoodlums, to "people who live by their wits" and seize opportunities when they see them. McDowell seemed to fit the profile created by the authorities.[71]

But George Fleary, a respected lawyer and vice president of the Brooklyn NAACP, expressed reservations. During the riot, he observed both looters and officers in person and from his office on Fulton. "I walked to Bedford and Fulton," he stated. "Just as I turned the corner somebody fired a gun right in front of my face. Police were running into a drug store and pulling a Negro out of the doorway toward a patrol car in the street." A World War II veteran who had served as a captain in the military police, Fleary had some experience with crowd control. "A lot of that firing was unnecessary," he asserted. The police, he contended, could have handled matters in a less violent manner.[72]

In Washington, Congressman Powell raised the same issue when he spoke with reporters at the airport Tuesday night after his flight from Geneva, where he had attended a conference on the impact of automation on cities. He called the NYPD "the most irresponsible police force in the nation" and contrasted it unfavorably with southern departments in Alabama and Mississippi that used tear gas and water hoses instead of live ammunition.[73]

"This was not a race riot," Powell asserted. "The black man is mad—mad with the continued brutality of white policemen." He added that he had no intention of returning to Harlem soon—he claimed that he was too busy with the antipoverty legislation awaiting action in Congress. But Powell contended that in "five minutes" the mayor and the commissioner could alleviate the crisis. "They can suspend that cop now," he stated. "They can name a civilian review board today and it can meet tomorrow. They can get an integrated force—not a black force—in Harlem immediately."[74]

By contrast, the Reverend Dr. W. Eugene Houston assigned blame more broadly. The chairman of the New York Presbyterian Church's Commission on Religion and Race was no apologist for the police—he supported the creation of a civilian review board and wanted Gilligan suspended until the grand jury had reached a verdict. But he also had little patience for the promoters of violence. In response to a question from reporters, he called for the arrest of Jesse Gray and the Reverend Nelson Dukes on charges of inciting the rioting and looting.[75] Soon the list of names would grow as the hunt for instigators began.

For Barbara Benson, a college-educated Brooklyn resident, the fundamental problem was the racial antagonism at the heart of police-community relations. "As a human being as well as a Negro I weep at the damage done to this city and the world by the Harlem riots," she wrote to the *New York Times*. Yet, she added, the uprising was predictable and understandable because of the underlying anger among many blacks. "Many of us," she stated, "have been stopped by the police and, yes, many frisked for no other reason than that a Negro in a certain neighborhood 'seems suspicious.'"[76]

At the root of the mistrust, continued Benson, was the unjustified animosity white officers felt toward African Americans. "Let no one be deceived," she concluded. "Many Harlem police are sadistic in their administration of the law, insatiable in their beatings, unable to discern men from children, and irrational in their fear of the black man."[77]

It was a heartfelt indictment, but not a universal sentiment. As the racial unrest moved into a fifth day, New Yorkers of all races, genders, ideologies, and ages remained deeply divided as to how to redress past grievances, alleviate present tensions, and prevent future violence.

CHAPTER 8

COMMUNISTS, CONSERVATIVES, AND CONSPIRACIES

"No, no, no," moaned the mayor
"It's not the way of the order
Oh, stay in your homes, please leave us alone
We'll be glad to talk in the morning"
    —Phil Ochs, "In the Heat of the Summer"

WEDNESDAY, JULY 22

On Tuesday afternoon, Lyndon Johnson had voiced his private suspicion to J. Edgar Hoover that communists were somehow behind the civil unrest in New York. Now on Wednesday morning the president's fears seemed confirmed and amplified, even if the conspiracy charge was unfounded. As he ate breakfast in bed he skimmed several newspapers, including the *Daily News*. The article that immediately captured his attention was "Blame Hate Groups, Red & White, for Harlem Terror" by three reporters. They broke the news that a five-month investigation spearheaded by the FBI and detectives with the Bureau of Special Service (BOSS) unit—the NYPD's "Red Squad"—had uncovered fifty paid operatives and a thousand "young fanatics dedicated to violence." Their instructions: "Deploy! Incite!" According to an unnamed source the communist conspirators were "beatniks, crumbums, addicts, and thieves" who received payment in cash and narcotics.[1]

The Powell shooting had placed the intelligence unit on full alert. It had "all of the explosive elements imaginable," recalled Anthony Bouza, then a

BOSS lieutenant and later the Minneapolis chief of police. He made Saturday visits to Central Harlem in civilian clothes to listen to various speakers. As a result, he was dismissive of the communist threat in general, but worried in particular about disaffected loners who would go to a meeting, complain that "this is a lot of bullshit," and then plan violent acts on their own. To keep tabs on dangerous individuals, Bouza used undercover infiltrators who worked in pairs—though unknown to each other so that he could cross-check their reports—to befriend and follow the "hot heads."[2]

According to the Daily News, the money trail allegedly led to an unnamed business on West 125th Street, perhaps Michaux's bookstore, where diplomatic attachés from African nations visited regularly and professional radicals received pay envelopes weekly. Other circumstantial evidence included the ambiguous involvement of Jesse Gray, the rent-strike activist who had spoken at the Sunday afternoon rally at Mount Morris Presbyterian Church. In testimony before the House Un-American Activities Committee (HUAC) several years earlier, Gray had denied under oath that he was currently a communist, but had repeatedly invoked the Fifth Amendment when asked about prior affiliation and other matters. Also in attendance at the Sunday rally, which had the support of the radical Progressive Labor Party (PLP), were Robert Thompson and William Patterson, both former national committee members of the Communist Party.[3]

The Daily News further claimed that an "unholy alliance" of left-wing agitators and right-wing extremists (backed by wealthy individuals like Texas millionaire H. L. Hunt) were funneling funds to the Black Muslims and Black Nationalists because they supposedly had plenty of weapons and were willing to use them. The conservatives hoped to provoke more violence and enhance Goldwater's chances for victory. The radicals wanted to discredit the mainstream civil rights organizations and spark a revolution. "The communists have been concentrating on these hate groups and Black Nationalists not because they believe in their philosophy," said the Reverend Richard A. Hildebrand, president of the New York branch of the NAACP, "but because they think they are the wildest and most extreme and through them they can promote the most unrest."[4]

The existence of a conservative conspiracy behind the riots was never proven, although Johnson remained interested in the possibility as a way of placing blame on Goldwater. In September he again asked Hoover about Hunt. "No, we've never been able to pin anything on him," replied the FBI director. But he was able to pass on to the president the story of how the wealthy Texan had allegedly made his money: he had operated a gambling den and whorehouse in Arkansas, then used his winnings to buy some land that had oil on it. The tale elicited several chuckles from Johnson.[5]

But the false charge of a communist conspiracy was no laughing matter. It was inflammatory and drew an immediate round of denunciations and denials from black radicals like Thompson and Patterson, who labeled the allegation a "big lie" and affirmed that they condemned "violence as a means of eliminating ghetto life and its monstrous evils." The PLP, which had split from the Communist Party three years earlier and distributed leaflets at the student protest on Friday morning, said that blaming "outside agitators" was the "oldest trick in the book" and was intended to "divide the people of Harlem against themselves."[6]

Although black liberals saw the communist question as a potential distraction, some were hesitant to dismiss it entirely. James Farmer of CORE stressed that the riot had begun spontaneously, but cautioned that "since the weekend certain elements have been trying to take control . . . and exploit it." The Reverend Milton Galamison, a key figure in the school boycott back in February, contended that "unseen forces" had launched a "whispering campaign" intended to stir up trouble in Bed-Stuy. "All winter we worked with peaceful, orderly demonstrations to try to get wrongs righted," he lamented. "We were vilified, called extremists and irresponsible." Now, he warned, "The brick throwers have taken over. Let the city deal with the brick throwers [since] they wouldn't deal with us."[7]

But other black leaders viewed the conspiracy theory as a side issue with little relevance. The riots may have given New York and the freedom movement a "black eye," but they were "not organized or financed by any group" according to Roy Wilkins of the NAACP, who by Wednesday had returned from his Wyoming vacation. "Raising the Communist cry won't solve very much at this time," he added. It would be a "dangerous mistake to conclude that the rioting was fundamentally the work of professional agitators," affirmed Alexander J. Allen, executive director of the Urban League.[8]

"Privation and despair"—not radical extremists—were the main causes of the civil unrest according to State Senator Constance Baker Motley, who in 1954 had assisted Thurgood Marshall with the *Brown* case and in 1966 became the first African American woman on the federal bench. Mistrust of the police exacerbated those conditions. "We never have rioting on Park Avenue between 59th and 96th Streets for the same reason that we do have rioting in Central Harlem and Bedford-Stuyvesant," she observed.[9]

Outside New York, the debate raged as white conservatives condemned the supposed radical role in hopes of putting more pressure on Johnson and providing more assistance to Goldwater. In Washington, Senator James Eastland of Mississippi charged that in Harlem "evidence of Communist participation and leadership in civil rights demonstrations is being brought into the open." Columnist David Lawrence, founder of *U.S. News & World Report*, added that the "Communist conspiracy" was now visible despite the efforts of liberals and leftists to hinder the work of HUAC. But Congressman Powell countered that the conservative accusation of radical involvement was "ridiculous." And from a rally in Jackson, Mississippi, King was withering in his scorn. "There are as many Communists in this Freedom Movement as there are Eskimos in Florida," he said in a mocking tone.[10]

The allegation of radical infiltration among the rioters nevertheless put the mainstream civil rights groups on the defensive. The executive secretary of the NAACP's New York branch denied that the communists had any real influence and insisted that his organization had weeded them out. The public relations director of CORE also insisted that his organization—especially the Brooklyn chapter—had expelled radical members because they might resort to violence in an effort to become "heroes" of the movement. "CORE, which was formerly considered too wild and militant, is now being condemned for conservatism and called an 'Uncle Tom,'" Marvin Rich told the *Daily News* reporters. "And why? Because we don't believe in killing people. And that's what they want to do up there—kill people."[11] The chilling comment may have unsettled Johnson as he read it that morning.

In the White House, Johnson's first long-distance phone call of the day went to New York. "Welcome back, my friend," he greeted Mayor Robert Wagner, who after seven hours of needed rest had awakened at 8 A.M. Stressing that he hoped to ease Wagner's burden as much as possible, the president declared that he wanted to "cooperate and coordinate" with the mayor. Johnson also vowed to "supplement and complement" whatever City Hall had in mind. "It's my own belief that some of these right-wingers, whether they're unmasked or not, are contributing something to this and financing a little of this and trying to start it," he told Wagner anxiously. "And I anticipate that Harlem's the first place and California will be the next place and Philadelphia will be the next place, to kind of prove what [Goldwater] said in his acceptance speech, that the cities of this country are going to be in a hell of a shape."[12]

Wagner interjected with his sixth "right" of the call as Johnson continued his monologue—it was almost impossible to interrupt him once he got on a roll. "I think it's a good thing to raise a question whether some of this stuff is being fomented and contributed from outside and make the other people stop and think a little bit, particularly Negroes, before they become the tools of some of these right-wing cranks." The situation, the president added, might not become "as dangerous to us as it might otherwise" if the administration could expose the conservative conspiracy. "That's right," replied Wagner again, who finally got a word in edgewise to tell the president that he had taken a ride through Harlem on Tuesday night with Commissioner Murphy and it was relatively calm.[13]

Johnson resumed by urging Wagner to make public any indication of conservative involvement, which was never found. "The good people of this country don't want this unrest fomented," he said, and with more evidence provided they might come to see Goldwater's defense of extremism as "almost like advocating rioting." The mayor concurred and observed that in Harlem he had seen youth wearing motorcycle helmets and carrying two-way radios (walkie-talkies). "Somebody must be giving them that equipment," he said. "I mean, they're not buying it themselves." The president agreed. "We have to be very, very cautious about it now," he declared. Pledging that Hoover would stay in close contact with Murphy, he promised Wagner he would support him "any way we can."[14]

Soon after speaking with Wagner, Johnson phoned Hoover. The day before, the FBI director had followed the president's instructions and spoken with Governor Nelson Rockefeller, who was still vacationing in Wyoming. According to Hoover, the governor said he was in close contact with City Hall and could mobilize five thousand State Police and National Guardsmen in less than two hours, but that it was "the last thing he wants to do."[15]

Hoover also said that Rockefeller thought the FBI should investigate both radical and conservative extremists, which the director agreed to do. The governor mentioned that during the California primary in late May he had met some Goldwater supporters who had said "there were going to be race riots this fall and it was going to be embarrassing." Not in New York, Rockefeller had replied, firmly and confidently. That's what you think, they had countered, adding that "they were going to see to it that [the riots] took place."[16]

In contrast to his one-sided dialogue with Wagner, Johnson let Hoover take the lead and report on his own conversation with the mayor earlier

Wednesday morning. "I think the Brooklyn situation is more of a looting of stores than a racial problem," commented the FBI director. "There no doubt is a great deal of Communist influence on the situation in Harlem." In response, the president urged Hoover to get a copy of the article in the *Daily News* and began to read an excerpt from it.[17]

Hoover then informed Johnson that he had sidestepped a direct request from the Justice Department "to investigate the police lieutenant who killed the colored boy" because he was reluctant to pressure Commissioner Murphy "by harassing his officers when he is doing everything he can to control them." According to Hoover, the president assigned the highest importance to the Harlem Riot and gave the agency complete authority to track down any and all extremist participation. It was unnecessary. As Johnson spoke, two hundred agents were already in New York conducting interviews, pursuing leads, and exploring every federal angle of the civil unrest, now entering a fifth day.[18]

Meanwhile, in Brooklyn on Wednesday morning more than one hundred merchants recited the refrain of woes that their Harlem counterparts had related on Sunday, Monday, and Tuesday. "We never had any trouble before," said Bill Kleinberg, proprietor of the Stop-N-Shop grocery on Nostrand Avenue for eighteen years. "Now—overnight—they put me out of business." Next door Newman Epps, a black man who had operated his small dry-cleaning business for twenty years, stared at a smashed plate-glass window that cost $250 to replace (he too had no insurance, which was expensive and hard to get). How, he wondered, would he make good on the more than $1,000 worth of suits, skirts, and shirts stolen from his store? "I got here in the middle of the looting," Epps recalled quietly as he surveyed the overturned racks and scattered clothes, "but I couldn't do anything about it. I had to stand by and watch [the looters] because I was afraid for my life."[19]

Hoping to help small business owners was Brooklyn Borough President Abe Stark, who was understandably sympathetic. Before he entered politics, Stark was a tailor who ran a clothing store on Pitkin Avenue. Few knew him until he paid for a promotion in Ebbets Field, home of the Dodgers. Located under the scoreboard near right center field, the billboard read "Hit Sign. Win Suit. Abe Stark. Brooklyn's Leading Clothier." The sign had made Stark a local legend, and in 1954 he became president of the New York City Council. But in 1961 he was forced to run for borough president, a mostly ceremonial position, which seriously strained his relations with Wagner.[20]

Now Stark saw an opportunity to seize the spotlight while the city waited for the mayor to give his speech and chart a course of action. In the morning, the borough president met with his deputy, various religious leaders, and Russell N. Service, executive director of the Bedford YMCA, who had hosted the meeting convened by Captain Jenkins on Tuesday. Presumably, Service informed Stark of how little it had accomplished. The borough president then called the mayor and the commissioner, who promised to provide the best police protection possible. Not entirely reassured by either conversation, Stark decided to send telegrams to no fewer than fifty-seven community activists, inviting them to a conference in his office at 4 P.M.

In his opening remarks, Stark told those assembled that he was there to listen. "The community itself, since it is closest to the situation, may best know what can be done and how to do it," he said. But he was quickly disabused of the notion that Bed-Stuy could handle the unrest, and what followed was a "heated discussion" according to an aide. "There's nothing that can stop us," declared the Reverend Walter Offutt of Bethany Baptist Church, speaking from the perspective of the demonstrators. "If Jesus Christ—if God Himself came down, He would have to shake us up before we would stop."[21]

Arthur Bramwell, the GOP leader of Bed-Stuy, believed that the top priority was the restoration of law and order, even if it meant firing at rioters and looters. Born in Brooklyn in 1918, the son of Jamaican immigrants, he had made campaign speeches for Mayor La Guardia in 1937 and joined the Republican Party at a time when most African Americans were switching their allegiance to the Democratic Party of Franklin Roosevelt and the New Deal. Now, more than a quarter century later, he contended that too many "decent people" had to live in fear. "If it means that some criminals have to be shot and killed, let's get on with it," said Bramwell, who represented a shrinking though still influential minority within the black community.[22]

Despite the lack of concrete progress, the meeting concluded with an agreement to impose a local moratorium on demonstrations similar to the national moratorium that Wilkins, Bayard Rustin, and A. Philip Randolph were attempting to organize. The community activists also decided upon a three-pronged communications strategy designed to reach those on the street in their own language. The first prong was a pamphlet drafted by George Fleary's law partners and distributed by the Brooklyn NAACP. Titled "Cool It Baby," it made an urgent appeal for voter registration after reassuring the demonstrators that their message was delivered.[23]

The second prong consisted of public service announcements promoting peace, which radio stations were encouraged to run. The idea was to have the disc jockeys speak directly in their own words to their youthful listeners. In Harlem, WLIB received special permission from the Federal Communications Commission to broadcast at night after Percy Sutton flew to Washington to meet with officials. "I was angry at prevailing police misconduct and at the mayor who could have changed things but failed to," he recalled. After contemplating his role Sutton decided that "all I could do was use the radio" to end what he saw as a rebellion.[24]

The final prong of the peace front was to deploy a sound truck to cruise the commercial streets of Bed-Stuy starting at 5:30 P.M. Plastered with NAACP voter-registration stickers, it was piloted by Fleary and three other members. For the first few hours, everything went smoothly. But then at dusk the sound truck parked at the corner of Nostrand and Fulton, site of the protests the night before, and several hundred onlookers quickly surrounded it.[25]

At first the mood was positive. "I don't want any outside agitators coming in here and destroying this community," said Fleary into the microphone to loud applause. "The press has exploded this thing out of proportion. Wallace, Goldwater, every southern figure is happy at what happened last night." The crowd clapped enthusiastically as a man yelled "Goldwater must go." The NAACP official described Bed-Stuy as a "community of law" and added that no one should "confuse New York City with Alabama."[26]

But then Fleary miscalculated. In the face of repeated questions from another man about police brutality, he opted to confront the issue head-on, even though he had intended to avoid it because it was so controversial. "We should not put the pressure on the cop on the beat," Fleary said. "He has a wife and a family and has to support them like you and me. We should put the pressure where it belongs—on the police commissioner." The statement was either courageous or foolhardy—as always, it was a matter of perspective.[27]

"Go home," jeered the crowd. "Go home." But Fleary was not done. "Mayor Wagner and the city will see that Jimmy Powell and his family get a square deal," he added. Suddenly, some listeners turned on him and began to beat on the roof of the car. Others started to rock it from side to side. Perhaps the hostile reaction was because Fleary had offered an unacceptable defense of a hated symbol—the white policeman. Or perhaps it was because (as he believed) organized agitators had chosen that moment to strike.[28]

Four men abruptly moved from the theater marquee across the street and positioned themselves at the four wheels of the NAACP vehicle. "These guys were in their upper twenties, early thirties," recalled Fleary. "They wore green berets and when I saw them coming at me, I knew they weren't coming for any good purpose. When they started to rock the station wagon, they knew what they were doing. They got the teenagers laughing, and then they started to help these men rock us. Then everything got out of hand."[29] It was no exaggeration.

"Let me finish," pleaded Fleary. "Please let me finish." It was too late—he lost control of the microphone. That was the signal for the police—who until then had watched from a distance—to intervene. Officers on both foot and horseback stormed into the crowd and rescued the NAACP officials. But in every direction—east and west on Fulton, north and south on Nostrand—clusters of rioters now scattered. And once they had evaded the thin blue line of officers stationed at the corners of the intersection, the sharp sounds of broken glass began to echo again through the darkness. "It was the same stores as before," recounted Ophelia Bryant of Herkimer Street. "Those people had put up signs saying the stores were owned by Negroes, but that didn't seem to make any difference."[30]

The police had hoped to make a difference on Wednesday night by changing tactics. Earlier in the day the decision was made to station mounted patrolmen at the four corners of Nostrand and Fulton. The use of horses, said Deputy Police Commissioner Walter Arm, was intended to "prevent the possibility of hand-to-hand conflict and to reduce injuries to rioters and police." Because Bed-Stuy had lower buildings and wider streets than Harlem, it seemed like the correct move—but as a precaution the department placed officers on several of the three- and four-story apartment houses on Fulton. With the high ground occupied and the police horses in plain view, the NYPD believed that it was in a better position to keep the traffic moving and the crowds under control.[31]

To improve communications, the department also established a mobile headquarters on a side street off Nostrand Avenue and across from Girls

High, which was no longer in use. And it brought in a fresh commander, Captain Anthony O'Connell, recalled from vacation. After forty-eight hours on duty, Inspector Walter Clerke and his deputy Dominic Hallinan could finally get some rest. The plan seemed sound, but execution and events would dictate otherwise.

At 9 P.M. Wagner settled into his seat at the CBS studio, flanked on his right by Murphy. With a sober demeanor on his tanned but tired face and a stack of paper on the desk in front of him, the mayor looked directly into the camera and began his much-anticipated speech on the unrest. "I am convinced," he said after reviewing his nighttime tour of the riot zone with the police commissioner, "that the overwhelming majority of those who live in the Harlem community neither participated in nor appreciated the violence and disorder." As he spoke, the mayor's words were broadcast live by all four local television stations and six local radio stations. Among them was WINS, the longest-running all-news station in the nation, whose tagline promised listeners, "You give us twenty-two minutes, we'll give you the world." But this time it was the world according to Wagner in twenty-three minutes.[32]

"The mandate to maintain law and order is absolute, unconditional, and unqualified," the mayor continued in a somber tone. Then he spoke directly to what he believed—or hoped—was the silent majority of Central Harlem and Bed-Stuy. "Law and order are the Negroes' best friend," he asserted. "Make no mistake about that. The opposite of law and order is mob rule, and that is the way of the Ku Klux Klan and the night riders and the lynch mobs." The subtext was clear—New York was not Alabama or Mississippi, regardless of what some black leaders like Farmer and Powell contended. Next Wagner spoke to what he viewed as the vocal or violent minority when he warned that "defiance of or attacks upon the police, whose mission it is to enforce law and order, will not be condoned or tolerated by me at any time."[33]

The language was unconditional and uncompromising, reinforced by the mayor's reaffirmation that he had "complete confidence" in the commissioner seated next to him in the studio. But Wagner also vowed to address the problems in housing, education, and employment that had served as fuel for the fire. "We are no richer than our poorest citizen," he said, "no stronger than the weakest among us." And in the face of reports that the tourist trade had suffered, he maintained that New York was a safe

FIGURE 13. Mayor Robert Wagner, with Police Commissioner Michael Murphy (left) at his side, addresses the citizens of New York in a televised speech. © Bettmann/ CORBIS.

city and appealed to visitors not to cancel their hotel reservations or change their travel plans. Criminals, the mayor wrongly claimed, had not seriously harmed a single tourist in the past three months, not one of the 150,000 Shriners presently in Manhattan or one of the 4.5 million visitors to the World's Fair in Queens. In fact, reporters soon discovered that on Tuesday night the manager of the Tournament of Roses in Pasadena was mugged in Midtown by a black youth and suffered a fractured pelvis as well as a brain concussion.[34]

As for the "spark" of the crisis, Wagner insisted that while the grand jury investigated the Powell shooting and the City Council contemplated changes to the current review board, it was premature for him to take executive action. Instead, he stressed that "ultimate authority" for the Police Department already rested in civilian hands—his own. As part of a nine-point program, he pledged that Deputy Mayor Edward Cavanagh would now evaluate every case of police brutality brought before the review board. He would also have the added responsibility of receiving brutality complaints at City Hall and referring them to the Police Department. And Wagner promised—as Screvane had on Monday—that his administration would recruit more minority officers, station more black patrolmen in Harlem, and expand outreach efforts to minority communities.[35]

These were, Wagner conceded, only first steps. More were needed and more would come. But he was careful to emphasize that in taking action "we are not bowing or surrendering to pressure. We will not be browbeaten by prophets of despair or by peddlers of hate, or by those who thrive on continued frustration." At the same time, the mayor counseled against overreaction in the other direction. Not on his watch would New York become a garrison state, with individual liberties sacrificed in the name of law and order, even though in his view they were the foundation of freedom and justice for all.[36]

Like Johnson in the coming years, Wagner charted a compromise course between what radicals and conservatives demanded. Neither appeasing the lawbreakers at any cost nor preserving the peace at any price were politically acceptable options for the moderate mayor. He was also determined not to bring in the National Guard—an "absolute last resort" and "the last thing in the world I wanted to do"—because it was not trained to handle the situation, as the results in many other cities would make abundantly clear.[37]

Wagner concluded with a fervent appeal to all citizens to lend a helping hand for the sake of the city. "The nation and the world have their eyes on New York," he asserted, and it was true. For five days, the international spotlight had shone, unflatteringly, on the financial and media capital of the United States. In Madrid, a headline blared "Harlem—U.S.A. Shame." In Lagos, the *West African Pilot* depicted the unrest as proof of the "ineffectiveness" of the Civil Rights Act. And in Moscow, *Izvestia* continued to exploit the riot, running a photo of a beaten and battered African American lying in the street with the caption "Another victim of the bloody persecution of Negroes by the New York police." To the dismay of the White House, the Soviet Union was winning this round of the Cold War propaganda fight.[38]

After the telecast, Wagner held a brief press conference at the Liederkranz Hall on the Upper East Side. In his address, the mayor had mentioned that the FBI director had supplied Murphy with "certain information which is of the greatest interest and use." Now Wagner insinuated to reporters that communist and conservative extremists might have encouraged or exploited the riots. "We have some evidence of that," he said, cryptically and cautiously. "We'll reveal it at the proper time. At present it's a matter between Mr. J. Edgar Hoover, the Police Commissioner, and myself." He would say no more and the issue was put aside for the moment.[39]

Of more immediate interest was the mixed reaction among black activists to Wagner's speech. Perhaps the most positive came, surprisingly, from the Reverend Nelson Dukes, who had led the march on the 28th Precinct in Central Harlem that triggered the explosion on Saturday night. "I think it was one of the best speeches he ever made," he said in an interview that night. "It came at a time when it was badly needed." Dukes added that he believed it would do some good. "I believe all citizens of goodwill will govern themselves accordingly," he predicted.[40]

Few others shared his optimism. Most criticized the mayor's failure to dismiss Gilligan or implement an independent review board. "Wagner did not go far enough," said CORE leader Farmer, who expressed disappointment that he had not put "the prestige of his office" behind civilian oversight of the Police Department. "Something concrete has to be done. We cannot restrain the people of Harlem without something concrete from the Mayor." NAACP leader Hildebrand was equally critical. "There was nothing new in Wagner's statement," he said. "There's no longer any need to deny police brutality. It exists just as plain as the news pictures from Harlem. There must be a civilian review board."[41]

The executive director of the New York Urban League agreed. The "racist streak" displayed by white officers in recent days, he asserted, demonstrated the necessity of a truly independent review board. More black officers in minority communities were also essential, even though they too drew the ire of the crowds at times. "You won't find Negro patrolmen addressing the residents of Harlem as 'nigger,'" Allen argued vehemently, "and you won't find Negro patrolmen addressing a Negro woman as 'black bitch.'" With emotions running high, the responses were unsurprising—officials like Allen, Farmer, and Hildebrand, although not elected like the mayor, were also embattled and under pressure from their constituents.[42]

It is doubtful that Wagner's words could or would have made a real difference on the tense streets of Bed-Stuy on Wednesday night, even if the mayor had promised to fire both Gilligan and Murphy, which he had not and would not. For the third evening in a row, the business district erupted in looting and vandalism. Although the destruction was less widespread than on Tuesday, in part because few stores were left untouched, the anger remained raw and visceral. At an intersection, a group of teens surrounded a car stopped at the light. Inside were two white journalists who hastily locked the doors and closed the windows. As the red turned green and the vehicle sped away, a black youth delivered a menacing message: "We're gonna kill every one of you white bastards."[43]

No one, white or black, was killed in Brooklyn or Harlem on Wednesday night. But three more looters in Bed-Stuy were shot when they were cornered by police and, according to Inspector Clerke, "figured they might as well try and fight their way out." Rufus Weaver was caught in a dry-cleaning store and critically injured by a bullet in the abdomen when he refused to surrender. Rufus Johnson was wounded in the leg when he ran at officers outside a liquor store. And William Bish was also hit in the leg when he ignored a warning shot and tried to flee from a furniture store. More than ninety windows were smashed and thirty-five people were arrested in the ten-block area surrounding the intersection of Nostrand and Fulton, where police had to fire a dozen shots to disperse an unruly crowd of six hundred. The rioting and looting began less than thirty minutes after Wagner had ended his telecast.[44]

Most of the looters were in their teens and twenties, but some were even younger. Father William Cullen of St. Peter Claver Catholic Church, who had attended the meeting organized by Stark, was one of the few whites walking the streets that night. At one point, he encountered an eleven-year-old black parishioner carrying clothes that he had taken from a store. "I'm sorry, Father," said the small boy sheepishly, "but everybody's doing it." Shaken, Cullen went to find the Reverend Richard Martin, the prominent black minister of St. Philips Church. Together, they broadcast a joint appeal for peace and unity from a phone booth. Whether it made a difference was impossible to tell.[45]

Assemblyman Thomas Jones lived close to the epicenter of the disorder. Although he was under no obligation to venture into the streets, he opted to see what he could do. It was pointless. "I am not a policeman; there was nothing I could do," he said with a mixture of regret and remorse. "I saw the wreckage, the undiscriminating attitude of the people. They didn't discriminate between stores owned by Negroes and white people. The kids who came around here don't know the places. Some guys were yelling,

FIGURE 14. A police officer restrains an angry demonstrator at the corner of Fulton and Nostrand. Photo by Stanley Wolfson. Library of Congress, Prints & Photographs Division, New York World-Telegram & Sun Collection.

'Don't hit that place,' but everybody was not made privy to it. Some knew it, but they couldn't communicate it to everybody." Frustrated, he departed to make his own plea for peace from the studio of a Manhattan radio station.[46]

Between 6 P.M. and midnight the Fire Department reported more than sixty false alarms. The police switchboard was also inundated with bogus calls, either because the perpetrators had already fled when officers arrived or because the callers wanted to distract attention from looters. Police were convinced that it was mostly the latter. Still, officers had no choice but to respond, and at times it almost resulted in tragedy. At Broadway and Fulton, patrol cars arrived simultaneously from several directions only to find themselves in an ambush as a barrage of glass and rocks rained down on them from nearby roofs and the elevated station. By sheer luck there were no injuries and only a windshield was smashed.[47]

The incident was not isolated—officers were increasingly the targets of projectiles because after three nights of vandalism most businesses had covered their windows, broken or unbroken, with plywood and taken other measures to protect property. "I saw [the teenagers] throwing rocks," recounted Jones after his foray into the riot. "They would come up, look around, see if a cop was nearby, or sometimes just stand across the street and heave, or they would come running along and heave it running. They'd laugh, and then run away. They didn't even bother to loot. The looters were the moochers and the same elements that operate after floods and catastrophes."[48]

After three nights of twelve- to eighteen-hour shifts, the police were exhausted and angered by the unrelenting physical and verbal abuse they had to endure. Fortunately, shortly after midnight rain began to fall and the crowds started to dissipate. By 1 A.M. the littered streets were empty and the mounted officers redeployed to the communications outpost across from Girls High. In the middle of the intersection at Nostrand and Fulton a group of police and reporters gathered. "Rain, rain, rain, come on and rain," said an officer as a photographer urged him to pose like the patrolman in the classic number in *Singing in the Rain*, the 1952 musical with Gene Kelly. "I don't know why it is," observed another patrolman. "Some of these people aren't afraid of horses, of nightsticks, even of guns. A couple of drops of rain and they run."[49]

In Central Harlem on Wednesday night it was quiet—quieter than usual, in fact. No arrests were made and only five windows were broken. Traffic flowed smoothly as the police lifted barricades and unsealed streets. Restaurants and bars were open. The only injury reported was to an officer who stopped his police car to remove trash cans from the intersection of 129th Street and Fifth Avenue and was struck on the hand by a tossed bottle. The only looting reported was at 127th Street and Lenox Avenue, where a grocery store was robbed by a dozen or so people who broke through a plywood barrier.[50]

But a major clash again took place in Lower Manhattan. For the second straight night, roughly one hundred black and white CORE demonstrators picketed in front of Police Headquarters on Centre Street. During the two-hour protest, which began around 9 P.M., they demanded an immediate end to police brutality and chanted "Jim Crow Must Go," "Freedom Now," and "Gilligan Must Go." As they marched, around three hundred neighborhood residents, most of them Italians of all ages, including small children, heckled the group. "Niggers must go," they yelled. "White trash go home." And they hurled rocks and eggs, cans and bottles at the demonstrators, although a patrolman suffered the sole injury when struck in the eye by broken glass. "They can't afford to throw away eggs in Harlem," commented a white protester. "We'd be a lot safer in Harlem," responded a black volunteer. "Or anywhere else."[51]

An elderly Italian had no objections. "They come down here and disturb us," he said. "They're an outside element. They ought to go home." It was echo of what the crowds in Harlem had chanted at the police on Saturday and Sunday night—once more the politics of race and place were intertwined. At 11:30 P.M. the demonstrators requested a police escort for the four-block walk to the IRT station at Spring Street. The department complied by forming a blue cordon of fifty officers to protect the picketers as they marched two-by-two to the subway. At every intersection the demonstrators were confronted by more than a hundred Italian teenagers armed with firecrackers, garbage can lids, and beer bottles—one of which narrowly missed the head of Chief Inspector Lawrence McKearney, who had assumed command of the escort.[52]

At one corner, a teenager defied a black officer's order to move. "Hit me, nigger, hit me and you're dead," he warned. Other patrolmen intervened and the youth suddenly doubled over in pain. "The nigger cop hit me," he moaned. "An Italian cop can hit me, but not a nigger." In all, the short stroll took almost fifteen long minutes and one demonstrator, a young white woman, was injured when hit by glass in the leg. "This is the backlash," said Herbert Callender, leader of the Bronx chapter of CORE, who was in charge of the pickets. "If the people in Harlem behaved like the whites here, there would be a lot more cracked heads."[53]

As the demonstrators rode home on the subway, an unprecedented unity meeting of black activists was ending at the Harlem Labor Center on 125th Street. Chaired by Percy Sutton, it included 150 delegates from the NAACP, Urban League, and CORE as well as the Black Nationalists and Black Muslims. Wilkins, Hildebrand, Farmer, and Rustin were not present, but their views were represented, and almost everyone else who was someone was there. It was a "stormy" but "satisfactory meeting of divergent groups not normally together in the past," said Sutton, sounding like Stark earlier in the day in Brooklyn. After three hours of debate and deliberations, those present agreed to send a telegram to Wagner demanding that he fire Murphy and two other top police officials.[54]

The delegates also agreed to send a five-man committee to the Harlem Youth Opportunities Unlimited (HARYOU) meeting on Friday evening at the 125th Street YMCA. The committee included Edward Davis of the African National Movement, James Lawson of the United African Movement, and a third Black Nationalist as well as Benjamin X of the Organization of Afro-American Unity (formed by Malcolm X, who remained in Egypt), and a representative from the Nation of Islam (led by Elijah Muhammad). None of the five had ever formally represented the black community, but it was time according to Sutton. "They control a lot of people on the streets and we must open channels of communication between them and other groups in Harlem," he said in words similar to what Wagner, Fleary, and others had recently uttered.[55]

But not everyone was prepared to climb aboard the unity committee's peace train. In the *Herald Tribune*, Jimmy Breslin was openly contemptuous. "Forget this Communist drivel," he wrote. "It is there, but in small doses. These are kids who can't spell Russia." But he was equally critical of self-proclaimed leaders such as Lawson, whom he described as a "buffoon" who liked to make death threats in front of television cameras. Lawson was also, Breslin charged, a drinker whose scam was to put out a weekly list of white people whom he claimed were anti-black—minus those merchants willing to pay to keep their names off the list. And the columnist reminded readers that on Sunday it was "Porkchop" Davis who had urged his black listeners to prepare to die.[56]

Breslin also expressed an opinion and raised a question on the minds of many whites and some blacks. "These riots by now have nothing to do with civil rights," he wrote. "They are criminal acts and they are being committed by criminals, and the most dangerous question of all . . . was how long can the police stand in the streets and have bottles thrown at them from rooftops or iron bars aimed at them from someplace in a dark street? How long are they going to take it?"[57] And how would angry youth in Harlem or Brooklyn react if an officer lost control or made a mistake? Few wanted even to contemplate the consequences.

As if in partial response, the police moved to reduce the chance of more deadly violence. Reportedly acting on an anonymous tip to a newspaper, a dozen detectives from the 28th Precinct raided Malcolm X's unoccupied office in the Hotel Theresa in the early hours of Thursday morning. What they found was a single, bolt-action Mauser, fully loaded, with over a hundred rounds of ammunition. No laws were violated—the weapon was properly licensed—and no conspiracies were uncovered, either radical or conservative. But what the rifle represented was as much of a mystery as who might bring peace to the troubled streets of New York—and when.[58]

CHAPTER 9

MAKE SOMEBODY LISTEN

> And when the fury was over
> And the shame was replacing the anger
> So wrong, so wrong, but we've been down too long
> And we had to make somebody listen
> In the heat of the summer . . .
> —Phil Ochs, "In the Heat of the Summer"

THURSDAY, JULY 23

In Washington, the Senate passed Lyndon Johnson's antipoverty bill by a sixty-two to thirty-three margin after almost ten hours of heated debate. Among the twenty-two Republicans to oppose the measure was Barry Goldwater, who had flown to the capital for the vote but was silent during the deliberations. In an appeal to the middle class, he later raised the threat of higher taxes and described the War on Poverty as "plainly and simply a war on your pocketbooks." For the president, however, the Senate action was an important victory because it was the first major piece of legislation initiated by him to pass either branch of Congress.[1]

But in the House the bill faced defeat at the hands of Democratic conservatives and the Republican leadership. In an urgent appeal to AFL-CIO President George Meany, who was born in Harlem, Johnson said that he had to swing the votes of fifteen liberal Republicans so that he could put more than one hundred thousand young men to work in the next ninety days. The union leader readily agreed to lend labor's muscle to the lobbying effort on Capitol Hill. "Where all this Harlem stuff comes from," the president insisted, "is that they've got no jobs. They can't do anything and they're just raising hell." He promised Texas Congressman George Mahon that "I'm going to take tax-eaters and make tax-payers out of them, and I'm going to stop these damn riots."[2]

But Johnson's commitment to helping the poor had other motivations and deeper roots, which stretched back to his upbringing in the Hill Country of Central Texas. As a child in a family that at times struggled financially, he understood that people often faced misfortunes beyond their control. The future president was also the admiring son of Sam Johnson, a state representative and agrarian populist who believed that the federal government had an obligation to assist those who encountered hard times. At the age of twenty, Lyndon spent a formative year teaching poor Mexican American children in a ramshackle school with no lunch facilities or playground equipment. "Those little brown bodies had so little and needed so much," he recalled. "I was determined to give them what they needed to make it in this world." Seven years later, the youngest state director in the National Youth Administration impressed both white and black New Dealers by avoiding symbolic actions on racial issues and delivering substantive benefits to African Americans who badly needed them in the 1930s.[3]

In the fall of 1964, Johnson nonetheless opted to sell the War on Poverty as a solution to the problem of "crime in the streets" identified by Goldwater. The conservative recipe for law and order was more police, harsher sentences, and larger prisons. The liberal response was to promise to address the "root causes" of ghetto conditions with job training and social programs for the disadvantaged and desperate. After the election the president would announce a War on Crime based on police professionalization. For now, although white anxiety over urban unrest had yet to reach critical levels, Johnson sensed the political danger and anticipated future trouble as he courted important constituencies.

At a Thursday luncheon for corporate leaders, Johnson set the tone. "I did not become president to preside over mounting violence and deepening disorder," he told the guests, who included the CEOs of U.S. Steel, AT&T, General Motors, Ford, NBC, CBS, and IBM. "I fully intend to use all the resources I have to make sure that those who claim rights—and those who deny them—bend their passions to peaceful obedience of the law." Johnson then appealed to the titans who were present to lend him a hand for the good of the country, "not just because it is good for business or for economic stability." The president added that he intended to make a similar appeal to labor leaders on Friday—just before he and Goldwater had a private summit at the White House about the racial turmoil in America's cities.[4]

"He wants to encourage a backlash," Johnson bluntly told Texas Governor John Connally, an old friend and political confidant, in a phone call Thursday afternoon. "That's where his future is." As the governor listened sympathetically, the president vented his frustration with the turmoil in Harlem and his fear that the politically unpredictable and psychologically unstable Goldwater might seek to exploit it. "I'm not going to do [anything] to incite or inflame anybody," promised Johnson. "What the hell are they rioting for?" asked Connally, who then listed many of the civil and legal rights that African Americans in New York supposedly enjoyed. "If they just keep on rioting in Harlem, you're going to have unshirted Hell, and you're going to have it . . . in Chicago and Iowa."[5]

The governor praised the president for making it clear that he was "not going to stand for disorderly conduct anywhere by anybody." But Johnson was hardly reassured. "Only trouble, I can't do that 'cause that's what Goldwater says," he replied. "He's for a national police force and I've got to leave it up to the governors and the cities and only help them when they let me." The president repeated his suspicions of communist agitation and conservative money from Texas millionaire H. L. Hunt; again he mentioned the presence of walkie-talkies and motorcycle helmets. "Somebody's financing them big, and they go into a different town every night," he commented. "It's Brooklyn one night and it's Harlem the next and it'll be another section of New York tonight."[6]

But on Thursday night the riots came to an end with a wet whimper, not a big bang. Although a few scattered incidents of looting and violence took place—including still another clash between demonstrators and counterdemonstrators in Lower Manhattan—they were isolated and contained by the police, who were nonetheless exhausted and awaited the weekend with worry. No group declared victory or admitted defeat as an uneasy peace returned. No single individual or organization could claim credit for the calm. Despite the rain, temperatures had not fallen—on the contrary, it was hotter than on Wednesday. But somehow the fever in Brooklyn had broken after seventy-two hours as in Harlem. By midnight everyone could sense that the crisis had concluded—for now. Yet no one knew precisely why—perhaps the participants were also exhausted.

On Thursday morning, City Hall boasted that the mayor's performance on Wednesday night had received overwhelming support, with 396 phone calls and telegrams expressing praise and only 44 expressing criticism. But the newspaper reviews were more mixed, a natural reflection of the ideological differences that roiled New York. The *Daily News* called the speech "powerful, courageous, and well-thought out." In particular, it praised Wagner's decision to reject the "Communist-'liberal' plan" for a civilian review board, which would make the police more hesitant to act and the streets less safe. By contrast, the *New York Post* was scathing. The "most conspicuous failure" according to the scornful editorial was the mayor's refusal to take the "decisive first step" and implement an independent review board, which was critical if white leaders wanted to offer "real reassurance" to black residents and provide real protection to police officers falsely or wrongly accused of brutality or misconduct.[7]

In Harlem, the *Amsterdam News* offered a balanced appraisal. "Mayor Wagner, without question, commands more respect and has done more to advance the cause of the Negro in New York City than any other public official, bar none," it editorialized. But the paper added that it was disappointed when the man "we like, admire, and respect" refused to use his executive authority to meet two reasonable and legitimate demands—suspend Lieutenant Gilligan until the grand jury reached a verdict and establish by executive authority a civilian review board without waiting for the City Council to act.[8]

The controversy over the causes of the riot and the need for civilian review would continue for years in New York. Of the fifty largest cities in the country in 1964, only four had some form of independent oversight, none of which seemed like a model that would satisfy the proponents of civilian review in New York. For the moment peace was the priority in Harlem. "Let's Play It Smart," urged the *Amsterdam News* in a front-page editorial. "These riots are only helping your enemies and ruining you." Don't get mad, it appealed to readers, get organized. "Let's stop these riots and go back to fighting the type of fight which was bringing us victory before these riots began," admonished the paper, which advised the Police Department to put black officers in charge of the Central Harlem station houses and suggested three candidates, all of whom had achieved the rank of captain in the past year: Eldridge Waith, Arthur Hill, and Lloyd Sealy, who in August received command of the 28th Precinct.[9]

The authorities also needed to restore order in Brooklyn, where fewer injuries were reported but the damage from looting was far more extensive. Over 550 businesses were vandalized or ransacked, including 40 of 47 on DeKalb Avenue. For the third day in a row, the police mobilized additional forces—including mounted officers—and deployed them on the street corners and rooftops of Bed-Stuy. They also investigated—and ultimately dismissed—rumors that black agitators from Philadelphia planned to join the unrest.[10]

Aiding the effort were more than forty black ministers who fanned out across the neighborhood in cars and on foot to encourage everyone to remain at home. Their efforts even won grudging praise from Commissioner Murphy. And two other clergy drove a sanitation truck equipped with a sound system from block to block for hours. "Kindly listen to law and order," they pleaded over and over. "This is the best for all concerned. Please get off the streets. This is worse than you think."[11]

By the early evening, Fleary was also back with the NAACP sound truck so, as he put it, "there would be no question in anybody's mind that we knew we were doing the right thing." Again, boos and jeers greeted him, although no one tried to overturn the vehicle. At Nostrand and Fulton, some in the crowd had messages for Fleary and the ministers printed on signs. Two read: "We Want NAACP to Stay Out of This" and "We Will Fight Now and Pray Later." Two others had ominous overtones: "The Dead Can't Talk We Can" and "We Will See That Killer Cop Gets a Fair Trial."[12]

On Thursday more than a thousand gang members appeared on the streets. Despite the hard work of the Youth Board, which had struggled to keep them away, they were in full force. "Buccaneers, Bishops, Chaplains, Warlords, Corsairs, tonight they're all around," pointed out a helpful young man to reporters. Whether by explicit treaty or implicit agreement, they were now a picture of harmony and unity, having set aside their wars and rivalries with the obvious hope of sharing in the spoils from the looting.[13] But they had missed their opportunity—there was no major rioting on this evening to cover their activities.

Instead, television crews and print journalists from across the country and around the world had arrived to witness and document Brooklyn's moment in the spotlight. But the drama was coming to a close. On the corner of Lewis and Gates Avenues, only two blocks from the 79th

FIGURE 15. Mrs. Anna Kelter reacts to the damage to her grocery store at the corner of Nostrand and Atlantic in Bed-Stuy. Photo by Stanley Wolfson. Library of Congress, Prints & Photographs Division, New York World-Telegram & Sun Collection.

Precinct, a group of youths smashed the windows of a drug store and robbed the window display. They might have taken more items, but photographer Mel Finkelstein of the *New York Journal-American* spotted them and took a photo. The flash startled the looters, who hurled bricks and bottles at him. He dropped his camera and escaped unharmed as his windshield was shattered. Three weeks later he was not so lucky—he and a fellow staffer were seriously injured when covering a riot in Paterson, New Jersey.[14]

In Manhattan, the center of the action was again Centre Street, where police had closed the block between Grand and Broome in an effort to separate 250 interracial CORE demonstrators and 1,500 counterdemonstrators from the Lower East Side neighborhood. On Mulberry Street, the heart of Little Italy, residents had no hesitation telling reporters what they thought of the "Nigger Communists" and "Beatniks" who were picketing Police Headquarters for the third night in a row. "The way they've been treated in the South they should be treated all over," said one teenager. "The cops let them get away with everything," chimed in a second. "A white person doesn't have as much civil rights as a colored, now." A third man argued that blacks should return to Africa. "Their whole basic argument is they want to be white," he said. "And they never will."[15]

The CORE pickets arrived at 8 P.M. and were greeted with jeers and epithets, eggs and garbage. Later, six youths in an automobile were arrested on charges of disorderly conduct after they hurled a sign at the picketers. On it was a crude drawing of a man in a turban, presumably black, with a dagger in his chest. Below the picture were the words "Get the smelly black bastards away from this block." With the demonstrators were two white Protestant ministers, one of whom said that he was doing what he considered his "pastoral duty." Among the counterdemonstrators was a local Catholic priest. On the archdiocese's orders he was trying "to make sure in so far as I can that none of the neighborhood young men get into trouble and to avert any incident if possible."[16]

The police and the priest were mostly successful. At 11 P.M., when it was time to leave, patrolmen escorted the picketers to the subway station at Canal Street instead of Spring Street. The alternate plan resulted in less trouble for the demonstrators. But a surging group of young whites cornered an automobile with six blacks inside. Before a mounted squad of police officers could reach the vehicle, the crowd had dragged the passengers from the car, punching, kicking, and beating them.[17]

The repeated clashes at Police Headquarters offered clear examples of racial animosity and bigotry. "I came here tonight to watch the cannibals," said an electrical engineer who was born in Little Italy and had since moved to Brooklyn. "I lived with them savages for nine years in a housing project. I know." He also knew what he was for—and against. "I'm for Social Security," he said. "I'm for Medicare, I'm for unions, but damn it, I'm gonna vote for Goldwater to show the politicians we're sick and tired of cannibals." It was the voice of what the media termed the "backlash"—exactly the reaction that Johnson most feared.[18]

Other whites, however, mixed pride with prejudice. "This is not a ghetto, this is a community," said a resident of Little Italy. "This is where you can walk the streets and not be mugged. This is where the streets are clean." A tax editor and Harvard Law School graduate echoed the sentiment. "This is a wonderful community," he said. "There is no reason for the CORE pickets to shout and sing until 11 o'clock. It keeps the kids up. The violence we had last night wasn't really racial. No matter who was making that kind of noise would have been attacked."[19]

Even the leader of the demonstration, New York CORE education chairman Roy Innis, acknowledged that the clashes in Little Italy were about more than race. "The people down here are not the most affluent in town," he said, "and I think they feel threatened by the civil rights movement." The observation was an important reminder that class and culture mattered too. Often the most vocal and visible opponents of racial integration were those who lacked the economic means to insulate themselves and their families from the social changes and physical dangers they associated with the freedom struggle. As moral traditionalists who could not afford to send their children to private schools or relocate to pricey suburbs, Italian Americans also reacted viscerally to the behaviors and attitudes expressed by black youths, who seemed to embody the negative consequences of permissive liberalism and threaten the community's values, both personal and property.[20]

In Bed-Stuy, the curtain call came around midnight. Police interrupted six youths who were looting a store. All escaped except for a teenager who was slammed against a patrol car and roughly searched. A black woman observed and objected. "Did you see what those——did to him? Did you see?" she asked over and over as a crowd gathered. Nervous, the police radioed for backup and soon several squad cars had raced to the scene to provide assistance. As tensions rose, the sanitation truck piloted by the two ministers arrived. "Ladies and gentlemen, please return to your homes," they repeatedly requested. "Help your community. Help make Bedford-Stuyvesant a safe place again."[21]

No one paid any attention until the police took the youth into custody. Suddenly, the woman heard the ministers and, visibly annoyed, made a move toward the vehicle. Officers stopped her and she unleashed a string of expletives. "Go to hell, these are our streets," she yelled. Then, as she prepared to launch more epithets, the rain returned—a steady downpour, stronger than on Wednesday night. "Oh-oh," said the woman in mid-sentence. "Guess I'll go in." And that was it. After six nights of rioting and looting, gunfire and night sticks, bricks and bottles, curses and confrontations, the racial unrest in New York had reached the finale.[22]

All that was left was the counting. According to the NYPD, the final toll in Harlem was one dead, thirty-eight police injured, eighty-five citizens injured, and 122 businesses damaged, looted, or vandalized. In Brooklyn it was ten civilians injured, twelve police injured, and 556 businesses damaged, looted, or vandalized. Many merchants would never reopen their doors—six months later, the commercial heart of 125th Street had almost seven times as many vacancies as a year earlier. In all, the police made 465 arrests and spent an estimated $1.5 million during the six days of racial unrest, 90 percent of which went for overtime pay. The official figures almost certainly understated civilian injuries since only those who went to the hospital for treatment were included. By contrast, police injuries were probably accurate since by law all officers injured in the line of duty had to seek medical attention.[23]

The effort to determine winners and losers began almost immediately. Among mainstream black activists the consensus was that the more extreme elements in Harlem and Brooklyn had gained influence at the expense of more moderate voices. "Black nationalism will increase because it represents the profound disgust and desperation of the black people," said Bayard Rustin on the television program *Who Speaks for Harlem?* James Farmer, Cleveland Robinson of the Human Rights Commission, and Basil Patterson of the NAACP concurred. "There has been a turning away from the drive for integration," said Patterson. "The leading Harlem weekly [the *Amsterdam News*] is printing things about nationalism that would never have appeared a few years ago."[24]

Among white officials the consensus was that the main victims were the small merchants who had suffered losses they could not recoup and the

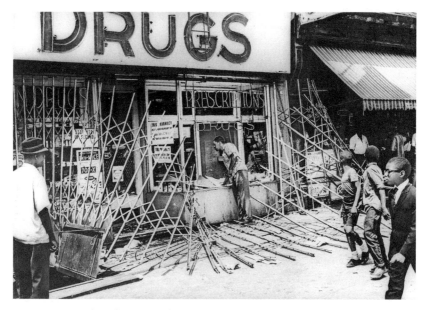

FIGURE 16. A Harlem drugstore after three nights of rioting and looting. Photo by
Warren K. Leffler. Library of Congress, Prints & Photographs Division, U.S. News &
World Report Magazine Collection (LC-U9-12259 frame 2).

law-abiding residents who had not supported or taken part in the disturbances. The "principal losers," wrote the *Herald Tribune*, were those black
men and women "who had the most to lose, who least deserved it, and
could least afford it." Now they not only had to live among those who had
victimized their community, but they had to suffer from increased racial
tension and decreased public respect for the rule of law—at precisely the
moment when their hopes and aspirations rested to a large degree on the
newly created Civil Rights Act.[25]

For black journalists, the unrest of the past six nights represented an
opportunity to shatter barriers and make history as they reported the news
for white-owned publications instead of black weeklies. "Harlem was our
coming out," recalled Earl Caldwell, who was on the staff of the Rochester
Democrat and Chronicle at the time. A product of small-town western Pennsylvania and a graduate of the University of Buffalo, Caldwell had not even
visited Harlem when his editor called him with the assignment. "Never had
the major media put so much of an important story in the hands of reporters

who were not white," he wrote later. "And there we were, smack in the middle of it, with notebooks in hand, dashing at the heels of the crowds, observing the battles and trying as best we could to record it all."[26]

Unlike most white reporters, who stayed close to the police, Caldwell and colleagues like Gerald Fraser, Austin Scott, Lester Carson, Ted Jones, Wallace Terry, Junius Griffin, Ted Poston, and Claude Lewis were usually at the heart of the action, where they faced questions and stares from white officers and Harlem residents, few of whom had encountered black journalists with press credentials from the Associated Press, *Time* magazine, and the metropolitan dailies. It was not easy handling the dangers of the disorder, the suspicion of the looters, and the hostility of the police. But the shared sense of purpose and opportunity bonded the reporters, who had all faced discrimination and overcome obstacles to break into the "big leagues" of print journalism. "The combination of our common history and the fires of the riot forged us into an instant fraternity," recalled Caldwell.[27]

For the police, the rain on Thursday brought a sense of relief that they were no longer at the center of the storm. By then many officers had lost patience with the citizens they had sworn to protect. "We have gone into these riots because the people in Harlem started them," said a patrolman. "We're trying to protect the lives of the residents—but after the rioting, all the leaders complain we were up there indiscriminately bashing heads, and it turns out we're the criminals." Other officers were confused and unsure as to their duty. On a street corner a rookie with less than a year on the force said, "I feel so foolish. I feel like I'm back in the Army. We have to treat these people like they were an enemy. That's not why I came on this job."[28]

On the job, frustration was widespread in the rank and file over what they saw as a misguided policy of restraint. Under strict orders and careful scrutiny from their superiors not to use excessive force or make arrests for minor infractions—since every arrest meant another officer had to leave the scene to handle processing and paperwork—they had to tolerate looting, harassment, assaults, and vandalism that normally would have brought a swift and sure response. The result in Bed-Stuy was more reported injuries to police than civilians—in sharp contrast to the three to one ratio of civilian to police injuries in Central Harlem. Nonetheless, even officers at the 28th and 32nd Precincts made fewer arrests during the days of rioting than in the previous week.[29]

After a tour of duty spent futilely trying to restore order in Brooklyn, an officer expressed weariness and exasperation. "Two of us would run to one store, and a hundred looters would run into another store down the street," he said. "And we couldn't do anything about it! We were told not to make arrests if we could possibly help it. And there just weren't enough of us." He paused, then added, "I just can't do it anymore." Even some senior officials had doubts about the policy of accommodation. "If they want to say terrible things about me, let 'em go ahead," said Brooklyn Inspector Walter Clerke. "But in the long run all this meant that it was just going to gather a crowd bent on force that couldn't be handled."[30]

"Thou shalt not police" was the implicit message many officers heard in the aftermath of the 1964 riots. When a "serious disorder" (as classified by the Kerner Commission) erupted in East Harlem in the summer of 1967, the NYPD adopted a policy of containment, not confrontation, and allowed hundreds of rioters and looters to run amok from 111th Street to 125th Street. After several days, the protests spread to Bed-Stuy and resulted in three deaths. The following year the city implemented the 911 emergency reporting system. In conjunction with urban unrest and the corruption investigation by the Knapp Commission, the new technology made the police less proactive and more reactive. "Twenty and out" was the motto of those on the force who simply wanted to put in their time, avoid trouble, and collect their pensions.[31]

The media formed another source of irritation for many officers in July 1964. In their view, newspaper editors and television reporters too often used, without proper analysis or context, selected photos or edited film of flailing nightsticks to bolster the repeated charges of police brutality. Some accusations were no doubt true, but others were false or exaggerated. "Let's see the toll of broken heads, arms, and legs," said an annoyed officer, who cited the low reported civilian casualty figures after six nights of street clashes. "With one swing of a club, we could break a head or a limb, but we've just been slapping them on the cans."[32] As in the case of firing over the heads of crowds and at rooftops, police discipline for the most part held despite continual provocations including a steady stream of extreme obscenities.

The deliberate restraint most officers exercised in most situations imposed a psychological burden. In particular, it worsened the intense and unrelenting strain they had to endure as they patrolled unfamiliar streets and faced unpredictable situations for which they were unprepared. Despite a set of established policies and practices, few officers—with the exception of TPF, which was pulled from the frontlines on Wednesday morning—had trained extensively for civil disturbances or were sufficiently experienced in handling them. "If they called out the National Guard," asked one patrolman, "do you think they'd take what we've been taking?" He received no answer. But another officer offered a simple statement: "There's no place I'd rather be than out of Harlem."[33]

The feeling was mutual among some black readers of the *Amsterdam News*. The police shooting of James Powell was "legalized murder" according to one resident, who asserted that "[Thomas Gilligan's] face should be blown up and spread all over Harlem billboards with the words 'Killer Cop' as a caption so that all Negroes may look upon the face of race hatred." A Bronx man expressed regret that he had not participated in the protests: "I have shamed myself as I saw the chilling specter of a police army stand poised to raise its mighty arsenal at a moment's notice against my people."[34]

But other readers vented their anger at those who preached or practiced violence. "All of you extreme militants, whether you know it or not, are really the black auxiliary of the White Citizens Council," contended a Brooklyn man. "Can't you understand that you are giving them the ammunition to push us back down into the gutter? The only difference between a Mississippi lynch mob and a bunch of smashing, rioting Negro hoodlums is the color of the participants." For the past seven days, wrote a group from Westchester, "The extremist and the ignorant have assaulted the citadels of law and order. This senseless battle must stop and the leaders of the Negro community must step forth and demand, not ask, that responsible colored Americans disassociate themselves from the criminal elements of society."[35]

Still others tried to find a middle ground. "I do not have to be in Harlem to be familiar with the kind of frenzied and sadistic brutality that many of the New York City police force feel they can get away with in dealing with Negro and Puerto Rican citizens," wrote Jackie Robinson, who left the Republican Party after the July convention. Yet in a guest editorial titled "Goldwater Ammunition" he also offered criticism of the looters and arsonists, as well as Jesse Gray and James Lawson: "I do not uphold the hoodlums who roved Harlem streets, taking advantage of the awful situation. I do not condone the actions or inflammatory words of some self-seeking leaders who can find glory only when there is grave crisis."[36]

In the meantime, a quieter crisis was consuming the attention of an older woman who worked at the Upper Park Avenue Baptist Church on

125th Street. "The biggest problem in Harlem is the pushers," she said. "They work right out on the streets—stand on the corners—and allow our children to see them openly pushing drugs in the community." But the police took no action, unlike in white neighborhoods, and every summer more kids were lost to addiction, which in turn led to purse-snatching and other crimes. "The parents are preaching constantly that this is right and this is wrong and you should abide by the right way," she commented, "and yet the most vicious and the most murderous of all things in Harlem is drug pushing and drug addiction and the kids see nothing done about it." In time they would, but whether the results were positive is open to debate.[37]

As the immediate crisis ended and the racial unrest subsided, three questions moved to the forefront: How many African Americans were active participants as opposed to passive bystanders? Who were the demonstrators and rioters? And how representative were they of the community as a whole? The official figures show that police officers arrested 465 individuals (overwhelmingly men) in Harlem and Brooklyn. The statistics are probably accurate as far as they go—a person is either arrested or not and leaves a paper trail. Whether the police could or should have taken more into custody is a different matter.

Historian Robert Fogelson, an expert on the disorders of the 1960s, calculated that the ratio between participants and those arrested was roughly five to one. So he estimated that approximately 3 percent of Harlem residents and 6 percent of Bed-Stuy residents were participants (compared to 11 percent in Watts in 1965 and 14 percent in Detroit in 1967).[38] The lower figures in New York might reflect in part the police reluctance to arrest individuals on lesser charges, but it is impossible to tell with any degree of precision.

Who were the participants? The white authorities—Mayor Wagner, Commissioner Murphy, City Council President Screvane, Borough President Stark—claimed that they were teenage hoodlums or punks, the community riffraff according to a popular expression. Among black leaders this view was also common, and even Rustin saw the rioters as youths on the margins of society, "forced to live by their wits, seeking out a living by gambling, selling numbers or dope, and sometimes selling themselves." They had, he added, "revolted in the only way left to them. They would make society listen."[39]

But the statistics indicate a more complicated picture. It is true that many of the participants were young—81 of the 465 arrested were under eighteen and another 81 were between eighteen and twenty. But 175 of those arrested were between twenty-one and twenty-nine and another 128 were over twenty-nine. Again, it is possible, though by no means certain, that the arrest records skew older than the perceptions of Rustin and others because the police concentrated on more serious, hardened offenders.[40]

Fogelson's research, however, strongly suggests that the relatively young and overwhelmingly single black men who were arrested were a representative minority, not a marginal element. Overall, they had similar levels of education and similar rates of employment to their peers. And more than 90 percent lived in Harlem and Bed-Stuy. "Thus to claim that the rioters were mainly the riffraff and outside agitators rather than fairly typical young adult males is to seriously misinterpret the riots," Fogelson concludes, which seems reasonable.[41]

The ideological stakes surrounding the "riffraff debate" were high. If the participants were a fringe element, then it was possible to dismiss their grievances as illegitimate and their actions as illegal. From this premise it was also plausible to conclude that the riot was formless and senseless. But if the participants were a representative minority, then it was logical to assume that they had broader support in the black community, at least among young African American males, although to what degree is difficult to tell. And it was not unreasonable to believe that the underlying conditions or "root causes" made the riot a form of rebellion, whether inchoate or not, even if it was marred by indiscriminate looting and vandalism.

Yet it is also important to remember that outside the center of the unrest and disorder most of Harlem remained calm and peaceful. "I recall a civility and orderliness that belies what was actually reported and printed, both on television and in newspapers," said black journalist George Barner. "The great riot was something that most people in Harlem read about in the newspaper just like everyone else."[42]

As liberals and conservatives chose sides in the dispute over who the rioters were, another issue emerged: Why now? Why was Saturday, July 18, the moment when two sparks—the Powell shooting and the street protest in front of the 28th Precinct—caused an explosion?

For liberals, the best explanation was that chronic ghetto problems had collided with two other, more recent, developments. The first was that the civil rights movements had generated rising expectations that, as of 1964, remained unmet. Despite promises and progress, albeit limited and uneven, blacks in the South and the North could clearly see that they failed to enjoy equal rights and equal opportunities for success in American society. And it was not apparent when they would, even with the recent passage of the Civil Rights Act.[43]

Liberals also identified and highlighted a second development—a growing sense of relative deprivation, reinforced by the spread of television. By 1964 the extraordinary economic prosperity of the past two decades had made the United States the richest nation in the history of the world. Now even poor Americans, especially in urban areas, had access to new technology unimaginable in earlier eras. But as a result they were less isolated and more likely to watch entertainment or news programs that depicted how wide the growing gap in consumption and incomes had become.

For conservatives, the best explanation for the Harlem Riot of 1964 was moral failure, not depressed ghetto conditions. The core conservative claim was that the unrest or rebellion was the responsibility of individuals, not society. Most of the poor were law-abiding and most immigrants in the past had peacefully endured far worse deprivation. Therefore the fault belonged first and foremost to the black rioters and looters themselves.

But, conservatives contended, white liberals had aided and abetted the civil unrest by raising false hopes and expectations. They had also encouraged a culture of dependency with the empty promise of government assistance. Finally, the detonation was primed by the insidious actions of black radicals like Jesse Gray—probably communists engaged in a conspiracy to destabilize society—and the invidious appeals of seeming moderates like King, who promoted the destructive doctrine of civil disobedience at the expense of respect for law and order.

"*Whose* law, one is compelled to ask, and *what* order?" retorted James Baldwin from Paris, where he was finishing a novel. The social problems of Central Harlem, he stressed, were most responsible for the riot. "These are conditions which almost no white American is willing to imagine, and from which he deliberately averts his eyes," he wrote. By contrast, black citizens were "exposed to the white world, and under the most intolerable conditions, every working day." From that basic yet crucial difference in racial perspective sprang the "fury and bitterness" of blacks, as well as the "anger and guilt" of whites whenever the ghetto exploded.[44]

For Dr. Charles Roberts, the black dentist and city alderman who had chaired the city commission for Mayor La Guardia in the tense aftermath of the 1935 riot, the 1964 disorders were easily understood and virtually inevitable. "You could have forecast them," he said from his elegant Harlem brownstone, where at age ninety-one he spent much of his time reading newspapers and talking politics. Then and now, he explained, prejudice and discrimination led to "emotional tension which seeks release at the slightest provocation." Sooner or later, the uprising was bound to occur.[45]

Another voice from the past belonged to Langston Hughes, the famous author and poet of the Harlem Renaissance. A resident of the community for decades, he had experienced the daily indignities, which may well have had a greater impact than police corruption, and witnessed the violent eruptions of 1935 and 1943. Now, after watching the rioting in Harlem over the weekend, Hughes agreed to write a series of columns for the *New York Post*.

After the Harlem Riot of 1935, Hughes recalled, white stores had started to hire a few black clerks. After the Harlem Riot of 1943, the Police Department had stationed more black officers in the area and integrated squad cars. It had also deployed "chocolate and vanilla teams" on corners so that black patrolmen could arrest black suspects without excessive brutality (according to Hughes, jazz musicians coined the term "bebop" from the sound made by "police clubs on Negro heads"). And after the Harlem Riot of 1964, he said, the community now awaited the deeds of Mayor Wagner "since man does not live by words alone."[46]

Hughes wondered in particular what city leaders could do for the "down boys" of Central Harlem, the "hoodlums and looters" who had no chance to escape the ghetto and join the "open society" of middle-class America as his generation of young men had. "When you are down as far as you can go, what difference does it make about the next step?" he asked. And he doubted whether the community's activists, whom he described as "pulpit or platform performers, not medicine men of the streets," could raise black youths by their bootstraps as many whites wanted them to do. "The problem is," he observed, "the down boys do not have any bootstraps. They wear mostly sneakers, often with broken shoe strings."[47]

The schools were not likely to help the "down boys" either. "What disgusts me [about the riots] is the pretense of shock, surprise, horror," said Kenneth Clark with a tone of bitterness and resignation. "The horrible living conditions, the sanitation, pushing people around—apparently nobody gives a damn about it. They send hundreds and hundreds and thousands of cops. They would do better to send one third as many building inspectors or a thousand sanitation workers, or just an attempt at proper schooling."[48]

On 125th Street, as a sense of normalcy slowly started to return, a black officer pondered the future. "You have to keep knocking on the door," he told *Time*. "If you don't knock, they won't hear you." The advice was sound, but as the newsweekly noted, "the question for New York and for every major U.S. city with a Harlem of its own was: how hard will Harlem knock next time?" For now no one had an answer.[49]

CHAPTER 10

CALMING THE WATERS

> New York City is the center of the Negro struggle for equality, the capital
> of Negro life, and the most liberal city in the country. What happens here
> affects the whole country.
> —Martin Luther King, Jr.

JULY 24–31

"Are you and Senator Goldwater ready to make a pact to eliminate the civil rights issue from the campaign?" *Washington Post* reporter Edward Folliard asked President Johnson. The question came shortly after the nationally televised press conference had begun at 3:30 P.M. on Friday, July 24.[1]

Unlike Goldwater on Monday, Johnson was not caught by surprise. With the assistance of a Secret Service agent, Press Secretary George Reedy had planted the question in advance with Folliard, whose unexpected query to the Arizona senator had led to his impromptu request to discuss the racial crisis with the president. Now their private meeting was scheduled for 5:30 P.M. that afternoon in the Oval Office. At the press conference, the obvious intent of the White House was to seize the initiative and preempt any attempt by the Republican candidate to exploit the summit for political gain.[2]

"I do not believe that any issue which is before the people can be eliminated from a campaign in a free society," said Johnson. Everyone, regardless of race, religion, or region, was entitled to the same basic constitutional rights, which was why he had backed the Civil Rights Act. Goldwater of course had not. "I propose to discuss and debate the hard and difficult issues," the president continued. If the senator and his advisers and supporters were willing to join him in "rebutting and rebuking bigots and those who seek to excite and exploit tensions, then it will be most welcome . . . [and] a very fine contribution to our political life in America."[3]

Was Johnson also willing to make urban unrest a campaign issue? "Well," he said with a hint of humor, "I am against sin, I am against lawlessness, and I am very much opposed to violence." He pledged to use the full resources of the national government to put a halt to it, but stressed again that street crime was a local and state responsibility. "I seem to have read and heard that other people, too, are opposed to the federal government usurping the rights of the states," commented the president in another indirect swipe at Goldwater.[4]

Johnson next reaffirmed his commitment to law and order. "No word or deed of mine has ever, or will ever, lend aid and comfort to the small minority who would take the law into their own hands for whatever cause," he promised. When questioned about the "small minority," the president stated that the FBI provided him with daily updates. "I would not hesitate to say that the impression I gain from reading those reports," he said, "is that there are extremist elements involved, and at the appropriate time I think their identity will be made known."[5]

Johnson would not reveal when. A few minutes after 4 P.M. he left the press conference and headed to the East Room to brief labor leaders on the economic and political climate. The Goldwater summit was little over an hour away.

Since Monday the president's staff had anxiously prepared for the private meeting. By Friday a flurry of meetings had led to a blizzard of suggestions for Johnson. Do not make any specific agreements, warned aide Bill Moyers. "Goldwater can only emerge brighter, whiter, and purer." Have him enter the Oval Office via the back door, counseled Reedy, and do not permit Goldwater to "use the White House as a backdrop for a television presentation." Listen to him and state your sincere hope for racial calm, advised speechwriter Richard Goodwin. But avoid a joint appearance with Goldwater at all costs and then swiftly show "him to the door." The preparations had reached the level of a presidential debate, which in a sense it was since the two candidates would not meet face-to-face for the rest of the campaign.[6]

Ultimately, the meeting was brief and anticlimactic, with both candidates offering pious banalities in place of incendiary remarks. Goldwater arrived by the southwest gate to avoid attention—he was early and, after wandering alone in the Rose Garden, had to wait in the Cabinet Room until Johnson escorted him to the Oval Office. Then he departed by the southeast gate to dodge reporters. No photos were taken. During the summit, the senator was silent until the president made a few innocuous comments about the need for harmony and the threat posed by "racist groups and communists who do not have the best interests of the Negro people or the United States at heart." The patriotic Goldwater concurred. "I told him I would not attack his position," he later wrote. "I hoped he would refrain from challenging mine."[7]

Johnson then retrieved the three-sentence "good faith" communiqué that his aides had drafted and placed on his desk (where he also had a longer, more detailed statement in case the Republican nominee, in Moyer's words, "wants to play games"). "The President met with Senator Goldwater and reviewed the steps he had taken to avoid the incitement of racial tensions," he read aloud. "Senator Goldwater expressed his opinion, which was that racial tension should be avoided. Both agreed on this position."[8] Goldwater had no objections and asked for a copy. Johnson said it was not a problem. More awkward silence followed.

Suddenly, the avid pilot erupted into a broad smile and said that he would like to test fly the new A-11, a supersonic jet designed to replace the U-2 spy plane. Johnson, struggling to contain his amusement, replied that it would be in development for another year and by then the White House might have a new occupant. Laughter ensued. On that light note, the meeting ended after sixteen minutes with back slaps and handshakes. Goldwater made no public comment and returned to his Washington apartment. "He got to say everything he wanted to say," declared a friend.[9]

Immediately after the summit, Reedy read the joint communiqué to reporters and joined Johnson, Moyers, and Jack Valenti for a brief recap. Then the president returned a call from Secretary of Defense Robert McNamara and told him that Goldwater had stated that "there are a lot of conservatives in this country—and I can't control 'em—but I want to do the best I can to keep down any riot. It just would hurt me terribly if somebody got killed because of something I said." The next morning, Johnson called Nicholas Katzenbach, the deputy attorney general, and informed him that the senator had noted that "he was a half Jew and that he didn't want to do anything that would contribute to any riots or disorders or bring about any violence."[10]

Whether for personal or political motives, Goldwater's restraint was a worthy gesture. But the simmering issue of urban crime and unrest was too volatile for the two candidates to contain with a "gentlemen's agreement." For the remainder of the campaign, Republican hopes and Democratic fears would rest in large measure on the impact of law and order on the electorate. And what neither Johnson nor Goldwater could have anticipated as they chatted in the Oval Office was that within hours racial tensions would again explode—this time in another city in the Empire State, which proved that the crisis was not confined to New York.

Rochester was a pleasant and prosperous place with plenty of civic pride. Home of Eastman Kodak and the Xerox Corporation, it was the third largest city in New York with a population of 320,000 and leafy neighborhoods filled with middle-class white families living in comfortable homes. But in the black community tensions were rising. Two months earlier, among other incidents, local leaders were insulted and embarrassed when the airport bar reportedly refused to serve the comedian and activist Dick Gregory, who had come to Rochester to participate in a civil rights rally.[11]

Police-community relations were also on edge after two high-profile cases of alleged police brutality, including the arrest of fifteen Black Muslims who had forcibly resisted when officers raided their meeting. Adding to the strain was the debate surrounding the creation of a Police Advisory Board in 1963. "You did not want to be arrested," recalled Trent Jackson, an Olympic athlete and NFL player who was born in Georgia in 1942 and moved to Rochester as a child. "There was a feeling that if you were arrested, the police would beat you."[12]

Most of the small businesses in the black areas were owned and operated by white merchants, leading to complaints about the high cost and low quality of the goods sold, as well as the lack of reinvestment in the community. And Rochester was experiencing the hottest July on record since 1955. But perhaps most important, large employers like Eastman Kodak had few positions for unskilled workers. "We're not in the habit of hiring bodies," said the company's industrial-relations director. "We seek skills. We don't grow many peanuts in Eastman Kodak." In Rochester, the unemployment rate for nonwhites was more than three times the rate for whites.[13]

Among black youth the jobless figures were even worse. "God knows I've tried to use this certificate," a recent female graduate of a job training program told an NAACP official as she gripped a piece of paper in one hand and a rock in the other. "I can't get a job anywhere. All the white girls from my class have jobs. I've tried to use this [certificate], but I've had better success using this [rock]. And baby, I'm ready to use this rock some more."[14]

On Friday, July 24, she had her chance. At 11:30 P.M. two uniformed white officers arrested twenty-one-year-old Randy Manigault, who was allegedly intoxicated and creating a disturbance at a block party on the corner of Joseph Avenue and Nassau Street in northeast Rochester. The street dance was sponsored by a mothers' group seeking to raise money to buy playground equipment for a children's park. As the young man protested and resisted, a crowd of several hundred gathered. When the police called for backup, the only available unit was a K-9 squad, which responded despite a 1960 agreement not to use German shepherds at black events.[15]

The arrival of the dogs inflamed the crowd. According to the police, a German shepherd attacked Manigault, as it was trained to do, after he had knocked an officer to the ground. But with images of Birmingham in their minds, some residents saw it differently. "Tell our side of it," yelled an eyewitness. "He turned that dog loose on Randy." Rumors quickly spread that a patrolman had slapped a pregnant woman and that a dog had also bitten a little girl. Neither story was true, which made no difference. Soon the crowd had swelled to at least three hundred, including blacks of all ages and some Puerto Ricans and Italian Americans—teenagers who reportedly belonged to street gangs.[16]

With no rapid mobilization plan in place, the department dispatched every available squad car to the scene as quickly as possible. But a shortage of handcuffs and a lack of experience at riot control hindered the outnumbered officers, who could not restore order amid a hail of cans, bottles, and rocks. Unlike in Harlem and Brooklyn, however, the police fired few shots and relied on tear gas, which had little effect.

At 12:30 A.M. Chief William Lombard arrived to assume direct command. He had spent Sunday, July 19 through Thursday, July 23 in New York City at a state convention of police chiefs, where he had followed the events in Harlem and Brooklyn closely. When he returned to his office on Friday morning, he immediately contacted all of his sources. "Everything was negative," he recounted, referring to the intelligence reports. "They said there was no reason to believe a riot would happen in Rochester. None whatsoever. Of all places, Rochester?" But of course, if it could happen there it could happen anywhere, which was an ominous sign.[17]

Then Lombard reached Joseph Avenue. "There was a roar in the sky," he vividly remembered, "a noise I'd never heard before." When he pleaded with the crowd to go home, he was booed, spat upon, and showered with rocks. His wrist watch was ripped from his arm. Bruised and shaken, Lombard could only stand by as the crowd smashed six police cars and over-turned his personal vehicle, denting the roof and shattering the windows before setting it ablaze. "I am surprised he didn't get killed," recalled a resident.[18]

By 1:30 A.M. police described the situation as "definitely out of control and critical," with selective rioting already under way. "There were just too many people," recalled Lombard. "There was no containing them." As the deputy chief later confirmed, the crowd deliberately targeted white-owned businesses and avoided black-owned businesses. Nusbaum's Department Store was the first to fall; others soon followed. Some white merchants with good reputations were spared—the corner deli operated by the immigrant father of jazz musician Chuck Mangione was not touched—but within hours most of the shops in the eight-block area of Joseph Avenue were ransacked.[19]

At the Public Safety Building pandemonium reigned. "You had white people running up and down the halls, saying things like 'Look what those niggers have done,' or 'You darn Democrats, you let the niggers tear up our town.' It was like they were insane," recalled Supervisor Constance Mitchell, who in 1961 had become the first black woman elected to public office in Monroe County. The week before, she had also witnessed the rioting in Harlem, where she predicted the same could happen in Rochester. "It was a lesson for me," she continued. "It was 'their' town. Blacks were living on someone else's plantation."[20]

At 4:24 A.M. City Manager Porter Homer declared a state of emergency. By then the crowd had grown to more than two thousand residents from all walks of life, and the rioting had spread down Clinton Avenue. "It was impossible to control," said a police captain. "We used fire hoses and they had no effect. We used tear gas and they threw the grenades back at us. Finally, we just withdrew and sealed off the area while Negro leaders circulated among them." Among the leaders was Mitchell, who appealed in vain for calm. "It was like a circus atmosphere," she recalled sadly.[21]

The decision to contain the riot rather than intervene to halt it was controversial among both officers and residents. "They panicked," said a black patrolman in disgust. Laplois Ashford, a Rochester native and national youth director of the NAACP, accused Chief Lombard of abandoning the neighborhood to looters. "That's either cowardice or condoning it," he said of the containment policy. In his view it only encouraged spectators to "get me some too." Plenty of white merchants no doubt felt the same way.[22]

For a time the cordon held and the crisis seemed to abate. But around 6:30 A.M. the crowd stormed the police line and forced a mass retreat from Joseph Avenue. "There were at least a thousand of them," said Detective Sergeant Tony Cuile. "Everything was coming from the top of the buildings. I saw a quart beer bottle heading for Inspector Harry Griswold. It caught him on the face and he fell. I stopped to pick him up and a young teenager belted me in the back with a two-by-four. Then the police had to charge them to save us."[23]

By sunrise the crowd had at last dispersed, exhausted but exultant. The initial toll was at least eighty-five persons injured, ninety arrested, and sixty stores looted or vandalized, with an estimated $1 million in property damage. In a television interview, Mitchell appeared simultaneously stunned and angry. "We are in the middle of a social revolution in this country," she said with fierce conviction, "and I think that the same thing that happened in Rochester Friday night can happen to any other city in America."[24]

Like the unrest in Harlem, which had erupted a week earlier, the violence in Rochester caught the Johnson administration by surprise. Ramsey Clark, an assistant attorney general at the time, later recalled "how distant Rochester and Harlem and the other major disturbances seemed to the Department of Justice. We just thought they've got big fine police departments and they can take care of it."[25] But in the White House the president remained focused on New York City.

On Saturday morning, Johnson called Katzenbach to relay Rockefeller's fear that Manhattan District Attorney Frank Hogan was not taking the radical threat—symbolized for the moment by rent-strike activist Jesse Gray—with sufficient seriousness. "I hear you ought to talk to [Mayor] Wagner about it," the president said, "and [not let] Goldwater say we scrubbed it under the rug." The deputy attorney general agreed to contact Hogan, but stressed that it was a local matter and that an arrest might cause even more trouble. To Johnson's evident disappointment, Katzenbach added that beyond "speculation and rumors" there was no evidence of involvement by conservative extremists from the John Birch Society or the Ku Klux Klan.[26]

Rockefeller was likely heartened by the arrest on Saturday afternoon of William Epton, a thirty-two-year-old electrician and father of two. The soft-spoken radical was vice chairman of the Progressive Labor Party and spokesman for the Harlem Defense Council, a paper organization that shared the same headquarters on Lenox Avenue. A week earlier, in the wake of the march on the 28th Precinct, Epton had called for a protest at the 32nd Precinct, which he described as a "meat grinder, a place that to Negroes is like Auschwitz to the Jewish people." In response, Commissioner Murphy on Friday had banned the demonstration because, he claimed, it represented a "clear and present danger" to public safety and the sponsors were "advocates of violence and disorder who proclaim their doctrines openly."[27]

Murphy's action generated immediate outrage among Harlem leaders— Bayard Rustin called it "irresponsible, criminal, and totalitarian"—who predicted that it would lead to more resentment. But they also strongly opposed the planned march, which they feared would lead to more violence. Thirty minutes before it was scheduled to start, the United Council of Harlem Organizations distributed leaflets warning that the "Trap is Set! Murphy plans to provoke! Mothers keep your children home!" Epton, however, contended that the ban was a violation of his constitutional right to assemble and demonstrate peacefully. At 4:20 P.M. he and his lawyer, radical activist Conrad Lynn, went ahead with the protest, which eventually attracted a crowd of more than one hundred. After twenty minutes, a black officer in plainclothes arrested both men, who were charged with disorderly conduct.[28]

For Epton it was only the start of a long and winding path through the judicial system. More than a year later, he was convicted of advocating criminal anarchy after undercover officers from the BOSS squad testified that he had made an inflammatory speech on July 18. "They declared war on us and we should declare war on them and every time they kill one of us, damn it, we'll kill one of them," read Epton's words in the indictment. "[W]e will not be fully free until we smash this state completely and totally." He also vowed, according to the police, that to achieve his goal "we're going to have to kill a lot of these cops, a lot of these judges, and we'll have to go against their army. We'll organize our own militia and our own army." Despite an appeal to the U.S. Supreme Court, Epton served a year in prison and became a footnote in state legal history, the first and last person convicted of criminal anarchy in New York since the Red Scare of 1919.[29]

Back in Rochester the police prepared for more trouble on Saturday evening as crowds gathered near the intersection of Jefferson Avenue and Bartlett Street, about a mile and a half from Friday's uprising. When officers arrived, they were greeted with showers of bricks and rocks from rooftops and alleys. Four were injured—one by a thrown hammer. The first and only fatality of the night occurred at 10 P.M. when Perry Judson Bryan, a sixty-one-year-old white salesman from a small town south of Rochester, was hit in the head with a lead pipe by black looters outside a store. Dazed, Bryan stumbled into the street and was struck by a car, which dragged him a hundred feet and then drove away without stopping.[30]

On Sunday afternoon, the tragedy deepened when a helicopter crashed into a three-story rooming house on Clarissa Street. On board was Monroe County Civil Defense Director Robert Abbott. Both the helicopter and the home immediately burst into flames. Two courageous black women were able to evacuate themselves and six small children. But the pilot and two men in the house were killed. Abbott also suffered severe burns and died from an infection a month later, raising the final death toll to five.[31]

Directing the rescue operation was Deputy Police Chief Henry Jensen, who collapsed from the heat and exhaustion—he had been on continuous duty since early Saturday morning. As stunned residents watched, he and an injured fireman were removed on stretchers. "Maybe that will satisfy them," commented a black officer. But a black teen had a different reaction as he saw the white firefighter wheeled away: "He should have got burned up long ago."[32]

On Sunday evening, Rochester police were reinforced by 450 state troopers (the largest contingent ever assembled in one location) and a thousand National Guardsmen under the command of General A. C. "Buzz" O'Hara. Governor Rockefeller also had additional supplies of tear gas rushed to the city by air. It was the first time the National Guard had intervened in a northern city in anyone's memory. During the Harlem Riot of 1943, troops were sent to city armories in case they were needed, which they were not.[33]

But now they were. And so at 9 P.M., in a show of force, an advance guard of 150 Guardsmen rode in ten trucks down Jefferson Avenue. Some carried M-1 rifles with fixed bayonets; others carried carbines or pistols. Following standard procedure, the weapons were not loaded—Army doctrine banned warning shots. Shoot only to wound or kill—with overwhelming force if possible—was the general directive. As the motorcade advanced, it was greeted with cheers and jeers, although the unrest abated.[34]

On Monday morning, after a weekend of disorder, 350 were injured (including 22 police officers) and 976 were in custody. Most were men in their twenties and thirties, employed and with no criminal record. The mass arrests left the county jail and penitentiary overflowing, while in the Public Safety Building the corridors and bullpen for the courtroom were jammed. Of the 893 prisoners who were eventually arraigned (128 of whom were white), most were hastily charged with minor offenses like disorderly conduct and curfew violation. Almost all received suspended sentences, lending credence to the NAACP contention that the arrests were random. Few looters were prosecuted, despite the more than two hundred stores ransacked and the millions in property damage.[35]

On Monday afternoon, Rockefeller arrived by private plane for a three-hour visit. He and his entourage, in three black limousines, first made an unannounced tour of the affected areas. "Have you been down to the streets where these riots took place and seen the boarded-up stores?" he asked of no one in particular. "I think that's clear evidence of extremism." He then went to a meeting with officials at the Culver Street Armory, where he spoke with Guardsmen and told them how proud the state was of them. Finally, Rockefeller held a press conference on the lawn outside the Armory, where a crowd of more than one hundred whites—and a solitary black couple with three children—had gathered.[36]

"The state of New York," Rockefeller said, "is determined to preserve law and order and to preserve the safety of lives and property." In response to a question, he said that he saw no "direct relation" between the disorder in Rochester and the violence in Harlem and Brooklyn. "There is no indication that I have from any source at the present time of outside agitation," the governor stressed. He concluded by stating that he could send the National Guard into New York City in two hours if needed and requested. Afterward, Rockefeller waded into the audience, shaking hands and signing autographs with enthusiasm. "This is the only kind of crowd I like," he commented, "not this other." Whether he meant the reporters or the residents of Joseph Avenue was unclear.[37]

Like Rockefeller, the special agent in charge of the FBI's Buffalo field office was quick to dismiss the likelihood of radical incitement. "We have no information that Communists or other subversive groups were involved in the riots," he said, adding that "from the information we have, it appears that the race riots were spontaneous as the result of the arrest of the youth [on Friday night]." But his description of the Rochester unrest as a "race riot" was not accepted by Mitchell, who vehemently protested that it "was not a race riot—this is war. Pull those National Guardsmen out and see what happens."[38]

In a more measured tone, NAACP official Arthur Whitaker shared Mitchell's objection to the FBI's characterization. A minister of the Mount Olivet Baptist Church and a sociologist at the University of Rochester, he noted later that there was plenty of evidence of white participation in the rioting—15 percent of those arrested were white youths. But there was no evidence of black residents attacking white residents or vice versa. On the contrary, neighbors of both races had gathered on front porches and in backyards to discuss how to protect their families, homes, and businesses. The rebellion or uprising was, he contended, primarily an emotional reaction by a small yet representative segment of the black community against police brutality by white officers and economic exploitation by white merchants.[39]

In Whitaker's view, the explosion was also caused by a breakdown in communications between poor and middle-class African Americans, as well as a lack of understanding by both races. In his thoughtful report to the NAACP, he wrote that blacks needed to stop believing that "every Negro in conference with the white power structure is an 'Uncle Tom.'" Conversely, whites needed to stop searching for a "black Messiah as leader and spokesman for all Negroes." According to Whitaker, it was as unreasonable and unrealistic to expect a single person to represent the black community as the white community.[40]

The point was fair and heartfelt. But as the preeminent black leader in America, the Reverend Martin Luther King, Jr., arrived in New York City on Monday evening at the invitation of Mayor Wagner, whites desperately turned to him in hopes of salvation from the violence and chaos that had consumed first Harlem, then Brooklyn, and now Rochester.

The sun was setting as King's plane touched down at Kennedy Airport. He had spent a sweltering Friday night in Meridian, Mississippi—the final stop on his four-day tour of places like Greenwood made famous by "Freedom Summer." While FBI agents scrambled to protect him from death threats, Student Nonviolent Coordinating Committee (SNCC) volunteers had to face white crowds on their own, and two black churches in nearby McComb were burned to the ground. On Saturday King returned to Atlanta for some rest and a chance to attend services at his father's church on Sunday. Now he would face a fresh challenge in a different world.

Waiting for King at the airport was Rustin, who remained a trusted if unofficial adviser after his ill-timed visit to the Soviet consulate in February. A week after the riot erupted in Harlem, King had called him and asked whether he should come to New York. Most certainly, replied Rustin, who according to a close friend and personal assistant always thought that a King appearance was "like chicken soup—it could not hurt." But Rustin urged him to keep his distance from Wagner and press for a civilian review board. Above all, it was imperative that the civil rights leader tie the racial unrest to the black struggle for better housing, schools, and jobs. He had to stress that "law and order do not exist in a vacuum; to the degree that you have justice—to that degree can law and order be maintained."[41]

No one knows what went through King's mind as he arrived in the city on Monday night. Perhaps he took heart from a survey that day in the *New York Times*, which revealed that African Americans in New York considered him by far the most influential and effective black leader, a man with "guts and sense" who "puts his life on the line for us." According to 73 percent of respondents, who could provide multiple answers, he was "doing the best for Negroes" compared to 22 percent for NAACP executive director Roy Wilkins and 21 percent for Congressman Adam Clayton Powell, Jr. Trailing well behind were CORE leader James Farmer and Malcolm X, with 8 and 6 percent, respectively.[42]

But from an institutional standpoint, it was a different story. More than half of the respondents—55 percent—identified the NAACP as "doing the best for Negroes." CORE came next at 23 percent, followed by the Urban League (led by Whitney Young) at 14 percent. The Southern Christian Leadership Conference (SCLC), which King headed, had the support of only 7 percent. Without a powerful local organization behind him, King had to rely on his moral stature and personal fame in his meetings with Wagner.[43]

King knew Harlem well and had many friends in the community. But in 1958, three years after he rose to national prominence during the Montgomery Bus Boycott, he had almost died there at age twenty-nine. During a book signing for *Stride Toward Freedom: The Montgomery Story* at Blumstein's Department Store, a middle-aged, mentally disturbed black woman stabbed him with a seven-inch steel letter opener. Another woman tried to remove it, but police officer Phil Romano instantly grabbed her hand and probably saved King's life. After he was rushed to Harlem Hospital with the blade imbedded in his chest, it took doctors more than four hours to repair the wound. "Had [he] sneezed or coughed the weapon would have penetrated the aorta," said a surgeon. "He was just a sneeze away from death."[44]

When officers arrested Izola Ware Curry, a recent arrival from Florida, they found that she was carrying a loaded automatic pistol. She was also harboring paranoid-schizophrenic delusions about the civil rights movement and alleged connections to the Communist Party. When charged with felonious assault and illegal possession of firearms, she retorted, "I'm charging him [King] with being mixed up with the Communists" and claimed that she had reported King to the FBI, which already had him under investigation. Curry was later found not competent to stand trial and was committed to a state hospital for the criminally insane, where she died at age ninety-eight.[45]

On Thursday, July 16, the day James Powell was shot in New York and Goldwater spoke in San Francisco, King was on his way to Florida after attending the Republican Convention. In St. Augustine that night, he described what it was like to witness the president signing the Civil Rights Act. "It was a great moment," King said, comparable to "the signing of the Emancipation Proclamation by Abraham Lincoln." But he also noted another, less positive, historical event taking place simultaneously in California. "While not himself a racist, Mr. Goldwater articulates a philosophy which gives aid and comfort to the racist," King stated. "His candidacy and philosophy will serve as an umbrella under which extremists of all stripes will stand."[46]

Five days later, King made his first public comment on the weekend riots in Central Harlem. Echoing the views of Wilkins and others, he described them as "very unfortunate in the cause of civil rights and the cause of freedom." Whites welcomed the words—and hoped for deeds to reinforce them. "Perhaps—probably—not even a Martin Luther King could have contained the savage fury that spilled into the hot streets of New York," editorialized the *Herald Tribune*. "But there comes a time when a man with power over his people has the duty to use it, the duty to try."

Although armed force was necessary at first, it was now time for King to employ his "moral force" to "keep the public peace and to help lead the way to understanding."[47]

Expectations were high—and King knew it as he arrived in New York on Monday at 8:45 P.M. Rustin pressed him to leave immediately for Harlem, where King was scheduled to meet with local black leaders before his private conference with Mayor Wagner at 10:15 P.M. But reporters forced him to hold an impromptu press conference. "Non-violence is still the best policy and the most effective," King told them. "I'm sure the majority of Negroes in New York feel the same way."[48] That was a fact.

King then offered some strong opinions. "It would have been wise to suspend the police lieutenant who murdered the Negro boy, and we feel that the Negro boy was murdered," he said, adding that the immediate creation of an independent review board and a massive jobs initiative were also essential. "So long as these conditions exist, these troubles will remain," he predicted. But it was after 9:15 P.M. before he left the airport, despite Rustin's almost frantic pleas. The delay meant King only had time for a brief tour of Harlem and a quick meeting with a few selected activists before he headed for Gracie Mansion, where he and Wagner spoke for almost four hours with aides present.[49]

While King and the mayor conferred, the United Council, representing two hundred delegates from sixty-nine organizations, concluded three and a half hours of constructive dialogue and debate. The emphasis was on unity and harmony. But the delegates also drew attention to the dual threat posed by Murphy's ban on the planned protest at the 28th Precinct and Epton's extremism, which had resulted in the arrest of the Progressive Labor Party leader on Saturday. The Black Nationalists, said James Lawson, "find ourselves united with [other groups] to save the people of Harlem from being entrapped by either the police or by the Peking or Moscow Communists."[50]

At the same time, Harlem activists sharply criticized Wagner for ignoring their demands and failing to meet with them. In the words of Livingston Wingate, president of Harlem Youth Opportunities Unlimited (HARYOU) who had met with King for ten minutes, they were "mad as hell at Mayor Wagner for importing Dr. King from Atlanta to discuss the problems of Harlem." Most of the anger was reserved for the mayor. But King also received flak for meeting with Wagner before he had consulted with the United Council and presuming that he could represent it. "I cannot envision Dr. King being able to speak on a local level for all Negro people everywhere," the Reverend Alvin Childs commented.[51]

Everyone was playing a complicated game. The mayor was using King to bypass the local black establishment; Wingate, Childs, and others were using him to elevate their status and put pressure on Wagner, while telling the community that King was an outsider who could not understand their concerns or defend their interests. "Wingate of course double-crossed Martin," asserted Rustin, who acted as a go-between and told both sides what they wanted to hear. On the one hand, he informed King that the Harlem leaders were "stupid crackpots" with few followers, and the street radicals were "dangerous dogs who will lash out at anything." On the other, he told various members of the United Council that King was not sophisticated or tough enough to achieve a meaningful settlement with City Hall.[52]

King would often hear that criticism in coming years—that as a southern black he could not fully understand the problems and despair in northern cities. As Wingate put it, "The Southern Negro wants things he can get—like going to a movie with whites or eating in a restaurant with whites. The Northern Negro wants vague things that may not be easy to get right away—jobs, better housing, integrated schools." The HARYOU official was frank: "Dr. King isn't able to negotiate miracles. There's a total breakdown in communication between the Negro 'haves' and the Negro 'have-nots' here and if the people have no confidence in the leadership we won't be able to restrain them."[53]

King also faced harsh recriminations from personal supporters like Ossie Davis and Ruby Dee, a celebrity couple who were actors and activists. "We were amazed and disappointed" that King had apparently fallen for "one of the most vicious 'white man tricks,'" they wrote in a scathing letter from their suburban home in New Rochelle. He had allowed the mayor to "invalidate, downgrade, and undercut the efforts of others who are much closer to the scene, and who have been working hard to construct some kind of racial peace in Harlem." The United Council was, they stressed, the "legitimate representative" of the black residents.[54]

"We respect your philosophy of non-violence," Davis and Dee continued, "but hate to see it, and you, used by cynical politicians to muffle the cries of an outraged community. If the Mayor had a little more respect for your philosophy maybe his police force would not be so trigger happy." Law and order, they added, was a "two way street: citizens must respect the law, but the law must equally respect, and protect, the citizen." The letter concluded with a blunt reminder that ultimately King had to choose sides: "The Mayor needs you, Dr. King. But not nearly so much as we, your own people, do."[55]

On Tuesday King spent the morning resting and relaxing. At 2:30 P.M. the summit resumed as he, Rustin, Cleveland Robinson of the City Commission on Human Rights, and others met with Wagner, City Council President Paul Screvane, and aides at Gracie Mansion. The major stumbling blocks were soon apparent—the mayor would not issue an executive order creating an independent review board or force the police commissioner, who reportedly threatened to resign, to suspend Gilligan. Nevertheless, the "cordial and fruitful" talks continued for four hours as city officials conferred with the White House on ways to pump more federal dollars into New York for job training and youth programs.[56]

By then news of King's visit had reached Rochester, where the curfew was lifted but the National Guard remained on duty and tensions remained high. "These kids tell me, 'We're gonna get some guns and start shooting.' And, if they do it, I'm going to be right in there with them," declared a black activist. "They say, 'That's the way the people get their freedom overseas; that's the way we'll get it here.' They say they're going to bring King around to talk to us. Don't give us King, give us Jesse Gray." On the streets of Harlem, it was a similar refrain—even though Gray, in a successful bid to avoid criminal charges, had claimed in court that he meant Mississippi, not New York, when he called for "guerrilla warfare" at a rally on the Sunday after the riot began.[57]

On Wednesday morning King resumed his talks with Wagner. At midday he held a press conference at the West 125th Street office of the Brotherhood of Sleeping Car Porters, which Rustin had recommended since it was close to the "seat of the problem." Flanked by A. Philip Randolph, founder and first president of the union, Robinson, Wingate, and C. B. Powell, publisher of the *Amsterdam News*, King said that it was his Christian duty to respond to Wagner's plea for assistance "because New York City is the center of the Negro struggle for equality, the capital of Negro life, and the most liberal city in the country. What happens here affects the whole country—from the sharecroppers of Mississippi longing for freedom to the followers of Barry Goldwater hoping to discredit liberalism."[58]

With a Black Muslim symbolically standing behind him, King said that he and Wagner had reached no agreement, aside from the need for more federal aid to New York, but that he had stressed to the mayor that "law

FIGURE 17. After meeting with New York Mayor Robert Wagner to discuss racial tensions in Harlem and Brooklyn, Dr. Martin Luther King, Jr. (right), Bayard Rustin (left), and Rev. Bernard Lee (center) leave Gracie Mansion. © Bettmann/CORBIS.

and order cannot exist in a vacuum. [It] must be based on the confidence of the people in the city's authorities." The language came from Rustin, who had earlier warned King that he had to be critical of the mayor's failure to address the housing, school, and employment problems. Otherwise he would find himself "in a box" with his image in jeopardy. "Well," King told Rustin, "I think you are exactly right."[59]

At the press conference, King also stated unequivocally that "I am not in New York to subvert the unity committee. It is the true representative of the Harlem community and I have made that clear to the Mayor." His words were intended to soothe at least some of the anger felt by Davis, Dee, and other local activists. But he had little time to wonder whether he had succeeded. The next item on his crowded agenda was a 4 P.M. meeting at NAACP national headquarters on West 40th Street; the other "Big Six" civil rights leaders intended to discuss the proposed moratorium on demonstrations until after the election.[60]

On July 2, President Johnson had initially floated the idea after the signing ceremony for the Civil Rights Act. It had gained momentum and urgency when Harlem exploded on July 18. Two days later, Randolph and Rustin had formally suggested a nationwide cessation of protests to Roy Wilkins, who like the others feared the threat from the Goldwater campaign and faced a backlash from white supporters. From around the country anxious liberals had flooded the major organizations with angry letters.

In a typical tirade, a Chicago woman wrote to James Farmer of CORE that after the Harlem Riot she had concluded that he was "a leading campaigner for Barry Goldwater." How else, she asked, could he accuse the NYPD of brutality when police officers had to "defend themselves and decent citizens against mobs of vicious, snarling savages"? She blamed Farmer for inciting violence and warned of the consequences of more unrest. "Every riot brings Barry thousands of votes," she wrote. "Every sit-down or roll-in-the-dust demonstration, interfering with the right of citizens to pursue their legitimate activities, promotes the objectives of Barry and his fascists."[61]

On Wednesday afternoon the "Big Six" engaged in three hours of spirited debate. Wilkins, moderate Whitney Young of the Urban League, and Randolph, who had headed the March on Washington in 1963, pressed for a temporary moratorium on the grounds of political expediency. They argued that more demonstrations—what some cynics were calling "Goldwater rallies"—would alienate white voters and might lead to Johnson's defeat, which would jeopardize the movement's gains. In particular, it might put at risk the implementation and enforcement of the Civil Rights Act.

But both Farmer and John Lewis, the twenty-four-year-old SNCC chairman, opposed the idea of a ban on protests because it would implicitly reinforce the conservative claim that nonviolent demonstrations contributed to urban violence. Lewis also objected to the moratorium because marches or picketing were the only leverage SNCC had against those in power—and he was reluctant to share credit for recent triumphs with the

NAACP and Urban League when their members had rarely placed their bodies directly on the line. Neither he nor Farmer would sign the pact—both said that they first had to consult with their boards of directors about the proposed change in tactics.[62]

"It seems to me quite essential now that we continue our pressure in order to keep our friends honest," said the CORE leader. "Otherwise, the tendency will be for our friends, President Johnson and the Democrats, to adopt the conventional political strategy of moving toward the middle when they're faced with a threat from the right, and this would be disastrous to the civil rights cause." Organized demonstrations, he added, were quite different from disorganized protests—and could serve as valuable outlets for community rage.[63]

"Demonstrations are CORE's only weapons," Farmer continued. "If we talk to wrongdoers and ask them to change their ways, they'll laugh at us. If we try to negotiate, we become an amateur Urban League. If we file suit, we become an amateur NAACP." The identity and viability of the organization were at stake. "For CORE to give up demonstrations, even for six months," he stated, "would be to give up its genius, its *raison d'etre*. It might sound our death knell." Farmer's rejection of the moratorium led to internal dissension and public resignations by top staffers. For the executive director, it was not quite the final straw, but he fully understood that the fate of his leadership was also on the line.[64]

Exhausted and frustrated, Farmer resigned from CORE in 1965. His immediate intent was to lead a nationwide literacy project on behalf of the War on Poverty, but it never moved beyond the planning stage. Four years later, he briefly and unhappily joined the Nixon administration as an assistant secretary in the Department of Health, Education, and Welfare. After his wife died, he retreated from public life and lived alone near Fredericksburg, Virginia, where he received few visitors and felt ignored until 1998, when President Bill Clinton awarded him the Medal of Freedom. A year later he died from complications related to diabetes, which had already claimed his sight and his legs.[65]

The racial unrest in New York placed King in a difficult position. On the one hand, he refused to condone lawlessness and looting "whether used by the racist or the reckless of any color." On the other, King stressed the urgent need for a "massive program" at the local, state, and federal levels to address the "environmental causes" of the recent riots. "As long as thousands of Negroes in Harlem and all the little Harlems of our nation are hovered up in odorous, rat-infested ghettoes; as long as the Negro finds himself smothering in the air-tight cage of poverty in the midst of an affluent society; as long as the Negro feels like an exile in his own land . . . [and] as long as the Negro finds his flight toward freedom constantly delayed by strong headwinds of tokenism and small handouts by the white power structure," he declared, "there will be an ever-present threat of violence and rioting."[66]

During the debate over the moratorium in the last week of July 1964, King as usual was the man in the middle. Seeing merit in both positions and seeking consensus, he urged Wilkins to soften his demand for a total ban on demonstrations to a "broad curtailment" of protests. The NAACP leader agreed. But at the press conference after the summit on Wednesday, Wilkins stressed his original concept of a full moratorium and implied that both Farmer and Lewis had personally accepted the idea. Farmer was not present to protest—he had to catch a plane to Boston—and Lewis kept his objections to himself both for the sake of unity and because no one bothered to ask him directly whether or not he approved.[67]

At the press conference Wilkins released two statements. The first announced the "broad curtailment" of organized demonstrations. It also contended that the Goldwater forces represented a serious threat to liberal democracy and blamed the Republican nominee for injecting racism into the election. "Race has been brought into this campaign head first, feet first, by the ears and everything," Wilkins told reporters. On that subject at least, Farmer and Lewis shared his sentiments.[68]

The second statement condemned the recent riots. It declared that the leaders wished to go "on record as strongly opposing looting, vandalism, or any type of criminal activities." But they drew a "sharp distinction" between unlawful acts and "legitimate protest" while asserting that justice and equality were as important as law and order. And they noted that "by word, deed, and constitution" their organizations had always rejected the participation of extremists such as communists. Of the "Big Six," only Lewis would not endorse the second statement because SNCC as a matter of policy never commented upon local developments in black communities.[69]

On Thursday the *New York Times* offered cautious praise for the curtailment or moratorium. It was "a welcome indication of maturity and responsibility in a period of national trial for Negro and white alike." But the paper warned that white resistance to needed change and black militancy in the nation's slums might render the pact irrelevant: "The big question now is how successful the Negro groups will be in discouraging more explosions." The *Amsterdam News* also supported the ban, which it called a "wise move," although solely as a means to deny votes for Goldwater and keep Johnson in power. "This tactic is not surrendering to the enemy," the weekly wrote. "It is a strategic withdrawal which should bring complete victory in the end."[70]

In the White House, the president voiced his guarded approval. "It is understandable," he said, "that those who are aggrieved will take to the streets, rightly or wrongly." But Johnson added that the Civil Rights Act had put in place the "machinery" to move the site of conflict from the streets to the courtroom and voting booth. It had also changed the "weapons of conflict from the club and the brick to the presentation of evidence and reasoned argument." Now was the time to give the law a chance to work. His careful position reflected his underlying concern that future demonstrations, which he could not control or prevent, might reflect poorly upon his leadership or suggest that many blacks repudiated the landmark legislation.[71]

But Jesse Gray had a negative reaction to the proposed moratorium. "We'll continue to have demonstrations in Harlem in spite of what Wilkins says," he promised. "The only guarantee that President Johnson will act in the best interest of the Negroes is if Negroes keep demonstrating. If Negroes don't demonstrate, Goldwater will move Johnson to the right." Other militants offered similar views. "As long as unjust conditions exist, we will demonstrate," pledged Herbert Callender, chairman of Bronx CORE. "Nobody is going to pay any attention to this ban," said the Reverend Milton Galamison of Brooklyn. "The people in the streets throwing bottles won't listen to these leaders anymore."[72]

In Mississippi, Lewis likewise refused to restrain SNCC's activism. "In the South and through this country, in communities like Harlem, people must be allowed to protest, must be allowed to demonstrate," he argued. "People are very frustrated, desperate, and restless. There's a need to let off steam." Lewis also expressed dismay at how the summit was handled, although he avoided direct criticism of Wilkins. "We tried to reach some consensus," he said, "but it's very difficult when you have certain organizations operating from one level and others operating from different levels. SNCC is not an NAACP-type or Urban League-type organization."[73]

With the movement fragmenting and the pact unraveling, Rustin tried to defend the moratorium. "Leadership often has to do what is right, whether or not people like it," he retorted, pledging that he would work tirelessly to make the ban or curtailment a reality. "Leadership often has to do what is politically sound, whether or not people like it. I think our leaders have taken a very courageous stand."[74] But his was a lonely voice— even Wilkins was silent for the moment. In the movement, the moratorium had become a litmus test in a new struggle between militants, who were convinced that Rustin had chosen the wrong side, and moderates, who were under increasing pressure.

In Egypt, Malcolm X was contemptuous of the ban. "I'd die before I'd tell Negroes to restrain themselves in the face of unjust attacks," he said. King and Wilkins "have sold themselves out and become campaign managers in the Negro community for Lyndon Johnson." From Washington Congressman Powell also offered a harsh assessment. The pact, he commented, was "rather nice but it is utterly meaningless." The national leaders, he stressed, lacked the power or influence to halt demonstrations in local communities.[75]

"Wonders Never Cease" was the editorial headline in the *Pittsburgh Courier*, which called the moratorium "an unusual document the Negro leaders signed to barter the votes of their followers (how many we don't know) for a wishful mess of pottage." But the black newspaper with a circulation of almost eighty thousand—larger than the *Amsterdam News*—was equally dismissive of what it called the "disgraceful orgies of civil disobedience, rioting, and vandalism" in Harlem and Rochester. They "set back the civil rights battle for years and destroyed what remained of the Negro image for sense and responsibility which decades of efforts had sought to build."[76]

Stung by the criticism from all sides, Rustin retreated. On WLIB, a radio station in New York popular with black listeners, he said that he could not and would not urge compliance with the moratorium. Citing the mayor's refusal to create an independent review board, he conceded that demonstrations "cannot be curtailed in a vacuum." The concession echoed the message he had given King about law and order on the eve of his visit to the city. But it was too late to save Rustin's reputation with militants, who increasingly viewed him as a sellout to the cause of freedom. "I got in trouble with the black community when I convinced Mr. Randolph that there should be a moratorium," he later admitted.[77]

On Thursday, with the rifts ever more visible, King returned to Gracie Mansion for a final round of face-to-face talks with Wagner. The effort proved fruitless. At 4:30 P.M. the mayor departed to pay his respects to the

family of a white officer killed in the line of duty three days earlier. Patrolman Henry Walburger, a twenty-four-year-old father of three whose wife
was pregnant, was shot by an intruder who had taken two black women, a
mother and daughter, hostage in their Lower East Side apartment. "A
young man has died," the daughter later wrote to the officer's widow. "And
because of him my mother and I are alive." She added that amid the
"screams of corruption and brutality which mushroom and condemn out
of hand an entire police force" she wanted to acknowledge Walburger's
sacrifice because he was an "example of how one would wish to live out a
good life."[78]

As King exited the official residence, he spoke to reporters from the
steps. The commissioner, he said, had refused to suspend Gilligan or support the creation of an independent police review board. Murphy was
"utterly unresponsive to either the demands or the aspirations of the Negro
people," charged King in a harsh statement drafted by Rustin. "He is
intransigent and has little understanding of the urgency of the situation."
Even though King declined to call for the commissioner's dismissal, the
strong comments led to a slander suit on behalf of Murphy from Roy Cohn,
the pugnacious former counsel to Senator Joseph McCarthy.[79]

"I trust the mayor has gained new insights" into the mood, feelings, and
"problems that face the Negro community," said King, who diplomatically
abstained from describing Wagner's reactions. Tired and frustrated after
eleven hours of direct discussions spread over four days, King appealed "to
all the people of New York, Negro and white, to refrain from bitterness and
violence." But he pointedly observed that in Central Harlem, "the explosive
possibilities are still there, and they will only subside to the degree the
Administration seeks to remove the conditions that brought them on at
first." His pessimism was palpable.[80]

On that discordant and despondent note, so different from the convivial
tone between Johnson and Goldwater, the summit between King and
Wagner concluded. The mayor had placed his hopes for peace on King,
who had placed his prestige on the line to resolve the crisis. But in the end
neither man could deliver what the other wanted and needed, although
Wagner would later credit King for "calming the waters." Like the presidential summit in the White House, expectations had exceeded what was possible or attainable. "Martin can win victories in the South," Rustin told a
white friend and ally, "but there are no victories for him to win in the
North."[81]

King instead faced sharp criticism. On his first visit to New York City since June, Congressman Powell told his congregants at Abyssinian Baptist Church that "no leader outside of Harlem should come into this town and tell us what to do." With King preaching at Riverside Church only blocks away, Powell implied that he was "used by the white power structure to keep the Negro in his place." But the congressman said he was not blaming King—he was simply offering "some words of advice from the old man of the black revolution" who was organizing protests and marches "before they put diapers on Martin Luther King." Later Powell denigrated King's signature legislative achievement to date, the Civil Rights Act, and touted what he called "my bill"—the antipoverty measure in Congress—which he had adroitly steered through the Education and Labor Committee as chairman. "If you haven't got a dime for a cup of coffee," Powell asked, "what good is a public accommodations act?"[82]

The barbed question undoubtedly nagged at King, who had long wrestled with similar thoughts about economic injustice. After five days in New York, King also had a firsthand sense of how intractable the racial problems were and how divided the freedom struggle was. Already the brief euphoria surrounding passage of the Civil Rights Act had faded, replaced by a sobering awareness of the complex challenges he and the movement faced. As King departed for Atlanta on Friday, he told reporters that he was now more optimistic about the South than the North, whose cities remained tinderboxes.[83]

That same day, Wagner left for his summer home on Long Island after releasing a statement. It offered nothing new—again he stressed the importance of law and order and the danger of demagogues who sought to exploit despair and turmoil. The mayor praised King as a "truly impressive American, a figure of deep spiritual insights and great world stature." But Wagner once more refused to implement an independent review board by executive authority and made no mention of Gilligan's possible suspension. Instead, the mayor proposed a seven-point economic program whose centerpiece was the creation of a thousand summer jobs with city agencies for high school dropouts recruited by HARYOU and the Mobilization for Youth in Bed-Stuy. It was too little, too late.[84]

As a hot and painful month came to a close, Wagner also announced that the commissioner had lifted the ban on demonstrations in Harlem and Brooklyn. And the mayor at last said that he was willing to meet with a "representative delegation" from the United Council the following week,

even though he remained privately dismissive of the "self-appointed leaders" in New York. "I tried to respect them and handle them," Wagner
recalled, "but I said, 'Who elected you? . . . I got 90 percent of the vote in
Harlem.'" Few thought, however, that another summit would make a real
or lasting difference. "It is no longer a question of who speaks for Harlem,"
admitted a founder of the coalition, "but rather who will listen."[85]

CHAPTER 11

ALL THE WAY WITH LBJ

> I do not as a Negro have the political and economic power to make a
> breakthrough. Therefore I need allies.
> —Bayard Rustin

JULY 27–NOVEMBER 3

The president's mood was tense on Monday morning after the weekend of unrest in Rochester. "This thing could get awfully dangerous for us," he told Roy Wilkins in a phone call. The NAACP leader agreed and said that he intended to meet in New York on Wednesday with the other major civil rights leaders to discuss a ban on future demonstrations and a focus on voter registration for the rest of the campaign.[1]

Johnson was supportive of the plan, especially if Wilkins could ensure the cooperation of Martin Luther King, Jr., but the White House remained anxious. "Further riots in other cities loom ahead," warned an aide on July 27. "This one issue could destroy us in the campaign. Every night of rioting costs us the support of thousands. Therefore we need to move swiftly to try to hold the line before it spreads like a contagion."[2]

To quarantine the disease of disorder, the adviser recommended that the president meet with Mayor Wagner, his aides, the police commissioner, and a select group of Harlem leaders, including NAACP officials, on his next trip to New York. "Appeal to the good sense and conscience of the city both white and Negro," he urged. "Denounce violence but recognize frustration. [Be] firm in the insistence on obedience to the law. Pinpoint the cause of the riots—poverty, squalor, hopelessness for the future."[3]

The liberal line was clear—strongly promise to defend law and order, but simultaneously pledge to address the "root causes" of civil unrest, especially with the antipoverty program. Quelling the violence, "calming the hot-heads and . . . blunting the further erosion of white voter passions" were vital according to the official. Otherwise further riots would damage the president's reputation and could open a "new issue for the opposition."[4]

The advice confirmed what Johnson already feared. "The first of several long, hot summers had begun," he later wrote in his memoirs. Harlem and Rochester "foreshadowed dark days of trial ahead."[5] But for now the president could run on his preferred themes of peace and prosperity. On every other major domestic and foreign issue he enjoyed a substantial advantage over Republican nominee Barry Goldwater, who had alarmed moderate voters with his talk of privatizing Social Security and using nuclear weapons against North Vietnam. Only law and order posed a serious danger to Johnson's hopes for a landslide victory of historic proportions.

For the rest of the campaign, the White House sought to highlight Goldwater's extremism, which a series of negative commercials skillfully accomplished. In the famous "Daisy" television spot, perhaps the most effective political ad in history, a young girl is picking petals from a flower when a countdown begins at ten. As it ends, a mushroom cloud fills the screen. "These are the stakes—to make a world in which all of God's children can live, or to go into the dark," intones the voice of Johnson. "We must either love each other or we must die."[6] The options were stark.

The president's campaign also worked hard to contain the political risk of urban unrest, which threatened to become the domestic equivalent of international communism. If conservatives could convincingly depict liberals as soft on crime and violence, Johnson stood little chance of persuading Congress to help him build the Great Society, his ultimate ambition. But at the moment he had an even more pressing matter on his mind.

On Monday afternoon, the president spoke by phone with the attorney general, who expressed little faith in the mayor of Rochester. The White House, asserted Robert Kennedy, had to take "some action" to provide "some hope" to young people. "Obviously with the Communists, with the Black Muslims, and just the no-gooders you're not going to be able to do anything," he said. But in Washington the city and federal authorities had prevented an explosion by integrating swimming pools and creating jobs programs. Sending speakers—especially athletes and entertainers—to the schools and opening channels of communication to disaffected teens had also helped. "Our experience in making the effort in juvenile delinquency," Kennedy added, "is that that makes a hell of a difference."[7]

Rochester was not necessarily a sign of further trouble. "But you could have that kind of explosion in a lot of these cities, and I would think that if it occurs during August and September and October, it could cause us some difficulty," Kennedy warned. "I don't know that it's going to go on, but the fact that you have Harlem and Rochester [is] going to give some of these people ideas in some of these other communities." Perhaps, he suggested, the president could convene a meeting with the mayors of other major cities such as Chicago, and then let officials like FBI Director J. Edgar Hoover and Sargent Shriver, acting head of the War on Poverty, describe the anticrime and antidelinquency programs of the federal government.[8]

"Obviously the Communists make an effort to infiltrate the civil rights movement," continued Kennedy. "They haven't been successful, but it's something that has to be watched continuously, and in certain instances they have achieved positions of importance which must be a concern to everybody." The president undoubtedly caught the allusion to some of King's advisers, who were under constant FBI surveillance. The attorney general further stressed that it was important to concentrate on more than just African Americans—Mexican Americans in cities like Phoenix also represented an "explosive situation" as well as a valuable opportunity to shift the focus away from civil rights "so that people don't think that we're just working on Negroes."[9]

Kennedy's thoughts and ideas met with vague approval from Johnson, who was nonetheless noncommittal, probably because he was preoccupied with a different problem. "I want you to come over sometime," the president told the attorney general. "I'll give you a ring and you might get this [proposal] up ahead of time. . . . I want to talk to you about some other matters and we can talk about this too."[10] Whether Kennedy knew it or not, his days in the administration were numbered. The split many saw as inevitable was coming—in two days.

Each man had loathed the other with a passion for years. Their bitter relationship was based on an extraordinary degree of mutual contempt, as speechwriter, historian, and cartoonist Jeff Shesol has aptly characterized their famous feud.[11] The animosity was in part due to their similarities—

both were thin-skinned and easily wounded, which left them vulnerable and volatile. Each man tended to harbor and obsess over slights, both real and imagined.

But the antagonism was also due to their differences. Physically, the imposing Johnson towered over the diminutive Kennedy, whom he called "that little shitass" and that "grandstanding little runt." Culturally, the attorney general, who had inherited a fortune and received an elite education at Harvard College, had disdain for the president. "Mean, bitter, vicious—an animal in many ways" was how he described Johnson, who was raised in the hill country outside Austin and had graduated from little-known Southwest Texas State Teachers College. Politically, Kennedy often disparaged elected officials in private, whereas Johnson usually liked and respected those who, like him, had battled in the arena and clawed their way to positions of power. He scorned the attorney general, who had never faced the judgment of voters and had received his appointment thanks to what the vice president (at the time) saw as a transparent act of blatant nepotism.[12]

By mid-July, when Goldwater received the Republican nomination, it was apparent to most insiders that Kennedy would not receive a spot on the ticket, since Johnson now had northern liberals in his pocket and could attract southern moderates if he selected someone less polarizing than Kennedy. On July 22, the president had a memo prepared with talking points for his fateful meeting with the attorney general. A week later, as King spoke to reporters at the office of the Brotherhood of Sleeping Car Porters in Harlem, the two men met in the Oval Office shortly after 1 P.M.

As Kennedy entered the room, Johnson ushered him to a seat by his desk rather than the sofa by the fireplace, where the president typically made guests feel welcome. The gesture was calculated—it enabled Johnson to showcase the power imbalance between the two men and tape the sensitive conversation in case Kennedy chose to dispute what took place (he later dictated his own record of the Wednesday meeting). Armed with the talking points, which lay on the desk, the president expressed his regard for the attorney general, his belief that he had a bright future, his hope that he would lend a hand with the campaign, and his willingness to get him any government job he wanted—except for the vice presidency.[13]

"Well, I'm sorry that you've reached this conclusion," said Kennedy as Johnson walked him to the door, "because I think I could have been of help to you." In the president's account, the words had a melancholy ring to them; in the attorney general's account, they had a sardonic tone. Both men were probably relieved, however, that at last they could end their uneasy partnership and go their separate ways. Now the issue was who would make the announcement because Johnson wanted Kennedy to remove himself from consideration, but he refused. So on Thursday evening the president stated, without mentioning the attorney general, that he would not select for vice president any member of the cabinet or any official who met with it, which also eliminated Shriver. The ploy fooled no one.[14]

The next day Johnson, who remained intensely insecure about Kennedy, inflamed their mutual animosity once more. Demonstrating a startling—though not surprising—lack of magnanimity, he invited three reporters—Douglas Kiker of the *Herald Tribune*, Tom Wicker of the *New York Times*, and Edward Folliard of the *Washington Post*—to the White House for a private lunch. For four hours the president entertained them with his version of the meeting, which included an impersonation of the attorney general reacting to his dashed hopes by gulping for air "like a fat fish" and moving his Adam's apple "up and down like a yo-yo."[15]

Outraged, Kennedy confronted Johnson, who denied that he had discussed their meeting with the press. Kennedy said he was a liar; Johnson said he would check his calendar. "He tells so many lies," Kennedy wrote later, "that he convinces himself after a while he's telling the truth. He just doesn't recognize truth or falsehood."[16] And so the feud would fester as Washington buzzed with rumors of the rivalry between the present king and the heir apparent. But with the coming of the weekend the president had more visitors to entertain and more politics to confront.

On Sunday, August 2, Johnson and his wife Lady Bird welcomed Mayor Robert Wagner and his sons, Robert III and Duncan, to the White House for a "social" visit. The three-day trip to Washington gave the mayor the opportunity to escape what he described as the "maelstrom" of New York and savor a brief vacation with his sons, who like their father remained deeply affected by the death of their mother Susan in March. Wagner also planned to meet the next day with administration officials to discuss how New York could get more federal funds from the War on Poverty program after it cleared the House of Representatives. Finally, he hoped to receive the president's blessing for a U.S. Senate bid so that he could again pursue his ambition of following in his father's footsteps.[17]

But Johnson had already resolved privately that he wanted Kennedy to run for the seat. If he was an active candidate, he would pose no threat to the president's nomination at the Democratic Convention in late August. Johnson also believed that Kennedy would benefit from some practical experience as a candidate and politician, especially if he planned to seek the White House in the future. And he represented the best opportunity the Democrats had to oust Republican Kenneth Keating and add to their majority in the Senate. Ever the loyal soldier, Wagner had to accede to the wishes of his party leader, see what favors or concessions he might negotiate in return, and decide how to bow out gracefully in the coming weeks.

For now the mayor avoided the topic. As he sat on the Truman Balcony and gazed across the South Lawn, he steered the conversation with the president and First Lady to the efforts he had made to keep New York from descending deeper into racial strife. Wagner described how the city had created summer jobs for Harlem youths, although he conceded it was a "drop in the bucket." He also spoke of how his administration had constructed huge blocks of public housing and tried to improve public health by allocating more than a million dollars for rat control. And the mayor emphasized how he had invited King to New York because of the "emotional hold" that he—unlike leaders such as Wilkins—had over the black community. Yet even King was powerless in the face of widespread anger and resentment toward the police.[18]

After the mayor had finished, the First Lady asked him a question. As an outsider, she said, civilian review of police actions seemed like a good idea. Why not implement it in New York? Because, he replied, "the morale of [the] police department would drop to zero overnight."[19] And if that happened the city would become ungovernable. The blunt answer revealed the basic calculation behind Wagner's refusal to implement civilian review despite the fervent pleas of white liberals and black leaders like King.

After fruitful discussions with cabinet officers and administration officials on Monday, the mayor returned to New York, where Governor Rockefeller, with the assent of local authorities, had withdrawn fifteen hundred members of the National Guard from Rochester; two hundred state police remained despite a week of calm. Harlem was also mostly peaceful. "There won't be any trouble for a month," a resident predicted. "Why should there be? The junkies have enough money now to keep going until next month." Like "piranha tearing flesh from bone," in the words of an observer, they had methodically stripped enough merchandise from stores to feed their habits for the near future.[20]

At the 28th Precinct, where in two weeks Lloyd Sealy would become the first black officer in Harlem history to assume command, Captain Casimir Kruszewski noted that in the past seven days he had not heard a single rumor of a weapons stash or secret meeting from his intelligence sources. "It's a period of relative calm now," he said as he sat in his rundown office. "Everything looks normal, but I don't know what they're thinking. I wish I did, but then, don't we all?" Local merchants also expected the peace to last—at least until the grand jury issued its report on the Powell shooting. "If they don't indict Gilligan," a black drugstore clerk warned, "this will blow right up again. And the second time will be a helluva lot worse than the first."[21]

But newspaper headlines on August 3 warned of immediate threats both overseas and closer to home. In the Gulf of Tonkin, three North Vietnamese PT boats had attacked a U.S. destroyer in international waters according to the Defense Department. In Jersey City, at least thirty were reported injured—including ten officers and a white family driving through the Lafayette neighborhood—when clashes erupted near the Booker T. Washington Housing Project on Sunday. The incident began with the arrest of a black couple for disorderly conduct. In response, forty or so residents marched on the station house to protest what they saw as police brutality. "Get the white cops out of Jersey City," chanted demonstrators as the entire force mobilized to restore order. "We're ready for you. Come on! Come on!"[22]

As the disorder spread, white conservatives questioned why the president was not assisting police officers or restraining black activists who used civil disobedience as a false pretense for unlawful deeds. For years southern politicians had warned that protests would lead to a wave of crime and a breakdown of society. Now federal action was needed. The White House, contended conservative columnist David Lawrence, had cited the harmful impact of racial prejudice on interstate commerce as legal justification for the Civil Rights Act. But when, he wondered, would Johnson recognize that "it is also discriminatory to allow civil rights to be taken away from white or colored people by means of riots and mob violence."[23]

With the bodies of CORE volunteers Schwerner, Chaney, and Goodman discovered in Mississippi and the president scheduled to give a speech in New York City the following week, the threat of more unrest triggered mounting concern in the White House. "It is by now clear that civil disorder will be the central domestic issue of the election," warned Adam Walinsky, a lawyer in the Justice Department and later a speechwriter for Robert

Kennedy. "Every Negro riot represents tens of thousands of Goldwater votes." Since black residents wanted more protection, he urged the prompt formation of civilian groups similar to the Maccabees in Brooklyn. Community patrols, whether they consisted of adult volunteers or unemployed youths paid with federal funds from the poverty program, could reduce racial tensions between officers and residents. They could also serve, Walinsky argued, "as an organizing point for the substantial majority of Negroes who resent and fear violence, whether from white police or Negro hoodlums."[24]

The president was ready to confront both the foreign and domestic crises of law and order when he arrived in New York on August 12 to address the annual meeting of the American Bar Association. With Goldwater on his mind though not in his text, Johnson told the three thousand delegates and their guests jammed into the Grand Ballroom of the Waldorf Astoria that he was opposed to "reckless action" in South Vietnam that might endanger "American boys" and risk nuclear war. At the same time, the president stressed "the right of every American to be secure in his home, his shop, and his streets. We will not permit any part of America to become a jungle where the weak are the prey of the strong and the many." Whether it was the South or the North made no difference.[25]

"There is no place in our federal system for a national police force," the president continued. "Under our Constitution, the local authorities have the central responsibility for civil peace." But Washington was prepared to provide assistance as needed and requested, whether the criminals were "hooded nightriders on our highways" (a reference to the murderers in Mississippi) or "hoodlums in the city streets." Finally, Johnson concluded with a call for racial justice and a swipe at Goldwater's platform: "The denial of rights invites increased disorder and violence, and those who would hold back progress toward equality, and at the same time promise racial peace, are deluding themselves and deluding the people." The twenty-one-minute speech was interrupted with applause sixteen times.[26]

But as Johnson spoke in New York, news arrived of more riots in Paterson and Elizabeth, New Jersey, two depressed industrial towns with sizable black populations. "These cops," said a bitter teen, "they'll stop your car and say, 'All right, nigger, get out,' and you'll have to swallow that. Then they'll say, 'You niggers get up against that wall,' and they'll smash you in the ribs, and you'll have to swallow that, too. And pretty soon you'll get tired of swallowing, so you wait for one of their cars to come by and you try to get it with a brick. Or you try to get into one of these stores around here, 'cause they're all the same—all these white people is the same."[27]

The day before the speech, Johnson had called Wagner in the afternoon. The two men chuckled as the mayor observed that he now had "a little of your former problem up here." Wagner indicated that he was unwilling to block Kennedy's bid by himself since "those boys play rough" and the unde-clared candidate already had the support he needed. "I just don't like to have him move in and get with some of the elements that are going to hurt us here," said the mayor, who emphasized that above all he wanted to protect the president. "I know that," replied Johnson, "and I'm going to do the same thing for you, Bob."[28]

The next day, the mayor met Johnson and accompanied him on his fifteen-minute limousine ride from the Wall Street Heliport to the Midtown Manhattan hotel. The details they discussed are not known. But five days earlier, Wagner had withheld his endorsement when he met with Kennedy, who insisted that he would not run without his approval. "Mayor Wagner doesn't like any 'other stars in the orbit' but . . . will accept the president's wishes," reported Averell Harriman, a former governor and longtime Dem-ocratic statesman. Apparently Johnson made his wishes clear because the mayor gave his assent to the Kennedy candidacy and was then invited back to the White House on August 20 when the president signed the antipov-erty bill.[29]

Five days later, a rather wistful and forlorn Wagner stood at the thirty-eight-year-old Kennedy's side as he declared that he intended to run for the U.S. Senate from New York. Perhaps, however, the mayor drew solace from the news that the White House had just awarded Harlem Youth Opportunities Unlimited (HARYOU), the antipoverty program, an initial grant of $1 million—the first federal funds it had received.[30]

On Tuesday afternoon, August 25, Bayard Rustin was huddled in the bedroom of Minnesota Senator Hubert Humphrey's suite at the Pageant Hotel in Atlantic City, site of the Democratic National Convention. With Rustin were, among others, King, Robert Moses of the Student Nonviolent Coordinating Committee (SNCC), and Walter Reuther, leader of the United Auto Workers. Also present were Aaron Henry and Edwin King of the Mississippi Freedom Democratic Party (MFDP), which with SNCC's assistance had registered voters, conducted elections, and held a state con-vention to choose an integrated slate of delegates as an alternative to the all-white slate of the regular Mississippi Democratic Party. Now the issue was which delegates would gain official recognition at the national convention.[31]

In late July, after the unrest in Harlem and Brooklyn had subsided, Rustin had traveled to Mississippi to meet with Moses and survey the situation. It was not good. SNCC workers were under intense pressure, he reported to King, and the MFDP campaign was in "bad shape around the state." Rustin predicted trouble. "They are going to try and accuse everybody of selling them out," he told King in a conversation recorded by the FBI. It was going to lead to "an assault on our friends"—the Johnson administration, white liberals, and labor unions. And it might provide an assist to their foes—the Goldwater conservatives.[32]

In search of unity and harmony, the White House proposed a compromise. It promised to enforce nondiscrimination standards at future conventions and require all delegates to sign a loyalty oath to the party's ticket and platform, which contained a civil rights plank. Humphrey, who was Johnson's representative in the negotiations and hoped to earn the vice presidential nomination as a reward, also offered to seat Henry and King of the MFDP as at-large delegates, although it would mean that they could not sit with the all-white Mississippi delegation and, legally, could not claim to represent anyone in the state.

The proposal was not well received by the MFDP representatives. So Reuther, a liberal who had backed the movement, offered the proverbial stick and carrot. "Your funding is on the line," he said to King. "The kind of money you got from us in Birmingham is there again for Mississippi, but you've got to help us and we've got to help Johnson." When Edwin King, one of only four white MFDP delegates, objected to the way the administration had peremptorily chosen Henry and him, Rustin suggested that substitutions were possible. But the negotiations were interrupted by news reports on the suite's television announcing that the Credentials Committee had just approved the compromise. "You cheated!" screamed Moses at Humphrey and Reuther as the MFDP supporters walked out of the room.[33]

That night Reuther spoke to Johnson, who was angry and upset. "I think the Negroes are going back to the Reconstruction period and going right where they were then," he said. "They're going to set themselves back a hundred years. . . . They don't understand that nearly every white man in this country would be frightened if he thought the Negro was going to take over." The UAW leader agreed. "They're completely irrational," he said. "They don't know the victory they've got is the proposition that next time no one can discriminate against Negroes."[34]

On Wednesday morning, discussion of the compromise resumed—this time at MFDP headquarters in the basement of Union Temple Baptist Church. Rustin now urged those assembled to reconsider their opposition to it. He praised their courage and their achievement. By persuading the Democratic Party to adopt a nondiscrimination policy in the future the MFDP had won a great victory. But blacks were only 10 percent of the population, and it was time, Rustin argued, to move from protests in the streets to politics in an arena where negotiation and compromise, with both allies and enemies, were essential to social and economic progress. "It was a very good talk," recalled Edwin King. "It was wrong, but it was very good." Others were less charitable.[35]

"You're a traitor, Bayard, a traitor," shouted Jehudah Menachem Mendel "Mendy" Samstein, a CORE volunteer in Mississippi. "Sit down!" Amid the uproar King attempted to restore order to the meeting. "I am not going to counsel you to accept or reject," he said. As a black leader, I would agree to the administration proposal, "but if I were a Mississippi Negro I would vote against it." SNCC leader John Lewis was more adamant. "We've shed too much blood," he said. "We've come much too far to back down now."[36]

After the guests departed, the MFDP delegates voted overwhelmingly to reject the compromise and most prepared to head home. Yet the convention continued. Johnson named Humphrey as his vice president and then the two candidates received a ringing endorsement from the Democratic faithful, followed by an emotional tribute from Robert Kennedy to his late brother.[37]

For Rustin, however, the fallout from Atlantic City was lasting. Once again he was the outsider, mistrusted by many of his former friends in the freedom struggle, who now saw him as part of the liberal establishment. "I think he flip-flopped," said Moses in retrospect. "The civil rights forces just had to move with the common people. And Bayard was moving with Humphrey and the administration." For Lewis the MFDP fight in Atlantic City "was the turning point of the civil rights movement." In the aftermath, hope and idealism gave way to despair and cynicism, as Johnson lost the faith of the people and they lost faith in their president. "We had played by the rules, done everything we were supposed to do . . . arrived at the doorstep, and found the door slammed in our face," he wrote in his memoir. It was an understandable reaction even though the convention compromise led to significant changes within the Democratic Party in future years.[38]

But if Atlantic City marked a watershed for SNCC, it was not a turning point for Rustin, whose philosophy had already evolved as a result of July's events—passage of the Civil Rights Act, the Harlem Riot, and the moratorium controversy. Three weeks earlier, in a television appearance in New York, he was clear about why the movement needed to build bridges, not burn them. "I do not as a Negro have the political and economic power to make a breakthrough," he explained. "Therefore I need allies."[39]

Rustin also knew who his enemies were. "Anything which can be done now which obstructs the election of Goldwater is good for America and the Negro people," he declared. "Anything which is done which helps him get elected is bad for America and bad for the Negro people." With implementation of the Civil Rights Act at stake, the fundamental objective was to appeal to white moderates. "They are fleeing into the Goldwater camp out of fear," Rustin continued. "We need to do those things which will assure them momentarily that we are trying to be militantly reasonable." It was the perfect encapsulation of his vision to transform the nation gradually and peacefully.[40]

And yet Rustin could empathize with the frustration and impatience of the SNCC leaders, who represented the viewpoint of a younger generation of black activists. "Those kids, who had been shot at, beaten up, brutalized, seen their buddies murdered, could scarcely have been prepared to accept compromise," he reflected later. "To a certain extent I would have been very disappointed in them if they had." Rustin added that "I understood them perfectly, but to understand is not to say they are right."[41] Not surprisingly, in coming years he would find less and less common ground with the militants in the movement as they embraced racial separatism and Black Power.

On August 31 pollster Louis Harris reported that 53 percent of Americans were more worried about safety in the streets than a year earlier. Although the level of anxiety varied by gender, region, and size of community, Harris concluded that "no section of the country or group of voters this fall will be immune from the volatile atmosphere" now surrounding the issue of personal security. In the nation as a whole, the fear of crime was foremost, but in the cities the fear of riots was the chief concern.[42] Nowhere was the unease greater than in New York, where black and white residents nervously awaited the findings of the grand jury, which had convened on July 21, five days after the Powell shooting.

On September 1, the verdict arrived. After holding fifteen meetings and listening to forty-five witnesses who offered sixteen hundred pages of oft-conflicting testimony, the grand jury unanimously found Lieutenant Thomas Gilligan not criminally liable in the shooting death of teenager James Powell. The twenty-three jurors refused to issue an indictment, which would have required at least twelve members to believe that a petit jury, after reviewing the evidence, would conclude beyond a reasonable doubt that Gilligan had not acted in self-defense. Under the law, both private citizens and police officers had the right to use deadly force in self-defense if they had a reasonable basis for fearing imminent harm or injury. Although Gilligan was off duty, he was obliged to intervene in the incident and not required to retreat if he had a reasonable basis for believing at the time that no safe alternative to the immediate use of deadly force existed, even if later inquiry or reflection proved him wrong.[43]

"In light of the great public interest evinced in the case," said District Attorney Frank S. Hogan with notable understatement, his office had prepared an unusual, fourteen-page summary of the grand jury's findings. As reporters received copies, Assistant District Attorney Alexander Herman, chief of the homicide bureau, removed from his pocket a clasp knife with a black handle and a three-inch blade. It was the same knife that Gilligan, who testified at least four times, said Powell had wielded and the grand jury had examined. A reporter who handled it claimed that the edge of the blade was dull. But reaction to the verdict was sharp among both moderate and militant black leaders.[44]

Roy Wilkins expressed deep disappointment and wondered why a 200-pound man could not handle a 120-pound teenager without resorting to deadly force. "I remain convinced that an experienced police officer should be able to arrest a fifteen-year-old boy without killing him," said Wilkins. "They can explain and explain until they're blue in the face, but they'll never explain why it's necessary for a police officer to shoot a fifteen-year-old kid." Frustrated, he added, "It just doesn't go down."[45]

Jesse Gray denounced the grand jury, whose finding he termed "the greatest whitewash since Emmett Till" (the black teenager murdered in Mississippi in 1955). Under an injunction preventing him from leading demonstrations in Harlem, Gray vowed that he would take no action. But at a rally on 125th Street his followers distributed a leaflet with the headline

"Powell's Murderer Set Free." Underneath it read, "Harlem knows that this grand jury decision means that any white policeman who wants to kill a Negro will not have to worry about being tried for murder."[46]

James Farmer of CORE was outraged. "If this killing was not a crime," he said in a statement, "then the law and Police Department policy are at fault." In particular, he took aim at the practice of allowing officers to use deadly force, making them "judge, jury, and executioner," even in the case of a misdemeanor like disorderly conduct. In a detailed response to the official summary, CORE now conceded that Powell was armed, but contended that Gilligan had not displayed his badge or fired a warning shot. At times the police had to resort to deadly force. But if it was not restricted to cases where a felony was in progress or likely to occur, more painful tragedies and innocent victims were inevitable. "The odds on every day greatly favor that a new incident will take place," the report concluded, "and that it will involve a Negro victim."[47]

But on this day Harlem remained quiet, probably because most residents had expected the verdict and were resigned to it. "What else did you expect?" said a barber who shrugged his shoulders at the news. "I would say that 95 percent of the people of Harlem felt it would be like that," said the pastor of the Upper Park Avenue Baptist Church. Richard Hildebrand, pastor of the Bethel African Methodist Church and president of the local NAACP chapter, was also not surprised. "These grand juries have a long record of exoneration of police officers accused of brutality against Negroes," he observed with accuracy.[48]

That was cold comfort to Annie Powell, the victim's mother, who learned of the verdict from a woman on the bus. "I just put my head down and cried," she said of her initial reaction. Alone since the death of James, her only child, she planned at some point to move in with her sister, who lived in Harlem. As for Gilligan, she had a simple message: "He'll have to answer to God for what he's done."[49]

For their part police officers expressed satisfaction and relief with the verdict. "Gilligan did the right thing," said an officer. Another agreed, stating, "If the grand jury exonerated him it must be because he was right." Still others took heart from the outcome, which they saw as good for the department and the citizens who depended on it. If Gilligan was indicted, an officer contended, it would have undermined the police and made them "damn good targets for all the punks in the city." That was the consensus among the men in blue.[50]

But the man of the hour was silent and invisible. Gilligan remained on sick leave with knife wounds to his right hand—he would not return to active duty until after the election in November. He was also out of sight— neighbors at the Stuyvesant Town housing complex where he lived with his wife and daughter had not seen him for weeks and police officials declined to identify where he was, probably for his own protection. And Gilligan continued to face a possible investigation by the Complaint Review Board, which had the authority to review the grand jury's findings and make a recommendation to the commissioner.[51]

That became far less likely when George S. Schuyler, one of two African Americans on the grand jury, spoke on the public record two days later and reported that the verdict was unanimous. "I did the right thing and so did the rest of the jury. We heard everything and we're more expert on the subject because we were there," he said of his fellow jurors. "I've been on juries for the last twenty years and so I think I know what I'm talking about." An editorial columnist with the *Pittsburgh Courier* (a black newspaper), Schuyler said that the grand jury was especially impressed by the eyewitness accounts of two teenagers, a boy and a girl, who confirmed the testimony from adults when they stated that Powell had a knife and threatened to use it.[52]

Schuyler's service on the grand jury was not his first time in the spotlight. After serving in the Army in World War I, he flirted with socialism in the 1920s and married a wealthy white woman from Texas named Josephine Codgell. During the Harlem Renaissance, he published *Black No More*, a satirical science fiction novel (one of the first by an African American) in which a black scientist invents a way to change skin color and "whiten" America. In the 1930s, his political views began to shift. By 1964 he was a staunch conservative who endorsed Goldwater and denounced the Civil Rights Act as a threat to personal liberty and freedom which would simultaneously stimulate white resistance to racial integration and equality.[53]

When Harlem erupted, Schuyler blamed King and Powell. "What must honest people think of these preachers who convert their pulpits into agitator's soapboxes spewing rabid racism, inciting the retardates to slick practices, delinquency, civil disobedience and crime?" Schuyler asked. Rustin and Farmer, he charged, were "leftist civil rights agitators" who had sparked the disorder by promising "poor and gullible Negroes things they knew they could never produce." The repeated charges of police brutality were a communist plot to weaken law enforcement, Schuyler maintained, and the black press was equally guilty of promoting violence. Although popular with conservatives, who showered him with awards, he was isolated and marginalized in his public life.[54]

But Schuyler's private life offered few consolations. Years earlier, his wife Josephine had become estranged and lavished her attention on their brilliant and beautiful daughter Philippa, a musical prodigy and concert pianist. At first she shared her father's conservative views on civil rights, but gradually she became a convert to Black Power. In her final letter to her mother, Philippa wrote, "Now if George, instead of letting himself be segregated all his life, had had the guts to go forth into integration and try to thrust his way into white companies and white neighborhoods, he would have found out why the Stokely Carmichaels are necessary." In 1967, at the age of thirty-five, she died in Vietnam when her helicopter crashed near Danang while on a mission to rescue Vietnamese children.[55]

Two years later, shortly before the second anniversary of Philippa's death, Josephine hanged herself in the doorway to her bedroom. For Schuyler the anguish was almost unbearable. "I have tried to fight the good fight for what I have considered right," he wrote in a letter to William Loeb, the conservative white publisher of the *Manchester Union Leader* and one of his few remaining friends, "but now the long battle has worn me down." Alone and forgotten, Schuyler died in 1977 at New York Hospital.[56]

In the White House, the Harris Poll of August 31 had generated more apprehension about the rising rates of street crime and juvenile delinquency. To counter Goldwater's attacks, wrote an aide, the administration needed to highlight the "positive and constructive" measures it had taken. Johnson took the advice to heart immediately. In a morning phone call to a *Dallas Morning News* editor, he reported that 16 percent of black youth were unemployed, at loose ends, and prone to crime. With the antipoverty program, said the president, "I'm going to put them to work, feed them, and clothe them." Otherwise, he warned, "the bottom's gonna blow off the teakettle."[57]

In the afternoon, Johnson discussed the Philadelphia Riot, which had broken out three days earlier, with Nicholas Katzenbach, the deputy attorney general. The president then asked if he would review a memo prepared by Abe Fortas, a longtime confidant whom Johnson would nominate for the Supreme Court in 1965. The memo urged the administration to ask

Congress to make assault on a police officer a federal crime. Katzenbach said that he would, and added that the Justice Department was already working on a statute to prevent the use of interstate facilities to foment acts of domestic violence. But, asked Johnson, aren't most of these riots caused by police incidents? "We certainly haven't discovered any conspiracies yet," agreed Katzenbach, "and I don't think it has much to do with civil rights. It's really just a lot of hoodlum stuff."[58]

The Philadelphia Riot led the White House to have Carl Rowan, a prominent African American journalist who was currently the director of the U.S. Information Agency, give a major speech on racial unrest. "Some Negroes believe that extremism in pursuit of the black man's liberty is no vice," he stated in a deliberate echo of Goldwater's slogan at the Republican Convention, "but I say that stupidity is never a virtue. . . . The hour has come when bold, uncompromising efforts must be made to free the civil rights movement from the taint of street rioters, looters, and punks who terrorize subways." When a presidential aide suggested more "non-political" speeches by Rowan, who decried the actions of the "ignorant and irresponsible," Johnson wrote in the margins of the memo, "I agree. Get him in 10 important states. NY, Illinois, Ohio, California, et al."[59]

Washington was another important concern for the president, although not for electoral reasons. As the seat of the federal government and, prior to passage of legislation in 1973, home to a disenfranchised population, it had symbolic significance and presented a unique opportunity for Johnson to demonstrate the effectiveness of his urban policies—or assume responsibility for their failure. We need, he told Katzenbach on the telephone, to reduce the rate of crime so "a woman can go out in the streets. Now we got control here—we don't have to mess with any states—and dammit . . . we ought to really go to town on that. . . . If we have to bring somebody in to clean it up, we ought to do it. But figure out what to do."[60]

Johnson was nervous for good reason. In the nation's capital, often within sight of the White House, crimes against persons occurred at four times the national average in the first six months of 1964. Goldwater wasted no time in publicizing the data. On September 10, he charged that violent crimes like rape, assault, and robbery had risen at more than double the national average in "the one city which should reflect most brightly the President's concern for law and order, for decent conduct. Instead, it is a city embattled, plagued by lawlessness, haunted by fears." Left unstated—

though widely understood—was Washington's image and reputation as a majority African American metropolis.[61]

Katzenbach responded to Goldwater eight days later with a clear statement of liberal principles. It was the only direct administration address of the fall campaign on the racial implications of law and order—evidence of the extreme sensitivity of the issue. Before the Federal Bar Association at the Shoreham Hotel in New York, the attorney general (he had replaced Kennedy by then) acknowledged that urban violence was a serious threat, but challenged the conservative equation of civil rights and civil disobedience with riots and crime. Emphasizing that poverty, not race, was the critical factor, he pointed out that juveniles in general, not blacks in particular, were responsible for most of the surge in disorder.[62]

"I do not mean to imply that Negroes do not commit crimes," said Katzenbach bluntly. "Of course they do. What I do mean to show is that to draw a causal connection between membership in the Negro race and crime is wrong. The relevant link is not between riots and race, but between riots and delinquency, between lawlessness and lawless environments." And the way to attack those environments was to wage war on those conditions—"the lack of food, shelter, education, work, self-respect, and hope"—that went "hand in hand with crime." Contrary to what Goldwater claimed, asserted Katzenbach, there were no simple or easy answers, no quick fixes. More police officers, fewer protections for accused individuals, and longer sentences for convicted criminals would not, by themselves, solve the growing problem of urban disorder.[63]

On the same day that Katzenbach spoke in Manhattan, the White House received a memo from a Democratic National Committee staffer. "I strongly urge that a quiet, serious study be made of the overall problem of crime," he wrote. "We obviously should not make an issue of it during the campaign, but the country is entitled to an honest statement of the problem on a long term basis; and a dispassionate study by a group of law enforcement officers, judges, statisticians, and public representatives could play a constructive role next year." Six days later, a deputy attorney general named Norbert Schlei delivered a comprehensive report. Titled "Riots and Crime in the Cities," it provided both a snapshot of the administration's views at the time and a roadmap of where they would lead in terms of policies in the future.[64]

"I was asked to focus on it by the White House," Schlei later recalled. "They said, 'Goldwater is making all this noise about crime in the streets.

Would you please focus on this issue and do a study of it for us and tell us what you think, what this issue is about, and where it is going?'" Schlei began by describing the Republicans' call for law and order as a racial appeal coded so that "those to whom racial issues are dominant will identify 'crime in the streets' with crime by Negroes in major urban centers" like New York and Philadelphia. Nevertheless, he insisted that street crime represented a real threat, not a statistical mirage or political smoke screen. To combat it, Schlei recommended that the Johnson administration place "principal emphasis" on initiatives already in place or under way, such as the Civil Rights Act and the War on Poverty.[65]

But, as Schlei readily conceded, focusing on social conditions was unlikely to yield "immediate and dramatic improvements" and might lend credence to Goldwater's claim that "something is basically wrong." The White House should therefore sit tight and enact no new measures "on a crash basis or upon the basis of an unbalanced or hysterical view of the [crime] problem." Instead, Schlei concluded, the president should appoint a commission to study the issue after the election. Katzenbach had already floated a similar proposal and Johnson would heed the idea in 1965 when, as part of his newly declared War on Crime, he formed the President's Commission on Law Enforcement and the Administration of Justice.[66]

The Schlei memo attracted wide notice inside the Johnson administration. But outside the White House, the Warren Commission Report on the assassination of President Kennedy, which was also distributed on September 24, dominated the headlines. It in turn overshadowed the FBI report on "Recent Civil Disturbances in Urban Areas," which was made public two days later, on a Saturday. The weekend release was not coincidental—neither Johnson nor J. Edgar Hoover wanted to draw undue attention to it.

The FBI report, which Johnson had commissioned in the aftermath of the Harlem Riot, was surprisingly moderate in tone and analysis. It stated that "there was no systematic planning or organization of any of the city riots," not by radical individuals or the Communist Party. It also refused to categorize the civil unrest as race riots or contend that they were the direct result of civil rights protest. "A common characteristic of the riots was a senseless attack on all constituted authority without purpose or object," declared the report, which stressed that both white and black business owners and police officers had suffered. Finally, it emphasized the causal impact of juvenile delinquency and slum conditions.[67]

The mention of "root causes" in the report led to praise from liberals. Conservatives, however, greeted it with scorn even though Hoover was critical of civilian review boards. *National Review* expressed outrage at the explicit "politicization" of the FBI and the implicit endorsement of the antipoverty program. "We must hope that future attempts to conscript the FBI as a propaganda agent for the Administration's policies will fail," wrote William F. Buckley Jr., a conservative intellectual and activist who would run for mayor of New York in 1965, "and one bases one's hopes that it will fail on a high regard for the integrity of John Edgar Hoover."[68] But the FBI director had hopes and designs of his own.

The report's ghostwriter was former Republican presidential candidate Thomas E. Dewey, whom Johnson had selected with the expectation that he would restrain Hoover and provide bipartisan political cover if needed. Dewey had offered his assistance because he was a friend of Frank Hogan, the district attorney. He also had vivid memories of the Harlem Riot of 1943, when he was governor of New York. Dewey insisted, however, that his participation remain strictly confidential. Although he had no intention of voting for Goldwater, he remained a loyal member of the GOP and feared that some "of the twenty-two million people who were nice enough to vote for me twice . . . will say I am a traitor and an ingrate."[69]

The president readily agreed to Dewey's demand. But contrary to Johnson's expectations, it was Hoover who moderated the tone of the report. "Endeavor to remove the basic economic factors underlying Negro unrest in our large cities which result in sub-standard living for Negroes," wrote the FBI director unexpectedly. "The Anti-Poverty Program and the program to keep teen-agers in school to avoid drop-outs are steps in this direction." In the end, the arrangement benefited both the president and the FBI director. As one historian has noted, Johnson "had covertly maneuvered a prominent Republican and overtly maneuvered his anticommunist director into issuing a report that endorsed the War on Poverty and helped blunt the Goldwater Republican challenge." In return, Hoover had gained a freer hand with surveillance operations aimed at black and white radicals in coming years.[70]

In the White House, the FBI report generated an internal debate. Katzenbach vigorously defended the analysis, calling it "factual and realistic" and lauding Hoover for disproving "the contention that the Civil Rights Act has led to strife." The attorney general also recommended sidestepping the civilian review board issue for now since it was "highly controversial and there is a good deal to be said on the other side." On balance, the report contained more good than bad, and withholding it could cause greater complications.[71]

But special assistant Bill Moyers strongly criticized the FBI report, warning of a "sharp backlash" among "Negroes who will object to the constant reference to their race." He also predicted that Goldwater would exploit the claim that decreased respect for the law among young people had led to increased crime. And Moyers counseled that white liberals would object to Hoover's claim that in cities like Philadelphia, civilian review boards had handcuffed police officers and endangered public safety. "If I were writing for the Senator from Arizona," he argued, "I could use this report."[72]

Although conservatives like Buckley were critical, radicals like Jesse Gray voiced the strongest objections. He charged that "the FBI swept under the official rug of the United States all the evidence and presented for all the world to see a fantastic report that could only have been born out of the wild dreams of sick minds." The report wrongly condemned civilian review of police officers, who were free to act as "prosecutor, jury, judge, and executioner," and falsely portrayed black youths as savage criminals. It also deliberately ignored the plight of the ghetto and maligned media coverage of the racial unrest to "keep from the eyes of the nation and the world the brutality and atrocities that are perpetrated on the Negro."[73]

After consideration Johnson sided with Katzenbach and publicly praised the FBI report. The president highlighted the assertions that the local police had acted with great restraint and the vast majority of blacks and whites had not participated in the civil unrest. But from his ranch in Austin, where he was spending the weekend, Johnson also directed the secretary of defense to expand the Army program for demonstrating techniques of riot control to the National Guard. And he instructed Hoover to make riot training available to local police through the FBI Academy in Quantico, Virginia. Five days later, the director informed the White House that he had taken "immediate action."[74]

The militarization and nationalization of riot control were under way. The president already had on his desk a recommendation to send small groups of specially trained federal troops to military bases across the country. From there they could quickly deploy to cities where the police needed and requested their intervention. The idea was an outgrowth of a proposal from the director of Law Enforcement Coordination within the Treasury Department, who argued that since the federal government currently helped communities with water pollution and communicable diseases, it should create a program to provide "technical assistance" to local and state police "to aid them in combatting crime and lawlessness, particularly in . . . civil disorders."[75]

According to the director, law enforcement had an urgent need for non-lethal weapons and police training in crowd-control techniques. When "dealing with violence and civil disturbances in our cities," it was vital that officers avoid the military model of riot control—"which in essence is to kill and destroy"—and employ "the minimum force necessary with a maximum humane, non-injurious effect." To limit fears of a federal takeover, he added that he had consulted with the International Association of Chiefs of Police, which was in favor of greater coordination and reported that 138 cities with populations of thirty thousand or more had requested "direct assistance for racial disturbances."[76]

At the same time, the director noted that almost thirty nations in Africa, Latin America, and Asia already received similar help through the Office of Public Safety in the Agency for International Development. By the time Congress terminated the controversial program in 1974, it had distributed $200 million in weapons and equipment to police forces around the world. It had also trained more than 7,500 senior officers in the United States and exported almost 1,500 American advisers, who had offered instruction to over a million foreign patrolmen. At home and abroad, the federal role in promoting what advocates touted as the professionalization and modernization of law enforcement was growing.[77]

But so too was presidential anxiety. As the campaign moved into the homestretch, the White House actively promoted the positive findings of the FBI report in the hope that they would serve as political cover for white Democrats in northern states, who continued to fear the Republican coupling of civil disobedience and black unrest.[78]

"You are doing well and will win big," wrote former Kennedy speech-writer Ted Sorensen to Johnson, who enjoyed a large lead in the polls over Goldwater in October. "The only possible, but not present, danger to such a margin is the 'violence in the streets—race mobs—Negro crime—white backlash' issue." The president should act, Sorensen advised, if—and "only if"—the Republicans managed to fan the fear to "ominous proportions." In that case, Johnson should address a "hostile northern white group" and underline that in terms of law and order "no man and no Administration can do more or is willing to do more or has pointed out what more can be done." The president agreed, although he remained convinced that "the less said about the subject the better."[79] In sum, that was the administration's strategy as the election neared.

As the president's popularity soared, Kennedy was struggling in New York. His Senate bid faced considerable skepticism from the *New York Times* and had not gained traction against Republican incumbent Kenneth Keating, who had a pleasant personality, waged a spirited campaign, and benefited from his refusal to back Goldwater. Reluctantly, Kennedy concluded that he would have to hitch his wagon to the president. In mid-September, posters with "Let's Put Bob Kennedy to Work for New York" were replaced by "Get on the Johnson, Humphrey, Kennedy Team." In mid-October, he remained unwilling to ask for the president's help, but swallowed his pride and agreed to a joint appearance with Johnson, who traveled to New York to endorse him and bolster the Democratic ticket.[80]

On the afternoon of October 14, the president landed at La Guardia Airport, where he was met by Wagner, Kennedy, and his wife Ethel. Security was tight—Johnson traveled in the bubbletop presidential limousine made bulletproof after the assassination in Dallas. On the way to the Waldorf Astoria, as helicopters patrolled overhead, a phalanx of motorcycles accompanied the motorcade as it drove through East Harlem, where crowds "six deep" and in the thousands lined the sidewalks and cheered Johnson. On the orders of Police Commissioner Michael Murphy, officers were stationed on roofs, bridges, and overpasses, while those on the street faced away from the president and scanned for signs of danger. It was the president's first visit to a northern ghetto since the start of the campaign, and it came amid news that King had won the Nobel Peace Prize.[81]

In the morning of October 15, Johnson flew with Kennedy, Wagner, and Harriman to the Rochester Airport. Present to greet them were a marching band, an excited crowd estimated at twenty-two thousand, and numerous dignitaries. In his speech, the president endorsed the former attorney general with public enthusiasm. "You don't often find a man who has the understanding, the heart and the compassion that Bobby Kennedy has," he said. Johnson also hailed his law enforcement expertise. "It's not enough just to talk about crime in September and October of every fourth year," he declared. "Crime is something you just don't talk against. Crime is something you must fight against."[82]

FIGURE 18. Lyndon Johnson and Robert Kennedy campaign together in New York in October 1964. LBJ Library photo by Cecil Stoughton.

Kennedy reciprocated by praising Johnson as "already one of the great Presidents of the United States" and a man whom he regarded with "affection and admiration." For the moment, the feud seemed forgotten. After a shuffle off to Buffalo for an afternoon speech at City Hall, Johnson, Wagner, and the Kennedys returned to New York at 5 P.M. This time the motorcade toured Brooklyn and stopped at least eight times so that the president and Kennedy could stand atop the bubbletop limousine. Then, to the evident dismay of the Secret Service, the two candidates switched to an open car, which they frequently exited to shake hands with the 750,000 bystanders who lined the twenty-two-mile route.[83]

"This isn't Goldwater country, is it?" asked Johnson, by then hoarse from a sore throat. "No," roared the enormous crowds, most of them Jewish, Irish, or Italian. Then go to the polls and elect Congressman John Murphy and Bob Kennedy, said the president, thrusting their arms into the air. "And don't forget about Hubert Humphrey or Lyndon Johnson, either." That evening he basked in the frenzied passion of twenty thousand members of the Liberal Party, who had gathered at Madison Square Garden and wildly applauded both him and Kennedy. Finally, an exhausted but exhilarated Johnson returned to the White House.[84]

The next morning, the president was greeted with bad news. A new Harris Poll showed that 61 percent of Americans—compared to 53 percent in August—now feared more for their personal safety than a year ago. But on October 16 Johnson had little time to worry because he had a campaign swing through Ohio. That evening, as the motorcade travelled from the Dayton airport to the County Court House, the president waved at the crowds and smiled at banners that read "All the Way with LBJ" and "Johnson Wax Shines Better Than Goldwater." In his speech, he spoke of how the pressures of urbanization in a mobile society negatively affected young people. "Children without roots, children without education, children who face discrimination—they all tend to become delinquent children," the president said. Then he uttered the sentence that would haunt his administration and liberalism in the years to come.[85]

"The war on poverty," declared Johnson, perhaps reacting to the latest Harris Poll, "is a war against crime and a war against disorder." Again, he implicitly criticized Goldwater as he hammered home the theme. "There is something mighty wrong when a candidate for the highest public office bemoans violence in the streets, but votes against the war on poverty, votes against the Civil Rights Act, and votes against major educational bills that have come before him as a legislator," said the president. "The thing to do is not to talk about crime; the thing to do is to fight and work and vote against crime."[86]

It was the liberal position, clearly and forthrightly articulated. But by coupling the War on Poverty that he had launched in 1964 to a War on Crime that he would announce in 1965, Johnson had exposed both crusades—and his larger ambition to build a Great Society—to a conservative crossfire that would reach a deadly crescendo by 1968. For now, however, it was the Republicans who were facing political defeat on a devastating scale. With the campaign at a climax, Goldwater supporters released a thirty-minute film that featured explicit footage of the Harlem Riot, including a nighttime scene where a black youth challenges a small group of white officers. "If you want to shoot, go to Vietnam," he yells with contempt, foreshadowing the third war that the president would expand a year later.[87]

Choice was produced by a supposedly independent organization called "Mothers for a Moral America," whose members included Nancy Reagan and Buckley's mother. But the film was conceived, funded, and backed by top officials in the Goldwater campaign, who saw it as a last-ditch chance to exploit the issue of law and order and win the election. The candidate himself gave initial approval, although without seeing a script. Later, in response to sharp criticism, he also made the ultimate decision not to show the incendiary film on national television. Yet *Choice* attracted widespread attention in the mainstream media, was aired on local stations in more than forty states, and was a forerunner of the notorious Willie Horton ad created for the George H. W. Bush campaign in the 1988 presidential race.[88]

The black-and-white film begins with a selective overview of American history and then presents voters with a "choice" between two nations: in Johnson's America, blacks constantly clash with police, interracial couples gyrate wildly to rock music, scantily clad women dance on tables, and pornographic books with titles like "Call Me Nympho" and "Jazz Me Baby" are available on every street corner; in Goldwater's America, well-scrubbed white children recite the Pledge of Allegiance, middle-class whites attend church, and neighborhood committees composed of white homeowners keep order in their communities. *Choice* features graphic footage of the Harlem Riot—"the best we have" according to a draft of the script. The film concludes with a personal appeal from Hollywood star John Wayne and a rapid montage of convention shots, including a sound bite of Goldwater warning that "tonight, there is violence in our streets."[89]

Between the history and the hysteria, the racial images and insinuations of *Choice* are numerous and obvious: white policemen confront unidentified blacks, perhaps rioters, looters, or demonstrators—the film offers no context or clarification. "In the name of God, please go home and protect the dignity of our Harlem community," pleads a minister as the crowd ignores him and the narrator warns of the dangers of "mobocracy." The only crime victim given a face is an ethnic white male beaten by a gang, and the only policeman given a voice is a white Philadelphia officer who complains that "during the riots we were told our only weapon was to be our night sticks. How the hell do we defend ourselves?"[90]

On October 22, the day before *Choice* was to air nationally on NBC-TV, news of it leaked and the illusion of independence was lost. Outraged, Wilkins telegrammed NBC President Robert Sarnoff and threatened to organize a boycott of the network if it showed the film, which he called "an unprincipled attempt to arouse anti-Negro feeling and to play upon the anxieties of some white people regarding the alleged criminality and irresponsibility of Negro citizens." The storm of criticism forced Goldwater to withdraw and then hastily repudiate *Choice*, which he termed "nothing but a racist film."[91]

But the damage was done. *Choice* discredited Goldwater's personal reputation for honesty and integrity. It also eroded the political appeal of law and order among moderate voters. And it distracted public attention from the vital issue the senator hoped to spotlight with the same martial rhetoric that the president favored. "Now we have heard of and seen many wars in the time of the present administration," said Goldwater, referring both to the War on Poverty and the war in Vietnam. "But have we yet heard of the only needed war—the war against crime?" He and the nation would soon hear of it—after the election.[92]

Ultimately, the administration's strategy of downplaying law and order and highlighting other issues paid great dividends—Johnson achieved the landslide victory he so eagerly sought. His popular vote margin was sixteen million (61 to 39 in percentage terms), and his Electoral College margin was 486 to 52. The president captured 94 percent of the black vote (putting him over the top in Virginia, Florida, Tennessee, Arkansas, and North Carolina), 90 percent of the Jewish vote, 62 percent of the women's vote, 20 percent of the Republican vote, and even a majority of the white vote (a feat no Democrat has managed since). He also carried every state, with the exception of Arizona and the Deep South (Mississippi, Alabama, South Carolina, Georgia, and Louisiana), which portended ill for the Democrats in the future.[93]

But on November 3 it was time to bask in the glow of victory. In New York, Johnson won by a margin of 2.5 million votes—more than in any other state. Kennedy won by only 700,000 votes, although it was the largest victory by a Democratic senator or governor since 1938. Could he have won without the support of the president? Perhaps—Kennedy later credited his television ad campaign and Keating's debate blunders for his triumph. But Johnson's coattails, which gave the Democrats two-to-one majorities in both the House and Senate, were a major factor. Yet on election night Kennedy thanked virtually everyone associated with his campaign except for the president, who watched on television in Austin. "I wonder why he doesn't mention me?" he asked. And so the mutual antagonism would continue, although it soon evolved into what a Kennedy loyalist described as an "armed truce."[94]

Johnson could, however, always count on Wagner. The two men spoke shortly after 6 P.M., a few hours before the polls closed in New York.

"Everything looks wonderful," the mayor reported. The voting was heavy across the state, especially in black areas like Central Harlem. "Well, Bob, it's a great tribute to you," said the president, who lavishly praised Wagner for being faithful, loyal, and competent. When the mayor tactfully suggested that Johnson probably had a "million people" who wanted to talk to him, the president replied, "No, I want to talk to you and I'm thanking your sweet wife. She's watching us in heaven."[95]

Together, Wagner and Johnson had weathered the storm and contained—for now at least—the political fallout from the racial unrest of the summer months. The immediate threat that the violence in Harlem, Brooklyn, and Rochester had posed to their hopes and ambitions had receded. The personal bonds between the two men, fortified by shared experience and mutual interests, were never stronger than at that moment, when the president again expressed his gratitude: "Anytime, anywhere, you just treat me like a brother."[96]

CHAPTER 12

THE WAR ON CRIME

> I will not be satisfied until every woman and child in this Nation
> can walk any street, enjoy any park, drive on any highway, and live in any
> community at any time of the day or night without fear of being harmed.
> —Lyndon Johnson

DECEMBER 1964–NOVEMBER 1968

"These are the most hopeful times in all the years since Christ was born in Bethlehem," declared an optimistic Lyndon Johnson as he pressed a button to light the National Christmas Tree on December 18. "Today—as never before—man has in his possession the capacities to end war and preserve peace, to eradicate poverty and share abundance, to overcome the diseases that have afflicted the human race and permit all mankind to enjoy their promise to life on this earth." For the president, it was typical rhetoric or bravado. But it was also emblematic of the extraordinary confidence that white liberals felt in the aftermath of the 1964 elections, when the Democrats had gained strong majorities in both the U.S. House and Senate. Amid a broad sense of economic prosperity—the gross domestic product had climbed for sixteen straight years and reached an all-time high—anything and everything seemed possible.[1]

But signs of trouble lay ahead. That same month, a Harris Poll showed that 73 percent of Americans—up from 61 percent in October—now believed that crime in their neighborhood had increased over the previous year, a figure that was consistent in rural areas, small towns, suburbs, and cities. The good news for the White House was that most accepted the liberal explanation that social conditions were responsible—only 20 percent took the conservative line and blamed racial unrest, declining morality, or lenient treatment by permissive judges. The bad news was that the rate of crime had risen five times as fast as the population since 1958. More ominously, young men between fifteen and twenty-four accounted for 70 percent of felony arrests in 1963—and that age cohort was expected to grow by 35 percent in the coming decade.[2]

In the White House, presidential aides had no shortage of suggestions about fighting crime. From the Department of Labor came the recommendation—courtesy of Daniel Patrick Moynihan, not yet notorious for his controversial report on black families—that the administration devote careful attention to juvenile delinquency, particularly among black teens. More funding for social programs and the War on Poverty was the predictable advice from the Department of Health, Education, and Welfare. Not surprisingly, the Department of Justice wanted Johnson to take a tougher stance. "We feel the president must place a much greater emphasis on crime and law enforcement if he is to strike the right note with Congress and the public," it urged.[3]

Johnson reached for that note in his State of the Union Address in January 1965. "Every citizen has the right to feel secure in his home and on the streets of his community," he told an audience of thirty-one million watching on television in the evening for the first time. Pledging federal assistance to local police departments, he also promised to convene a presidential commission to study every aspect of criminal justice and law enforcement. The comments attracted favorable notice from an unlikely source—*The Nation*. "Violence in the streets has become so much a part of the American way of life that most of our citizens are personally alarmed," asserted the liberal journal, which contended that the $1 billion spent on the War on Poverty paled in comparison to the $27 billion lost to crime every year.[4]

On March 8, in what would become an annual ritual, Johnson delivered a Special Message on Law Enforcement. It was the same day that more than three thousand Marines came ashore at Danang, north of Saigon. Their mission was to protect the airfields for Operation Rolling Thunder, the bombing campaign against North Vietnam, which had begun in February after three hundred communist guerrillas had launched a deadly predawn raid against a U.S. helicopter base at Pleiku in the Central Highlands. The president's speech also came the day after Bloody Sunday in Selma, Alabama. Marchers peacefully protesting for the right to vote were savagely attacked and beaten on the Edmund Pettus Bridge by state troopers and a local posse armed with tear gas, bullwhips, nightsticks, and rubber tubes wrapped with barbed wire.

"No right is more elemental to our society than the right to personal security and no right needs more urgent protection," Johnson told Congress without a trace of irony and in language reminiscent of Goldwater's acceptance speech at the Republican National Convention. "Experience and wisdom dictate that one of the most legitimate functions of government is the preservation of law and order." In effect, the president had now committed the nation to a War on Crime in addition to the War on Poverty and the War in Vietnam. The risks were real and the stakes were high. But Johnson had to show that he and liberals took the threat of crime and riots seriously or conservatives would relentlessly exploit their inaction.[5]

The presidential message as a whole was balanced and tempered. Johnson stressed that lawlessness was an ancient and complicated problem, national in scope, which would "not yield to quick or easy answers." In the long term, the best response was "jobs, education, and hope," but he conceded that "not all crime is committed by those who are impoverished or those denied equal opportunity." The president also acknowledged the basic political reality that "crime will not wait while we pull it up by the roots." In the short term, the federal government had to offer immediate assistance to the brave officers in harm's way, although Johnson restated his opposition to a national police force.[6]

Among the initiatives announced was a presidential commission on law enforcement and the administration of justice. Composed of a nonpartisan body of impartial experts, it had a broad mandate to explore every facet of the crime crisis. The White House also recommended more treatment facilities for drug users and fewer applications of mandatory-minimum sentences for nonviolent offenders so that they would have, "consistent with the public safety," the opportunity to return to "useful, productive lives." Most important, Johnson called for the creation of an Office of Law Enforcement Administration (OLEA), which would provide small grants to local and state police for experimental programs, research projects, specialized training, and modern equipment—all in the name of greater professionalism and effectiveness.[7]

By offering federal dollars directly to police departments, the OLEA represented a significant moment in the gradual intervention of the national government in police practices and criminal justice at the local

level. Within three years more than twenty states had received funding to
purchase new equipment and provide more training for police officers,
especially in riot control. Radicals would soon grow sharply critical of what
they viewed as the "police-industrial complex" and the growing militarization of law enforcement. But for now the War on Crime enjoyed broad
support, although conservatives saw a deliberate and concerted effort to
steal their more popular issues. A widely syndicated political cartoon by
Reg Manning showed the president behind a desk with two position papers:
"Aggressive Policy in Vietnam" and "War on Crime." Under the heading
"Any More Good Ideas in There?" an aide rummaged in a file cabinet
labeled "Goldwater Campaign Speeches."[8]

Johnson was unwilling to take any chances. "I got 38 percent of these
young Negro boys out on the streets," he lobbied Arkansas Senator John
McClellan, a conservative Democrat, on March 23. "They've got no school
to go to and no job. And by God, I'm just scared to death what's going to
happen in June and July." The president bemoaned the pace of urbanization and how "this damn world is shifting and changing so fast." Then he
predicted "ten times" more violence and unrest: "What you've seen in
Selma was nothing. You just wait until this thing gets going in Harlem and
Chicago." The very next day trouble arrived for Johnson—but it was at the
University of Michigan, where hundreds of faculty and thousands of students discussed and debated Vietnam from dusk until dawn during the first
major antiwar teach-in.[9]

Bayard Rustin was at the state capitol in Montgomery, Alabama, on
March 25 to witness the final rally of the Selma March. From his seat on
the speakers' platform he was able to gaze out at the sea of faces who had
gathered to hear Martin Luther King, Jr. proclaim that "we are on the
move and no wave of racism can stop us." Ten days earlier, Johnson had
introduced the voting rights bill on national television and concluded with
the freedom struggle's signature phrase: "And we shall overcome." Now
King praised Johnson for delivering "an address that will live in history as
one of the most passionate pleas for human rights ever made by a president
of our nation." Later Rustin was even more effusive. No president, he told
a confidant, not Lincoln or Kennedy, had ever given "as forthright a speech
in defense of our movement as Johnson."[10]

Selma capped yet another whirlwind chapter in Rustin's life. Back in
January he had ended almost a quarter century with the peace movement

by resigning as executive secretary of the War Resisters League. Rustin had also announced the creation of the A. Philip Randolph Institute, which sought to strengthen ties between progressive labor unions and civil rights organizations. Then he published his most important strategic analysis, "From Protest to Politics: The Future of the Civil Rights Movement," in the February issue of *Commentary* magazine. In the article, Rustin outlined his vision of the goals and tactics needed for the next stage of the freedom struggle.

During the decade from 1954 to 1964, the civil rights movement had won a great victory—it had ended legal discrimination and segregation. But the institutions that were successfully integrated—lunch counters, bus terminals, and swimming pools—were the "most anachronistic, dispensable, and vulnerable" as well as "relatively peripheral" to the basic needs of black people and the economic order in modern America. Rustin then posed the same question that many others were now asking: "What is the value of winning access to public accommodations for those who lack the money to use them?" The freedom struggle had to move beyond civil rights and address social conditions if it hoped to turn opportunity into equality and alleviate the frustration in the slums.[11]

The violent protests in Harlem and Brooklyn the previous summer, Rustin argued, "were outbursts of class aggression in a society where class and color definitions are converging disastrously." Automation had widened the unemployment and income gap between blacks and whites. By weakening or removing the lower rungs of the economic ladder it had rendered traditional self-help doctrines less relevant than in the past and made education more important than ever for both unskilled and skilled workers. Yet school segregation had increased since the *Brown* decision. The only way to confront these larger problems, contended Rustin, was to build a progressive and lasting coalition that could turn the Democratic Party into a powerful vehicle for transformative change. Black Americans could not do it on their own. Racial separatism was not the answer. And time was running short—the president's mandate came with an expiration date. "We need allies," pleaded Rustin, who urged radicals to see that the "main enemies" of the "revolutionary struggle" he wanted to wage within the existing order were conservatives like Goldwater, not liberals like Johnson.[12]

In the weeks leading to Selma, Rustin was active behind the scenes and as an intermediary between the White House and local organizers. In

February he traveled with King to Washington, where they pressed administration officials and congressional leaders to take strong action on voting rights. Two days after Bloody Sunday, a federal judge issued an injunction against further marches and King agonized over whether to violate it. From his experiences in Harlem, Rustin knew firsthand that the movement risked a crucial loss of credibility and another outbreak of unrest if it failed to act. "Martin, there is only one answer to . . . the people in the street," he said in a conference call wiretapped by the FBI. "That is that the people who believe in non-violence are not now going to retreat."[13]

On March 14, a week after Bloody Sunday, Rustin followed his own advice in Harlem. Accompanied by James Farmer of CORE and John Lewis of SNCC, he led fifteen thousand peaceful marchers on a silent parade that began and ended at the Hotel Theresa, followed by a rally with music and speeches. "Johnson got our votes, but he must be told that he hasn't got us in his pocket," Farmer told the integrated crowd, which included priests, ministers, nuns, and rabbis as well as college students and union members. It was precisely the kind of progressive coalition that Rustin had envisioned in *Commentary*, brought together by a common vision of racial justice and a shared sense of political urgency. "We will stay in these damn streets until every Negro in the country can vote," he vowed.[14]

After the crisis in Selma had abated, Rustin shifted his focus back to Harlem. Like the president, he worried about what might happen in the coming months. Rustin reminded Mayor Wagner in mid-May that he had not addressed the underlying roots of racial unrest, such as youth unemployment and police brutality, although he had accepted the resignation of Commissioner Murphy. "The choice before you is clear; either you creatively meet the causes of discontent in spring, or negatively face another long, hot summer," warned Rustin. But neither he nor Johnson expected the explosion to take place in a community of wide boulevards and single-family homes more than three thousand miles away from the crowded streets and run-down tenements of New York.[15]

On August 11, five days after the president had signed into law the Voting Rights Act with Rustin in attendance, the Watts section of Los Angeles erupted in violence. Like the Harlem Riot, it began on a hot evening after an alleged act of police brutality, when a white officer with the Highway Patrol arrested a black motorist for drunk driving. A hostile crowd rapidly gathered in support of the young man and the tense situation quickly escalated. Within hours it was out of control. By the next day ministers in Watts were appealing to King and Rustin to come to Los Angeles, but at first they declined, believing that they could do little and not wanting to repeat what had happened in New York in July 1964.

King, however, had a change of heart and asked Rustin to accompany him. He agreed and the two men toured the riot zone, where they heard repeated references to the "Watts Manifesto." Confused, Rustin asked for a copy from a youth, who produced a match and lit it. "Daddy, that was our manifesto, and the slogan was Burn, Baby, Burn," he told Rustin. And, he added, "We won." Rustin asked how and what he had won. For years, the teen replied, he and others had "asked [whites] to come and talk with us. They didn't come. We tried to get some war on poverty. It didn't come. But after our manifesto, daddy, the Mayor, the Governor, you, Dr. King, everybody came."[16]

It was another sobering moment for Rustin. "If you wait until youngsters are forced to riot to listen to their grievances," he said later, "woe unto you and damn you, for you will get nothing but violence." By August 17 the Los Angeles Police Department and the National Guard had restored a semblance of peace, but by then thirty-four people were killed (most of them black), around a thousand were injured, almost five thousand were arrested (most of them adults), and nearly one thousand buildings were damaged at a cost of $40 million. In the words of the *Los Angeles Times*, Watts was a "holocaust of rubble and ruins not unlike the aftermath in London when the Nazis struck, or Berlin after Allied forces finished the demolition."[17]

For the first few days of the riot, the president reacted with stunned silence. Then he vented his anger and disbelief. Why now, after all that he had done? After he calmed down a bit he expressed an understanding that he had not done enough, that the social conditions in Watts—high unemployment, poor schools, and substandard housing—were the same as in Harlem and Brooklyn. But in private Johnson remained convinced that the violence was the deliberate result of a communist conspiracy. "I sure don't think [Watts was] an accident," he told Attorney General Nicholas Katzenbach. "I think it's premeditated." The president was also deeply concerned that conservatives intended to exploit the racial unrest for political gain by claiming that the civil rights movement had encouraged disrespect for the law and the War on Poverty had rewarded rioters with federal aid.[18]

"A rioter with a Molotov cocktail is not fighting for civil rights any more than a Klansman with a sheet on his back and a mask on his face,"

Johnson told the White House Conference on Equal Employment Opportunity on August 19. "They are both . . . lawbreakers, destroyers of constitutional rights and liberties, and ultimately destroyers of a free America." We need to help the poor and disadvantaged, the president continued with a genuine sense of personal conviction and political urgency. "But never let us confuse the need for decent work and fair treatment with an excuse to destroy and to uproot." The balancing act for white liberals had become far more difficult in the wake of Watts, which shattered the bright vision of a Great Society built on economic prosperity and racial harmony.[19]

The next day Johnson had a painful conversation with King, who said that he was "not optimistic" about the future and feared a cycle of violence leading to a "full-scale race war." Morose, the president asked why he had not received more credit for his commencement speech at Howard University. There in June he had declared, similar to Rustin, that in "the next and more profound stage of the battle for civil rights" the nation had to pursue "not just equality as a right and a theory but equality as a fact and equality as a result." No president, King tried to reassure Johnson, had ever said or done more. But the president remained glum. "All of it comes to naught if you have a situation like a war in the world [Vietnam] or a situation like in Los Angeles," he replied. "What we've all got to do is obey the law." Of course, the crisis in the slums made it harder. "We're not doing enough to alleviate it," admitted Johnson, "and we're not doing it quickly enough. And I'm having hell up here with this Congress."[20]

Conservatives were making life increasingly difficult for the president. But he won a decisive victory when Congress overwhelmingly approved the Office of Law Enforcement Assistance (OLEA)—the removal of "administration" from the title reflected traditional concerns about federal intervention in local matters. The measure sailed through the House by a vote of 326 to 0; it cleared the Senate by voice vote. A rare consensus had formed about the pressing need for police professionalization, reinforced by public fear of rising crime and urban unrest. The new program's modest scope—the Justice Department received only $10 million to award in grants—was also a factor. The largest single grant of almost $200,000 went to Los Angeles so that the Sheriff's Department could purchase surveillance helicopters for Project Sky Knight.[21]

But beneath the apparent unity lurked different agendas. Many liberals believed that professionalization would promote racial fairness and enhance police legitimacy in minority neighborhoods. More training and higher standards would lead to better policing, which in turn would reduce the chance of unrest by improving community relations and teaching "slum children to respect the law" according to Maryland Senator Joseph Tydings. By contrast, most conservatives believed that professionalization would strengthen riot control and discredit false charges of police brutality. "Martin Luther King and Bayard Rustin and other agitators," contended Alabama Representative James Martin, could no longer call for the "ouster of good police officers." It might also, asserted Nebraska Senator Roman Hruska, help the police achieve the same objective as the military—the "deterrence of aggression."[22]

The thin blue line had to hold. At the signing ceremony for the OLEA in September, Johnson recycled the uncompromising language John Kennedy had employed in his inaugural address. "I will not be satisfied," the president declared, "until every woman and child in this Nation can walk any street, enjoy any park, drive on any highway, and live in any community at any time of the day or night without fear of being harmed." The rhetorical oversell was vintage Johnson—ambitious and risky. By hailing the police officer as "the frontline soldier in our war against crime" and promising unconditional victory—but committing only limited resources—he had staked a great deal of the credibility of his presidency and the fate of the Great Society on the domestic equivalent of the Vietnam quagmire.[23]

At the moment few were critical. By December, however, the growing danger was apparent to Katzenbach, who trenchantly advised Johnson that he had to lower expectations or face the consequences. "Fear and frustration about crime," he cautioned, "[are] already making people susceptible to unfair, yet effective, political appeals and to a tendency to find simple answers to complex problems." Like the war in Vietnam, the War on Crime promised no instant or complete victory, only attrition and stalemate. Johnson therefore had to temper his penchant for grandiose promises. "It makes no political sense," warned the attorney general, "for the president annually to engage in an all-out war on crime and annually lose."[24]

Robert Wagner had tears in his eyes and a lump in his throat as he faced a horde of reporters, cameramen, and photographers in the packed City Hall reception room on June 10. "I shall not seek or agree to re-election," said the five-foot-eight-inch mayor, seated on telephone books and a plush cushion in an armchair behind a desk. "I am not willing under any circumstances to be a candidate for this office." His voice cracking, Wagner then revealed that after twelve years in Gracie Mansion he was ready to fulfill a 1961 pledge he had made to his late wife Susan, who had asked him to make his third term his last so that he could give their two sons, Robert III and Duncan, "the guidance of a full-time father."[25]

It was a rare display of inner emotion from a phlegmatic politician who admitted that he had initially made the decision not to run back in March, although he had kept it a secret to avoid lame-duck status and allow time for "mature" reconsideration. But in mid-May Republican Congressman John Lindsay, a liberal reformer who represented the Silk Stocking District of the Upper East Side, had declared his candidacy for mayor. Contending that New York was in crisis, he had briefly altered Wagner's calculations. "If there is anything I relish it is a good political fight," he said. "I began to feel the old excitement of political combat. I knew I could take this candidate's measure." Polls, however, showed the aging and tired Wagner losing to the youthful and vigorous Lindsay, who at forty-three was tall, handsome, and radiated change, which was what the city desperately needed.[26]

"New York is a city crying for help," wrote *Look* magazine. "It is dirty, thirsty, tired, scared, old, worn, fouled, and poor." Scared was especially apt—the murder rate had doubled since Wagner took office despite the hiring of almost seven thousand new officers, who had increased the size of the department by 35 percent. But New York had a host of other ills including a severe water shortage. It was hemorrhaging white middle-class residents, more than a million of whom had decamped for the suburbs between 1955 and 1965. To replace the lost income tax revenue, the city raised property taxes by 75 percent. But the move backfired when many businesses joined the exodus, costing the city hundreds of thousands of jobs and tens of millions of dollars in revenue. During the last year of the Wagner administration, the budget deficit almost tripled to more than $250 million.[27]

The state of the city—combined with the exit of Wagner and the entry of Lindsay, who also accepted the nomination of the Liberal Party—prompted William F. Buckley Jr., the wealthy founder and editor of *National Review*, to join the race. Five days after Wagner's bombshell, "Buckley for Mayor" appeared as a teaser on the cover of the conservative magazine. Inside was a reprint of a column titled "Mayor, Anyone?" in which he sardonically wrote that Lindsay, a personal and political rival, was singularly unqualified—except for the "brilliance of his teeth"—to meet the critical challenges faced by New York. Buckley then presented his own

ten-point program that included innovative ideas to fight juvenile delinquency and ease traffic congestion (with bikeways) as well as libertarian
proposals to legalize gambling and drugs. He even recommended allowing
anyone with a driver's license and without a criminal record to operate a
car as a taxi.[28]

Whether Buckley was merely testing the waters remains a matter of
conjecture, but after some wooing he held a press conference on June 24 to
announce that he was running on the Conservative Party ticket because the
Republican Party in New York was not amenable to his principles. To
defuse the subject of eligibility, the well-known Connecticut resident joked
to reporters that he had owned an apartment in the city longer than Robert
Kennedy had when he ran for the U.S. Senate. The patrician and youthful
Buckley—he was not yet forty—also made it clear that as a part-time candidate he would issue press releases, give media interviews, and debate other
candidates, but not engage in retail politics in ethnic communities—no
corned beef, baked ziti, or cheese blintzes for him. His objective was to
raise issues and promote ideas, not win votes. When asked how many he
expected to receive, he quipped, "Conservatively speaking, one."[29]

Despite the playful humor, Buckley had serious aims: to highlight what
he saw as the symbolic failure of urban liberalism in New York and to
discredit Lindsay, whose solutions to the problems of the city—more
spending on social programs, higher taxes, and task forces staffed with tech-
nocratic "experts"—were anathema to the Goldwater-style conservatism
championed by National Review. If Buckley could draw enough votes to
deny Lindsay the election, he might hasten the conservative purification of
the Republican Party and leave the Democratic Party saddled with the liberal label. To Buckley's surprise, he ultimately attracted fewer disenchanted
Republicans and more disgusted Democrats than he expected. He proved
especially popular with working-class whites. Angry and frustrated, they
deserted in droves from Comptroller Abe Beame, a short and bland Jewish
American. In the Democratic primary, he had come from behind to defeat
City Council President Paul Screvane, whose handling of the Harlem Riot
had not helped him.[30]

Back in April Buckley had tapped into some of that anger when he
spoke to almost six thousand Catholic officers (a quarter of the force) at
the Holy Name Society Communion breakfast after Mass at St. Patrick's
Cathedral. The speech became notorious when a reporter wrote that Buckley had defended the actions of the police in Selma and implied that the

Klan murder of Viola Liuzzo, the Detroit housewife and activist, was her own fault. But most of his remarks focused on how declining morality and a growing tendency to view criminals as victims of society rather than as agents of evil had caused too many New Yorkers to see the police as "guilty unless proved innocent." Buckley reassured the officers that although a vocal minority despised and criticized them, they had the gratitude and respect of what would later become known as the "silent majority." Not surprisingly, he received an ovation from the audience, which included Commissioner Murphy and Mayor Wagner.[31]

The controversy surrounding Buckley's comments about Selma receded as fears of another "long, hot summer" arose. But by mid-July an "uneasy calm" prevailed in Harlem according to the New York Times. With Captain Lloyd Sealy in command of the 28th Precinct and another African American officer, Eldridge Waith, now the community relations officer for the area, the police were better prepared to communicate with residents. The sense in Harlem, said the Reverend Eugene Callender, was that although problems remained, at least "people were listening and hands were working" on them. In particular, he cited Lindsay's endorsement of a majority-civilian review board.[32]

For Lindsay it was critical to gain the votes of African Americans and middle-class Jewish Democrats who were liberal in orientation. The modified civilian review board seemed to fit the bill since it promised to improve police-community relations until City Hall could address the root causes of racial disorder. "As long as inequity remains a dominant fact of life for millions," conceded the congressman, "New York will be a powder keg of unrest." But Buckley had no patience with civilian review—the priority was law and order. "The problem in New York is too much crime, not too much police brutality," he declared as Irish-American teens in Queens heckled Lindsay with placards that read SUPPORT YOUR LOCAL POLICE and DOWN WITH SO-CALLED REVIEW BOARDS.[33]

Public safety was the most important issue for white voters, regardless of class or ethnicity. In mid-October, as the campaign reached a climax, a senseless murder seemed to capture the random nature of life and death in a city spinning out of control. Trudy Collins, a young white mother riding the IRT Lexington line with her infant daughter in her arms, had to watch helplessly as her husband Arthur bled to death after he was stabbed by a drunk man in their subway car at the 125th Street station in Harlem. "This place is a jungle," said the victim's father. "It stinks. You know what I think

FIGURE 19. Congressman John Lindsay speaking at a rally in October 1965 during his campaign for mayor. Photo by Walter Albertin. Library of Congress, Prints & Photographs Division, New York World-Telegram & Sun Collection (LC-USZ62-132503).

Trudy's going to do? Pack up and get out of this jungle. I'd like to do it myself." In response, Lindsay demanded that she receive financial restitution because she "lost her husband through 25 years of neglect in New York City."[34]

In the spring, the *Herald Tribune* had provided Lindsay with the motivation and theme for his campaign when it ran daily features on "New York City in Crisis." Now the newspaper gave him a final boost in late October with a week-long series on "The Lonely Crimes," which described how lawlessness had altered behavior in the city. "Women carry tear-gas pens in their pockets," wrote Jimmy Breslin and Dick Schaap. "Cab drivers rest iron bars on the front seat next to them. Store owners keep billy clubs next to the cash register. And people enter the parks and the subways and the side streets of New York, the most important city in the world, only in fear. The fear is justified. The weapons are justified."[35]

Lindsay promised to make fighting crime his top priority. If elected mayor, he told a gathering of elderly Jews in Manhattan, he would "spare no money and no effort—I WILL SPARE NOTHING—to insure the safety of the streets, your homes, hallways." Lindsay also went to Kew Gardens in Queens where Kitty Genovese was murdered in March 1964. "Something has gone out of the heart and soul of New York City," he said with the clear implication that Wagner and the Democrats were responsible after a dozen years in power.[36]

On election night, most expected Beame to win despite his unimpressive appearance, lackluster campaign, and a last-minute Lindsay endorsement by Ed Koch, a reform Democrat and district leader in Greenwich Village who later became mayor himself. But in the end the congressman earned 40 percent of the black vote, held his own district as well as most of the Republican base, and gained enough middle-class Jewish votes to triumph by 43 to 39 percent. The margin was 100,000 votes and turnout was 81 percent—the third-highest in New York City history. After polling as high as 20 percent, Buckley received 340,000 votes or 13 percent of the total. The next day Lindsay, the first Republican to occupy Gracie Mansion in twenty years, decided not to celebrate on the Upper East Side. Instead, he symbolically chose to visit Rego Park in Queens, which had a large Jewish population. And then he went to Central Harlem and Bedford-Stuyvesant, where expectations for a new civilian review board were high.[37] The new mayor of what he soon called "Fun City" was about to step squarely into a political minefield.

To meet Harlem's expectations and fulfill the campaign promise he had made a year earlier, Lindsay issued an executive order in May 1966 creating a Civilian Complaint Review Board with three police officials (including an African American deputy commissioner) and four civilians (two white liberals, a Latino activist, and a black professor). The modified board would have its own investigators, but would still have limited power—it could only recommend to the department whether to press charges against officers. The new police commissioner, Howard Leary, who had worked with an independent civilian review board in Philadelphia, would retain the authority to make all final disciplinary decisions.[38]

In a further bid for police acceptance, unproven complaints would no longer go automatically into an individual's personnel record, which Leary said "has scarred the records of many conscientious officers." Instead, the file would reflect only substantiated charges. President John J. Cassese of the Patrolmen's Benevolent Association (PBA) nevertheless vowed to fight the plan to the end. The association first had a bill introduced in the state legislature in June to reverse the executive order and then tried in vain to get a court injunction. Finally, the union circulated petitions and gathered almost a hundred thousand signatures to place a referendum opposing the new civilian review board on the ballot in the fall.[39]

Worried liberals now mobilized and formed the Federated Association for Impartial Review (FAIR), but the odds were against them. "There seems little question that if the referendum were to be voted on today it would pass overwhelmingly," the board of directors of the New York Civil Liberties Union privately concluded. "The chances for influencing public opinion to vote against the PBA proposal in November do not appear overly bright." The pessimism was justified—from the outset the grim specter of racial unrest and rising crime loomed menacingly over the referendum.[40]

Conservative opponents of civilian review contended that it would hinder the ability of officers to respond to present lawlessness and future riots. A television commercial offered stark footage of the property damage from the Philadelphia Riot in August 1964 as the announcer commented that "the police were so careful to avoid accusations that they were virtually powerless." A newspaper advertisement warned that "the addict, the criminal, the hoodlum—only the policeman stands between you and him." And a neighborhood pamphlet posed a series of leading and loaded questions: "Does the policeman protect the law-abiding citizen? OF COURSE he does. Then WHO is calling for the chains to shackle our police? Who is screaming 'police brutality'? WHO WANTS A CIVILIAN REVIEW BOARD?"[41]

Liberal supporters of the new board retorted that it would act as a riot preventive. Civilian review would ease police-minority relations by providing appropriate oversight of law enforcement and a legitimate outlet for community anger. As evidence, Lindsay noted that New York had a peaceful summer in 1966, unlike other cities. FAIR also sought to make civilian review a political measure of personal commitment to civil rights. Although strapped for cash compared to the PBA, it managed to distribute thousands of posters that read DON'T BE A YES MAN FOR BIGOTRY—VOTE NO on the referendum. "This is an historic moment," asserted the mayor. "This fight is the guts of it."[42]

In the fall, both sides at first tried to present moderate positions. FAIR was careful to keep minority advocates in the background to dispel the idea that civilian review was a "protective agent" for them. The PBA in turn replaced the blunt Cassese as chief spokesman after he made a series of inflammatory statements. "Racial minorities would not be satisfied until you get all Negroes and Puerto Ricans on the board and every policeman who goes in front of it is found guilty," he said in a television interview. Both FAIR and the PBA hoped to appeal to Jewish voters on the assumption that minority voters were overwhelming in favor of civilian review and Catholic voters—especially Italian Americans and Irish Americans, who dominated the top ranks of the Police Department—were strongly opposed.[43]

Although Jewish Americans in New York were firm supporters of civil rights, civilian review divided them along class lines. In the boroughs outside Manhattan, lower-middle-class and working-class Jews were wary of the new board—a fact highlighted when the Bronx chapters of the American Jewish Congress voted unanimously to disregard the parent body's backing of it. But in Manhattan even professional Jews with college degrees proved reluctant to oppose the referendum unless they combined an overriding commitment to civil rights with a powerful sense of personal security. At Temple Rodeph Shalom in the heart of the Upper West Side, for example, congregants barraged Lindsay's press secretary with questions about why the mayor always seemed to side with lawless minorities against law-abiding taxpayers.[44]

The image that dominated the campaign featured a young and scared white woman in a raincoat exiting from the subway and emerging alone onto a dark and deserted street. "The Civilian Review Board must be stopped! Her life . . . your life . . . may depend on it," read the advertisement plastered on billboards across the city. It warned that if a police officer hesitated to take action, "the security and safety of your family may be jeopardized." On November 4, a WCBS-TV poll showed that a clear majority of those surveyed believed that civilian review would hinder police performance. Four days later, buoyed by a near-record turnout—over two million voters cast ballots, more than in the 1964 presidential race—the referendum passed by an almost two-to-one margin. Of the five boroughs, only Manhattan narrowly voted to retain the Civilian Complaint Review Board.[45]

The outcome was not a surprise. Yet it sent shockwaves through the increasingly fragile liberal coalition in New York. As expected, minority voters opposed the referendum by huge margins. But in Brooklyn a postelection sample of white voters revealed that 83 percent of Catholics had backed the referendum—a level of support greater than John Kennedy had received in 1960. More shockingly, only 40 percent of Jews had voted to retain civilian review even after almost every prominent liberal organization and politician had related it to civil rights and endorsed the new board. Although most whites rejected extreme forms of racial prejudice according to the survey, they associated blacks with crime and disorder. What united ethnic voters in Brooklyn was fear—only 25 percent reported that they felt "very safe" in their homes after dark compared to 50 percent of all Americans.[46]

Other politicians had noticed. As Republican Governor Nelson Rockefeller prepared to announce his bid for a third term, he told the state legislature in January that because heroin users committed a large percentage of street crimes he wanted to impose compulsory treatment on addicts and mandatory sentences on pushers, "those men without conscience who wreck the lives of innocent youngsters for profit." In Harlem, where a state of emergency existed according to a black assemblyman, the *Amsterdam News* praised Rockefeller's plan to "wage an all-out war on narcotics addiction," which he launched in the spring after his legislation was approved. In the fall, the governor was also careful not to endorse the review board publicly, on the ostensible grounds that it was a local issue, even though he privately supported it.[47]

Despite these steps, Rockefeller found himself trailing his Democratic opponent, Queens District Attorney Frank O'Connor, in late October. With the election less than three weeks away, the governor opted to make curbing crime his main issue and unleashed a massive negative ad campaign to spotlight the district attorney's support of civilian review and opposition to compulsory treatment for drug addicts. "If you want to keep the crime rates high O'Connor's your man," Rockefeller growled in a television commercial, "but if you want to protect yourself and your children vote for me." Five days before the ballots were cast, the governor declared that O'Connor was willing to let heroin users roam free "on the streets for purse snatching, mugging, and murder." Rockefeller stressed that his opponent "wants the drug addict—a sick, desperately dangerous man—to decide voluntarily if he needs the treatment."[48]

Gone at least for the moment was an earlier view of the narcotics user as a helpless victim who needed therapeutic care, not compulsory treatment or punitive confinement. Now he was an enemy of society, beyond understanding or sympathy. The message was effective—on Election Day Rockefeller won with a plurality. But it also marked a turning point in the political career of the nation's preeminent liberal Republican, whose outlook on criminals and drugs had hardened well before his abortive 1968 presidential bid or the 1971 Attica Prison riot. Two years later, the governor signed the nation's toughest antinarcotics law, which inspired other states and paved the road from the War on Crime to the War on Drugs.

In November 1966, the desire for law and order contributed to Republican gains in the midterm elections. Former actor Ronald Reagan, a political newcomer, attracted national attention when he easily upset California Governor Edmund "Pat" Brown, the two-term incumbent Democrat. A charismatic Republican who two years earlier had electrified conservatives with "A Time for Choosing," his televised speech on behalf of Goldwater, Reagan benefited from widespread alarm over the Watts Riot, the Berkeley "Free Speech" protests, and the soaring crime rate. Overall, the Democrats lost three Senate seats, eight governorships, and forty-seven House seats. "The president must grasp the nettle of violence in the streets very firmly and unequivocally," warned Johnson's pollster. "This is one problem that will not go away and which will cause even more difficult political problems in the next two years unless some dramatic and successful efforts are made."[49]

On election night in New York, Cassese exulted in the PBA victory. "Thank God we saved this city," he said. But why, a reporter asked Lindsay, had the review board lost so decisively? "Emotion and misunderstanding and fear," he replied. Then, shrugging aside suggestions that he had also suffered a personal defeat, the mayor added that "the important thing is that we did what we thought was right. It was worth fighting for, even though we lost." Perhaps it was. The outcome, however, boded ill for the Johnson administration as it struggled to maintain control of the War on Crime and contain the politics of law and order.[50]

"They have lost control in Detroit," FBI director J. Edgar Hoover grimly informed the president late in the evening of July 24, 1967. "Harlem will break loose within thirty minutes. They plan to tear it to pieces." The White House was again in an uproar, only a week after the Newark Riot had ended with dozens of deaths and hundreds of injuries. Now, for the second night in a row, Detroit was convulsed by violence after undercover officers had raided a "blind pig" or unlicensed club, where a black soldier safely home from South Vietnam was celebrating with friends. Neither the local police nor the National Guard could restore order despite the widespread use of indiscriminate gunfire. "The situation is continuing to deteriorate," reported former Deputy Secretary of Defense Cyrus Vance, who recommended that Johnson place the Michigan Guardsmen under federal control and deploy paratroopers from the 82nd and 101st Airborne, already assembled at Selfridge Field outside the city.[51]

"Well," the president said forlornly as he signed the proclamation, "I guess it's just a matter of time before federal troops start shooting women and children." But his worst fears for Detroit were not realized. The U.S. Army soon restored relative peace with minimal resort to deadly force—the soldiers fired only two hundred rounds in comparison to the thousands discharged by officers in Harlem and Brooklyn in 1964. The military also maintained tight discipline—unlike the Detroit police and National Guard, the paratroopers were not even permitted to load their weapons unless they received a direct order. By July 27 the worst civil disorder of the century to date—until the Los Angeles Riot of 1992—was over. The human cost, however, was tragically high—forty-three dead, thirty-three of whom were black. And the estimated damage from looting and arson was at least $40 million.[52]

Federal intervention had undoubtedly saved lives and property. But the president's position that public safety was a local responsibility lay in ruins. The administration's attempt to draw a clear and convincing distinction between crime and riots had also collapsed. And the clamor by conservatives for more assistance to the overmatched police and less aid to the undeserving poor had left liberals in a difficult position. As White House special counsel and chief speechwriter Harry McPherson Jr. put it, "We talk about the multitude of good programs going into the cities, and yet there are riots, which suggests that the programs are no good or the Negroes past saving." Even as paratroopers patrolled the streets of Detroit, officials tabulated telegrams to see if whites blamed the War on Poverty for the unrest in the cities.[53]

At the cabinet meeting on August 2, heated arguments flared over whether black radicals like Stokely Carmichael and H. Rap Brown had incited the most recent round of riots. In his presentation, Attorney General Ramsey Clark said that conspiracy theories deflected attention from the root causes of social unrest—not to mention the real danger that untrained and undisciplined local police and National Guardsmen might trigger a "guerrilla war in the streets" between the races. More training and professionalism were essential, said Clark, who added that at present the Justice Department could not build a case against Carmichael or Brown. The reaction among his fellow cabinet members was a mixture of anger and incredulity.[54]

"It is incredible to think that you can't make a case," declared Secretary of the Treasury Henry Fowler. Clark replied that the arrest figures showed little evidence of a wider conspiracy. "But there are fifty-two cities potentially about to explode," sputtered Vice President Hubert Humphrey. Secretary of State Dean Rusk said that Carmichael had personally threatened his life as well as the lives of other officials including the president. And HEW Secretary John Gardner warned that "those who organize or incite riots are generally the last to be picked up and arrested." The final word came, naturally, from Johnson, whose views on radical agitators had not changed since 1964. "I don't want to foreclose the conspiracy theory now," he stated. "Keep that door open. . . . I have a very deep feeling that there is more to that than we see at the moment."[55]

To get a feel for whether Harlem was about to "break loose" again, as Hoover had predicted during the Detroit Riot, the president dispatched the trusted and respected McPherson to New York on the weekend of August 12–13. Johnson had known the courtly Texan since 1956, when as Senate Majority Leader he had hired him fresh out of law school, sight unseen, to serve as assistant general counsel to the Democratic Policy Committee. Now he would rely on McPherson to discover the facts on the ground and report back to him. But because the white Texan would have little access or credibility on his own, he was accompanied by two black officials—Louis Martin and Clifford Alexander, Jr.—from very different backgrounds.[56]

Martin was a sixty-five-year-old journalist and Democratic powerbroker from Savannah, Georgia, who was known as the "Godfather of black politics." During the New Deal, he had joined Franklin Roosevelt's "black Cabinet." He had also watched in horror as the Detroit Riot of 1943 spawned "blind hatred" and transformed humans into "monsters"; the images were permanently seared into his memory. By the 1960s, he was formally a deputy chairman for the Democratic National Committee and informally a political troubleshooter who organized voters and recruited officials for Kennedy and Johnson.[57]

Alexander was a thirty-four-year-old Harlem native whose parents were fixtures in the community—his father was an immigrant from Jamaica who had risen to the position of superintendent of the Riverton Houses, the Met

Life apartment complex, and his mother was the politically active daughter of Duke Ellington's personal physician and best friend. Alexander attended elite private schools in New York, then earned degrees from Harvard College in 1955 and Yale Law School in 1958. But major corporations and law firms would not interview or hire him because of his race. So he entered government service and served as executive director of Harlem Youth Opportunities Unlimited (HARYOU). With Martin's assistance, Alexander joined the White House in 1964 and was soon promoted to special counsel—the first black on the senior staff. On August 4, 1967, eight days before he escorted McPherson to New York, Alexander became the third chairman of the Equal Employment Opportunity Commission.[58]

The three men traveled to Bed-Stuy, which McPherson described as "incredibly depressing," with block after block of dingy bars, liquor stores, hair parlors, and storefront churches. "Every tenth car" was a late-model Cadillac, Buick, or Chrysler, "double-parked before a busted, decaying house." Martin was suspicious. "You can't get one honestly," he said. "It's got to be numbers or something like that." At Fulton and Stuyvesant they listened to a woman harangue a crowd about the need to meet white violence with black violence. When she finished she received considerable applause but few donations. "Everybody knows how you got that Poverty job," she accused a well-dressed black man with a cigar. "They're paying you $11,200 a year over the table and God knows how much underneath. You ought to give some of that to your brothers." Laughter rippled as several black officers scanned the street.[59]

Although Central Harlem was also "depressing" according to McPherson, in contrast to Bed-Stuy it had "an electricity, an exciting gaminess that even communicates to a visiting WASP." But he was not blind to the radical agitators on the street corners or the unemployed youths "looking for trouble." The rundown housing was also evident, with the blame shared by absentee landlords, city officials, and poor residents. Much of Harlem, conveyed McPherson, "looks like Calcutta: filthy streets, broken doorways (affording no security for those who live there), trash in the halls, [and] condemned buildings where junkies sleep overnight and sometimes start fires that threaten the whole neighborhood."[60]

The word in Central Harlem, reported McPherson, was that it would not explode for a number of reasons: Mayor Lindsay was a regular and popular presence; business leaders, white and black, desired peace; and organized crime wanted no additional police presence in the area (whether true or not, it was widely believed that "Bumpy" Johnson, a black mobster, had personally threatened to kill Rap Brown if he instigated a riot). Federal, state, and local money was also pouring into Harlem. "When the baby's got his mouth on the nipple he can't holler" was a phrase McPherson heard several times. Finally, he had great respect and lavish praise for the black commander of the 28th Precinct, Inspector Arthur Hill, who had replaced Sealy in 1966. In the early hours of Sunday morning, Hill met with the visitors from Washington after they had toured the area in a squad car.[61]

When asked how he kept the peace, Hill answered, "I talk to everybody. If trouble starts, I get there in a hurry. By the time I arrive thirty white officers may already be there, among two or three hundred Negroes. I get the [white] officers out of there fast—if somebody drops a bottle on them from the rooftop, they'll start swinging and the thing will get out of hand in a hurry." Because Harlem residents saw white policemen, even if not brutal or corrupt, as hostile outsiders, Hill wanted to recruit more black officers, who comprised less than 15 percent of the roster in the 28th Precinct. Drug addicts also posed a challenge. "You have to wait until they commit some offense," the inspector said. "There's no treatment program that reaches enough of them now."[62]

During the "long, hot summer" of 1967, New York managed to avoid another riot on the scale of Newark or Detroit, although police shootings resulted in rioting and looting in East Harlem and Bed-Stuy. Much of the credit belonged to officers like Hill, a talented member of the "police establishment" who was also "a cat—he never stopped being street" according to George Barner of the *Amsterdam News*. Hill's mentor was Sealy, who led by example and invited the senior black police officials to his home every year. Sealy had received a promotion to assistant chief inspector in February 1966, the highest rank ever attained by an African American at that time. Six months later, he achieved another first when he assumed command of Brooklyn North, which included Bed-Stuy, where in July 1967 he coolly defused a dangerous confrontation between seventy officers and a large group of black youths. Although a pitched battle appeared imminent, Sealy ordered the officers to put away their nightsticks and kept his composure despite taunts like "Take off your black mask and show us your white face."[63]

For the next two years, Sealy often walked the streets with Lindsay as together they tried to maintain order. When he was bypassed for promotion to chief inspector in 1969, he resigned from the department and joined the faculty at John Jay College of Criminal Justice, where he was a respected and dedicated teacher. On his sixty-eighth birthday in 1985, Sealy suffered a heart attack in the classroom and died, five years after his stepson, an off-duty patrolman with the Metropolitan Transit Authority, was shot and killed while attempting to stop an armed robbery in Brooklyn. "To black officers in particular Lloyd Sealy was an inspiring model of what a top-notch policeman can be," eulogized Commissioner Benjamin Ward, who in 1966 was appointed executive director of the Civilian Complaint Review Board by Lindsay and in 1984 became the first African American to lead the NYPD.[64]

Democratic Congressman Emanuel Celler was an anxious man in August 1967—and with good reason. A member of the House since 1923—his maiden speech was in opposition to the National Origins Act, which imposed immigration quotas—and chairman of the Judiciary Committee since 1949, he had helped guide the Civil Rights Acts of 1957, 1960, and 1964 to passage, earning respect as a liberal voice for racial equality and civil liberties. But the seventy-nine-year-old Jewish American knew that he was likely to face a serious primary challenge in the coming year.[65]

Celler also knew that he represented a Brooklyn district not far from Bed-Stuy and not insulated from urban conflict. Even those faithful constit-uents who had regularly voted for him and strongly supported the freedom struggle in the early 1960s were now terrified of crime and unrest. "Your actions for civil rights are commendable," wrote a rabbi from Midwood. "But the simple, decent, law-abiding people—Jew and non-Jew—want a CIVIL RIGHTS LAW to protect them from the rapists, murderers, rioters, looters. . . . Personally, I give Brooklyn no more than five to seven years. It's finished!"[66]

In the spring, Celler had shepherded the administration's omnibus crime bill through the Judiciary Committee. It reflected the modernization and professionalization impulse generated by the presidential commission on law enforcement, which Johnson had convened in 1965. The Safe Streets Act (as it was known) authorized the attorney general to distribute $50 million (the figure rose to $300 million in two years) in categorical grants to police departments in cities over fifty thousand in population. A new agency, the Law Enforcement Assistance Administration (LEAA), would administer the funds. Among the categories eligible for federal dollars were the recruitment and training of police; the upgrading of equipment, such as two-way radios for better communications; and alternative forms of prison rehabilitation, such as work-release programs. Finally, the crime legislation banned electronic surveillance unless a federal judge or the attorney general deemed it vital to national security. Not surprisingly, liberal groups such as the American Civil Liberties Union (ACLU) endorsed the Safe Streets Act in original form.[67]

But in the summer Newark and Detroit altered the political equation. In the wake of the riots, conservatives in Congress blamed organizations like SNCC and CORE, as well as individuals like Carmichael and Brown, for inciting the unrest. The House as a whole rejected the administration bill and replaced the categorical grants for local departments with block grants for state agencies, which could distribute the federal funds largely at their discretion. In place of the focus on professionalization and rehabilitation was an emphasis on riot control, with an additional $25 million earmarked specifically for that purpose. The revised measure passed by an overwhelming margin of 377 to 23. Suddenly, the White House was no longer in command of the War on Crime even as it was on the verge of escalation.[68]

In the fall, both Celler and Johnson tried in vain to reassure anxious voters and reassert the liberal position on public safety. White racism was in part responsible for black unrest, Celler told the American Jewish Committee in November. But he hastily added that he was "no apologist" for looters or arsonists and that law and order was essential for all. "Riots are a form of self-indulgence and ultimately boomerang," he said. "That we understand the reasons for the riots is important. That we do not use the reasons for excuses is equally important." The balanced and reasoned speech likely satisfied few in the audience.[69]

"Our big problem is to get at the causes of these riots," Johnson declared in a mid-December interview on national television. The violence was the work of a "very small minority" and reflected underlying social factors, which the War on Poverty and the Great Society would tackle. "The answer is jobs," he told Dan Rather of *CBS News*. "The answer is education. The answer is health care. Now, if we refuse to give them those answers, people are going to lose hope, and when they do, it is pretty difficult to get them to be as reasonable as we think they should be." Rioting, looting, and "taking the law into your own hands is not going to produce better health or better housing," the president stated firmly. "It is going to produce anarchy. And that cannot be tolerated." At that moment, the optimism he had expressed three years earlier as he lit the National Christmas Tree seemed like a distant memory.[70]

By January 1968 public safety was the most important domestic issue for white Americans—and perhaps the most important overall despite the Tet Offensive. "Overwhelmingly," reported the Associated Press after polling members of Congress about their districts, "anger over riots and crime overshadowed all other domestic issues and, in many cases, even the war in Vietnam." *Time* contended that "law and order looms, with the possible exception of Vietnam, as the nation's prime preoccupation in Election Year 1968." And in February the Gallup Poll stated that, for the first time in history, "crime and lawlessness" (including riots) was at the top of the domestic agenda for white voters.[71]

As the Senate deliberated over the crime bill, a tragedy in Memphis led to violent unrest in more than one hundred cities, large and small. On April 4, James Earl Ray shot and killed King outside his motel room, four days after the president had shocked the political world when he announced that he would not seek a second term. Within twenty-four hours the nation was on fire. The White House immediately went into crisis mode, mobilizing more than fifty thousand U.S. Army soldiers and National Guard troops across the country. At 14th and U Streets in Washington, Carmichael brandished a pistol. "If you don't have a gun, go home," he advised the crowd. By the afternoon the burning and looting had spread to within blocks of the White House, where Johnson could smell the smoke and see the flames. By 5 P.M. a company of soldiers with bayonets patrolled the grounds and a machine-gun post guarded the Capitol steps. But panic remained in the air.[72]

"That's just insanity," Walter Washington, the African American mayor-commissioner, complained to the White House when he learned that the authorities planned to release looters because the detention centers were overwhelmed and could not process more serious offenders. "I don't give a Goddamn what the Constitution says. We just can't release them and let them go out again." Democratic Senator Robert Byrd of West Virginia telephoned to state for the record that he wanted martial law imposed and looters shot (killed if they were adults, wounded if they were juveniles). By April 10 calmer voices had prevailed and the fires had cooled, but not before the nation had suffered thirty-nine deaths, more than twenty-six hundred injuries, and twenty-one thousand arrests.[73]

On the very day of the King assassination, the Senate Judiciary Committee had rejected a motion to amend the crime bill so that it regulated the sale, distribution, and importation of all firearms. Then came the massive unrest. Two days later, the committee reconsidered and approved the amendment, although for handguns only. The action reflected a dramatic and temporary shift in public opinion—by late April a white public fearful of racial violence favored regulating gun sales and registering gun purchases by a seventy-one to twenty-three margin. Even owners of weapons, like Charlton Heston, the famous actor and future president of the National Rifle Association, were in favor by a sixty-five to thirty-one margin. But with the exception of gun control, which liberals eagerly embraced as the antidote to violence, the politics of law and order in the spring of 1968 favored conservatives.[74]

Like the House bill, the Senate version of Safe Streets ultimately bore little resemblance to the original measure and, with the exception of Title IV (gun control), reflected the conservative desire to exploit public fear and enhance police discretion. Title II stated that in federal cases a confession was admissible as long as the judge deemed it voluntary—a direct swipe of dubious constitutionality at the Supreme Court's *Miranda* ruling, which hindered interrogations and limited confessions according to police officials. Title III expanded electronic surveillance by permitting, with judicial approval, any federal assistant attorney general and any state or local district attorney to plant a bug or tap a phone if the crime in question carried a sentence of at least one year. If a crime was imminent, no court order was necessary for forty-eight hours. And Title V disqualified from federal employment (including the antipoverty program) any person convicted of a felony committed in a riot. Despite strong though inconsistent opposition from the White House and liberal groups like the ACLU, the Senate bill passed in May by a seventy-two to four margin.[75]

Celler's only hope in early June was to convene a conference committee, where he and other liberals might reconcile the virtues and remedy the flaws of the two bills. But events again conspired against him. On the very day the House was debating his motion, news reached the floor that an assassin had shot Senator Robert Kennedy after he had won the California Democratic primary. Motion adjourned. The next day Kennedy died and the House voted 368 to 17 to accept the Senate bill. "The old man was most articulate and magnificent in his defiance of the mood of the House," observed a presidential aide. But it was little consolation to Celler, who fully understood the price he would pay for his staunch opposition to the Safe Streets Act.[76]

"How in God's name you would obliterate the only ray of hope existing for millions of victims of crime-ridden cities defies the imagination," declared a letter typical of the hundreds that poured into Celler's office. "Thousands of people of the Jewish faith have stood by helplessly to see their businesses destroyed, their lives in constant peril as politicians blithely court the Negro vote and ignore those who elected them to office. Why is it your sworn duty to protect robbers, muggers, and rapists? If you think this is the road to your re-election you are doomed to disappointment." Presumably, the writer was disappointed when Celler, after forty-five years in Congress, barely survived a bitter primary fight.[77]

The fate of the Safe Streets Act and the future of the War on Crime now rested in Johnson's hands. If he issued a veto, Congress could easily override it or pass an even worse bill. And he might jeopardize the presidential aspirations of Vice President Hubert Humphrey. Given the political climate, McPherson advised Johnson that he had little choice even though "it is the worst bill you will have signed since you took office." Ultimately, the president bowed to the pressure in mid-June. "I have decided," he said as he penned the Safe Streets Act with great reluctance, "that this measure contains more good than bad and that I should sign it into law."[78]

That was political spin. In fact, most of the Safe Streets Act represented little more than symbolic attempts at crime control, regardless of who set the agenda. Contrary to what conservatives claimed, police interrogations without the Miranda warning (Title II) were unlikely to lead to more confessions and convictions. Electronic surveillance (Title III) was also unlikely to prevent most street crimes or urban riots. Contrary to what liberals claimed, sales restrictions on handguns (Title IV) were unlikely to prevent experienced criminals from acquiring firearms.

What mattered far beyond the debates between liberals and conservatives was that Congress had opened the floodgates to federal aid with block grants to state agencies (Title I). Police departments could now seek large grants for punitive purposes with few restrictions. The federal role in local and state law enforcement was set to reach new heights.

After New York exploded in 1964, Johnson had ordered the FBI and the Army to provide more riot training to police officers and the National Guard. Then he had declared a bipartisan War on Crime in 1965 with the express goal of police professionalization. By 1968 the president had lost influence and the nation was firmly on the path to a more nationalized and militarized system of law enforcement. Amid a great deal of sound and fury, the Safe Streets Act ensured that a War on Crime both broader in scale and narrower in scope than what Johnson had originally intended three years earlier would continue. Now the pressing question as the presidential election neared was who would assume leadership for the next four years.

"Which presidential candidate do you feel could do the best job in handling law and order?" That was the question the Harris Poll asked voters in September. By 36 to 23 percent they favored the conservative Republican, Richard Nixon, over the liberal Democrat, Hubert Humphrey. By 26 to 23 percent they also preferred the reactionary independent, Alabama Governor George Wallace, over the vice president. "Humphrey is soft in the area of law and order, and this softness is hurting him more than anything else," confided his pollster, citing private surveys. "Crime prevention is at the top of what people—as many as 89 percent—want."[79]

Humphrey could never find a clear and consistent voice on what was more important, social order or social justice, in part because the Democratic Party was deeply divided between conservatives and liberals, whites and blacks. His inability to take a firm stand on law and order, reported his pollster in October, was harming him "far more than any position he does or does not take on bombing pauses [in Vietnam]." In the final weeks, the vice president opted for a strategy of silence on crime and unrest similar to Johnson's tactic in 1964. But this time it would not work, largely because public anxiety was much stronger and Humphrey's opponent was better positioned to exploit it.[80]

Unlike Humphrey, Nixon had a clear audience—white voters alarmed at the loss of public safety in the nation's communities. "Freedom from fear is a basic right of every American," he declared in his acceptance speech at the Republican Convention, borrowing from Franklin Roosevelt. Nixon also had a consistent explanation for crime and unrest—the Great Society had reaped great disorder by rewarding rioters, the Supreme Court under Chief Justice Earl Warren had coddled dangerous criminals and handcuffed police officers, and the White House had failed to protect or promote traditional values such as respect for authority. It was the Goldwater prescription for law and order, updated and presented by a candidate without the Arizona senator's racial baggage.[81]

On Election Day Nixon won the popular vote by a close margin (a quarter million votes out of sixty-eight million cast). But the result was misleading—together he and Wallace had received 57 percent of the vote compared to the 61 percent Johnson had received four years earlier. Almost twelve million Americans—including five million from urban areas—had either abstained or defected from Humphrey and the Democrats. The outcome was a crushing defeat for liberals and a convincing victory for conservatives. A new commander with a different strategy would now lead the War on Crime.[82]

During the campaign, the Republicans released a series of powerful and innovative political ads produced by Roger Ailes, the future chairman of Fox News. The commercial known as "Order" featured collage images, dissonant music, jump cuts, and a voice-over from Nixon, who acknowledged that dissent was necessary. "But in a system of government that provides for peaceful change," he asserted, "there is no cause that justifies a resort to violence." Nixon then repeated a popular line from his acceptance speech at the national convention: "Let us recognize that the first civil right of every American is to be free from domestic violence."[83]

"Security from domestic violence" was what Barry Goldwater had promised at the Republican Convention in San Francisco on July 16, 1964. Hours earlier James Powell had bled to death on a sidewalk in Manhattan. After two days of rising tensions, Central Harlem erupted in anger and protest, marking a new dynamic in the racial struggles of a turbulent decade. The unrest also galvanized the War on Crime and ushered in the age of law and order, which has shaped and shadowed American politics and society for more than fifty years.

ON A GRAY spring day three decades after President Johnson had signed
the Safe Streets Act, Nicholas Katzenbach ruefully recalled the War on
Crime, which the racial unrest of July 1964 had done so much to initiate.
"It proved to be a dreadful mistake," the former attorney general reflected
in his comfortable Princeton home, surrounded by photos and memora-
bilia of his long career in public service. "You are meant to win wars, and
the War on Crime was in a sense an unwinnable war." Like the war in
Vietnam, which the White House escalated in 1965 amid public optimism,
the War on Crime soon dissolved into a costly quagmire of unintended
consequences and collateral damage.[1]

Responsibility for the War on Crime rested after 1968 with Richard
Nixon, who entered office determined to prevent more "long, hot summers," which the Harlem Riot had originated. Under his direction the Law
Enforcement Assistance Administration (LEAA) pumped billions of dollars
to police departments so they could acquire modern equipment battle-
tested in South Vietnam. From the Pentagon to the police went armored
personnel carriers, electronic movement sensors, improved tear gas, and
sophisticated scout helicopters. Louisiana even received a tank, which was
later used in an assault on the New Orleans headquarters of the Black Pan-
ther Party. Perhaps partly for this reason, urban unrest declined sharply in
the 1970s.[2]

Radicals voiced prescient criticisms of the LEAA. They argued that it
had militarized policing to a dangerous degree. By promoting professionalization the agency had also reinforced the belief in police infallibility and
eroded the credibility of police critics. And radicals asserted that the LEAA
was constructing a national police force with mass surveillance capabilities

and stimulating a prison-industrial complex eager to pursue profits from privatization.[3]

But a bipartisan consensus between Democrats and Republicans securely surrounded the War on Crime. Liberals were either vocal in their support or silent in their opposition. Most conservatives abandoned any reservations they might once have had. Few objected to the federal government's intervention in local law enforcement, probably because a large chunk of LEAA funds were distributed by state agencies as block grants to police departments in Republican suburbs, where voters were plentiful, rather than to Democratic cities, where crime was prevalent. And the political benefits of taking a "tough on crime" stance were clear to both Congress and the president, who stumped for law and order at every opportunity.[4]

In October 1970, on the eve of midterm elections, Nixon signed the Comprehensive Drug Abuse Prevention and Control Act, which attracted only six dissenting votes. The bipartisan measure toughened mandatory-minimum sentences for "dope pushers"—which had existed since the 1950s—but reduced marijuana possession to a misdemeanor offense. The action reflected the long-standing though ill-founded distinction between the "casual user"—typically portrayed as a white middle-class youth from the suburbs—and black or Latino dealers who lived in the cities and supposedly preyed on innocent victims from "good" families. Heroin, the president stated, was now "America's Public Enemy Number One."[5]

Bayard Rustin was not impressed with Nixon's "cheap and repressive" measures or his exploitation of law and order to further his "own deplorable ends." But according to the executive director of the Randolph Institute it was a "myth" that the slogan was "conservative and racist" because blacks stood to benefit greatly from more and better police protection. In a majority of violent crimes they were the victims, and in Central Harlem and Bed-Stuy narcotics revenues exceeded welfare payments. The real issue, Rustin argued in November 1970, was how to improve the justice system. In his view the police needed to hire reinforcements and implement reforms to curtail corruption and brutality. The prisons had to foster rehabilitation, not recidivism. And the federal government had to make a sincere commitment to full employment; otherwise, Rustin concluded, the president was not truly fighting crime—he was merely "debasing the meaning of law and order."[6]

As the urban upheavals of the 1960s faded into memory, the War on Crime receded into history. But it left a political foundation for the War on

Drugs, which Nixon loudly proclaimed in June 1971 even as he quietly approved methadone treatment and research. Three months later, more than twelve hundred largely minority inmates rebelled at the Attica Correctional Facility in upstate New York. Incensed by brutal conditions and treatment, they seized control and took hostages. After four days of tense negotiations, the authorities agreed to most of the demands made by the prisoners, although not the removal of the superintendent or a complete amnesty from criminal prosecution for their actions, which included the killing of a guard. Governor Rockefeller, however, refused to go to Attica despite a warning that storming the maximum-security prison might lead to riots in Harlem and Bed-Stuy.[7]

Rockefeller instead sent an aide accompanied by Major General A. C. "Buzz" O'Hara, the commander of the National Guard when it used minimal force during the Rochester Riot in July 1964. Now O'Hara stood by the superintendent when he pleaded with the governor to reconsider his refusal to negotiate in person. Rockefeller again declined and then ordered the state police to retake the facility and rescue the white hostages from the black inmates. Amid a hail of gunfire and cries of "coon hunting," twenty-nine prisoners and ten correctional officers or civilian employees were killed. "It really was a beautiful operation," Rockefeller told Nixon by phone the next day.[8]

Rockefeller saw the minority inmates at Attica Prison as violent revolutionaries. The bloody assault strengthened his resolve to address the intersection between crime and race because in his mind—and the popular imagination—the typical pusher or dealer was a young black or Latino man. They were responsible for a drug epidemic sweeping New York, where half of the heroin addicts in the United States reportedly lived. Central Harlem and Bed-Stuy were especially afflicted. "The crime, the muggings, the robberies, the murders associated with addiction continue to spread a reign of terror," Rockefeller informed the state legislature in January 1973. "Whole neighborhoods have been effectively destroyed by addicts as by an invading army. We face the risk of undermining our will as a people—and the ultimate destruction of our society as a whole."[9]

The governor then announced that he wanted life sentences imposed on anyone—addict, pusher, or dealer—who sold hard drugs in any quantity. No plea bargaining was possible, and after conviction there was no chance of probation or parole. The "Attila Law" attracted conservative support—Nixon was an admirer—and liberal opposition from Mayor

Lindsay, the American Civil Liberties Union, and the *New York Times*, as well as many African Americans—though by no means all and probably not even a majority. But in April the legislators passed a modified version of Rockefeller's law with stiff mandatory-minimum sentences of at least fifteen years to life imprisonment for the sale or possession of small quantities of heroin, cocaine, and marijuana. In September, two years after the Attica uprising, the harshest antinarcotics measure in the nation went into effect.[10]

Three months later, the governor stepped down, and in December 1974 he became vice president under Gerald Ford, who had replaced Nixon when he resigned amid the Watergate scandal. But in New York the Rockefeller legacy was significant—the prisons were soon crowded with non-violent drug offenders, most of them poor minorities from urban communities. And in the following decade, forty-eight other states passed similar antidrug laws, which swelled prison populations and created a demand for ever-larger police forces and ever-more correctional facilities.[11]

At the federal level, the War on Drugs escalated under President Ronald Reagan, who militarized interdiction programs aimed at reducing the supply of marijuana and cocaine from Central America. The administration also endorsed the Sentencing Reform Act of 1984, which had bipartisan backing from Republican conservatives like Utah Senator Orrin Hatch, who wanted less judicial leniency, and Democratic liberals like Massachusetts Senator Ted Kennedy, who wanted more racial fairness. The legislation eliminated indeterminate sentencing for federal crimes and instituted a comprehensive grid of mandatory minimums. And with the endorsement of the Congressional Black Caucus, the president signed the Anti-Drug Abuse Act of 1986, which imposed a five-year sentence for dealing five hundred grams of powder cocaine or five grams of crack cocaine. African Americans soon constituted the vast majority of federal crack cocaine convictions.[12]

Despite Reagan's focus on interdiction and incarceration, public anxiety over a supposed "crack crisis" grew in the 1990s. To demonstrate that he was a "New Democrat" who was not soft on crime or opposed to law and order, President Bill Clinton warned that "gangs and drugs have taken over our streets" and stated that—like Goldwater, Johnson, and Nixon before him—"the first duty of any government is to keep its citizens safe." Accordingly, Clinton signed the largest law enforcement bill in history in 1994, shortly before the mid-term elections. It increased the number of federal crimes eligible for the death penalty, mandated life sentences for "three strikes" violent felons, and pumped billions of dollars to the states to hire a hundred thousand more police officers and build more prisons.[13]

By 2010 the social, economic, and political impact of the War on Drugs and mass incarceration was evident. As the Defense Department distributed surplus equipment from the wars in Iraq and Afghanistan, the militarization of policing expanded. Although the growth of public prisons brought some jobs and revenue to rural, usually white, communities, the benefits were marginal. By contrast, the proliferation of private prisons, as radicals had predicted, generated sizable corporate profits, especially in the region a scholar has dubbed Flocatex—Florida, California, and Texas. The drive to create "factories with fences" and exploit prison labor also weakened trade unions in certain industries and eroded wage levels for black and white workers.[14]

At the same time, the War on Drugs altered the balance of power between the executive, legislative, and judicial branches of government. It also affected behavior in schools and the workplace. And widespread felon disenfranchisement laws stripped a basic right of citizenship from both prisoners and those who had already served their time, with important implications for liberals and conservatives. In the 2000 presidential election, for example, almost two million black men could not cast ballots— including more than a hundred thousand in Florida, where Republican George W. Bush defeated Democrat Al Gore by a narrow margin.[15]

Yet by then violent crime was already on the decline. In New York City, homicides rose from 1,444 in 1970 to 2,228 in 1980 and 2,605 in 1990 before starting to decrease under Democratic Mayor David Dinkins. Under Republican Mayor Rudolph Giuliani, who was in office from 1994 to 2001, the NYPD practiced an aggressive style of preventive policing. It featured the regular use of stop-and-frisk based on "reasonable suspicion"—or what critics termed "racial profiling"—and stressed "zero tolerance" for minor violations or quality-of-life offenses, such as public drinking and urination. Whether the tactics were legal, justified, or effective remains contentious, but by 2000 murders had dropped to 952 and by 2014 they had plunged to a record low of 328.[16]

The trend was nationwide, with few exceptions. Why violent crime plummeted so dramatically and consistently during the last decade of the twentieth century and the first decade of the twenty-first century was a matter of debate among criminologists and policymakers, who could not agree on the relative importance of such factors as police strategies, gun control, economic opportunity, drug preferences, and demographic change. But most experts concurred that the expensive system of mass incarceration had limited effect.[17]

The fall in crime led many liberals and conservatives to reconsider their earlier commitment to prison expansion. "The judicial system has been a critical element in keeping violent criminals off the street," said Democratic Senator Richard Durbin of Illinois in 2015. "But now we're stepping back, and I think it's about time, to ask whether the dramatic increase in incarceration was warranted." Other senators, including Republicans Mike Lee of Utah and Rand Paul of Kentucky, joined Durbin in supporting reduced federal drug sentences for nonviolent offenders. Conservatives even launched a campaign of reform and retrenchment titled Right on Crime.[18]

More than a half century after New York erupted in violence and Lyndon Johnson announced a War on Crime, a new consensus had seemingly emerged. In July 2015, Barack Obama commuted the sentences of forty-six persons, most of them serving terms of twenty years or more for nonviolent drug crimes. He then became the first president to visit a federal prison. "These are young people who made mistakes that aren't that different than the mistakes that I made, and the mistakes that a lot of you guys made," Obama told reporters fifty-one years—to the day—after James Powell was shot. At the NAACP convention Clinton also apologized for his contribution to mass incarceration. "I signed a bill that made the problem worse," he said. "And I want to admit it."[19]

Less than a year after Nixon declared the War on Drugs in June 1971, Rustin was in Houston to deliver the opening address at the third national conference of the Randolph Institute when he learned that Lyndon Johnson had suffered a heart attack while visiting his daughter in Virginia. Recalling with "special poignancy" his own massive heart attack in upstate New York months earlier, from which he had only recently recovered, Rustin sent a floral bouquet and personal note to the former president, whom he had privately considered little more than a "shrewd politician" and the "lesser of two evils" back in October 1964.[20]

But now the passage of time and, more important, the Voting Rights Act had softened Rustin's view of Johnson, who had given him a pen after the signing ceremony. "You represented political leadership in the area of civil rights unequaled since the time of Lincoln," Rustin wrote in April

1972, "leadership we have sorely missed since your retirement from public office." A week later, Johnson replied with a gracious note of his own: "How could I not help but be cheered by your generous memory of me and my administration in connection with civil rights? It is a cause close to my heart. I only wish I could have done more."[21]

Soon the ailing heart of the former president could do no more. Since his retirement he had led a quiet life (for him), attending to the daily details of ranch life on his sizable spread along the Pedernales River and overseeing the construction of his presidential library at the University of Texas in Austin. Johnson had also resumed his habit, abandoned after a 1955 heart attack, of smoking three packs of cigarettes a day. Believing that he would follow in the footsteps of his grandfather and father, both of whom had died before they reached sixty-five, he resisted the entreaties of his daughters, who pleaded with him to quit again. "I've raised you girls," he told them, "I've been president, and now it's my time." Johnson's time came on January 22, 1973, two days after he would have finished his second full term if he had sought and won reelection in 1968. He was sixty-four years old.[22]

The next day, as Nixon announced a ceasefire in Vietnam, Rustin wired private condolences to Lady Bird and then composed a public tribute for the NAACP. In the twentieth century, he eulogized, "no president contributed as much to the struggle for racial equality as did Lyndon Johnson. Important as they were, the accomplishments of Roosevelt, Truman, and Kennedy pale beside those of Johnson." Whereas the other Democrats "acted only after incessant prodding," wrote Rustin, "Johnson took the initiative, responding to the needs of black people with all the moral leadership and political skills at his command." The praise was lavish, even fulsome. It was also reflective of Rustin's disenchantment with Republican racial policies and dismay at the changing political landscape of the 1970s.[23]

But in his personal life he unexpectedly found love. On a warm afternoon in April 1977, a month after his sixty-fifth birthday, Rustin exchanged glances with Walter Naegle at the corner of Times Square and 42nd Street. A musician from New Jersey, the twenty-seven-year-old Naegle had left college during the Vietnam era to join Volunteers in Service to America, the domestic counterpart to the Peace Corps, and had planned to move to San Francisco until he met Rustin. As they built a life together, Naegle gradually persuaded him to become more open about his homosexuality and more active in the fight for gay rights, including lobbying Mayor Ed

Koch and the New York City Council to ban discrimination on the basis of sexual orientation. But their love could not conquer all of the challenges they faced—Rustin ultimately had to adopt Naegle to assert his legal rights as next of kin.[24]

"The struggle must be continuous," Rustin often said in his late years, "for freedom is never a final act." But in August 1987 the curtain fell on his enduring commitment to racial, economic, and sexual equality. A decade after Rustin had first laid eyes on Naegle and five months after he had celebrated his seventy-fifth birthday at a fundraiser for the Randolph Institute, he had emergency surgery for acute peritonitis and a ruptured appendix. Three days later, Rustin suffered a heart attack and died at Lenox Hill Hospital on the Upper East Side, less than two blocks from where James Powell was killed.[25]

Powell's body rests in an unmarked grave amid the lush lawns and rolling hills of Ferncliff Cemetery in Westchester County, far from the hustle and bustle of New York. Buried near him are such black luminaries as singer-activist Paul Robeson, jazz pianist Thelonious Monk, James Baldwin, and Malcolm X. Also interred in the cemetery are Broadway icons like Oscar Hammerstein, Moss Hart, Jerome Kern, and Alan Jay Lerner as well as notable figures like film director Preston Sturges, disc jockey Alan Freed, singer Judy Garland, actor Basil Rathbone, and Madame Chiang Kai-Shek.

Ferncliff does not permit headstones—the policy is intended to limit distinctions between those who are privileged and those who are not. But today the gravesite of Powell lacks even a plaque with his name or that of his father with whom he is buried. Among the cemetery's famous and obscure residents, James remains invisible, a young man whose short, troubled life would have passed unnoticed by virtually everyone except his mother were it not for what his untimely death sparked.

Thomas Gilligan quietly returned to work in November 1964. His duty assignment remained a departmental secret, but he again attracted public notice seven months later, when he came to the aid of a middle-aged black man, Allen Hopwood, who had suffered an epileptic seizure near 62nd and Broadway. Gilligan, who was on his way to an undisclosed location, stopped when he saw the stricken individual surrounded by concerned bystanders. He administered medical care, calmed the crowd, and summoned an ambulance, which took Hopwood to Roosevelt Hospital, where he was treated and released.[26]

Gilligan then slipped back into the shadows, never to return to the limelight. He retired from the NYPD in April 1968 on three-quarters disability pay. Gilligan's departure came after he had spent the previous year on sick leave due to a back injury he had sustained before the Powell shooting when a patrol car in which he was riding collided with another vehicle. At age forty-two, he had spent almost twenty-one years on the force and received nineteen citations for outstanding service.[27]

In 2014, fifty years after the shooting of Powell, Gilligan died at age eighty-eight. To the end he refused to answer questions or speak about what had transpired on that Thursday morning in front of 215 East 76th Street across from Wagner Junior High School. Almost a decade earlier, I had discovered that Gilligan was living in a small house with a tree-lined driveway in East Hampton on Long Island. But when I sent him letters, he would not respond. When I paid him a visit, he would not open the door. And when I reached him by telephone it was apparent that he remained deeply pained and scarred by the incident.

"It was a long time ago and I don't ever want to get into it again," Gilligan told me before declining to grant an interview. "That chapter of my life is closed." When I informed him that I had no hidden agenda or ax to grind, that I was simply a historian who wanted to give him the opportunity to tell his side of the story and set the record straight, he said, flatly but forcefully, "Then you'll look at all the facts and tell the truth."

NOTES

The folllowing abbreviations are used in the notes.

AHF   Arizona Historical Foundation, Tempe, Arizona
BCAH   Barker Center for American History, Austin, Texas
CUOHP   Columbia University Oral History Project, New York, New York
HIA   Hoover Institution Archives, Stanford University, Palo Alto, California
JFK Library   John F. Kennedy Presidential Library, Boston, Massachusetts
LBJ Library   Lyndon Baines Johnson Presidential Library, Austin, Texas
LCC   LaGuardia Community College, Long Island City, New York
LOC   Library of Congress, Washington, D.C.
MACNY   Municipal Archives of the City of New York, New York
MHS   Minnesota Historical Society, St. Paul, Minnesota
MLK MF   Martin Luther King, Jr. Main File
NPMP   Nixon Presidential Materials Project, National Archives II, College Park,
               Maryland
NUL   National Urban League, LOC
NYAN   *New York Amsterdam News*
NYDN   *New York Daily News*
NYHT   *New York Herald Tribune*
NYP   *New York Post*
NYT   *New York Times*
NYWTS   *New York World-Telegram & Sun*
PCF   Presidential Campaign Files, AHF
RAC   Rockefeller Archives Center, Tarrytown, New York
RDC   *Rochester Democrat and Chronicle*
RMN Library   Richard M. Nixon Presidential Library, Yorba Linda, California
SCRBC   Schomburg Center for Research in Black Culture, New York, New York
URL   University of Rochester Library, Rochester, New York
WHCF   White House Central Files, LBJ Library
WHOF   White House Office Files, LBJ Library
WHSF   White House Subject Files, LBJ Library

PROLOGUE

1. Sue Reinert, "Near Riot—Student Slain by Policeman," *NYHT*, July 17, 1964.

2. William Travers, "Negro Boy Is Slain by Cop; Pupils Riot," *NYDN*, July 17, 1964.

3. Republican National Convention, July 16, 1964, Box 10, 1964, PCF, Goldwater Papers, AHF.

4. See, among others, Marie Gottschalk, *The Prison and the Gallows: The Politics of Mass Incarceration in America* (Cambridge University Press, 2006); Edward L. Ayers, *Vengeance and Justice: Crime and Punishment in the Nineteenth-Century American South* (Oxford University Press, 1984); David M. Oshinsky, *"Worse Than Slavery": Parchman Farm and the Ordeal of Jim Crow Justice* (Free Press, 1996); Rebecca McLennan, *The Crisis of Imprisonment: Protest, Politics, and the Making of the American Penal State, 1818–1938* (Cambridge University Press, 2008); Samuel Walker, *Popular Justice: A History of American Criminal Justice* (Oxford University Press, 1980); Claire Bond Potter, *War on Crime: Bandits, G-Men, and the Politics of Mass Culture* (Rutgers University Press, 1998); and James Gilbert, *A Cycle of Outrage: America's Reaction to the Juvenile Delinquent in the 1950s* (Oxford University Press, 1986).

5. It is impossible to calculate precisely, but the best estimates are that only around one percent—or eight thousand of the approximately three-quarters of a million blacks living in Harlem and Bed-Stuy—took part in some way. Robert M. Fogelson, *Violence as Protest: A Study of Riots and Ghettos* (Doubleday, 1971), 38. Only two of two hundred sample respondents in Brooklyn indicated that they had any direct or personal contact with the riot. Joe R. Feagin and Paul B. Sheatsley, "Ghetto Resident Appraisals of a Riot," *Public Opinion Quarterly* 32 (Fall 1968): 357.

6. The terminology or language of urban unrest was and is contested. The most common term—"riot"—has a precise legal meaning as well as a broad public understanding. The Kerner Commission popularized "civil disorder," which troubled many liberals because it seemed to connote civil disobedience. By contrast, both radicals and conservatives often preferred "uprising," "revolution," or "rebellion" because they presumed political intent and even premeditation. Insurance companies frequently favored the term "insurrection" because it voided coverage, although starting in the summer of 1967 they agreed to honor all claims regardless of the specific terminology used by local officials. This account will use "unrest," "riot," and "disorder" interchangeably because they seem more neutral than the alternatives. But as society becomes more diverse, other customs may come to the forefront. Latino Americans, for example, often use *los quemazones* ("the great burnings") to describe the Los Angeles Riot of 1992, while Korean Americans generally follow their tradition of using the date—sa-i-ku (4-2-9). Todd S. Purdum, "Legacy of Los Angeles Riots: Divisions amid the Renewal," *NYT*, April 27, 1997.

7. Khalil Gibran Muhammad, *The Condemnation of Blackness: Race, Crime, and the Making of Modern Urban America* (Harvard University Press, 2011).

8. Naomi Murakawa, *The First Civil Right: How Liberals Built Prison America* (Oxford University Press, 2014), 9, 58–61.

9. Michael W. Flamm, *Law and Order: Street Crime, Civil Unrest, and the Crisis of Liberalism in the 1960s* (Columbia University Press, 2005).

10. Matt Lassiter, "Suburban Imperatives of the War on Drugs," *Journal of American History* 102 (June 2015): 126–140.

11. David Cole, "The Disgrace of Our Criminal Justice," *New York Review of Books*, December 4, 2014; National Research Council, *The Growth of Incarceration in the United States: Exploring Causes and Consequences* (National Academies Press, 2014), 2; Marie Gottschalk, "Hiding in Plain Sight: American Politics and the Carceral State," *Annual Review of Political Science* 11 (2008): 238.

12. Jake Halpern, "The Cop," *The New Yorker*, August 10 and 17, 2015.

13. The only full-length account was published by two reporters with the *New York Herald Tribune*, Fred C. Shapiro and James W. Sullivan. *Race Riots: New York 1964* (Thomas Y. Crowell, 1964) is based on their personal experiences and contemporary newspaper reports. It is a lively read, but contains no archival or background research and makes no effort to explore the larger political significance of the Harlem Riot. And of course the authors could not have foreseen how the "race riots"—which they were not—would facilitate the War on Crime in 1965.

14. For example, the *New York Times* had no major retrospectives on the Harlem Riot in 1974, 1984, 1989, or even 2014. Yet it published front-page articles on the anniversaries of the riots in Watts, Newark, and Detroit.

15. See, among others, Gerald Horne, *The Fire This Time: The Watts Uprising and the 1960s* (University of Virginia Press, 1995); Sidney Fine, *Violence in the Model City: The Cavanaugh Administration, Race Relations, and the Detroit Riot of 1967* (University of Michigan Press, 1989); and Clay Risen, *A Nation on Fire: America in the Wake of the King Assassination* (John Wiley, 2009); Carvin Eison and Chris Christopher, *July '64* (Independent Lens, 2006).

16. Dudley Flamm to Edward F. Cavanaugh, July 27, 1964, Folder 111, MA Series, Robert F. Wagner Papers, MACNY. "Cops in those days had no PR [public relations] sense," admitted then-Lieutenant Anthony Bouza. It was like the classic joke: "Officer, how do I get to Columbus Circle or should I just go fuck myself?" Author interview with Anthony Bouza.

17. Most complaints to the NYPD continue to center on language. "A lot of the training that we're doing with our officers" is aimed at seeing "if we can rid of the F-word," said Police Commissioner William Bratton. "We joke that if we got rid of three, four words from a cop's vocabulary we'd solve half the problem." Ken Auletta, "Fixing Broken Windows," *New Yorker*, September 7, 2015.

CHAPTER 1. THE GROWING MENACE

1. Theodore Jones, "Few Present as Boy Shot by Policeman Is Buried," *NYT*, July 21, 1964; "Text of Report by District Attorney on Investigation into Gilligan Case," *NYT*, September 2, 1964.

2. Theodore Jones, "Few Present as Boy Shot by Policeman Is Buried," *NYT*, July 21, 1964; "Text of Report by District Attorney on Investigation into Gilligan Case," *NYT*, September 2, 1964.

3. The information in this paragraph and those that follow is primarily from newspaper accounts, FBI records, and the released findings of the grand jury.

4. FBI Report, September 18, 1964, Box 20, WHOF of Richard Goodwin, LBJ Library.

5. Ibid.

6. Sue Reinert, "The Bitter Students . . . The Watchful Police," *NYHT* July 18, 1964.

7. Ibid.

8. Ibid.

9. Ralph Blumenfeld and Kenneth Gross, *NYP*, July 17, 1964.

10. Sue Reinert, "Near Riot—Student Slain by Policeman," *NYHT*, July 17, 1964.

11. "Text of Report by District Attorney," *NYT*, September 2, 1964.

12. Shapiro and Sullivan, *Race Riots*, 2.

13. "Text of Report by District Attorney," *NYT*, September 2, 1964.

14. Ibid.

15. Shapiro and Sullivan, *Race Riots*, 5 6.

16. "Text of Report by District Attorney," *NYT*, September 2, 1964.

17. Theodore Jones, "Negro Boy Killed; 300 Harass Police," *NYT*, July 17, 1964.

18. James Lardner, *Crusader: The Hell-Raising Police Career of Detective David Durk* (Random House, 1996), 57. The value of eyewitness testimony is open to challenge. See Adam Benforado, *Unfair: The New Science of Criminal Injustice* (Crown, 2015). According to a former officer, some plainclothes detectives also carried and used "gypsy guns." Author interview with Robert Leuci.

19. Theodore Jones, "Negro Boy Killed; 300 Harass Police," *NYT*, July 17, 1964; Sue Reinert, "Near Riot—Student Slain by Policeman," *NYHT*, July 17, 1964.

20. Ibid.

21. "The Slain Boy: Neighborhood Views Conflict," *NYP*, July 17, 1964.

22. Sue Reinert, "Near Riot—Student Slain by Policeman," *NYHT*, July 17, 1964.

23. Transcript, Robert Joseph Allen interview with Goldwater, July 3, 1963, Box 4, Denison Kitchel Papers, HIA.

24. Barry Goldwater to Elizabeth Churchill Brown, July 19 and 27, 1963, Box 2, Elizabeth Churchill Brown Papers, HIA.

25. John F. Kennedy, "Radio and Television Report to the American People on Civil Rights," June 11, 1963, http://www.jfklibrary.org/Asset-Viewer/LH8F_0Mzv0e6Ro1yEm74 Ng.aspx (accessed January 2, 2015).

26. Ibid.

27. Lee Edwards, *Goldwater: The Man Who Made a Revolution* (Regnery, 1995), 295.

28. Quoted in David Farber, "Democratic Subjects in the American Sixties: National Politics, Cultural Authenticity, and Community Interest," in David Farber and Jeff Roche, eds., *The Conservative Sixties* (Peter Lang, 2003), 10.

29. F. Clifton White, *Suite 3505: The Story of the Draft Goldwater Movement* (Arlington House, 1967), 117.

30. Robert Alan Goldberg, *Barry Goldwater* (Yale University Press, 1995), 171.

31. Ibid., 179, 181.

32. Naomi Murakawa, "The Origins of the Carceral Crisis," in Joseph Lowndes, Julie Novkov, and Dorian T. Warren, eds., *Race and American Political Development* (Routledge, 2008), 241–242.

33. Speech at the University of New Hampshire, March 3, 1964, Reel 9, Political Speeches, Goldwater Papers, AHF.

34. Speech at Keene High School, Keene, New Hampshire, March 4, 1964, Reel 9, Political Speeches, Goldwater Papers, AHF; Flamm, *Law and Order*, 3–4.

35. "Text of Goldwater's Address to G.O.P. Rally Here," *NYT*, May 13, 1964; Goldberg, *Barry Goldwater*, 178; "Goldwater's Rights Stand Challenged by Roy Wilkins," NAACP press release, Box A247, Group III, NAACP Papers, LOC.

36. Theodore White, *The Making of the President* (Atheneum, 1965), 125.

37. Clay Risen, *The Bill of the Century: The Epic Battle for the Civil Rights Act* (Bloomsbury Press, 2014), 228–229; Robert Dallek, *Flawed Giant: Lyndon Johnson and His Times, 1961–1973* (Oxford University Press, 1998), 119–120.

38. *Congressional Record* 110, June 18, 1964, 14319.

39. Ibid., 14319; Ezra Taft Benson to Goldwater, June 19, 1964, Reel 1.1, Goldwater General Files 1963–1964, Goldwater Papers, AHF.

40. Goldberg, *Barry Goldwater*, 202; White, *Making of the President 1964*, 200.

41. Republican National Convention, July 16, 1964, Box 10, PCF, Goldwater Papers, AHF; White, *Making of the President 1964*, 228.

42. Republican National Convention, July 16, 1964, Box 10, PCF, Goldwater Papers, AHF; "Wake Up America!" *NYAN*, July 25, 1964.

43. Republican National Convention, July 16, 1964, Box 10, PCF, Goldwater Papers, AHF.

44. "Copy of Final Notes on Acceptance Speech," Folder 4, Box 20, 1964 Campaign Files, Goldwater Papers, AHF.

45. Remarks at the Mark Hopkins Hotel, ABC News, July 16, 1964, Box 10, PCF, Goldwater Papers, AHF.

46. Remarks at the Mark Hopkins Hotel, ABC News, July 16, 1964, Box 10, PCF, Goldwater Papers, AHF; press release, July 20, 1964, Box 535, Papers of Emanuel Celler, Manuscript Division, LOC.

47. President's Daily Diary, July 16, 1964, LBJ Library.

48. Johnson and Ernest McFarland, 8:20 P.M., July 16, 1964, Citation 4255 (WH6407.09), LBJ Library.

49. Ibid.

50. Moyers and LBJ, 6:20 and 6:26 P.M., July 17, 1964, Citations 4267 and 4268 (WH6407.9), LBJ Library.

51. Hobart Taylor Jr. to LBJ, July 17, 1964, attached to memo, Jack Valenti to Lee White, July 17, 1964, Ex Hu 2, Box 3, WHCF, LBJ Library.

52. Press Conference, July 18, 1964, "Report of the U.S. Senate Committee on Commerce," Box 16, 1964 Campaign Files, Goldwater Papers, AHF.

CHAPTER 2. THE GREAT MECCA

1. Gerald Early, "Great Adventurer," *New York Review of Books*, April 8, 2004; Eric Pace, "Bayard Rustin Is Dead at 75; Pacifist and a Rights Activist," *NYT*, August 25, 1987.

2. Quoted in John D'Emilio, *Lost Prophet: The Life and Times of Bayard Rustin* (Free Press, 2003), 23.

3. Quoted in Kevin Boyle, *Arc of Justice: A Saga of Race, Civil Rights, and Murder in the Jazz Age* (Henry Holt, 2004), 201.

4. "No Place Like Home," *Time*, July 31, 1964; Gilbert Osofsky, *Harlem: The Making of a Ghetto: Negro New York, 1890–1930* (HarperCollins, 1966), 83.

5. Osofsky, *Harlem*, 107.

6. Ted Poston, "Violence in Harlem," *Midstream* (September 1964): 23. See also Kevin McGruder, *Race and Real Estate: Conflict and Cooperation in Harlem, 1890–1920* (Columbia University Press, 2015).

7. Cheryl Lynn Greenberg, *Or Does It Explode? Black Harlem in the Great Depression* (Oxford University Press, 1991), 15.

8. Quoted in Boyle, *Arc of Justice*, 201.

9. David Levering Lewis, *When Harlem Was in Vogue* (Knopf, 1981).

10. Osofsky, *Harlem*, 141.

11. George S. Schuyler Oral History, CUOHP, 232; Greenberg, *Or Does It Explode?*, 186–187, 192.

12. Thomas A. Johnson, "A Man of Many Roles: Adam Clayton Powell, Former Harlem Representative, Dies," *NYT*, April 5, 1972. See also Wil Haygood, *King of the Cats: The Life and Times of Adam Clayton Powell Jr.* (Harper, 2006).

13. Greenberg, *Or Does It Explode?*, 61, 122.

14. James Baldwin, *Notes of a Native Son* (Beacon, 1955), 68.

15. Inspector John M. De Martino to the police commissioner, NYPD Report of Disorder, March 20, 1935, "Harlem Riot 1935" Box, LaGuardia Papers, LCC; "Police Shoot into Rioters, Kill Negro in Harlem Mob," *NYT*, March 20, 1935; C. C. Nicolet, "One Dead in Wake of Harlem Riots," *NYP*, March 20, 1935; "Police Criticized on Harlem Unrest," *NYT*, March 31, 1935; Robert M. Fogelson and Richard E. Rubenstein, advisory eds., *The Complete Report of Mayor La Guardia's Commission on the Harlem Riot of March 19, 1935* (Arno Press and *NYT*, 1969), 7–8; Thomas Kessner, *Fiorello H. La Guardia and the Making of Modern New York* (McGraw-Hill, 1989), 368; Mark Naison, *Communists in Harlem during the Depression* (University of Illinois Press, 1983), 140–141.

16. Inspector John M. De Martino to the police commissioner, NYPD Report of Disorder, March 20, 1935, "Harlem Riot 1935" Box, LaGuardia Papers, LCC; "Police Shoot into Rioters, Kill Negro in Harlem Mob," *NYT*, March 20, 1935; C. C. Nicolet, "One Dead in Wake of Harlem Riots," *NYP*, March 20, 1935; "Police Criticized on Harlem Unrest," *NYT*, March 31, 1935; Fogelson and Rubenstein, *Complete Report of Mayor La Guardia's Commission*, 7–8; Kessner, *Fiorello H. La Guardia and the Making of Modern New York*, 368; Naison, *Communists in Harlem During the Depression*, 140–141.

17. Inspector John M. De Martino to the police commissioner, NYPD Report of Disorder, March 20, 1935, "Harlem Riot 1935" Box, LaGuardia Papers, LCC; "Police Shoot into Rioters, Kill Negro in Harlem Mob," *NYT*, March 20, 1935; C. C. Nicolet, "One Dead in Wake of Harlem Riots," *NYP*, March 20, 1935; "Police Criticized on Harlem Unrest," *NYT*, March 31, 1935; Fogelson and Rubenstein, *Complete Report of Mayor La Guardia's Commission*, 7–8; Kessner, *Fiorello H. La Guardia and the Making of Modern New York*, 368; Naison, *Communists in Harlem During the Depression*, 140–141.

18. "How Nieuw Haarlem Sank into Squalor," *Life*, July 31, 1964.

19. Ibid.

20. Ralph Ellison, *Invisible Man* (Modern Library, 1952; rev. ed., 1994), 529–530.

21. Inspector John M. De Martino to the police commissioner, NYPD Report of Disorder, March 20, 1935, "Harlem Riot 1935" Box, LaGuardia Papers, LCC; "Police Shoot into Rioters, Kill Negro in Harlem Mob," *NYT*, March 20, 1935; C.C. Nicolet, "One Dead in Wake of Harlem Riots," *NYP*, March 20, 1935; "Police Criticized on Harlem Unrest,"

NYT, March 31, 1935; Fogelson and Rubenstein, *Complete Report of Mayor La Guardia's Commission*, 7–8; Kessner, *Fiorello H. La Guardia and the Making of Modern New York*, 369–370. Naison, *Communists in Harlem During the Depression*, 140–141.

22. Kessner, *Fiorello H. La Guardia and the Making of Modern New York*, 373–374.

23. "Police Criticized on Harlem Unrest," *NYT*, March 31, 1935.

24. Kessner, *Fiorello H. La Guardia and the Making of Modern New York*, 370; Naison, *Communists in Harlem During the Depression*, 142.

25. "Harlem Editor Blames Outside Reds for Race Rioting in Harlem," *World-Telegram Journal*, March 20, 1935, and Edgar T. Rouzeau, "The Man in the Street," *NYAN*, March 22, 1935.

26. Ford to La Guardia, March 20, 1935, "Harlem Riot 1935" Box, LaGuardia Papers, LCC.

27. Kessner, *Fiorello H. La Guardia and the Making of Modern New York*, 370; Edgar T. Rouzeau, "The Man in the Street," *NYAN*, March 22, 1935; Nannie Helen Burroughs, "The Causes of the Harlem Riot," in Gerda Lerner, ed., *Black Women in White America*, repr. ed. (Vintage, 1992), 407–409.

28. Fogelson and Rubenstein, *Complete Report of Mayor La Guardia's Commission*, 128.

29. Ibid., 128.

30. Ibid., 1, 5.

31. Kessner, *Fiorello H. La Guardia and the Making of Modern New York*, 376–377.

32. D'Emilio, *Lost Prophet*, 29.

33. Ibid., 36.

34. Martha Biondi, *To Stand and Fight: The Struggle for Postwar Civil Rights in New York* (Harvard University Press, 2003), 3.

35. Charles V. Hamilton, *Adam Clayton Powell Jr.: The Political Biography of an American Dilemma* (Cooper Square Press, 1991), 125–126.

36. Dominic J. Capeci, *The Harlem Riot of 1943* (Temple University Press, 1977), 72.

37. Kessner, *Fiorello H. La Guardia and the Making of Modern New York*, 530–531.

38. W. Marvin Dulaney, *Black Police in America* (University of Indiana Press, 1996), 69.

39. "500 Police Sent into Harlem as Riot Threatens," *NYHT*, August 2, 1943; Capeci, *Harlem Riot of 1943*, 100; Kessner, *Fiorello H. La Guardia and the Making of Modern New York*, 531.

40. "Memo for the Chief Inspector," August 2, 1943, Papers of Thomas Dewey, URL; "500 Police Sent into Harlem as Riot Threatens," *NYHT*, August 2, 1943; Capeci, *Harlem Riot of 1943*, 100; Kessner, *Fiorello H. La Guardia and the Making of Modern New York*, 531.

41. Capeci, *Harlem Riot of 1943*, 101–103.

42. Claude Brown, *Manchild in the Promised Land* (New American Library, 1965), 12–13.

43. Kessner, *Fiorello H. La Guardia and the Making of Modern New York*, 531; Ralph Ellison, "Harlem 24 Hrs. After—Peace and Quiet Reign," *NYP*, August 3, 1943; Arnold Rampersad, *Ralph Ellison: A Biography* (Knopf, 2007), 167.

44. Baldwin, *Notes of a Native Son*, 111; Ralph Ellison, "Harlem 24 Hrs. After—Peace and Quiet Reign," *NYP*, August 3, 1943.

45. Transcript of broadcast, August 2, 1943, "Harlem Riot 1943" Box, LaGuardia Papers, LCC.

46. Malcolm Logan, "Harlem Stores Open Under Heavy Guard," *NYP*, August 3, 1943; Capeci, *Harlem Riot of 1943*, 102, 104, 123.

47. "The Policemen's Responsibility," *NYAN*, August 28, 1943.

48. Laurie F. Leach, "Margie Polite, the Rioter Starter: Harlem, 1943," *Studies in the Literary Imagination* 40.2 (Fall 2007): 25–48.

49. Fogelson, *Violence as Protest*, 19–21.

50. Walter Davenport, "Harlem . . . Dense and Dangerous," *Colliers*, September 23, 1944.

51. Gerald Early, "Great Adventurer," *New York Review of Books*, April 8, 2004; Eric Pace, "Bayard Rustin Is Dead at 75; Pacifist and a Rights Activist," *NYT*, August 25, 1987; D'Emilio, *Lost Prophet*, 93–120.

52. Gerald Early, "Great Adventurer," *New York Review of Books*, April 8, 2004; Eric Pace, "Bayard Rustin Is Dead at 75; Pacifist and a Rights Activist," *NYT*, August 25, 1987; D'Emilio, *Lost Prophet*, 191–193.

53. Gerald Early, "Great Adventurer," *New York Review of Books*, April 8, 2004; Eric Pace, "Bayard Rustin Is Dead at 75; Pacifist and a Rights Activist," *NYT*, August 25, 1987; Michael G. Long, ed., *I Must Resist: Bayard Rustin's Life in Letters* (City Lights Books, 2012), 238.

54. Biondi, *To Stand and Fight*, 3; Joshua Freeman, *Working-Class New York: Life and Labor Since World War II* (Norton, 2000), 172, 182.

55. Kenneth B. Clark, *Dark Ghetto: Dilemmas of Social Power* (Harper & Row, 1965), 30; Ralph Ellison, *Shadow and Act* (Random House, 1964), 296.

56. Clark, *Dark Ghetto*, 27.

57. Adina Black, "Exposing the 'Whole Segregation Myth': The Harlem Nine and New York City's School Desegregation Battles," in Jeanne Theoharis and Komozi Woodard, eds., *Freedom North: Black Freedom Struggles Outside the South, 1940–1980* (Palgrave Macmillan, 2003), 65–91.

58. Biondi, *To Stand and Fight*, 113, 123–124, 131, 135.

59. Clark, *Dark Ghetto*, xv, 59.

60. Freeman, *Working-Class New York*, 181.

61. Clark, *Dark Ghetto*, 60–61; Fred Powledge, "Negro Riots Reflect Deep-Seated Grievances," *NYT*, August 2, 1964.

62. Fred Powledge, "Negro Riots Reflect Deep-Seated Grievances," *NYT*, August 2, 1964; Clark, *Dark Ghetto*, 60–61.

63. Barry Gottehrer, *New York City in Crisis: A Study in Depth of Urban Sickness* (D. McKay, 1965), 16; Jonathan J. Bean, "'Burn, Baby, Burn': Small Businesses in the Urban Riots of the 1960s," *Independent Review* 5 (Fall 2000): 165–188; Fred Powledge, "Fighting the System," *NYT*, August 6, 1964.

64. Fred Powledge, "Negro Riots Reflect Deep-Seated Grievances," *NYT*, August 2, 1964; Clark, *Dark Ghetto*, 34–37, 60–61.

65. Clark, *Dark Ghetto*, 37.

66. "Strong Arm of the Law," *Time*, July 7, 1958.

67. William H. Harris, *The Harder We Run: Black Workers since the Civil War* (Oxford University Press, 1982); press release, October 1, 1959, "Crime–Juvenile Delinquency, 1958–62," Box 91A, Group III, NAACP Papers, Manuscript Division, LOC.

68. Brown, *Manchild in the Promised Land*, 263; author interviews with Sonny Grosso and Elliott Bovelle.

69. "No Place Like Home," Time, July 31, 1964; Fred Powledge, "Negro Riots Reflect Deep-Seated Grievances," *NYT*, August 2, 1964; Edward Conlon, *Blue Blood* (Riverhead Books, 2004), 173.

70. Author interview with Barney Cohen; Michael Harrington, *The Other America: Poverty in the United States* (Macmillan, 1962), 67.

71. Joseph Tirella, *Tomorrow-Land: The 1964–1965 World's Fair and the Transformation of America* (Lyons Press, 2014), 197.

72. William Brink and Louis Harris, eds., *The Negro Revolution in America* (Simon & Schuster, 1964), 112, 123; Thomas J. Sugrue, *Sweet Land of Liberty: The Forgotten Struggle for Civil Rights in the North* (Random House, 1988), 288; D'Emilio, *Lost Prophet*, 336.

73. D'Emilio, *Lost Prophet*, 338–339.

74. Author interview with Rachelle Horowitz.

75. Ben Keppel, *The Work of Democracy: Ralph Bunche, Kenneth B. Clark, Lorraine Hansberry, and the Cultural Politics of Race* (Harvard University Press, 1995), 133–134.

76. Ibid., 139.

CHAPTER 3. THE GATHERING STORM

1. William Travers and Henry Lee, "Police Say Slain Boy Left for School with 2 Knives," *NYDN*, July 18, 1964.

2. Theodore Jones, "Teen-Age Parade Protests Killing," *NYT*, July 18, 1964; William Travers and Henry Lee, "Police Say Slain Boy Left for School with 2 Knives," *NYDN*, July 18, 1964; Shapiro and Sullivan, *Race Riots*, 13.

3. Ibid. and author interview with Val Coleman.

4. http://www.oopau.org/2.html (accessed February 20, 2014).

5. Ibid.

6. Tirella, *Tomorrow-Land*, 137.

7. Shapiro and Sullivan, *Race Riots*, 13.

8. Ibid., 14.

9. "Gangs Beat and Rob 2 Riders on Upper Manhattan Subways," *NYT*, July 18, 1964.

10. "Rise in Murders Reported by City," *NYT*, July 18, 1964.

11. "The Policemen's Responsibility," *NYAN*, August 28, 1943.

12. Lardner, *Crusader*, 33, 49.

13. Layhmond Robinson, "Negroes' View of Plight Examined in Survey Here," *NYT*, July 27, 1964.

14. Ibid.

15. "Harlem: Hatred in the Streets," *Newsweek*, August 3, 1964; Barbara Benson, "Letters to the Times," *NYT*, July 22, 1964.

16. Taylor Branch, *Pillar of Fire: America in the King Years, 1963–1965* (Simon & Schuster, 1998), 42–44; Hamilton, *Adam Clayton Powell Jr.*, 430–437.

17. Poston, "Violence in Harlem," 23; Branch, *Pillar of Fire*, 42–44; Hamilton, *Adam Clayton Powell Jr.*, 430–437.

18. Lardner, *Crusader*, 170.

19. Jim O'Neil with Mel Fazzino, *A Cop's Tale: NYPD The Violent Years* (Barricade Books, 2009), 34–35.

20. Robert Leuci, *All the Centurions* (HarperCollins, 2004), 105.

21. *Knapp Commission Report on Police Corruption* (George Braziller, 1972), 1, 4, 67, 71, 89–90.

22. James Baldwin, *The Fire Next Time* (Vintage, 1963), 21, 23.

23. Biondi, *To Stand and Fight*, 60.

24. Ibid., 192–193.

25. Ibid., 193–194.

26. Layhmond Robinson, "Negroes' View of Plight Examined in Survey Here," *NYT*, July 27, 1964.

27. O'Neil, *Cop's Tale*, 24.

28. James Baldwin, *Nobody Knows My Name* (Dell, 1962), 65–67.

29. Andrew T. Darien, "Patrolling the Borders: Integration and Identity in the New York City Police Department, 1941–1975" (Ph.D. diss., New York University, 2000), 161; *Report of the National Advisory Commission on Civil Disorders* (Bantam, 1968), 321–322.

30. O'Neil, *Cop's Tale*, 16–18.

31. Ibid., 18–21.

32. Michael F. Armstrong, *They Wished They Were Honest: The Knapp Commission and New York City Police Corruption* (Columbia University Press, 2012), 65–66; Leuci, *All the Centurions*, 8, 25.

33. Leuci, *All the Centurions*, 46–47.

34. Author interviews with Percy Sutton and Anthony Bouza.

35. Clarence Taylor, *Knocking at Our Own Door: Milton A. Galamison and the Struggle to Integrate New York City Schools* (Lexington Books, 2001), chap. 5.

36. "Man in the News: Bayard Rustin," *NYT*, February 4, 1964; Daniel Levine, *Bayard Rustin and the Civil Rights Movement* (Rutgers University Press, 2000), 162.

37. Leonard Buder, "Boycott Cripples City Schools," *NYT*, February 4, 1964; Fred Powledge, "Leaders of Protest Foresee a New Era of Militancy Here," *NYT*, February 4, 1964.

38. "Boycott Chief Soviets' Guest," *NYDN*, February 5, 1964; SAC NY to FBI director, February 6, 1964, Rustin FBI Files (http://vault.fbi.gov/bayard-rustin/bayard-rustin-part -01-of-07/view).

39. D'Emilio, *Lost Prophet*, 370–373.

40. Kevin Cook, *Kitty Genovese: The Murder, the Bystanders, the Crime That Changed America* (Norton, 2014), 40, 214.

41. Ibid., 215–220.

42. Quoted in ibid., 96; Anthony Scaduto, "Murphy of the Police," *NYP*, July 26, 1964.

43. Anthony Scaduto, "Murphy of the Police," *NYP*, July 26, 1964; Lynda Richardson, "Michael J. Murphy, 83, Dies; Led New York Police in 1960s," *NYT*, May 18, 1997.

44. Scaduto, "Murphy of the Police," *NYP*, July 26, 1964; Richardson, "Michael J. Murphy, 83, Dies; Led New York Police in 1960s," *NYT*, May 18, 1997.

45. Quoted in Cook, *Kitty Genovese*, 96; Anthony Scaduto, "Murphy of the Police," *NYP*, July 26, 1964.

46. LeRoi Jones, *Dutchman and The Slave: Two Plays* (Morrow Quill Paperbacks, 1964).

47. Ibid., 33.

48. Margalit Fox, "Amiri Baraka, Polarizing Poet and Playwright, Dies at 79," *NYT*, January 9, 2014; Howard Taubman, "The Theater: 'Dutchman,'" *NYT*, March 25, 1964.

49. "Liberalism and the Negro," *Commentary*, March 1964, 39.

50. Tirella, *Tomorrow-Land*, 179–182. The most complete account is Brian Purnell, *Fighting Jim Crow in the County of Kings* (University Press of Kentucky, 2013), 249–278.

51. Tirella, *Tomorrow-Land*, 183.

52. Ibid., 183–197.

53. "75 in Harlem Throw Fruit at Policemen," *NYT*, April 18, 1964; Junius Griffin, "Harlem: The Tension Underneath," *NYT*, May 29, 1964; Shapiro and Sullivan, *Race Riots*, 38–39.

54. Arthur Gelb, *City Room* (Marian Wood, 2003), 307.

55. Todd S. Purdum, *An Idea Whose Time Has Come: Two Presidents, Two Parties, and the Battle for the Civil Rights Act of 1964* (Henry Holt, 2014), 252, 272.

56. Junius Griffin, "Whites Are Targets of Harlem Gang," *NYT*, May 3, 1964; Junius Griffin, "Anti-White Harlem Gang Reported to Number 400," *NYT*, May 6, 1964; Junius Griffin, "Harlem: The Tension Underneath," *NYT*, May 29, 1964.

57. Ibid.

58. Susan E. Tifft and Alex S. Jones, *The Trust: The Powerful and Private Family Behind the New York Times* (Back Bay Books, 2000), 277; Gelb, *City Room*, 381.

59. Earl Caldwell—*Journal* (chapters 8–12), Robert C. Maynard Institute for Journalism Education, http://www.maynardije.org/news/features/caldwell/Chapter9/; Southwest Virginia Historical State Park, http://www.swvamuseum.org/juniusgriffin.html (accessed December 3, 2015).

60. Poston, "Violence in Harlem," 26–27; Junius Griffin, "N.A.A.C.P. Assails Reports of Gang," *NYT*, May 11, 1964.

61. Gay Talese, *The Kingdom and the Power* (Anchor Press, 1978), 377.

62. Cook, *Kitty Genovese*, 95; Gelb, *City Room*, 281, 394; author interviews with Arthur Gelb and Gay Talese.

63. Truman Nelson, *The Torture of Mothers* (Beacon, 1968), 49.

64. "Maccabees and the Mau Mau," *National Review*, July 16, 1964, 479–480.

65. Arnold Fein to Robert Wagner, May 19, 1964, Box 4, Folder 31, City Council Papers of Paul Screvane, LCC.

66. Fred Powledge, "Screvane to Meet Rights Leaders," *NYT*, July 20, 1964; Ruth Cowan, "The New York City Civilian Review Board Referendum of November 1966: A Study in Mass Politics" (Ph.D. diss., New York University, 1970), 116–117, 126.

67. Cassese to Wagner, May 21, 1964, Box 14, Folder 278, Screvane Papers, LCC.

68. Ibid.

69. Martin Arnold, "Murphy Discounts Fears of Violence This Summer," *NYT*, June 9, 1964.

70. Press Conference, June 4, 1964, "News Media on the Manifestation of Teenage Violence," Box 43, Part II, NUL Papers, Manuscript Division, LOC.

71. Ibid.

72. "New York: The Jitters," *Newsweek*, June 15, 1964.

73. Richard Goodwin to Lyndon Johnson, May 4, 1964, Ex Hu2/Gen Hu2, Box 2, WHCF, LBJ Library.

74. "A Bad Law," *NYAN*, March 7, 1964; Alex Elkins, "Fifty Years of Get-Tough: Remembering Harlem and the Urban Street Justice of the 1960s Riots," http://urbanhistorians.wordpress.com/2014/07/16/fifty-years-of-get-tough/ (accessed July 22, 2014).

75. Junius Griffin, "Harlem: The Tension Underneath," *NYT*, May 29, 1964.

76. "Maccabees and the Mau Mau," *National Review*, July 16, 1964.

77. Brown, *Manchild in the Promised Land*, 313, 315.

CHAPTER 4. THE FIRE THIS TIME

1. Paul L. Montgomery and Francis X. Clines, "Thousands Riot in Harlem Area; Scores Are Hurt," *NYT*, July 19, 1964.

2. "Timetable of Violence," *NYHT*, July 20, 1964; Shapiro and Sullivan, *Race Riots*, 47–48, 62; Paul L. Montgomery, "Night of Riots Began with Calm Rally," *NYT*, July 20, 1964.

3. William Borders, "More Than 100 Injured Get Aid at 2 City Hospitals in Harlem," *NYT*, July 20, 1964; "Casualty List in Battle of Harlem," *NYAN*, July 25, 1964.

4. "Harlem Is a Study in Contrasts as Sun Rises on Scene of Riots," *NYT*, July 20, 1964.

5. A veteran black journalist estimated that Harlem "leaders" like Nelson Dukes, Jesse Gray, and James Lawson had at most a total of five thousand followers in a community of half a million. Poston, "Violence in Harlem," 26.

6. "Mother Hysterical at Boy's Bier," *NYT*, July 19, 1964.

7. Ibid.

8. Paul L. Montgomery, "Night of Riots Began with Calm Rally," *NYT*, July 20, 1964; Shapiro and Sullivan, *Race Riots*, 44–45.

9. Ibid.

10. Paul L. Montgomery, "Night of Riots Began with Calm Rally," *NYT*, July 20, 1964; Shapiro and Sullivan, *Race Riots*, 45–46; Paul L. Montgomery and Francis X. Clines, "Thousands Riot in Harlem Area; Scores Are Hurt," *NYT*, July 20, 1964.

11. Ibid.

12. Gelb, *City Room*, 391.

13. Paul L. Montgomery, "Night of Riots Began with Calm Rally," *NYT*, July 20, 1964; Shapiro and Sullivan, *Race Riots*, 42.

14. Shapiro and Sullivan, *Race Riots*, 42.

15. Author interviews with Wayne Moreland and Quentin Hill (Basir Mchawi).

16. Paul L. Montgomery, "Night of Riots Began with Calm Rally," *NYT*, July 20, 1964; Shapiro and Sullivan, *Race Riots*, 48–49; author interviews with Wayne Moreland and Quentin Hill (Basir Mchawi); Paul L. Montgomery and Francis X. Clines, "Thousands Riot in Harlem Area; Scores Are Hurt," *NYT*, July 19, 1964.

17. Author interviews with Wayne Moreland and Quentin Hill (Basir Mchawi).

18. Ibid.; Clarence Major, ed., *The New Black Poetry* (International Publishers, 1969), 68.

19. Paul L. Montgomery, "Night of Riots Began with Calm Rally," *NYT*, July 20, 1964; Shapiro and Sullivan, *Race Riots*, 48–49; Paul L. Montgomery and Francis X. Clines, "Thousands Riot in Harlem Area; Scores Are Hurt," *NYT*, July 19, 1964.

20. Paul Montgomery, "Night of Riots Began with Calm Rally," *NYT*, July 20, 1964.

21. Leuci, *All the Centurions*, 61; Paul L. Montgomery and Francis X. Clines, "Thousands Riot in Harlem Area; Scores Are Hurt," *NYT*, July 19, 1964.

22. Author interview with Peter Drew.

23. Shapiro and Sullivan, *Race Riots*, 49; Francis X. Clines, "Policemen Exhaust Their Ammunition in All-Night Battle," *NYT*, July 20, 1964.

24. Paul L. Montgomery, "Night of Riots Began with Calm Rally," *NYT*, July 20, 1964.

25. George Barner, "Three Violent Days: Saturday Night," *NYAN*, July 25, 1964; Paul L. Montgomery, "Night of Riots Began with Calm Rally," *NYT*, July 20, 1964; Thomas Toolen and Richard Henry, "Cops Battle Thousands in Riot," *NYDN*, July 19, 1964.

26. UPI photo and caption, *NYAN*, July 25, 1964; "When Night Falls," *Time*, July 31, 1964.

27. "When Night Falls," *Time*, July 31, 1964.

28. Francis X. Clines, "Policemen Exhaust Their Ammunition in All-Night Battle," *NYT*, July 20, 1964.

29. Leuci, *All the Centurions*, 60–61.

30. Shapiro and Sullivan, *Race Riots*, 52.

31. Paul L. Montgomery, "Night of Riots Began with Calm Rally," *NYT*, July 20, 1964.

32. Paul L. Montgomery and Francis X. Clines, "Thousands Riot in Harlem Area; Scores Are Hurt," *NYT*, July 19, 1964.

33. Ibid.; Shapiro and Sullivan, *Race Riots*, 66.

34. O'Neil, *Cop's Tale*, 41.

35. Ibid.

36. Author interview with Robert Leuci; O'Neil, *Cop's Tale*, 42.

37. O'Neil, *Cop's Tale*, 42–44.

38. Ibid. O'Neil identifies the officer as Jimmy Denton, but the newspapers listed him as James Dexter.

39. Ibid.

40. Ibid., 44; author interview with Lez Edmond.

41. Bill Whitworth, "Tinderbox Harlem: Saturday Night and Sunday Morning," *NYHT*, July 20, 1964.

42. Paul L. Montgomery, "Night of Riots Began with Calm Rally," *NYT*, July 20, 1964; O'Neil, *Cop's Tale*, 44–45.

43. Ibid.

44. "Harlem: Hatred in the Streets," *Newsweek*, August 3, 1964; George Barner, "Three Violent Days: Saturday Night," *NYAN*, July 25, 1964; Francis X. Clines, "Policemen Exhaust Their Ammunition in All-Night Battle," *NYT*, July 20, 1964.

45. Edward Cumberbatch and Alfred T. Hendricks, "Woman Accuses Cop in Shooting," *NYP*, July 21, 1964.

46. George Barner, "Three Violent Days: Saturday Night," *NYAN*, July 25, 1964; Francis X. Clines, "Policemen Exhaust Their Ammunition in All-Night Battle," *NYT*, July 20, 1964.

47. Fred Ferretti and Martin G. Berck, "Tinderbox Harlem: New Outbursts Snap Uneasy Truce," *NYHT*, July 20, 1964; Ed James, "Harlem: By 2 Who Were There," *NYP*, July 20, 1964; George Barner, "Three Violent Days: Saturday Night," *NYAN*, July 25, 1964.

48. George Barner, "The Negro Cop in a Race Riot," *NYAN*, July 25, 1964.

49. James Farmer, *Lay Bare the Heart* (New American Library, 1985), 279–280; author interview with Alan Gartner; James Farmer Oral History, CUOHP, 294–300.

50. Farmer, *Lay Bare the Heart*, 279–280; author interview with Alan Gartner; James Farmer Oral History, CUOHP, 294–300.

51. Farmer, *Lay Bare the Heart*, 280–281; Farmer Oral History, 294–300.

52. Farmer, *Lay Bare the Heart*, 280–281; Farmer Oral History, 294–300.

53. Farmer, *Lay Bare the Heart*, 282–283; Farmer Oral History, 294–300.

54. Farmer, *Lay Bare the Heart*, 282–283; Farmer Oral History, 294–300.

55. Farmer, *Lay Bare the Heart*, 282–283; Farmer Oral History, 294–300.

56. O'Neil, *Cop's Tale*, 45–46.

57. Ibid., 45–46; Francis X. Clines, "Policemen Exhaust Their Ammunition in All-Night Battle," *NYT*, July 20, 1964.

58. Nicholas Alex, *New York Cops Talk Back: A Study of a Beleaguered Minority* (John Wiley, 1976), 75.

59. Anthony Mosca, "Riot Control" (M.A. thesis, John Jay College, 1979), 30–31; author interview with Anthony Bouza.

60. "New York City Deep in Trouble," *U.S. News & World Report*, August 3, 1964.

61. Lez Edmond, "Harlem Diary," *Ramparts*, October 1964, 25.

62. R. W. Apple Jr., "Police Defend the Use of Gunfire in Controlling Riots in Harlem," *NYT*, July 21, 1964.

63. "Uneasy Calm Hangs over New York City," *Pittsburgh Courier*, August 1, 1964.

64. William Borders, "More Than 100 Injured Get Aid at 2 City Hospitals in Harlem," *NYT*, July 20, 1964; author interview with Lester Carson.

65. William Borders, "More Than 100 Injured Get Aid at 2 City Hospitals in Harlem," *NYT*, July 20, 1964; author interview with Lester Carson.

66. Author interview with Francis X. Clines.

67. Ibid.

68. Shapiro and Sullivan, *Race Riots*, 54–56.

69. Ibid., 56.

70. Gelb, *City Room*, 391; author interviews with Francis X. Clines and Fred Powledge.

71. Paul L. Montgomery, "Night of Riots Began with Calm Rally," *NYT*, July 20, 1964.

72. Francis X. Clines, "Policemen Exhaust Their Ammunition in All-Night Battle," *NYT*, July 20, 1964; Anthony Scaduto, "Murphy of the Police," *NYP*, July 26, 1964.

73. Author interview with Lez Edmond.

74. Author interview with Lez Edmond; Edmond, "Harlem Diary," 17, 19.

75. Bill Whitworth, "Tinderbox Harlem: Saturday Night and Sunday Morning," *NYHT*, July 20, 1964.

76. Edmond, "Harlem Diary," 19–20.

77. "Text of Murphy Appeal," *NYT*, July 20, 1964, 1964.

78. Shapiro and Sullivan, *Race Riots*, 65.

79. Dr. Kenneth Clark, "Behind the Harlem Riots—Two Views," *NYHT*, July 20, 1964.

80. "Harlem: Hatred in the Streets," *Newsweek*, August 3, 1964.

81. Leonard Katz and Normand Poirier, "Crowd Awaits the Injured at the Hospital," *NYP*, July 20, 1964.

82. "Harlem Is a Study in Contrasts as Sun Rises on Scene of Riots," *NYT*, July 20, 1964.

CHAPTER 5. THIS MOST MARVELOUS CITY

1. Fred Ferretti and Martin G. Berck, "Tinderbox Harlem: New Outbursts Snap Uneasy Truce," *NYHT*, July 20, 1964.

2. Ibid.

3. Herb Goldstein and Edward Cumberbatch, "After a Boy's Funeral, a Rights Leader Weeps," *NYP*, July 20, 1964; Fred Ferretti and Martin G. Berck, "Tinderbox Harlem: New Outbursts Snap Uneasy Truce," *NYHT*, July 20, 1964.

4. Ibid.

5. Fred Ferretti and Martin G. Berck, "Tinderbox Harlem: New Outbursts Snap Uneasy Truce," *NYHT*, July 20, 1964; "Warning by Malcolm X," *NYDN*, July 21, 1964.

6. Manning Marable, *Malcolm X: A Life of Reinvention* (Viking, 2011), 300.

7. Author interview with Percy Sutton; Peter Goldman, *The Death and Life of Malcolm X* (University of Illinois Press, 1979), 206. Some believe that Malcolm X might have had the ability to halt the unrest. Author interview with Lez Edmond.

8. Farmer Oral History, 294.

9. R. W. Apple Jr., Violence Flares Again in Harlem; Restraint Urged," *NYT*, July 20, 1964; Jimmy Breslin, "Fear and Hate—Sputtering Fuse," *NYHT*, July 20, 1964.

10. Fred Ferretti and Martin G. Berck, "Tinderbox Harlem: New Outbursts Snap Uneasy Truce," *NYHT*, July 20, 1964.

11. Terry Smith, "How Some of the White Merchants Fared—Disastrously," *NYHT*, July 20, 1964.

12. Ibid.

13. Ibid.; Bean, " 'Burn, Baby, Burn,' " 169–171.

14. Terry Smith, "How Some of the White Merchants Fared—Disastrously," *NYHT*, July 20, 1964.

15. Fred Powledge, "Screvane to Meet Rights Leaders," *NYT*, July 20, 1964; "Texts of Screvane and Murphy Appeals," *NYT*, July 20, 1964.

16. Fred Powledge, "Screvane to Meet Rights Leaders," *NYT*, July 20, 1964; "Texts of Screvane and Murphy Appeals," *NYT*, July 20, 1964.

17. William Travers and Joseph McNamara, "Harlem Is Urged to Simmer Down," *NYDN*, July 20, 1964; Fred Powledge, "Screvane to Meet Rights Leaders," *NYT*, July 20, 1964.

18. William Travers and Joseph McNamara, "Harlem Is Urged to Simmer Down," *NYDN*, July 20, 1964; Fred Powledge, "Screvane to Meet Rights Leaders," *NYT*, July 20, 1964; Ted Poston and Ralph Blumenfeld, "Riot Toll: 1 Killed, 119 Hurt," *NYP*, July 20, 1964.

19. Thomas Toolen, "Arm Assails Race Leaders and Criminals," *NYDN*, July 20, 1964; Fred Powledge, "Screvane to Meet Rights Leaders," *NYT*, July 20, 1964; Ted Poston and Ralph Blumenfeld, "Riot Toll: 1 Killed, 119 Hurt," *NYP*, July 20, 1964.

20. Thomas Toolen, "Arm Assails Race Leaders and Criminals," *NYDN*, July 20, 1964; Fred Powledge, "Screvane to Meet Rights Leaders," *NYT*, July 20, 1964; Ted Poston and Ralph Blumenfeld, "Riot Toll: 1 Killed, 119 Hurt," *NYP*, July 20, 1964.

21. Thomas Toolen, "Arm Assails Race Leaders and Criminals," *NYDN*, July 20, 1964, 3, 18; R. W. Apple Jr., "Violence Flares Again in Harlem; Restraint Urged," *NYT*, July 20, 1964, 1, 16.

22. Gertrude Schwebell to Rockefeller, July 19, 1964, Reel 17, RG 15, Gubernatorial Office Records, Subject Files, RAC.

23. R. W. Apple Jr., "Violence Flares Again in Harlem; Restraint Urged," *NYT*, July 20, 1964.

24. Thomas Toolen, "Arm Assails Race Leaders and Criminals," *NYDN*, July 20, 1964; R. W. Apple Jr., "Violence Flares Again in Harlem; Restraint Urged," *NYT*, July 20, 1964.

25. Herbert Geist to James Farmer, July 23, 1964, Reel 3, A1:85, CORE Papers, Manuscript Division, LOC.

26. James Fallon to James Farmer, July 19, 1964, Reel 3, I:34; Mason Gaffney to James Farmer, September 9, 1964, Reel 2, A1:76. Both are in the CORE Papers, Manuscript Division, LOC.

27. Jeff Sklansky, *James Farmer* (Chelsea House, 1992), 20–25; Richard Severo, "James Farmer, Civil Rights Giant in the 50's and 60's, Is Dead at 79," *NYT*, July 21, 1999.

28. Sklansky, *James Farmer*, 20–25; Richard Severo, "James Farmer, Civil Rights Giant in the 50's and 60's, Is Dead at 79," *NYT*, July 21, 1999.

29. Sklansky, *James Farmer*, 53–71; Richard Severo, "James Farmer, Civil Rights Giant in the 50's and 60's, Is Dead at 79," *NYT*, July 21, 1999.

30. Sklansky, *James Farmer*, 53–71; Richard Severo, "James Farmer, Civil Rights Giant in the 50's and 60's, Is Dead at 79," *NYT*, July 21, 1999.

31. Sklansky, *James Farmer*, 88–91; Richard Severo, "James Farmer, Civil Rights Giant in the 50's and 60's, Is Dead at 79," *NYT*, July 21, 1999.

32. August Meier and Elliot Rudwick, *CORE: A Study in the Civil Rights Movement, 1942–1968* (Oxford University Press, 1973), 292–326; "Civil Rights Leader out of Bellevue," *NYT*, July 21, 1964.

33. "The Ghetto Ignites," *The Nation*, August 10, 1964; Richard Severo, "James Farmer, Civil Rights Giant in the 50's and 60's, Is Dead at 79," *NYT*, July 21, 1999; author interview with Fred Powledge.

34. "Is Harlem Mississippi?" flyer, Folder 5, Box 5, James Haughton Papers, SCRBC.

35. "Rally to Protest Housing Is Held on Harlem Block," *NYT*, May 31, 1964; "The Negroes' Leaders: Right, Left and In-Between," *NYHT*, August 9, 1964.

36. Junius Griffin, "'Guerrilla War' Urged in Harlem," *NYT*, July 20, 1964; John Mallon and Richard Henry, "Missiles Are Hurled at Police; Throngs Jam Streets," *NYDN*, July 20, 1964.

37. Junius Griffin, "'Guerrilla War' Urged in Harlem," *NYT*, July 20, 1964; Henry Beckett, "Jesse Gray Back on Stand," *NYP*, July 29, 1964.

38. George Todd, "James Powell's Funeral Tears—Then Violence," *NYAN*, July 25, 1964; John Mallon and Richard Henry, "Missiles Are Hurled at Police; Throngs Jam Streets," *NYDN*, July 20, 1964.

39. George Todd, "James Powell's Funeral Tears—Then Violence," *NYAN*, July 25, 1964; John Mallon and Richard Henry, "Missiles Are Hurled at Police; Throngs Jam Streets," *NYDN*, July 20, 1964; Shapiro and Sullivan, *Race Riots*, 74–75.

40. Junius Griffin, "'Guerrilla War' Urged in Harlem," *NYT*, July 20, 1964.

41. Ibid.; Theodore Jones, "Uneasy Calm Prevails in Harlem," *NYT*, July 17, 1965.

42. "New York: When Night Falls," *Time*, July 31, 1964.

43. Fred Ferretti and Martin G. Berck, "Tinderbox Harlem: New Outbursts Snap Uneasy Truce," *NYHT*, July 20, 1964; John Mallon and Richard Henry, "Missiles Are Hurled at Police; Throngs Jam Streets," *NYDN*, July 20, 1964.

44. Author interview with Percy Sutton; "The Negroes' Leaders: Right, Left, and In-Between," *NYHT*, August 9, 1964.

45. Fred Ferretti and Martin G. Berck, "Tinderbox Harlem: New Outbursts Snap Uneasy Truce," *NYHT*, July 20, 1964; John Mallon and Richard Henry, "Missiles Are Hurled at Police; Throngs Jam Streets," *NYDN*, July 20, 1964.

46. Fred Ferretti and Martin G. Berck, "Tinderbox Harlem: New Outbursts Snap Uneasy Truce," *NYHT*, July 20, 1964; John Mallon and Richard Henry, "Missiles Are Hurled at Police; Throngs Jam Streets," *NYDN*, July 20, 1964.

47. Long, *I Must Resist*, 291; D'Emilio, *Lost Prophet*, 384–385.

48. Bayard Rustin, "The Harlem Riot and Nonviolence," in Staughton Lynd, ed., *Non-Violence in America* (Orbis Books, 1995), 495; Murray Kempton, "How Cops Behave in Harlem," *New Republic*, August 27, 1964.

49. D'Emilio, *Lost Prophet*, 383; author interview with Rachelle Horowitz; Rustin, "Harlem Riot & Nonviolence," 496–497.

50. Rustin, "Harlem Riot & Nonviolence," 496–497.

51. Junius Griffin, "'Guerrilla War' Urged in Harlem," *NYT*, July 20, 1964.

52. Gelb, *City Room*, 390; author interview with Joseph Lelyveld.

53. Branch, *Pillar of Fire*, 394, 446; Joseph Lelyveld, "Breaking Away," *NYT Magazine*, March 6, 2005; author interview with Joseph Lelyveld.

54. Author interview with Lester Carson; Edward Cumberbatch, "Harlem: By 2 Who Were There," *NYP*, July 20, 1964.

55. Thomas R. Brooks, "New York's Finest," *Commentary*, August 1965; Shapiro and Sullivan, *Race Riots*, 66; R. W. Apple Jr., "Violence Flares Again in Harlem; Restraint Urged," *NYT*, July 20, 1964.

56. "Police Use Helicopters," *NYT*, July 20, 1964.

57. R. W. Apple Jr., "Violence Flares Again in Harlem; Restraint Urged," *NYT*, July 20, 1964; Fred Ferretti and Martin G. Berck, "Tinderbox Harlem: New Outbursts Snap Uneasy Truce," *NYHT*, July 20, 1964.

58. Jack Roth, "Dynamite Threat in Riot Disclosed," *NYT*, September 22, 1964.

59. Ibid.

60. Ibid.

61. Kareem Abdul-Jabbar and Peter Knobler, *Giant Steps: The Autobiography of Kareem Abdul-Jabbar* (Bantam, 1983), 4, 6, 70.

62. Ibid., 61.

63. Ibid.

64. Ibid., 72.

65. Ibid.

66. Ibid., 72–73.

67. Ibid., 74–75.

68. Jimmy Breslin, "Fear and Hate—Sputtering Fuse," *NYHT*, July 20, 1964.

69. Ibid.; Shapiro and Sullivan, *Race Riots*, 70.

70. Jimmy Breslin, "Fear and Hate—Sputtering Fuse," *NYHT*, July 20, 1964.

71. Fred Powledge, "Screvane to Meet Rights Leaders," *NYT*, July 20, 1964.

CHAPTER 6. HEAT AND DIRT, ANGER AND FURY

1. "Civil Rights: The White House Meeting," *Newsweek*, August 3, 1964; Richard Dougherty, "Campaign Ground Rules on the Rights Issue?" *NYHT*, July 21, 1964.

2. Richard Dougherty, "Campaign Ground Rules on the Rights Issue?" *NYHT*, July 21, 1964.

3. Johnson and Reedy, 7:40 P.M., July 20, 1964 (6407.11), LBJ Library.

4. Moyers, Goodwin, and Valenti to Johnson, July 21, 1964, Diary Backup, Box 7, LBJ Library.

5. Horace Busby to Johnson, July 24, 1964, Diary Backup, Box 7, LBJ Library.

6. "Send Troops to Harlem, Alabama Mayor Urges," *NYT*, July 22, 1964.

7. Johnson and Reedy, 7:40 P.M., July 20, 1964 (6407.11), LBJ Library.

8. Sue Reinert, "Harsh Words, No Violence at Boy's Funeral," *NYHT*, July 21, 1964; Theodore Jones, "Few Present as Boy Shot by Policeman Is Buried," *NYT*, July 21, 1964.

9. Sue Reinert, "Harsh Words, No Violence at Boy's Funeral," *NYHT*, July 21, 1964; Theodore Jones, "Few Present as Boy Shot by Policeman Is Buried," *NYT*, July 21, 1964.

10. Sue Reinert, "Harsh Words, No Violence at Boy's Funeral," *NYHT*, July 21, 1964; Theodore Jones, "Few Present as Boy Shot by Policeman Is Buried," *NYT*, July 21, 1964.

11. Junius Griffin, "Harlem Businessmen Put Riot Losses at $50,000," *NYT*, July 21, 1964.

12. Ibid.

13. David Halberstam, "White Harlem Merchants Tense; Many Would Like to Sell Stores," *NYT*, July 22, 1964.

14. Ibid.

15. Fred Powledge, "Screvane to Meet Rights Leaders," *NYT*, July 20, 1964; "Texts of Screvane and Murphy Appeals," *NYT*, July 20, 1964.

16. Peter Kihss, "City to Increase Negro Policemen on Harlem Duty," *NYT*, July 21, 1964; "Harlem Riots Make Headlines in Europe," *NYHT*, July 22, 1964; "European Papers Report on Rioting," *NYT*, July 21, 1964.

17. "Harlem Riots Make Headlines in Europe," *NYHT*, July 22, 1964; "European Papers Report on Rioting," *NYT*, July 21, 1964; "Happy Days!" *NYDN*, July 21, 1964; Mary L. Dudziak, *Cold War Civil Rights: Race and the Image of American Democracy* (Princeton University Press, 2000).

18. Peter Kihss, "City to Increase Negro Policemen on Harlem Duty," *NYT*, July 21, 1964; Maurice C. Carroll and Edward J. Silberfarb, "Harlem Seethes for 3d Night; Mayor Summoned from Spain," *NYHT*, July 21, 1964.

19. Peter Kihss, "City to Increase Negro Policemen on Harlem Duty," *NYT*, July 21, 1964; Maurice C. Carroll and Edward J. Silberfarb, "Harlem Seethes for 3d Night; Mayor Summoned from Spain," *NYHT*, July 21, 1964.

20. Maurice C. Carroll and Edward J. Silberfarb, "Harlem Seethes for 3d Night; Mayor Summoned from Spain," *NYHT*, July 21, 1964.

21. George Barner, "The Negro Cop in a Race Riot," *NYAN*, July 25, 1964; Gay Talese, "A Negro Policeman in Harlem Faces Taunts and Loneliness," *NYT*, July 22, 1964.

22. Theodore Jones, "Witnesses Praise Two Negro Officers in Harlem," *NYT*, July 23, 1964.

23. Bernard Lefkowitz, "Man in the Middle: A Negro Cop," *NYP*, July 22, 1964.

24. Ibid.

25. Gay Talese, "A Negro Policeman in Harlem Faces Taunts and Loneliness," *NYT*, July 22, 1964.

26. George Barner, "The Negro Cop in a Race Riot," *NYAN*, July 25, 1964; Gay Talese, "A Negro Policeman in Harlem Faces Taunts and Loneliness," *NYT*, July 22, 1964.

27. George Barner, "The Negro Cop in a Race Riot," *NYAN*, July 25, 1964.

28. Author interview with George Barner.

29. Maurice C. Carroll and Edward J. Silberfarb, "Harlem Seethes for 3d Night; Mayor Summoned from Spain," *NYHT*, July 21, 1964; Peter Kihss, "City to Increase Negro Policemen on Harlem Duty," *NYT*, July 21, 1964.

30. Maurice C. Carroll and Edward J. Silberfarb, "Harlem Seethes for 3d Night; Mayor Summoned from Spain," *NYHT*, July 21, 1964; Peter Kihss, "City to Increase Negro Policemen on Harlem Duty," *NYT*, July 21, 1964.

31. "Tragedy in Harlem," *NYT*, July 20, 1964; "Harlem and the Police," *NYT*, July 21, 1964.

32. "After New York's Tragic Weekend: A Challenge and a Program," *NYP*, July 20, 1964.

33. "Kibitzer Kouncil," *NYDN*, July 22, 1964.

34. Hobart Taylor Jr. to Lyndon Johnson, December 3, 1963, Ex Hu2/Gen Hu 2, Box 2, WHCF, LBJ Library; "Harlem's Plea," *NYAN*, July 25, 1964.

35. "Boy's Slaying Is Going to Grand Jury Today," *NYHT*, July 21, 1964; Peter Kihss, "City to Increase Negro Policemen on Harlem Duty," *NYT*, July 21, 1964; Maurice C. Carroll and Edward J. Silberfarb, "Harlem Seethes for 3d Night; Mayor Summoned from Spain," *NYHT*, July 21, 1964.

36. "Boy's Slaying Is Going to Grand Jury Today," *NYHT*, July 21, 1964; Peter Kihss, "City to Increase Negro Policemen on Harlem Duty," *NYT*, July 21, 1964; Maurice C. Carroll and Edward J. Silberfarb, "Harlem Seethes for 3d Night; Mayor Summoned from Spain," *NYHT*, July 21, 1964.

37. Peter Kihss, "City to Increase Negro Policemen on Harlem Duty," *NYT*, July 21, 1964.

38. Ibid.

39. "Tragedy in Harlem," *NYT*, July 20, 1964.

40. Wilkins to King, Farmer, Young, Randolph, and Lewis, n.d., Box 247, Group III, Series A, LOC.

41. "Violence Erupts for Third Night," *NYT*, July 21, 1964.

42. Lael Scott and Marvin Smilon, "What Negroes Think of the Riots in Harlem," *NYP*, July 22, 1964.

43. "Violence Erupts for Third Night," *NYT*, July 21, 1964; Shapiro and Sullivan, *Race Riots*, 87–88.

44. C. Gerald Fraser, "Lewis Michaux, 92, Dies; Ran Bookstore in Harlem," *NYT*, August 27, 1976.

45. Maurice C. Carroll and Edward J. Silberfarb, "Harlem Seethes for 3d Night; Mayor Summoned from Spain," *NYHT*, July 21, 1964; "Violence Erupts for Third Night," *NYT*, July 21, 1964.

46. "Violence Erupts for Third Night," *NYT*, July 21, 1964; Shapiro and Sullivan, *Race Riots*, 92.

47. Maurice C. Carroll and Edward J. Silberfarb, "Harlem Seethes for 3d Night; Mayor Summoned from Spain," *NYHT*, July 21, 1964; "After New York's Tragic Weekend: A Challenge and a Program," *NYP*, July 20, 1964.

48. Ted Poston, "50 Injured in Harlem," *NYP*, July 21, 1964.

49. "The Negroes' Leaders: Right, Left and In-Between," *NYHT*, August 9, 1964; Shapiro and Sullivan, *Race Riots*, 94–95; author interview with Lester Carson.

50. Gay Talese, "CORE 'Imprisons' a White Member to Keep Him Safe," *NYT*, July 21, 1964; Sue Reinert, "CORE's Harlem Office—Where the Wounded Talk," *NYHT*, July 22, 1964; author interview with Gay Talese.

51. "Violence Erupts for Third Night," *NYT*, July 21, 1964; Shapiro and Sullivan, *Race Riots*, 95.

52. Jimmy Breslin, "North of 110th Street," *NYHT*, July 21, 1964; author interviews with Sergeant Barney Cohen and Detective Sonny Grosso.

53. Michael W. Flamm, "Lloyd Sealy," in Henry Louis Gates Jr. and Evelyn Brooks Higginbotham, eds., *African American National Biography*, vol. 7 (Harvard University Press, 2008), 130–131.

54. Flamm, "Lloyd Sealy," 130–131; "Harlem Police Leader: Lloyd George Sealy," *NYT*, August 15, 1964; "Welcome, Captain," *NYAN*, August 22, 1964; "Capt. Sealy Seeks Cooperation of All," *NYAN*, August 22, 1964.

55. Flamm, "Lloyd Sealy," 130–131; "Harlem Police Leader: Lloyd George Sealy," *NYT*, August 15, 1964; Robert D. McFadden, "Sealy Leaves Police Post for Teaching," *NYT*, September 4, 1969.

56. Thomas Toolen and I. Eeds Moberly, "Gangs Use Walkie-Talkies in Harlem War on Police," *NYDN*, July 21, 1964; Theodore Jones, "Witnesses Praise Two Negro Officers in Harlem," *NYT*, July 23, 1964; Albin Krebs, "Capt. Sealy Made His Mark during Riots," *NYHT*, August 15, 1964.

57. Author interview with Wayne Moreland; Ted Poston, "50 Injured in Harlem," *NYP*, July 21, 1964.

58. Shapiro and Sullivan, *Race Riots*, 94.

59. Ted Poston, "50 Injured in Harlem," *NYP*, July 21, 1964; "Violence Erupts for Third Night," *NYT*, July 21, 1964.

60. Edmond, "Harlem Diary," 21–22.

61. Ted Poston, "50 Injured in Harlem," *NYP*, July 21, 1964; Shapiro and Sullivan, *Race Riots*, 99–101.

62. "Violence Erupts for Third Night," *NYT*, July 21, 1964; Shapiro and Sullivan, *Race Riots*, 99–101.

63. White, *Making of the President*, 243–244.

64. Kay Gardella, "Harlem Riot Coverage Poses Questions for TV," *NYDN*, July 21, 1964.

65. "Violence Erupts for Third Night," *NYT*, July 21, 1964.

66. "Mobs Fight Police Again in Brooklyn and Harlem Area," *NYT*, July 22, 1964.

67. Albert Ellenberg, "B'klyn Rally Sparks Riot," *NYP*, July 21, 1964; "Mobs Fight Police Again in Brooklyn and Harlem Area," *NYT*, July 22, 1964.

CHAPTER 7. TAKE THE "A" TRAIN

1. Cartha "Deke" DeLoach, *Hoover's FBI: The Inside Story by Hoover's Trusted Lieutenant* (Regnery, 1995), 279.

2. Johnson and Kennedy, 12:25 P.M., July 21, 1964, Citation 4288 (6407.11), LBJ Library.

3. Ibid.

4. Johnson and Screvane, 12:35 P.M., July 21, 1964, Citation 4289 (6407.11), LBJ Library.

5. Johnson and Hoover, 12:40 P.M., July 21, 1964, Citation 4290 (6407.11), LBJ Library; Richard Gid Powers, *Secrecy and Power: The Life of J. Edgar Hoover* (Macmillan, 1987), 409.

6. Johnson and Hoover, 12:40 P.M., July 21, 1964, Citation 4290 (6407.11), LBJ Library.

7. Powers, *Secrecy and Power*, 418–419.

8. Ibid., 353–392.

9. Johnson and Kennedy, 1:00 P.M., July 21, 1964, Citation 4291 (6407.11), LBJ Library.

10. Ibid.

11. Johnson and Hoover, 1:06 P.M., July 21, 1964, Citation 4292 (6407.11), LBJ Library.

12. Ibid.; S. J. Dzikowski and Frances Adler to Lyndon Johnson, July 20, 1964, Box 41, Gen HU 2/ST 32–50, WHCF, LBJ Library.

13. "Statement by President," *NYT*, July 22, 1964.

14. Ibid.

15. "Editorial Comments From around Nation on Outbreak of Violence," *NYT*, July 22, 1964.

16. Ibid.

17. Ibid.

18. "Riots and Reds," *NYDN*, July 21, 1964.

19. Peter Kihss, "Screvane Links Reds to Rioting," *NYT*, July 22, 1964; "Screvane on the Communists," *NYP*, July 26, 1964.

20. Peter Kihss, "Screvane Links Reds to Rioting," *NYT*, July 22, 1964; "Screvane on the Communists," *NYP*, July 26, 1964.

21. James F. Clarity, "Robert Wagner, 80, Pivotal New York Mayor, Dies," *NYT*, February 13, 1991.

22. Joshua M. Zeitz, *White Ethnic New York: Jews, Catholics, and the Shaping of Postwar Politics* (University of North Carolina Press, 2007), 172–173; James F. Clarity, "Robert Wagner, 80, Pivotal New York Mayor, Dies," *NYT*, February 13, 1991.

23. James F. Clarity, "Robert Wagner, 80, Pivotal New York Mayor, Dies," *NYT*, February 13, 1991.

24. David Halberstam, "Mrs. Wagner Dead at 54 of Cancer," *NYT*, March 2, 1964; James F. Clarity, "Robert Wagner, 80, Pivotal New York Mayor, Dies," *NYT*, February 13, 1991.

25. "A Survey of the Political Climate in New York City," August 1964, Oliver Quayle and Company, Folder 6, Box 01B2, MI Series, Robert F. Wagner Papers, LCC.

26. Maurice C. Carroll and Edward J. Silberfarb, "Wagner Takes over in Riots; Johnson Orders FBI to City," *NYHT*, July 22, 1964; Peter Kihss, "Screvane Links Reds to Rioting," *NYT*, July 22, 1964; Maurice C. Carroll and Edward J. Silberfarb, "Mayor's Nine Points to Protect Peace," *NYHT*, July 23, 1964.

27. Maurice C. Carroll and Edward J. Silberfarb, "Mayor's Nine Points to Protect Peace," *NYHT*, July 23, 1964.

28. Maurice C. Carroll and Edward J. Silberfarb, "Wagner Takes over in Riots; Johnson Orders FBI to City," *NYHT*, July 22, 1964; Peter Kihss, "Screvane Links Reds to Rioting," *NYT*, July 22, 1964.

29. Purnell, *Fighting Jim Crow*, 48–52; Shapiro and Sullivan, *Race Riots*, 137–138.

30. "Teenagers Throw Eggs at CORE Unit Picketing the Police," *NYT*, July 22, 1964; Maurice C. Carroll and Edward J. Silberfarb, "Wagner Takes over in Riots; Johnson Orders FBI to City," *NYHT*, July 22, 1964.

31. "Teenagers Throw Eggs at CORE Unit Picketing the Police," *NYT*, July 22, 1964; Maurice C. Carroll and Edward J. Silberfarb, "Wagner Takes over in Riots; Johnson Orders FBI to City," *NYHT*, July 22, 1964.

32. Maurice C. Carroll and Edward J. Silberfarb, "Mayor's Nine Points to Protect Peace," *NYHT*, July 23, 1964; Peter Kihss, "Wagner Asserts Disorders Harm Negroes' Cause," *NYT*, July 23, 1964; "Text of Wagner's Radio-TV Appeal for Restoration of Law and Order in City," *NYT*, July 23, 1964.

33. Ted Poston, "Rioting Ebbs in Harlem," *NYP*, July 22, 1964; "Mobs Fight Police Again in Brooklyn and Harlem Area," *NYT*, July 22, 1964; Maurice C. Carroll and Edward J. Silberfarb, "Wagner Takes over in Riots; Johnson Orders FBI to City," *NYHT*, July 22, 1964.

34. Email correspondence from Bernard Witlieb to the author, July 17, 2014.

35. Shapiro and Sullivan, *Race Riots*, 186–187.

36. Ibid.

37. Ibid., 187.

38. Maurice C. Carroll and Edward J. Silberfarb, "Wagner Takes over in Riots; Johnson Orders FBI to City," *NYHT*, July 22, 1964; Shapiro and Sullivan, *Race Riots*, 187–188.

39. Edmond, "Harlem Diary," 22.

40. "Bed-Stuy," *NYT*, July 23, 1964; Gerald Sorin, *The Nurturing Neighborhood: The Brownsville Boys Club and Jewish Community in Urban America, 1940–1990* (New York University Press, 1992), 91, 159–163.

41. Suleiman Osman, *The Invention of Brownstone Brooklyn: Gentrification and the Search for Authenticity in Postwar New York* (Oxford University Press, 2011), 42. See also Craig Steven Wilder, *A Covenant with Color: Race and Social Power in Brooklyn* (Columbia University Press, 2000).

42. Tirella, *Tomorrow-Land*, 180; Osman, *Invention of Brownstone Brooklyn*, 42.

43. Freeman, *Working-Class New York*, 183; Jack Newfield, "Bedford-Stuyvesant: Portrait of a Ghetto," *NYP*, August 2, 1964; Jason Sokol, *All Eyes Are upon Us: Race and Politics from Boston to Brooklyn* (Basic Books, 2014), 49; Wilder, *Covenant with Color*, 206.

44. Osman, *Invention of Brownstone Brooklyn*, 42; "Biggest City's Nightmare—Its Crime-Ridden Schools," *U.S. News & World Report*, February 7, 1958.

45. Osman, *Invention of Brownstone Brooklyn*, 22, 61; Jack Newfield, "Bedford-Stuyvesant: Portrait of a Ghetto," *NYP*, August 2, 1964; Shapiro and Sullivan, *Race Riots*,

111, 115; Janet L. Abu-Lughod, *Race, Space, and Riots in Chicago, New York, and Los Angeles* (Oxford University Press, 2007), 160–161.

46. Jack Newfield, "Bedford-Stuyvesant: Portrait of a Ghetto," *NYP*, August 2, 1964; "The Negroes' Leaders: Right, Left and In-Between," *NYHT*, August 2, 1964.

47. Milton Galamison, "Bedford-Stuyvesant—Land of Superlatives," *Freedomways* 3 (Summer 1963): 414.

48. Purnell, *Fighting Jim Crow*, 97–127; Sokol, *All Eyes Are upon Us*, 50–53.

49. Jack Newfield, "Bedford-Stuyvesant: Portrait of a Ghetto," *NYP*, August 2, 1964; Shapiro and Sullivan, *Race Riots*, 116–120; "What We Need Most," *NYAN*, August 8, 1964.

50. "Mobs Fight Police Again in Brooklyn and Harlem Area," *NYT*, July 22, 1964.

51. Shapiro and Sullivan, *Race Riots*, 135.

52. Ibid.

53. Ibid., 135–137.

54. Ibid., 138.

55. Ibid., 138–139.

56. Maurice C. Carroll and Edward J. Silberfarb, "Wagner Takes over in Riots; Johnson Orders FBI to City," *NYHT*, July 22, 1964; Alfred T. Hendricks, "Looters on Brooklyn Rampage," *NYP*, July 22, 1964.

57. Maurice C. Carroll and Edward J. Silberfarb, "Wagner Takes over in Riots; Johnson Orders FBI to City," *NYHT*, July 22, 1964; Alfred T. Hendricks, "Looters on Brooklyn Rampage," *NYP*, July 22, 1964.

58. "Brooklyn Riots Continue; Police Shoot 2 as Looters," *NYT*, July 23, 1964; Robert W. White and Fred C. Shapiro, "Mayor's Nine Points: The Protest," *NYHT*, July 23, 1964; Maurice C. Carroll and Edward J. Silberfarb, "Wagner Takes over in Riots; Johnson Orders FBI to City," *NYHT*, July 22, 1964; Alfred T. Hendricks, "Looters on Brooklyn Rampage," *NYP*, July 22, 1964.

59. Shapiro and Sullivan, *Race Riots*, 149.

60. Ibid., 142, 147.

61. Ibid., 142–144.

62. Ibid.

63. Ibid., 144–145.

64. "Mobs Fight Police Again in Brooklyn and Harlem Area," *NYT*, July 22, 1964; Maurice C. Carroll and Edward J. Silberfarb, "Wagner Takes over in Riots; Johnson Orders FBI to City," *NYHT*, July 22, 1964.

65. O'Neil, *Cop's Tale*, 47.

66. Ibid., 47–48.

67. Ibid., 48.

68. Shapiro and Sullivan, *Race Riots*, 145, 203.

69. O'Neil, *Cop's Tale*, 49.

70. "Brooklyn Riots Continue; Police Shoot 2 as Looters," *NYT*, July 23, 1964.

71. Ibid.

72. Shapiro and Sullivan, *Race Riots*, 148.

73. Jesse H. Walker, "'Not a Race Riot' Says Adam Powell," *NYAN*, July 25, 1964.

74. Ibid.

75. "Arrest All Agitators," Negro Cleric Urges," *NYDN*, July 22, 1964; "Cleric Assails 2 as Inciters or Riots," *NYT*, July 22, 1964.

320 Notes to Pages 167–173

76. Barbara Benson, "Letters to the Times," *NYT*, July 22, 1964.

77. Ibid.

CHAPTER 8. COMMUNISTS, CONSERVATIVES, AND CONSPIRACIES

1. Presidential Daily Diary, July 22, 1964, LBJ Library; Jack Mallon, William Federich, and Henry Lee, "Blame Hate Groups, Red & White, for Harlem Terror," *NYDN*, July 22, 1964.

2. Author interview with Anthony Bouza.

3. Jack Mallon, William Federich, and Henry Lee, "Blame Hate Groups, Red & White, for Harlem Terror," *NYDN*, July 22, 1964.

4. Jack Mallon, William Federich, and Henry Lee, "Blame Hate Groups, Red & White, for Harlem Terror," *NYDN*, July 22, 1964; Shapiro and Sullivan, *Race Riots*, 205; "The Negroes' Leaders: Right, Left and In-Between," *NYHT*, August 9, 1964.

5. Johnson and Hoover, 5:25 P.M., September 9, 1964, Citation 5555 (6409.08), LBJ Library.

6. Peter Kihss, "Wagner Appeals for End to Riots," *NYT*, July 23, 1964; William Federici and Henry Lee, "A Lot of Secret Cash Spurred Riots," *NYDN*, July 23, 1964.

7. Peter Kihss, "Wagner Appeals for End to Riots," *NYT*, July 23, 1964; Bill Whitworth, "Rights Chiefs Deny Reds Incited Riots," *NYHT*, July 23, 1964; William Federici and Henry Lee, "A Lot of Secret Cash Spurred Riots," *NYDN*, July 23, 1964.

8. Peter Kihss, "Wagner Appeals for End to Riots," *NYT*, July 23, 1964; Bill Whitworth, "Rights Chiefs Deny Reds Incited Riots," *NYHT*, July 23, 1964; William Federici and Henry Lee, "A Lot of Secret Cash Spurred Riots," *NYDN*, July 23, 1964; "The Negroes' Leaders: Right, Left, and In-Between," *NYHT*, August 9, 1964.

9. Alexander Wohl, *Father, Son, and Constitution: How Justice Tom Clark and Ramsey Clark Shaped American Democracy* (University Press of Kansas, 2013), 297; Julie A. Gallagher, *Women in American History: Black Women and Politics in New York City* (University of Illinois Press, 2012), 142–143.

10. Bill Whitworth, "Rights Chiefs Deny Reds Incited Riots," *NYHT*, July 23, 1964; David Lawrence, "Role of the Communists in Race Riots," *NYHT*, July 23, 1964.

11. Jack Mallon, William Federich, and Henry Lee, "Blame Hate Groups, Red & White, for Harlem Terror," *NYDN*, July 22, 1964; author interview with Marvin Rich.

12. Johnson and Wagner, 8:39 A.M., July 22, 1964, Citation 4304 (6407.12), LBJ Library; Maurice C. Carroll and Edward J. Silberfarb, "Mayor's Nine Points to Protect Peace," *NYHT*, July 23, 1964.

13. Johnson and Wagner, 8:39 A.M., July 22, 1964, Citation 4304 (6407.12), LBJ Library.

14. Ibid.

15. Hoover to Tolson, DeLoach, et al., July 21, 1964, Section 13, MLK MF, 100-106670, FBI Papers.

16. Ibid.

17. Johnson and Hoover, 9:26 A.M., July 22, 1964, Citation 4305 (6407.12), LBJ Library.

18. Hoover to Tolson, DeLoach, et al., July 22, 1964, Section 13, MLK MF, 100-106670, FBI Papers; Branch, *Pillar of Fire*, 418.

19. "Plundered Storekeepers of Brooklyn Take Stock," *NYP*, July 23, 1964.

20. Michael Pollak, "F.Y.I.," *NYT*, April 22, 2007.

21. Shapiro and Sullivan, *Race Riots*, 155–156.

22. Jonathan P. Hicks, "For a Staunch Republican, Ousting a Rival Superseded Party Loyalty," *NYT*, November 17, 1996; John McGee and Sidney Kline, "Fire Murphy and Arm, Negroes Demand," *NYDN*, July 23, 1964.

23. "The Word Goes Out," Series I, Box 332, Democratic National Committee Papers, LBJ Library.

24. Author interview with Percy Sutton.

25. Shapiro and Sullivan, *Race Riots*, 161.

26. Ibid., 161–162.

27. Alfred T. Hendricks and Edward Cumberbatch, "More Looting in Brooklyn; Harlem Quiet," *NYP*, July 23, 1964.

28. Ibid.

29. Shapiro and Sullivan, *Race Riots*, 163.

30. Ibid., 163–164.

31. "Brooklyn Rioting Goes on 3D Night," *NYT*, July 23, 1964.

32. "Remarks by Mayor Robert F. Wagner," July 22, 1964, Folder 9, Wagner Papers, LCC; Peter Kihss, "Wagner Appeals for End to Riots," *NYT*, July 23, 1964.

33. "Remarks by Mayor Robert F. Wagner," July 22, 1964, Folder 9, Wagner Papers, LCC.

34. Ibid.; R. W. Apple Jr., "Tourism in City Hurt by Rioting," *NYT*, July 23, 1964.

35. "Remarks by Mayor Robert F. Wagner," July 22, 1964, Folder 9, Wagner Papers, LCC.

36. Ibid.

37. Robert Wagner Oral History, CUOHP, 992–995, 1020.

38. "Remarks by Mayor Robert F. Wagner," July 22, 1964, Folder 9, Wagner Papers, LCC; "Harlem Is Big News in Soviet Union and Spain," *NYT*, July 24, 1964; Dudziak, *Cold War Civil Rights*, 215.

39. "The Communist Angle," *NYP*, July 23, 1964.

40. "Harlem Minister Hails Mayor's Talk on Riots," *NYT*, July 23, 1964.

41. Ralph Blumenfeld, "Negroes to Mayor: 'Not Enough,'" *NYP*, July 23, 1964; Maurice C. Carroll and Edward J. Silberfarb, "Mayor's Nine Points to Protect Peace," *NYHT*, July 23, 1964; NAACP press release, July 23, 1964, Box C103, Series III, NAACP Papers, LOC.

42. Robert W. White and Fred C. Shapiro, "Mayor's Nine Points: The Protest," *NYHT*, July 23, 1964.

43. Shapiro and Sullivan, *Race Riots*, 172.

44. "Brooklyn Rioting Goes on 3D Night," *NYT*, July 23, 1964; Shapiro and Sullivan, *Race Riots*, 169; "Relative Calm Is Restored to Riot-Torn Areas Here," *NYT*, July 24, 1964; John McGee and Sidney Kline, "Fire Murphy and Arm, Negroes Demand," *NYDN*, July 23, 1964.

45. Shapiro and Sullivan, *Race Riots*, 168, 170.

46. Ibid., 169–170.

47. "Brooklyn Rioting Goes on 3D Night," *NYT*, July 23, 1964; Shapiro and Sullivan, *Race Riots*, 168.

48. Shapiro and Sullivan, *Race Riots*, 170.

49. Ibid., 172.

50. Alfred T. Hendricks and Edward Cumberbatch, "More Looting in Brooklyn; Harlem Quiet," *NYP*, July 23, 1964; "Brooklyn Rioting Goes on 3d Night," *NYT*, July 23, 1964.

51. Kenneth Gross, "Whites Stone CORE Pickets," *NYP*, July 23, 1964; "White Youths Clash with CORE Pickets," *NYT*, July 23, 1964.

52. Kenneth Gross, "Whites Stone CORE Pickets," *NYP*, July 23, 1964; "White Youths Clash with CORE Pickets," *NYT*, July 23, 1964.

53. Kenneth Gross, "Whites Stone CORE Pickets," *NYP*, July 23, 1964; "White Youths Clash with CORE Pickets," *NYT*, July 23, 1964.

54. Ralph Blumenfeld, "Negroes to Mayor: 'Not Enough,'" *NYP*, July 23, 1964.

55. Ibid.

56. Jimmy Breslin, "More to Come?" *NYHT*, July 23, 1964; Jimmy Breslin, *I Want to Thank My Brain for Remembering Me: A Memoir* (Little, Brown, 1996), 258–259.

57. Jimmy Breslin, "Our Town's Nightmare," *NYHT*, July 24, 1964.

58. Peter Kihss, "Cavanagh Picks 6 to Aid His Review of Police Cases," *NYT*, July 24, 1964; Alfred T. Hendricks and Edward Cumberbatch, "More Looting in Brooklyn; Harlem Quiet," *NYP*, July 23, 1964.

CHAPTER 9. MAKE SOMEBODY LISTEN

1. Marjorie Hunter, "Antipoverty Bill Passed in Senate by 62–33 Vote," *NYT*, July 24, 1964; Rick Perlstein, *Before the Storm: Barry Goldwater and the Unmaking of the American Consensus* (Hill and Wang, 2001), 430.

2. Johnson and Meany, July 28, 1964, Citation 4360 (6407.15), LBJ Library; Johnson and Mahon, July 29, 1964, Citation 4407 (6407.18).

3. Mitchell Lerner, "'To Be Shot at by the Whites and Dodged by the Negroes: Lyndon Johnson and the Texas NYA," *Presidential Studies Quarterly* 39 (June 2009): 245–274.

4. Frank Holeman, "We Will Enforce Civil Order Laws, Too: LBJ," *NYDN*, July 24, 1964.

5. Johnson and Connally, 5:31 p.m., July 23, 1964, Citations 4321 and 4322 (6407.13), LBJ Library.

6. Ibid.

7. Robert W. White and Fred C. Shapiro, "Violence Subsides on 6th Night; Police Brace for Weekend," *NYHT*, July 24, 1964; "Fine Speech, Mr. Mayor," *NYDN*, July 24, 1964; "What the Mayor Didn't Say," *NYP*, July 23, 1964.

8. "Justified Demands," *NYAN*, August 1, 1964.

9. Foster Hailey, "Survey Shows Few Cities Use Civilian Boards," *NYT*, July 24, 1964; Gertrude Samuels, "Who Shall Judge a Policeman?" *NYT Magazine*, August 2, 1964; "Come on Harlem—Let's Play It Smart," *NYAN*, July 25, 1964.

10. "Brooklyn Riots Continue; Police Shoot 2 as Looters," *NYT*, July 24, 1964; Robert W. White and Fred C. Shapiro, "Violence Subsides on 6th Night; Police Brace for Weekend," *NYHT*, July 24, 1964.

11. Robert W. White and Fred C. Shapiro, "Violence Subsides on 6th Night; Police Brace for Weekend," *NYHT*, July 24, 1964; "Brooklyn Riots Continue; Police Shoot 2 as Looters," *NYT*, July 24, 1964.

12. Shapiro and Sullivan, *Race Riots*, 174; Robert W. White and Fred C. Shapiro, "Violence Subsides on 6th Night; Police Brace for Weekend," *NYHT*, July 24, 1964.

13. Shapiro and Sullivan, *Race Riots*, 175.

14. "Brooklyn Riots Continue; Police Shoot 2 as Looters," *NYT*, July 24, 1964.

15. Robert W. White and Fred C. Shapiro, "Violence Subsides on 6th Night; Police Brace for Weekend," *NYHT*, July 24, 1964; Fred Powledge, "Mulberry Street Is Angered Over CORE Pickets," *NYT*, July 24, 1964.

16. Robert W. White and Fred C. Shapiro, "Violence Subsides on 6th Night; Police Brace for Weekend," *NYHT*, July 24, 1964; "Relative Calm Is Restored to Riot-Torn Areas Here," *NYT*, July 24, 1964.

17. Patrick Doyle, Sidney Kline, and Richard Henry, "Sixth Night: Mob Beats Up Six COREmen," *NYDN*, July 24, 1964; Robert W. White and Fred C. Shapiro, "Violence Subsides on 6th Night; Police Brace for Weekend," *NYHT*, July 24, 1964; "Relative Calm Is Restored to Riot-Torn Areas Here," *NYT*, July 24, 1964.

18. "Behind Little Italy's Riot: Pride—and Prejudice," *NYHT*, July 26, 1964.

19. Ibid.

20. Robert W. White and Fred C. Shapiro, "Violence Subsides on 6th Night; Police Brace for Weekend," *NYHT*, July 24, 1964; author interview with Roy Innes; Jonathan Rieder, *Canarsie: The Jews and Italians of Brooklyn against Liberalism* (Harvard University Press, 1985), 132–141.

21. Shapiro and Sullivan, *Race Riots*, 179–180.

22. Ibid.

23. "The Week's Riot Toll," *NYP*, July 26, 1964; Peter Kihss, "Harlem Planner Urges More City Aid," *NYT*, February 12, 1965; Emanuel Perlmutter, "Police Costs in Riot Put at $1.5 Million," *NYT*, July 26, 1964.

24. Terry Smith, "Harlem Leaders on Harlem Riots—Gain for Black Nationalists," *NYHT*, July 27, 1964.

25. "The Principal Losers," *NYHT*, July 26, 1964.

26. Author interviews with C. Gerald Fraser and Earl Caldwell; Earl Caldwell, *The Caldwell Journals*, chaps. 8–11, http://mije.org/historyproject/caldwell_journals (accessed May 5, 2015).

27. Author interviews with C. Gerald Fraser and Earl Caldwell; Earl Caldwell, *The Caldwell Journals*, chaps. 8–11, http://mije.org/historyproject/caldwell_journals (accessed May 5, 2015).

28. William Federici and Henry Lee, "Cops & Commissioner Wonder: What about Civilian Brutality?" *NYDN*, July 24, 1964.

29. Ibid.

30. William Federici and Henry Lee, "Cops & Commissioner Wonder: What about Civilian Brutality?" *NYDN*, July 24, 1964; Shapiro and Sullivan, *Race Riots*, 167.

31. James Lardner and Thomas Reppetto, *NYPD: A City and Its Police* (Henry Holt, 2000), 280–284; Vincent J. Cannato, *The Ungovernable City: John Lindsay and His Struggle to Save New York* (Basic Books, 2001), 132–141.

32. Sam Rubenstein, "The Bedford-Stuyvesant Toll," *NYHT*, July 24, 1964; William Federici and Henry Lee, "Cops & Commissioner Wonder: What about Civilian Brutality?" *NYDN*, July 24, 1964.

33. William Federici and Henry Lee, "Cops & Commissioner Wonder: What about Civilian Brutality?" *NYDN*, July 24, 1964. Even the TPF was trained primarily in handling political demonstrations, not civil disorders. Author interview with Robert Leuci.

34. "Calls It Murder," *NYAN*, August 1, 1964; "He's Sorry," *NYAN*, August 1, 1964.

35. "Sounds of Violence" and "No Excuse," *NYAN*, August 1, 1964.

36. Jackie Robinson, "Goldwater Ammunition," *NYAN*, August 1, 1964; Michael Beschloss, "Jackie Robinson and Nixon: Life and Death of a Political Friendship," *NYT*, June 6, 2014.

37. Edmond, "Harlem Diary," 26–27, See also the telegram from the women of the Abyssinian Baptist Church to Lyndon Johnson, August 2, 1964, Box 28, Ex JL 3, WHCF, LBJ Library.

38. Fogelson, *Violence as Protest*, 38.

39. Rustin, "Harlem Riot & Nonviolence," 495.

40. Shapiro and Sullivan, *Race Riots*, 206.

41. Fogelson, *Violence as Protest*, 42–43.

42. Author interview with George Barner.

43. For a defense of the "rising expectations" thesis, see Siddharth Chandra and Angela Williams Foster, "The 'Revolution of Rising Expectations,' Relative Deprivation, and the Urban Social Disorders of the 1960s," *Social Science History* 29 (Summer 2005): 299–332.

44. "James Baldwin on the Harlem Riots," *NYP*, August 2, 1964. Baldwin was "merchandising the mythology of mayhem," asserted Talese, who nonetheless knew and liked him. Author interview with Gay Talese.

45. "Where Are They Now?" *Newsweek*, August 3, 1964.

46. Langston Hughes, "Harlem—IIII," *NYP*, July 23, 1964.

47. Langston Hughes, "The Down Boys," *NYP*, July 26, 1964.

48. Poston, "Violence in Harlem," 27–28.

49. "No Place Like Home," *Time*, July 31, 1964.

CHAPTER 10. CALMING THE WATERS

1. Bill Moyers to Lyndon Johnson, Box 32, WHOF of Bill Moyers, LBJ Library.

2. "The Campaign: The Proper Stance," *Time*, July 31, 1964; Bill Moyers to Lyndon Johnson, Box 32, WHOF of Bill Moyers, LBJ Library.

3. Bill Moyers to Lyndon Johnson, Box 32, WHOF of Bill Moyers, LBJ Library; "Civil Rights: The White House Meeting," *Newsweek*, August 3, 1964.

4. James W. Sullivan and Maurice C. Carroll, "Harlem Marchers to Defy Ban," *NYHT*, July 25, 1964.

5. "Civil Rights: The White House Meeting," *Newsweek*, August 3, 1964; Marjorie Hunter, "'Extremist Elements' Involved in Rioting Here, Johnson Says," *NYT*, July 24, 1964.

6. Moyers to LBJ, July 24, 1964, Box 7, Diary Backup; Reedy to LBJ, July 24, 1964, Box 7, Diary Backup; Goodwin to LBJ, July 24, 1964, Box 7, Diary Backup. All in LBJ Library.

7. Dallek, *Flawed Giant*, 134; Jack Bell, *The Johnson Treatment: How Lyndon B. Johnson Took over the Presidency and Made It His Own* (Harper & Row, 1965), 173; "Civil Rights: The White House Meeting," *Newsweek*, August 3, 1964, 15; Barry Goldwater, *With No Apologies: The Personal and Political Memoirs of United States Senator Barry M. Goldwater* (William Morrow, 1979), 192–193.

8. Lee White, Bill Moyers, Jack Valenti, and Douglass Cater to LBJ, July 24, 1964, attached to Moyers to LBJ, n.d., WHOF of Bill Moyers, Box 32, LBJ Library; presidential statement, July 24, 1964, Box 10, 1964, PCF, Goldwater Papers, AHF.

9. Edwards, *Goldwater*, 242; Jack Valenti Oral History, LBJ Library; "Civil Rights: The White House Meeting," *Newsweek*, August 3, 1964.

10. Michael Beschloss, ed., *Taking Charge: The Johnson White House Tapes, 1963–1964* (Simon & Schuster, 1997), 472, 474.

11. William H. Rudy, "80 Hurt as Negroes Battle Rochester Cops," *NYP*, July 26, 1964; "Rochester Police Battle Race Riot," *NYT*, July 25, 1964; Fred Ferretti, "Why 'Serene' Rochester Exploded," *NYHT*, July 26, 1964.

12. Arthur L. Whitaker, "Racial Disorder in Rochester, New York," n.d., Box C106, Administrative File (III), NAACP Papers, LOC; Eison and Christopher, *July '64*.

13. Arthur L. Whitaker, "Racial Disorder in Rochester, New York," n.d., Box C106, Administrative File (III), NAACP Papers, LOC; James W. Sullivan, "Copter Crash, Three Die in Negro Area," *NYHT*, July 27, 1964; Joseph Lelyveld, "Kodak Says Rochester Offers Few Skilled Negroes," *NYT*, July 29, 1964.

14. "Report of Youth Secretary," n.d., Box C106, Administrative File (III); NAACP Papers, LOC.

15. Jim Myers and James Goodman, "The Night the City's Streets Erupted," *RDC*, July 22, 1984.

16. James W. Sullivan, "Violent Mobs Defy Curfew—Man Killed," *NYHT*, July 26, 1964; "Rochester Beset by New Rioting; White Man Dead," *NYT*, July 26, 1964.

17. Jim Myers and James Goodman, "Few Whites Could Believe It, but the City Was Ripe for Rage," *RDC*, July 22, 1984.

18. Jim Myers and James Goodman, "The Night the City's Streets Erupted," *RDC*, July 22, 1984; William H. Rudy, "80 Hurt as Negroes Battle Rochester Cops," *NYHT*, July 26, 1964; "Rochester Beset by New Rioting; White Man Dead," *NYT*, July 26, 1964; Eison and Christopher, *July '64*.

19. Jim Myers and James Goodman, "The Night the City's Streets Erupted," *RDC*, July 22, 1984; "Rochester Police Battle Race Riot," *NYT*, July 25, 1964; James W. Sullivan, "Violent Mobs Defy Curfew—Man Killed," *NYHT*, July 26, 1964; "Rochester Beset by New Rioting; White Man Dead," *NYT*, July 26, 1964; Sean Dobbin, "Five Decades," *RDC*, February 2, 2014; James Goodman, "Three Days That Shook Rochester," *RDC*, July 20, 2014.

20. Jim Myers and James Goodman, "Few Whites Could Believe It, but the City Was Ripe for Rage," *RDC*, July 22, 1984; Jim Myers and James Goodman, "The Night the City's Streets Erupted," *RDC*, July 22, 1984.

21. "Rochester Beset by New Rioting; White Man Dead," *NYT*, July 26, 1964; Eison and Christopher, *July '64*.

22. Fred Powledge, "In One Part of the City, Looting; In Another, 'Nothing Left to Loot,'" *NYT*, July 26, 1964; James W. Sullivan, "Rockefeller Visit . . . ," *NYHT*, July 28, 1964; "Report of Youth Secretary," n.d., Box C106, Administrative File (III); NAACP Papers, LOC.

23. James W. Sullivan, "Violent Mobs Defy Curfew—Man Killed," *NYHT*, July 26, 1964.

24. "Rochester Beset by New Rioting; White Man Dead," *NYT*, July 26, 1964; Eison and Christopher, *July '64*.

25. Ramsey Clark Oral History, LBJ Library.

26. Johnson and Katzenbach, 10:15 A.M., July 25, 1964, Citation 4337–4339 (6407.14), LBJ Library.

27. "Violence Subsides," *NYHT*, July 24, 1964; James W. Sullivan and Maurice C. Carroll, "Harlem Marchers to Defy Ban," *NYHT*, July 25, 1964.

28. R. W. Apple Jr., "Police Ban March in Harlem Today; Sponsors Defiant," *NYT*, July 25, 1964; R. W. Apple Jr., "Protest Leaders Seized in Harlem," *NYT*, July 26, 1964; Edward J. Silberfarb and Maurice C. Carroll, "Harlem 'March': Leader Arrested," *NYHT*, July 26, 1964.

29. Jack Roth, "Criminal Anarchy Charged to Epton in Indictment Here," *NYT*, August 6, 1964; Douglas Martin, "William Epton, 70, Is Dead; Tested Free-Speech Limits," *NYT*, February 3, 2002.

30. James W. Sullivan, "Violent Mobs Defy Curfew—Man Killed," *NYHT*, July 26, 1964; "Rochester Beset by New Rioting; White Man Dead," *NYT*, July 26, 1964.

31. James W. Sullivan, "Copter Crash, Three Die in Negro Area," *NYHT*, July 27, 1964; James Goodman, "Three Days That Shook Rochester," *RDC*, July 20, 2014.

32. Joseph Lelyveld, "1000 National Guardsmen Are Sent into Rochester to Help Halt Race Riots," *NYT*, July 27, 1964; Bernard Gavzer, "The Faces in the Crowd," *New York Post*, July 27, 1964.

33. "After Action Report," Major General A. C. O'Hara to Rockefeller, July 27, 1964, Folder 37, Box 17, RG 15, RAC; Joseph Lelyveld, "1000 National Guardsmen Are Sent into Rochester to Help Halt Race Riots," *NYT*, July 27, 1964.

34. "After Action Report," Major General A. C. O'Hara to Rockefeller, July 27, 1964, Folder 37, Box 17, RG 15, RAC; James W. Sullivan, "Copter Crash, Three Die in Negro Area," *NYHT*, July 27, 1964; Hanson W. Baldwin, "Army's Methods of Riot Control Vary with Area and Conditions," *NYT*, July 28, 1964.

35. Governor's Commission on the Los Angeles Riots, "Violence in the City—An End or a Beginning?" in Anthony M. Platt, ed., *The Politics of Riot Commissions, 1917–1970* (Macmillan, 1971), 284n1; James W. Sullivan, "Rockefeller Visit . . .," *NYHT*, July 28, 1964; James Goodman and Brian Sharp, "Riots Spawned FIGHT, Other Community Efforts," *RDC*, July 20, 2014.

36. James W. Sullivan, "Rockefeller Visit . . . ," *NYHT*, July 28, 1964.

37. Transcript of Governor Rockefeller's News Conference, July 27, 1964, Folder 345, Box 17, Series 25, RG 15, RAC; James W. Sullivan, "Rockefeller Visit . . . ," *NYHT*, July 28, 1964.

38. James W. Sullivan, "Copter Crash, Three Die in Negro Area," *NYHT*, July 27, 1964; James W. Sullivan, "Rockefeller Visit . . . ," *NYHT*, July 28, 1964.

39. Arthur L. Whitaker, "Racial Disorder in Rochester, New York," n.d., Box C106, Administrative File (III), NAACP Papers, LOC.

40. Ibid.

41. Author interview with Rachelle Horowitz; Levine, *Bayard Rustin*, 164.

42. Layhmond Robinson, "Negroes' View of Plight Examined in Survey Here," *NYT*, July 27, 1964.

43. Ibid.

44. "Dr. King's Knifer Sent to Bellevue," September 22, 1958, http://mlk-kpp01 .stanford.edu/index.php/encyclopedia/encyclopedia/enc_curry_izola_ware_1916/ (accessed

August 28, 2014); Breslin, *I Want to Thank My Brain*, 260–261; David Garrow, *Bearing the Cross: Martin Luther King, Jr., and the Southern Christian Leadership Conference* (Vintage, 1988), 109–111.

45. "Dr. King's Knifer Sent to Bellevue," September 22, 1958, http://mlk-kpp01.stanford.edu/index.php/encyclopedia/encyclopedia/enc_curry_izola_ware_1916/ (accessed August 28, 2014); Margalit Fox, "Izola Ware Curry, Who Stabbed King in 1958, Dies at 98," *NYT*, March 21, 2015.

46. Branch, *Pillar of Fire*, 396.

47. "Riots Hurt Cause: King," *NYDN*, July 22, 1964; "Now Let's Hear from Dr. King," *NYHT*, July 23, 1964.

48. Edward J. Silberfarb, "King and Wagner in Conference," *NYHT*, July 28, 1964.

49. Ibid.

50. Larry Klein, "Wagner-King Talks Go On; Capital Calls," *NYHT*, July 29, 1964; Edward J. Silberfarb, "King and Wagner in Conference," *NYHT*, July 28, 1964.

51. Larry Klein, "Wagner-King Talks Go On; Capital Calls," *NYHT*, July 29, 1964; Philip Benjamin, "Harlem Leaders Charge Dr. King Is Ignoring Them," *NYT*, July 29, 1964.

52. Branch, *Pillar of Fire*, 423; memos to Hoover, July 28 and 30, 1964, Section 14, MLK MF, 100-106670, FBI Papers.

53. Kenneth Gross and Ted Poston, "Wagner and King Draft 'Peace,'" *NYP*, July 28, 1964.

54. Ruby Dee and Ossie Davis to King, July 28, 1964, Bayard Rustin Papers, Reel 3, LOC.

55. Ibid.

56. Larry Klein, "Wagner-King Talks Go On; Capital Calls," *NYHT*, July 29, 1964.

57. James W. Sullivan, "The Soul Searching Begins in Rochester," *NYHT*, July 29, 1964; Henry Beckett, "Jesse Gray Back on Stand," *NYP*, July 29, 1964.

58. Memo to Hoover, July 29, 1964, Section 14, MLK MF, 100-106670, FBI Papers; "Dr. King Explains How, Why He Came to New York," *NYAN*, August 8, 1964.

59. Memos to Hoover, July 27 and 29, 1964, Section 14, MLK MF, 100-106670, FBI Papers; Sue Reinert, "Leaders Call for Negro Action in Voting Booths, Not Streets," *NYHT*, July 30, 1964.

60. Sue Reinert, "Leaders Call for Negro Action in Voting Booths, Not Streets," *NYHT*, July 30, 1964.

61. Irene Kawin to James Farmer, July 24, 1964, Reel 3, A1:33, CORE papers, LOC.

62. Nick Kotz, *Judgment Days: Lyndon Baines Johnson, Martin Luther King Jr., and the Laws That Changed America* (Houghton Mifflin, 2005), 185.

63. "The Ghetto Ignites," *The Nation*, August 10, 1964.

64. Kotz, *Judgment Days*, 185; author interviews with Norman Hill, Velma Hill, Marvin Rich, and Alan Gartner; "Farmer's Top Aide Resigns; CORE's Ranks Split by Rift," *NYAN*, September 5, 1964.

65. Richard Severo, "James Farmer, Civil Rights Giant in the 50's and 60's, Is Dead at 79," *NYT*, July 21, 1999; author interview with Fred Powledge.

66. Dr. Martin Luther King, Jr., "Negroes-Whites Together," *NYAN*, August 15, 1964.

67. Sue Reinert, "Negroes' Summit Pact Begins to Come Apart," *NYHT*, July 31, 1964; minutes, NAACP Board of Directors meeting, September 14, 1964, Box A26, Series III, NAACP Papers, LOC.

68. NAACP press release, July 31, 1964, Box C106, Series III, NAACP Papers, LOC; Sue Reinert, "Leaders Call for Negro Action in Voting Booths, Not Streets," *NYHT*, July 30, 1964.

69. "Texts of Statements by Negro Leaders," *NYT*, July 30, 1964.

70. "Who Speaks for the Negro?" *NYT*, July 30, 1964; "Wise Move," *NYAN*, August 1, 1964; "No Surrender," *NYAN*, August 8, 1964.

71. "Rights Protest Curb Favored by Johnson," *NYT*, July 31, 1964.

72. Sue Reinert, "Negroes' Summit Pact Begins to Come Apart," *NYHT*, July 31, 1964; R. W. Apple Jr., "Negro Leaders Split over Call to Curtail Drive," *NYT*, July 31, 1964.

73. Sue Reinert, "Negroes' Summit Pact Begins to Come Apart," *NYHT*, July 31, 1964.

74. R. W. Apple Jr., "Negro Leaders Split over Call to Curtail Drive," *NYT*, July 31, 1964.

75. "Civil Rights: Calculated Risk," *Newsweek*, August 10, 1964; Sue Reinert, "Negroes' Summit Pact Begins to Come Apart," *NYHT*, July 31, 1964; R. W. Apple Jr., "Negro Leaders Split over Call to Curtail Drive," *NYT*, July 31, 1964.

76. "Wonders Never Cease," *Pittsburgh Courier*, August 8, 1964; Hobart Taylor Jr. to Lyndon Johnson, December 3, 1963, Ex Hu 2/Gen Hu 2, Box 2, WHCF, LBJ Library.

77. D'Emilio, *Lost Prophet*, 386.

78. "Patrolman Slain by East Side Thug," *NYT*, July 28, 1964; "Simple Eloquence," *Spring 3100*, September 1964.

79. "Statement of Dr. King," Folder 487, Box 109095B, MACNY; Branch, *Pillar of Fire*, 423; Sue Reinert, "Dr. King Ends Talks; Bitterness at Murphy," *NYHT*, July 31, 1964.

80. Ibid.

81. Robert Wagner Oral History, CUOHP, 993; Levine, *Bayard Rustin*, 164–165.

82. Paul L. Montgomery, "CORE to Continue Its Direct Action," *NYT*, August 10, 1964; "Adam Blasts Dr. King and Mayor," *NYAN*, August 15, 1964; M. C. Blackman, "Powell Claims the Leadership of Harlem; Poverty Bill, Too," *NYHT*, August 17, 1964; Julian E. Zelizer, *The Fierce Urgency of Now: Lyndon Johnson, Congress, and the Battle for the Great Society* (Penguin, 2015), 140–141.

83. Thomas F. Jackson, *From Civil Rights to Human Rights: Martin Luther King, Jr. and the Struggle for Economic Justice* (University of Pennsylvania Press, 2006); Garrow, *Bearing the Cross*, 344.

84. "Text of Wagner's Statement on Harlem," *NYT*, August 1, 1964.

85. Robert Wagner Oral History, CUOHP, 997–998; Junius Griffin, "Coalition of 69 Negro Groups Gives Shaky Unity to Harlem," *NYT*, August 1, 1964.

CHAPTER 11. ALL THE WAY WITH LBJ

1. Johnson and Wilkins, 8:54 A.M., July 27, 1964, Citation 4361 (6407.16), LBJ Library.

2. Unsigned memo, July 27, 1964, Box 25, Ex JL3, WHCF, LBJ Library.

3. Ibid.

4. Ibid.

5. Lyndon Baines Johnson, *The Vantage Point: Perspectives of the Presidency, 1963–1969* (Holt, Rinehart and Winston, 1971), 95, 160.

6. Robert Mann, *Daisy Petals and Mushroom Clouds: LBJ, Goldwater, and the Ad that Changed American Politics* (Louisiana State University Press, 2011).

7. Johnson and Kennedy, 5 P.M., July 27, 1964, Citation 4359 (6407.15), LBJ Library.

8. Ibid.

9. Ibid.

10. Ibid.

11. Jeff Shesol, *Mutual Contempt: Lyndon Johnson, Robert Kennedy, and the Feud That Defined a Decade* (Norton, 1998).

12. Ibid., 3, 56.

13. Dallek, *Flawed Giant*, 139–140; Arthur M. Schlesinger, Jr., *Robert Kennedy and His Times* (Ballantine Books, 1978), 711–713; Shesol, *Mutual Contempt*, 207.

14. Dallek, *Flawed Giant*, 140–141; Schlesinger, *Robert Kennedy*, 713; Shesol, *Mutual Contempt*, 207.

15. Schlesinger, *Robert Kennedy*, 714; Dallek, *Flawed Giant*, 141–142.

16. Schlesinger, *Robert Kennedy*, 715.

17. Lady Bird Johnson [Claudia T. Johnson], *A White House Diary* (Holt, Rinehart and Winston, 1970), 187.

18. Ibid.

19. Ibid.

20. "Governor Orders Guard Recalled from Rochester," *NYT*, August 3, 1964; Terry Smith, "Harlem: Return to 'Normal Tension' after the Explosive Days of Rioting," *NYHT*, August 2, 1964; Edmond, "Harlem Diary," 26.

21. Terry Smith, "Harlem: Return to 'Normal Tension' after the Explosive Days of Rioting," *NYHT*, August 2, 1964.

22. "Negroes and Police Clash in Jersey City," *NYT*, August 3, 1964; "Viet Reds Fire on Our Warship" and "Rioting Erupts in Jersey City," *NYHT*, August 3, 1964.

23. David Lawrence, "Federal Powers and Racial Riots," *NYHT*, August 4, 1964.

24. Yarmolinsky would later promote the idea of a Police Corps similar to the Peace Corps. Adam Yarmolinsky to Douglass Cater, August 10, 1964, Box 17, WHOF of S. Douglass Cater, LBJ Library.

25. Anthony Lewis, "Johnson Pledges Restraint Abroad and in Race Issue," *NYT*, August 13, 1964; "Text of Address by Johnson to Lawyers," *NYT*, August 13, 1964.

26. Anthony Lewis, "Johnson Pledges Restraint Abroad and in Race Issue," *NYT*, August 13, 1964; "Text of Address by Johnson to Lawyers," *NYT*, August 13, 1964.

27. "Civil Rights: White Boycott," *Newsweek*, August 24, 1964.

28. Johnson and Wagner, 4 P.M., August 11, 1964, Citation 4888 (6408.17), LBJ Library.

29. Presidential Daily Diary, August 12, 1964, LBJ Library; Shesol, *Mutual Contempt*, 213–214.

30. "Mr. Kennedy Declares," *NYT*, August 25, 1964; Sydney H. Schanberg, "HARYOU Will Get U.S. and City Fund of $4.4 Million," *NYT*, August 25, 1964.

31. Branch, *Pillar of Fire*, 469.

32. D'Emilio, *Lost Prophet*, 387.

33. Branch, *Pillar of Fire*, 470.

34. Johnson and Reuther, 8:25 P.M., August 25, 1964, Citation 5165 (6408.35), LBJ Library.

35. James T. Patterson, *Eve of Destruction: How 1965 Transformed America* (Basic Books, 2012), 6; Levine, *Bayard Rustin*, 168.

36. Dina Weinstein, "Mendy Samstein (1938–2007): Unsung Hero of Freedom Summer," *Moment*, http://www.momentmag.com/mendy-samstein-1938-2007-unsung-hero-freedom-summer/ (accessed March 10, 2015); Branch, *Pillar of Fire*, 473–474; John Lewis, *Walking with the Wind: A Memoir of the Movement* (Simon & Schuster, 1998), 289.

37. Lewis, *Walking with the Wind*, 292.

38. Levine, *Bayard Rustin*, 169; Lewis, *Walking with the Wind*, 291.

39. Joseph Lelyveld, "Negro Leadership Split," *NYT*, August 3, 1964.

40. Ibid.

41. D'Emilio, *Lost Prophet*, 392.

42. Louis Harris, "53 Per Cent of Voters More Worried Now about Safety on the Streets," *Washington Post*, August 31, 1964.

43. Jack Roth, "Gilligan Cleared by Grand Jury in Killing of Boy," *NYT*, September 2, 1964; "Text of Report by District Attorney," *NYT*, September 2, 1964.

44. Jack Roth, "Gilligan Cleared by Grand Jury in Killing of Boy," *NYT*, September 2, 1964; "Negro Juror Voted to Whitewash Lt. Gilligan: Verdict Satisfies Schuyler," *NYAN*, September 5, 1964.

45. David Halberstam, "Jury's Exoneration of Gilligan Scored by Negro Leaders," *NYT*, September 2, 1964; NAACP press release, September 4, 1964, Box A247, Series III, NAACP Papers, LOC.

46. "Negroes Denounce Gilligan Whitewash," *NYAN*, September 5, 1964; David Halberstam, "Report on Gilligan Assailed by CORE," *NYT*, September 3, 1964.

47. "CORE Report on Gilligan Case," September 2, 1964, Reel 3, Series I, CORE Papers, LOC; David Halberstam, "Report on Gilligan Assailed by CORE," *NYT*, September 3, 1964.

48. David Halberstam, "Jury's Exoneration of Gilligan Scored by Negro Leaders," *NYT*, September 2, 1964. The barber shop was a common place to go when a reporter needed a comment. See Quincy T. Mills, *Cutting along the Color Line: Black Barbers and Barber Shops in America* (University of Pennsylvania Press, 2013).

49. "A Mother's Verdict," *NYAN*, September 5, 1964.

50. David Halberstam, "Jury's Exoneration of Gilligan Scored by Negro Leaders," *NYT*, September 2, 1964.

51. Charles Crutzner, "Gilligan's Leave Is Still in Force," *NYT*, September 2, 1964.

52. Robert Alden, "All on Jury Agreed to Absolve Gilligan," *NYT*, September 4, 1964.

53. George Goodman Jr., "George S. Schuyler, Black Author," *NYT*, September 9, 1977; Jeffrey Leak, ed., *Rac[e]ing to the Right: Selected Essays of George S. Schuyler* (University of Tennessee Press, 2001), 103; George S. Schuyler, "Views and Reviews," *Pittsburgh Courier*, August 15, 1964; Oscar R. Williams, *George S. Schuyler: Portrait of a Black Conservative* (University of Tennessee Press, 2007).

54. Leak, *Rac[e]ing to the Right*, 108; George S. Schuyler, *Black and Conservative: The Autobiography of George S. Schuyler* (Arlington House, 1966), 346–348; Harry McKinley Williams, Jr., "When Black Is Right: The Life and Writings of George S. Schuyler" (Ph.D. diss., Brown University, 1988), 359.

55. Williams, *George S. Schuyler*, 162.

56. Ibid., 163–164.

57. Paul Southwick to Jack Valenti, August 1, 1964, Box 481, WHOF of Jack Valenti, LBJ Library; Johnson and Dick West, 9:52 A.M., August 31, 1964, Citation 5279 (6408.43), LBJ Library.

58. Johnson and Nicholas Katzenbach, 2:35 P.M., August 31, 1964, Citation 5288 (6408.43), LBJ Library.

59. Moyers to Johnson, September 7, 1964, Handwriting File, Box 4, LBJ Library.

60. Johnson and Nicholas Katzenbach, 2:35 P.M., August 31, 1964, Citation 5288 (6408.43), LBJ Library.

61. Speech, Minneapolis, September 10, 1964, Box 10, 1964, PCF, Goldwater Papers, AHF.

62. Katzenbach to the Federal Bar Association, September 18, 1964, Box 33, Katzenbach Papers, JFK Library.

63. Ibid.

64. Fred Dutton to Bill Moyers, September 18, 1964, Box 84, Ex PL2, WHCF, LBJ Library; Norbert Schlei to Lee White, September 24, 1964, Box 5, WHOF of Lee White, LBJ Library.

65. Author interview with Norbert Schlei; Norbert Schlei to Lee White, September 24, 1964, Box 5, WHOF of Lee White, LBJ Library.

66. Norbert Schlei to Lee White, September 24, 1964, and Nicholas Katzenbach to Lee White, September 8, 1964, Box 5, WHOF of Lee White, LBJ Library.

67. FBI Report, September 18, 1964, Box 20, WHOF of Richard Goodwin, LBJ Library.

68. "Bulletin," *National Review*, October 13, 1964.

69. Johnson and Thomas Dewey, 5:05 P.M., September 8, 1964, Citation 5530 (6409.07), LBJ Library.

70. Hoover to Walter Jenkins, September 9, 1964, Box 5, WHOF of Lee White, LBJ Library; Kenneth O'Reilly, "The FBI and the Politics of the Riots, 1964–1968," *Journal of American History* 75 (June 1988): 94–98. See also Kenneth O'Reilly, *"Racial Matters": The FBI's Secret File on Black America* (Free Press, 1989), 233–236.

71. Katzenbach to Johnson, September 24, 1964, Box 39, WHOF of Bill Moyers, LBJ Library; "Civil Rights Points for Democratic Speakers," attached to memo, Lee White to Johnson, September 28, 1964, Box 5, WHOF of Lee White, LBJ Library.

72. Moyers to Johnson, September 23, 1964, Box 4, WHOF of Bill Moyers, LBJ Library.

73. "FBI Whitewash the Riots," September 28, 1964, Folder 5, Box 5, James Haughton Papers, SCRBC.

74. Statement by the President, September 26, 1964, Box 39, WHOF of Bill Moyers, LBJ Library; Hoover to Walter Jenkins, October 1, 1964, Ex Hu 4, Box 59, WHCF, LBJ Library.

75. Lee White to Lyndon Johnson, September 8, 1964, Box 5, and Arnold Sagalyn to Lee White, September 2, 1964, Box 5, Office Files of Lee White, LBJ Library.

76. Arnold Sagalyn to Lee White, September 2, 1964, Box 5, WHOF of Lee White, LBJ Library.

77. Arnold Sagalyn to Lee White, September 2, 1964, Box 5, WHOF of Lee White, LBJ Library; Micol Seigel, "Objects of Police History," *Journal of American History* 102 (June 2015): 153.

78. "Civil Rights Points for Democratic Speakers," attached to Lee White to Lyndon Johnson, September 28, 1964, WHOF of Lee White, Box 5, LBJ Library.

79. Sorensen to Johnson and Jack Valenti, September 14, 1964, and Valenti to Sorensen, October 3, 1964, Box 84, Ex PL2, WHCF, LBJ Library.

80. Shesol, *Mutual Contempt*, 223.

81. Presidential Daily Diary, October 14, 1964, LBJ Library; R. W. Apple Jr., "President Takes Unnoticed Trip," *NYT*, October 15, 1964.

82. Presidential Daily Diary, October 15, 1964, LBJ Library; *Public Papers of the Presidents of the United States: Lyndon B. Johnson, 1963–1964*, book 2 (U.S. Government Printing Office, 1965), 1339.

83. Homer Bigart, "Johnson Hailed at Liberal Rally," *NYT*, October 16, 1964; Presidential Daily Diary, October 15, 1964, LBJ Library.

84. Homer Bigart, "Johnson Hailed at Liberal Rally," *NYT*, October 16, 1964; Presidential Daily Diary, October 15, 1964, LBJ Library.

85. Hazel Erskine, "The Polls: Demonstrations and Riots," *Public Opinion Quarterly* 31 (Winter 1967–1968): 670; Presidential Daily Diary, October 16, 1964, LBJ Library; Speech, Dayton, OH, October 16, 1964, Box 16, PCF, Goldwater Papers, AHF.

86. Presidential Daily Diary, October 16, 1964, LBJ Library; Speech, Dayton, OH, October 16, 1964, Box 16, PCF, Goldwater Papers, AHF.

87. *Choice*, copy in the author's possession and the Audio-Visual Department of the JFK Library.

88. The Goldwater campaign contributed $100,000 in production and national airtime costs. See George Hamilton Combs, Mutual Broadcasting System, October 22, 1964, Box 18, PCF, Goldwater Papers, AHF. See also Samuel G. Freedman, "The First Days of the Loaded Political Image," *NYT*, September 1, 1996. A campaign poster listed forty-one states where *Choice* would air, including air times and specific stations. Advertisement, "1964 Presidential Campaign Advertising: Choice," Box 3H514, Series VI, Goldwater Collection, BCAH.

Like the *Choice* film, the Willie Horton spot was created by a supposedly independent organization and derived most of its impact from the attention devoted to it by the mainstream news media. See David C. Anderson, *Crime and the Politics of Hysteria: How the Willie Horton Story Changed American Justice* (Random House, 1995).

89. *Choice*, author's copy; *Choice* transcript, First Draft, "1964 Presidential Campaign Advertising: Choice," Box 3H514, Series VI, Goldwater Collection, BCAH.

90. *Choice*, author's copy.

91. Roy Wilkins to Robert Sarnoff, October 21, 1964, Box A247, Series III, NAACP Papers, LOC; Edwards, *Goldwater*, 330; White, *Suite 3505*, 414–415.

92. Speech, St. Petersburg, FL, September 15, 1964, Box 10, 1964, PCF, Goldwater Papers, AHF. See also David Zarefsky, *President Johnson's War on Poverty: Rhetoric and History* (University of Alabama Press, 1986).

93. Goldberg, *Barry Goldwater*, 232–235; Flamm, *Law and Order*, 48.

94. Shesol, *Mutual Contempt*, 229–230; Schlesinger, *Robert Kennedy*, 729, 741.

95. Johnson and Wagner, 6:14 P.M., November 3, 1964, Citation 6125 (6411.01), LBJ Library.

96. Ibid.

CHAPTER 12. THE WAR ON CRIME

1. Lyndon B. Johnson, "Remarks at the Lighting of the Nation's Christmas Tree," December 18, 1964, http://www.presidency.ucsb.edu/ws/?pid = 26766 (accessed May 5, 2015).

2. Louis Harris, "Crime Rise Laid to Social Problems, Not Breakdown in Law Enforcement," *Washington Post*, December 7. 1964; J. Edgar Hoover to Norbert Schlei, November 13, 1964, Statements of LBJ File, Box 136, LBJ Library.

3. Daniel Patrick Moynihan to Richard Goodwin, November 20, 1964, Box 25, Ex JL 3, WHSF, LBJ Library; Staff memo, December 1, 1964, Box 28, WHOF of Horace Busby, LBJ Library; Norbert Schlei, December 2, 1964, Box 70, SP 2-3/1965/JL, WHSF, LBJ Library.

4. Annual Message to Congress on the State of the Union, January 4, 1965, *Public Papers of the Presidents of the United States: Lyndon B. Johnson, 1965,* book 1 (U.S. Government Printing Office, 1965), 1–9; Patterson, *Eve of Destruction*, 36; Woody Klein, "Crime in the Streets," *The Nation*, January 11, 1965.

5. Special Message to Congress on Law Enforcement and the Administration of Justice, March 8, 1965, *Public Papers of the Presidents of the United States,* book 1, 263–271.

6. Ibid.

7. Ibid.

8. Annual Report to the President and the Congress on Activities under the Law Enforcement Assistance Act of 1965, 3rd ed.; Joseph C. Goulden, "The Cops Hit the Jackpot"; Lee Webb, "Repression—A New 'Growth Industry' "; and Vince Pinto, "Weapons for the Homefront," all in Anthony Platt and Lynn Cooper, eds., *Policing America* (Prentice Hall, 1974), 31–40, 77–83, and 84–90; *Bridgewater Post*, March 15, 1965, Goldwater post-election correspondence, Microform Reel 4, Cornell University Collection, Ithaca, N.Y.

9. Johnson and McClellan, March 23, 1965, Citation 7135 (WH6503.11), LBJ Library; Patterson, *Eve of Destruction*, 100–101.

10. Martin Luther King, Jr., "Our God Is Marching On," March 25, 1965, http://mlk-kpp01.stanford.edu/index.php/kingpapers/article/our_god_is_marching_on/ (accessed May 11, 2015); Levine, *Bayard Rustin*, 183.

11. Bayard Rustin, "From Protest to Politics: The Future of the Civil Rights Movement," *Commentary*, February 1964.

12. Ibid.

13. Levine, *Bayard Rustin*, 183.

14. Philip Benjamin, "15,000 March through Harlem to Protest the Racial Strife in Selma," *NYT*, March 15, 1965.

15. Rustin to Mayor Wagner, May 19, 1965, Reel 18, Bayard Rustin Papers, LOC.

16. Levine, *Bayard Rustin*, 184–185.

17. Ibid., 185–186; Patterson, *Eve of Destruction*, 179–180.

18. Johnson and Katzenbach, August 17, 1965, Citation 7854 (WH6508.05), LBJ Library.

19. John Herberts, "Johnson Rebukes Rioters as Destroyers of Rights," *NYT*, August 21, 1965.

20. Lyndon Johnson, "To Fulfill These Rights," June 4, 1965, http://www.lbjlib.utexas.edu/johnson/archives.hom/speeches.hom/650604.asp (accessed May 8, 2015); Johnson and King, August 20, 1965, Citation 8578 (WH6508.07), LBJ Library.

21. Murakawa, *First Civil Right*, 79; Elizabeth Hinton, "'A War within Our Own Boundaries': Lyndon Johnson's Great Society and the Rise of the Carceral State," *Journal of American History* 102 (June 2015): 105.

22. Murakawa, *First Civil Right*, 80; Roman Hruska to Nicholas Katzenbach, Senate Judiciary Committee hearing, August 19, 1965, cited in Hinton, "'A War within Our Own Boundaries,'" 103.

23. Lyndon Johnson, "Statement by the President Following the Signing of the Law Enforcement Bill," September 22, 1965, http://www.presidency.ucsb.edu/ws/?pid=27270 (accessed May 10, 2015).

24. Katzenbach to Johnson, December 8, 1965, attached to Califano to Johnson, December 9, 1965, Box 25, Special Files, LBJ Library; Katzenbach to Califano, February 25, 1966, Box 77, Special Files, LBJ Library.

25. Richard Witkin, "Wagner Says He Won't Run for Fourth Term," *NYT*, June 11, 1965.

26. Ibid.

27. Cannato, *Ungovernable City*, 22; Kenneth T. Jackson, ed., *The Encyclopedia of New York City* (Yale University Press, 1995), 298; Kevin M. Schultz, *Buckley and Mailer: The Difficult Friendship That Shaped the Sixties* (Norton, 2015), 151.

28. William F. Buckley Jr., "Mayor, Anyone?," *National Review*, June 15, 1965.

29. Schultz, *Buckley and Mailer*, 157–158; Timothy J. Sullivan, *New York State and the Rise of Modern Conservatism: Redrawing Party Lines* (State University of New York Press, 2009), 58–59.

30. Schultz, *Buckley and Mailer*, 161–167; Robert D. McFadden, "Abraham Beame Is Dead at 94; Mayor During 70's Fiscal Crisis," *NYT*, February 11, 2001.

31. Roy Wilkins, "That Buckley Speech," *NYAN*, April 17, 1965; William F. Buckley Jr., "Remarks to the NYPD Holy Name Society," *National Review*, April 20, 1965; William F. Buckley Jr., *The Unmaking of a Mayor* (Bantam, 1966), 9–15.

32. Theodore Jones, "Uneasy Calm in Harlem," *NYT*, July 17, 1965.

33. Cannato, *Ungovernable City*, 40, 52, 68.

34. "Transit Authority Says Slaying on IRT Train Was Preventable," *NYT*, October 12, 1965; Cannato, *Ungovernable City*, 60.

35. Jimmy Breslin and Dick Schaap, "The Lonely Crimes," *NYHT*, October 26, 1964.

36. Cannato, *Ungovernable City*, 61.

37. Ibid., 69–70, 73.

38. Thomas R. Brooks, "'No!' Says the P.B.A.," *NYT Magazine*, October 16, 1966; press release, May 2, 1966, Box 68, Departmental Correspondence, Lindsay Papers, Yale University.

39. Ibid. and Cowan, "New York City Civilian Review Board," 300.

40. Cowan, "New York City Civilian Review Board," 301.

41. Bernard Weinraub, "Kennedy Sees Peril to Civilian Control of Police," *NYT*, November 4, 1966; advertisement, *NYT*, November 3, 1966; flyer, New York Citizens Committee to Support Your Local Police, Box 19, Legal Department (1956–65), NAACP Papers, LOC.

42. Woody Klein, *Lindsay's Promise: The Dream That Failed* (Macmillan, 1970), 232; press release, September 22, 1966, Box 68, Departmental Correspondence, Lindsay Papers.

43. "PBA Head Denies Charge of Racism," *NYT*, July 18, 1966. See also Frank to Lindsay, July 22, 1966 and Lindsay to Frank, August 10, 1966, Box 68, Departmental Correspondence, Lindsay Papers.

44. Cowan, "New York City Civilian Review Board," 317, 331; Klein, *Lindsay's Promise*, 255.

45. Cowan, "New York City Civilian Review Board," 6, 393. In South Harlem, the margin was 10,507 to 3,332 in opposition to the referendum; in Central Harlem, it was 11,044 to 2,658; and in East Harlem, it was 15,206 to 3,255. In Brooklyn similar figures were reported from Bedford-Stuyvesant, where the margin was three to one. See "Tally of Votes for Governor, Statewide Offices, Police Review Board, and Judgeships," *NYT*, November 10, 1966; Flamm, *Law and Order*, 76, 79.

46. David W. Abbott, Louis H. Gold, and Edward T. Rogowsky, *Police, Politics, and Race: The New York City Referendum on Civilian Review* (American Jewish Committee and the Joint Center for Urban Studies of MIT and Harvard, 1969), 7–8.

47. "All Our Fight," *NYAN*, January 8, 1966; Les Matthews, "Harlemites Decry Crime in Streets, Demand Police Act," *NYAN*, March 5, 1966; Richard Norton Smith, *On His Own Terms: A Life of Nelson Rockefeller* (Random House, 2015), 492.

48. "1966 Campaign Commercials," RAC; Ralph Blumenthal, "Governor Warns on Street Crimes," *NYT*, November 4, 1966.

49. Flamm, *Law and Order*, 68–76; Richard Scammon to LBJ, January 6, 1967, attached to Marvin Watson to LBJ, January 12, 1967, Box 77, PL 2, WHSF, LBJ Library.

50. Bernard Weinraub, "Police Review Board Panel Killed by Large Majority in City," *NYT*, November 8, 1966; Klein, *Lindsay's Promise*, 255–276.

51. Tom Johnson's Notes of the President's Activities during the Detroit Crisis, July 24, 1967, Box 1, Cabinet Papers, LBJ Library; Garry Wills, *The Second Civil War* (New American Library, 1968), 56.

52. Tom Johnson's Notes of the President's Activities during the Detroit Crisis, July 24, 1967, Box 1, Cabinet Papers, LBJ Library; *Report of the National Advisory Commission on Civil Disorders*, 100, 106–108.

53. Joseph Califano to Lyndon Johnson, July 26, 1967, Box 22, WHOF of John Robson and Stanford Ross, LBJ Library; Fred Nimetz to Califano, August 9, 1967, Box 58, WHOF of Joseph Califano, LBJ Library.

54. Notes of the President's Meeting with the Cabinet, August 2, 1967, Box 9, Cabinet Papers, LBJ Library. The Kerner Commission later found that the average patrolman received only eighteen hours of riot training, most of it inappropriate and all of it when he was a recruit. Command-level officers received almost no training. *Report of the National Advisory Commission on Civil Disorders*, 327.

55. Notes of the President's Meeting with the Cabinet, August 2, 1967, Box 9, Cabinet Papers, LBJ Library.

56. Harry McPherson, *A Political Education: A Washington Memoir* (University of Texas Press, 1994), 5–7; Harry McPherson Oral History, LBJ Library; author interview with Harry McPherson.

57. Alex Poinsett, *Walking with Presidents: Louis Martin and the Rise of Black Political Power* (Rowman & Littlefield, 1997), 2, 31–32, 102; Louis Martin Oral History, CUOHP.

58. "Boss Man of the Army," *Ebony*, June 1977; Poinsett, *Walking with Presidents*, 128, 144; author interview with Clifford Alexander, Jr.

59. McPherson to Johnson, August 14, 1967, Box 32, WHOF of Harry McPherson, LBJ Library.

60. Ibid.; author interview with Harry McPherson.

61. McPherson to Johnson, August 14, 1967, Box 32, WHOF of Harry McPherson, LBJ Library; author interviews with Arthur Hill, Harry McPherson, and Clifford Alexander, Jr.

62. McPherson to Johnson, August 14, 1967, Box 32, WHOF of Harry McPherson, LBJ Library; author interview with Arthur Hill.

63. Flamm, "Lloyd Sealy," 130–131; author interviews with Arthur Hill and George Barner.

64. Flamm, "Lloyd Sealy," 130–131; author interview with Alton Waldon, Jr.; Leonard Buder, "Transit Officer Slain in Bar as He Seeks to Stop Holdup," *NYT*, March 1, 1980; Peter Kerr, "Lloyd G. Sealy Is Dead at 69; Held High Posts with Police," *NYT*, January 5, 1985.

65. Zelizer, *Fierce Urgency of Now*, 53–54; Roche to Johnson, March 7, 1968, WHOF of Charles Roche, Box 3, LBJ Library; Kevin M. Kruse, *One Nation Under God: How Corporate America Invented Christian America* (Basic Books, 2015), 208.

66. Pincus Dachowitz to Celler, May 23, 1967, Box 299, Celler Papers, Manuscript Division, LOC.

67. Murakawa, *First Civil Right*, 85.

68. Malcolm M. Feeley and Austin D. Sarat, *The Policy Dilemma: Federal Crime Policy and the Law Enforcement Administration, 1968–1978* (University of Minnesota Press, 1980), 45–46, 89–90.

69. Celler to the American Jewish Committee Appeal for Human Relations, November 2, 1967, Box 540, Celler Papers, Manuscript Division, LOC.

70. "A Conversation with the President," December 19, 1967, *Public Papers of Lyndon Johnson*, http://www.presidency.ucsb.edu/ws/index.php?pid = 28621&st = answer&st1 = jobs (accessed May 29, 2015).

71. "The Cities: The Crucible," *Time*, January 26, 1968; Richard Harris, *The Fear of Crime* (Praeger, 1968), 67; George Gallup, *The Gallup Poll: Public Opinion, 1935–1971* (Random House, 1972), 2107–2108.

72. Risen, *Nation on Fire*, 58; Johnson, *Vantage Point*, 538.

73. Joseph A. Califano, Jr., *The Triumph and the Tragedy of Lyndon Johnson: The White House Years* (Simon & Schuster, 1991), 279; Califano to LBJ, April 5, 1968, Box 39, Ex JL 6, WHSF, LBJ Library; Risen, *Nation on Fire*, 4.

74. Louis Harris, "Tight Gun Rules Favored 71–23," *Washington Post*, April 22, 1968.

75. Fred Nimetz to Califano, June 8, 1968, Box 5, WHOF of James Gaither, LBJ Library; Linda Greenhouse, "Justices Reaffirm Miranda Rule, 7–2," *NYT*, June 27, 2000.

76. Tom Finley to Ramsey Clark, June 6, 1968, Box 107, Papers of Ramsey Clark, LBJ Library.

77. George Kamenow to Celler, May 23, 1968, Box 298, Celler Papers, Manuscript Division, LOC.

78. McPherson to Johnson, June 14, 1968, Box 32, WHOF of Harry McPherson, LBJ Library; "Statement by the President upon the Signing of the Omnibus Crime Control and

Safe Streets Act," June 19, 1968, *Public Papers of Lyndon Johnson*, http://www.presidency .ucsb.edu/ws/index.php?pid = 28939 (accessed May 29, 2015).

79. Louis Harris and Associates, Inc., "Harris Survey," iPOLL Databank, Roper Center for Public Opinion Research, University of Connecticut (accessed May 23, 2015); confidential minutes, September 27, 1968, Box 1, 1968 Campaign Papers, Hubert Humphrey Papers, MHS.

80. Kirkpatrick to Freeman, October 4, 1968, Box 1, 1968 Campaign Papers, Hubert Humphrey Papers, MHS.

81. Presidential Nomination Acceptance Speech, August 8, 1968, PPS 208 (1968).58.11.2, Speech Files, RMN Library.

82. "The Way the Voting Went—and Why," *U.S. News & World Report*, November 18, 1968; "Nixon's Hard-Won Chance to Lead," *Time*, November 15, 1968.

83. Joe McGinniss, *The Selling of the President 1968* (Trident Press, 1969); "Order," Nixon campaign commercial, 1968, Museum of Television and Radio, New York.

EPILOGUE

1. Author interview with Nicholas Katzenbach.

2. Goulden, "Cops Hit the Jackpot," 31–40.

3. Webb, "Repression" and Pinto, "Weapons for the Homefront," 77–83 and 84–90.

4. Feeley and Sarat, *Policy Dilemma*, 40–41; Michael W. Flamm, "Politics and Pragmatism: The Nixon Administration and Crime Control," *White House Studies* 6 (February 2006): 151–162.

5. Lassiter, "Suburban Imperatives of the War on Drugs," 133–135; Adam Rathage, "Pondering Pot: Marijuana's History and the Future of the War on Drugs," *American Historian* (August 2015): 35; Eric Schneider, *Smack: Heroin and the American City* (University of Pennsylvania Press, 2009), 159–164.

6. Bayard Rustin, "Let's Talk Sense About Crime," *NYAN*, November 28, 1970.

7. David T. Courtwright, "The Cycles of American Drug Policy," *American Historian* (August 2015): 27; Michael Massing, *The Fix* (Simon & Schuster, 1998); Smith, *On His Own Terms*, 597.

8. Smith, *On His Own Terms*, 590, 599, 604–605.

9. Julilly Kohler-Hausmann, "'The Attila the Hun Law': New York's Rockefeller Drug Laws and the Making of a Punitive State," *Journal of Social History* 44 (Fall 2010): 76, 80; Michael Javen Fortner, "The 'Silent Majority' in Black and White: Invisibility and Imprecision in the Historiography of Mass Incarceration," *Journal of Urban History* 40 (March 2014): 5–9.

10. Kohler-Hausmann, "'Attila the Hun Law,'" 80–85; Courtwright, "Cycles of American Drug Policy," 28; Fortner, "'Silent Majority' in Black and White," 19–20. See also Michael Javen Fortner, *Black Silent Majority: The Rockefeller Drug Laws and the Politics of Punishment* (Harvard University Press, 2015).

11. Kelefa Sanneh, "Body Count," *New Yorker*, September 14, 2015; Kohler-Hausmann, "'Attila the Hun Law,'" 88.

12. Donna Murch, "Crack in Los Angeles: Crisis, Militarization, and Black Response to the Late Twentieth-Century War on Drugs," *Journal of American History* 102 (June 2015): 163; Murakawa, *First Civil Right*, 91, 121–122.

13. "Crime Bill: What Passed," *USA Today*, August 29, 1994.

14. Taylor Wofford, "How America's Police Became an Army: The 1033 Program," *Newsweek*, August 13, 2014; Heather Ann Thompson, "Why Mass Incarceration Matters: Rethinking Crisis, Decline, and Transformation in Postwar American History," *Journal of American History* 97 (December 2010): 716–725, 732–734; Alex Lichtenstein, "Flocatex and the Fiscal Limits of Mass Incarceration: Toward a New Political Economy of the Postwar Carceral State," *Journal of American History* 102 (June 2015): 113–125.

15. Jonathan Simon, *Governing Through Crime: How the War on Crime Transformed American Democracy and Created a Culture of Fear* (Oxford University Press, 2009); and Erika L. Wood, "Florida: How Soon We Forget," *NYT*, April 5, 2012.

16. Ken Auletta, "Fixing Broken Windows," *The New Yorker*, September 7, 2015.

17. Alfred Blumstein and Joel Wallman, eds., *The Crime Drop in America* (Cambridge University Press, 2000); National Research Council, *The Growth of Incarceration in the United States*, 155.

18. Eric Eckholm, "In a Safer Age, U.S. Rethinks Its 'Tough on Crime' System," *NYT*, January 13, 2015; Bill Keller, "Prison Revolt," *New Yorker*, June 29, 2015.

19. "President Obama Takes on the Prison Crisis," *NYT*, July 17, 2015.

20. Long, *I Must Resist*, 297, 325.

21. Ibid., 387.

22. Leo Janos, "The Last Days of the President: LBJ in Retirement," *Atlantic*, July 1973, http://www.theatlantic.com/magazine/archive/1973/07/the-last-days-of-the-president/376281/ (accessed March 3, 2015); Jonathan Darman, *Landslide: LBJ and Ronald Reagan at the Dawn of a New America* (Random House, 2014), 364–366.

23. Long, *I Must Resist*, 392–393.

24. D'Emilio, *Lost Prophet*, 484–491; Eric Pace, "Bayard Rustin Is Dead at 75; Pacifist and a Rights Activist," *NYT*, August 25, 1987.

25. D'Emilio, *Lost Prophet*, 492–494.

26. "Another Day in Life of Lt. Gilligan," *NYHT*, June 3, 1965.

27. "Gilligan Retiring from City Police," *NYT*, January 22, 1968.

PERSONAL INTERVIEWS AND CORRESPONDENCE

Alexander, Clifford, Jr., September 13, 2004
Barner, George, June 9, 2005
Bouza, Anthony, February 10, 2005
Bovelle, Elliott, May 27, 2005
Caldwell, Earl, May 13, 2005
Carson, Lester, June 21, 2005
Clines, Francis, December 13, 2004
Cohen, Barney, January 28, 2005
Coleman, Val, April 7, 2005
Drew, Peter, December 6, 2004
Edmond, Lez, March 19, 2005
Fraser, C. Gerald, May 10, 2005
Garelik, Sanford, July 7, 2005
Gartner, Alan, June 28, 2005
Gelb, Arthur, February 2, 2005
Grosso, Sonny, February 4, 2005
Hill, Arthur, August 12, 2004
Hill, Norman, May 26, 2005
Hill, Velma, May 31, 2005
Horowitz, Rachelle, July 27, 2006
Innes, Roy, May 11, 2005
Katzenbach, Nicholas, March 6, 1998
Lelyveld, Joseph, May 11, 2005
Leuci, Robert, May 19, 2005
Marius, Everard, August 13, 2004
Mchawi, Basir, November 29, 2004
McPherson, Harry, August 10, 2004

Moreland, Wayne, November 22, 2004
Powledge, Fred, June 21, 2005
Rich, Marvin, May 11, 2005
Schlei, Norbert, July 6, 1995
Sutton, Percy, August 17, 2004
Talese, Gay, August 11, 2004
Waldon, Alton, Jr., June 9, 2005
Witlieb, Bernard to the author, July 17, 2014

INDEX

Page numbers in italics represent illustrations.

Murphy, Michael J., 252, 263, 269; background of, 66–67; and black officers, 128, 138; on proposed civilian review board, 74–75
—during Harlem 1964 Riot, 55, 97, 105, 212; analysis of causes by, 145, 200; and community leaders, 97, 126, 191, 212, 218; and federal officials, 145, 147, 179–80; and Mayor Wagner, 104, 151–53, 177, *178*, 180; public statements by, 98–99; tactical decisions by, 87, 116–17, 128
—as target of protesters, 78, 79, 87, 111, 227; calls for resignation or firing of, 110, 152, 184
Muste, A. J., 39, 44, 45

Naegle, Walter, 293–94
Nation, The, 259
National Association for the Advancement of Colored People (NAACP), 49, 60, 216, 230, 292; in Brooklyn, 166, 175–76, 191; and civilian review, 73–74; and crime legislation, 77; and legal processes over Powell shooting, 12, 17; New York branch of, 169, 171 (*see also* Hildebrand, Richard A.); and 1964 protest moratorium, 222–24; in Rochester, 208, 210–11, 214, 215; ties of, to Harlem, 30, 32, 72, 184. *See also* Wilkins, Roy
National Guard, 106, 199, 214, 250, 264, 284; reluctance to use, in Harlem, 151, 172, 179
—in other cities, 282; Detroit (1967), 276; Los Angeles (1965), 264; Rochester (1964), 213–15, 220, 235, 289
National Negro American Labor Council, 126
National Review, 73, 77, 249, 268. *See also* Buckley, William F., Jr.
Nation of Islam, 50, 55, 169, 220; in Harlem, 184, 185, 220
Newark Riot of 1967, 4, 275, 281
Newsweek, 76
New York Age, 36–37

New York Civil Liberties Union, 272
New York Daily News, 65, 171, 190; on civilian review board proposals, 131–32, 190; on 1964 Harlem Riot, 127, 149, 168, 169, 173
New York Herald Tribune, 86, 105, 234, 270; on 1964 Harlem Riot, 99, 119–20, 163, 164, 196, 217–18. *See also* Breslin, Jimmy
New York Journal-American, 65, 193
New York Post, 42, 58–59, 72, 77; and civilian review, 131, 190; and 1964 Harlem Riot, 116, 136, 203
New York school boycott (February 1964), 64–65, 101, 170
New York Times, 68, 155, 234, 269, 290; black reporters for, 71 (*see also* Griffin, Junius); "Blood Brothers" story in, 71–73, 75; editorial opinion in, 131, 133, 167, 224–25, 252; news policies of, 70, 71; Harlem Riot coverage by, 96–97, 114–15, 136 (*see also* Montgomery, Paul); surveys of black opinion in, 61, 216. *See also* Rosenthal, Abe
New York World's Fair (1964–65), 110, 150, 178; planned stall-in at, 69, 109
New York World Telegram and Sun. See Carson, Lester
Nixon, Richard M., 287, 290, 293; presidential campaigns of, 20, 285–86; and War on Drugs, 4–5, 288–89, 292
"No Knock" law, 77
nonviolent resistance: Bayard Rustin and, 8, 50, 101–2, 113, 114; conservatives' hostility to, 4, 21, 202, 222, 236, 244, 251; growing impatience with, 81, 92, 109; James Farmer and, 44, 102–3, 108; Martin Luther King and, 4, 69
numbers racket, 49, 59

Obama, Barack, 292
Ochs, Phil, 6, 66; "In the Heat of the Summer" by, 6, 10, 29, 53, 78, 101, 122, 144, 168, 187
O'Connell, Anthony, 177
O'Connor, Frank, 274

ACKNOWLEDGMENTS

This book was many years in the making and many people helped make it possible. Without the inspiration and support of my colleagues, students, friends, and family I simply could not have finished it. To all of you—as well as numerous others—I owe a tremendous debt of gratitude, which I wish to repay here in some small way.

My fellow historians have immensely improved this work with their critical insights. At meetings of the Social Science History Association and the Institute for Policy History, panelists and participants offered useful suggestions. At the Ohio State University, the modern U.S. History seminar debated the premises of the project and dissected a chapter on the aftermath of the riots. It is a great privilege to be part of such a vibrant intellectual community. I am also deeply appreciative of the busy scholars—Alan Brinkley, Edward Foley, Eric Foner, Clayton Howard, KC Johnson, Mitch Lerner, Clay Risen, Jonathan Schoenwald, David Stebenne, David Steigerwald, Heather Thompson, Timothy Thurber, and Eric Wakin—who took the time to read all or part of the manuscript and offer perceptive comments. Two others merit particular mention. Vincent Cannato deserves special praise for his thoughtful feedback. And Michael Kazin has become far more than a colleague over the years—I cannot begin to list his numerous acts of kindness and generosity.

Research assistance came from many institutions and individuals, who often went above and beyond the obligations of professionalism. As a historian, I benefitted enormously from the expert guidance of Leanora Gidlund at the Municipal Archives, Doug DiCarlo and Steven Levine at La Guardia Community College, Phyllis Andrews and Mary Huth of the Rush Rhees Library at the University of Rochester, and Ellen Belcher of the Lloyd Sealy Library at John Jay College. At the Library of Congress, Jeff Bridgers was most helpful when it came to identifying photos, and at the Lyndon Baines Johnson Presidential Library Allen Fisher once again made it a pleasure to explore the collection and spend time in Austin. At Ohio Wesleyan University, which backed this project with faculty research grants and special scholarly leave, four talented and dedicated reference librarians—Paul Burnam, Ben Daigle, Jillian Maruskin, and Deanne Peterson—aided my efforts. Sarah Richmond, a promising undergraduate, also helped me transcribe the oral history interviews that I conducted. Finally, Nicole Hemmer of Columbia University tirelessly tracked down newspaper and magazine articles. At the time she was a graduate student—now she is a gifted historian and commentator in her own right.

Although I was born in New York, I am by no means a native. My understanding of the city was immeasurably strengthened by my interviews with reporters, officers, activists, and participants who directly experienced the events of 1964 and graciously agreed to answer my questions. I only wish that I could have completed this book sooner so that more of those with whom I spoke could read it. Special thanks are due to George Barner, Arthur Hill, and Percy Sutton, who generously shared their encyclopedic knowledge of Central Harlem. Earl Caldwell, Francis Clines, Joseph Lelyveld, Fred Powledge, and Gay Talese taught me a great deal about the intricacies of journalism, while Anthony Bouza and Sonny Grosso offered fascinating insights into the practices and politics of the NYPD. The latter also treated me to a memorable evening at Rao's in East Harlem. Jerry Palace, a retired detective, made a valiant attempt to reach out to Thomas Gilligan. And Walter Naegle was extremely accommodating when I decided to make Bayard Rustin a central figure.

Writing is often a lonely and difficult task. I am therefore thankful for the support provided by my newer friends in Ohio: Brent and Dana Adler, Bud Barnes, David Bernstein, Cathy Bindewald, Lauren Bonfield, Lavea Brachman, Nicholas Breyfogle, Robert Coleman, Adam Davis, Theodora Dragostinova, Julian Halliday, Dennis Hirsch and Suzanne Goldsmith-Hirsch, Steve Keyes, Scott Levi, Dodie McDow, Andrew Mills, Fred and Shannon Nelson, Allison Norris, Piers and Abby Norris-Turner, Brian Roe, Alexandra Schimmer, Inna Simakovsky, Karen Simonian, Andrew Smith, Karen Spierling, Jim and Kim Wilson, and Eric and Katrina Zidel. At the same time, I remain grateful for the encouragement offered by my older friends like Jonathan Engel, Chris Fischer, Wif Petersberger, Phil Prince, John Stoner, and Margaret Usdansky. When the book was at an early stage,

Ethan Anderson offered an invaluable critique. At a late stage, Bennett Singer responded without hesitation when I needed to draw upon his deep knowledge of Bayard Rustin. Finally, words cannot express my gratitude to Tom Maguire, who combed through the manuscript line-by-line, polishing the prose and clarifying the claims. More than twenty-five years ago, we taught history together at Scarsdale High School. Now I believe that he might have missed his true calling as a copy editor, although a generation of students would surely disagree.

At Ohio Wesleyan the History Department has provided me with a congenial and collegial home, where I feel honored to count Ellen Arnold, Jeremy Baskes, and Barbara Terzian as colleagues. I am also fortunate to have had the opportunity to work with the outstanding editorial, production, and marketing staff at the University of Pennsylvania Press, including Noreen O'Connor-Abel and Joseph Dahm. In particular, I must express my deepest appreciation to my exceptional editor, Robert Lockhart. From the start he promised that he would provide hands-on editorial attention, which I eagerly wanted and have rarely received. But he was not merely making a sales pitch. His enthusiasm for, and commitment to, this project have made it better in countless ways.

As always, I am profoundly thankful for the love of my family. My parents, Dudley and Ellen Flamm, have never failed to provide me with unconditional reassurance when I most needed it. Their respective life partners, Beth Wickum and Richard Peterson, have also warmly embraced me. Since childhood my brother Eric has stood by my side, and I treasure the time that we have spent together in Hood River, Oregon, with his wife Robin and their children Olivia and Jonah.

My largest debt is to my wife Jennifer, who is an incredible partner and person. Since we met in 2001 she has filled my life with love and adventure. Although deeply invested in her own causes and career, she has sustained me and tolerated the crankiness that often came from writing late at night after the children were in bed and early in the morning before they awoke. Above all, I am forever grateful to her for giving me the greatest gifts that I will ever receive: my son Austin and my daughter Alexandra. For their entire lives I have been researching or writing this book. And for years they have asked when I would complete it. Now at last I have and I dedicate it to them. You mean the world to me and I love you with all my heart.